FROMMER'S EasyGuide TO CUBA

By
Claire Boobbyer

Easy Guides are • Quick To Read • Light To Carry
• For Expert Advice • In All Price Ranges

CA

FrommerMedi

Published by
FROMMER MEDIA LLC

ISBN 978-1-62887-234-7 (paper), 978-1-62887-235-4 (e-book)

Editorial Director: Pauline Frommer
Editor: Alexis Lipsitz
Production Editor: Lindsay Conner
Editorial Assistant: Ross Walker
Cartographer: Liz Puhl
Cover Design: Howard Grossman

Frommer Media LLC also publishes its books in a variety of electronic formats. Some content that appears in print may not be available in electronic formats.

Manufactured in the United States of America

5 4 3 2 1

FROMMER'S STAR RATINGS SYSTEM

Every hotel, restaurant and attraction listed in this guide has been ranked for quality and value. Here's what the stars mean:

★ Recommended
★★ Highly Recommended
★★★ A must! Don't miss!

AN IMPORTANT NOTE

The world is a dynamic place. Hotels change ownership, restaurants hike their prices, museums alter their opening hours, and busses and trains change their routings. And all of this can occur in the several months after our authors have visited, inspected, and written about, these hotels, restaurants, museums and transportation services. Though we have made valiant efforts to keep all our information fresh and up-to-date, some few changes can inevitably occur in the periods before a revised edition of this guidebook is published. So please bear with us if a tiny number of the details in this book have changed. Please also note that we have no responsibility or liability for any inaccuracy or errors or omissions, or for inconvenience, loss, damage, or expenses suffered by anyone as a result of assertions in this guide.

CONTENTS

ABOUT THE AUTHOR

Claire Boobbyer is a Cuba travel expert. She has been writing about the island for the last 15 years for guidebooks, newspapers, and magazines. She writes for the U.K.'s *Daily Telegraph*, the *Guardian*, the *Independent*, *Time Out*, and *National Geographic Traveller UK*, among other publications. For the last two years she has led tours to Cuba for New York Times Journeys, Smithsonian Journeys, and the Environmental Defense Fund.

ACKNOWLEDGMENTS

I would like to thank the many Cubans who helped me along my way during my extensive research trip across the island in 2015. Thank you, also, to my editor Alexis Lipsitz Flippin.

ABOUT FROMMER'S TRAVEL GUIDES

For most of the past 50 years, Frommer's has been the leading series of travel guides in North America, accounting for as many as 24% of all guidebooks sold. I think I know why.

Though we hope our books are entertaining, we nevertheless deal with travel in a serious fashion. Our guidebooks have never looked on such journeys as a mere recreation, but as a far more important human function, a time of learning and introspection, an essential part of a civilized life. We stress the culture, lifestyle, history and beliefs of the destinations we cover, and urge our readers to seek out people and new ideas as the chief rewards of travel.

We have never shied from controversy. We have, from the beginning, encouraged our authors to be intensely judgmental, critical—both pro and con—in their comments, and wholly independent. Our only clients are our readers, and we have triggered the ire of countless prominent sorts, from a tourist newspaper we called "practically worthless" (it unsuccessfully sued us) to the many rip-offs we've condemned.

And because we believe that travel should be available to everyone regardless of their incomes, we have always been cost-conscious at every level of expenditure. Though we have broadened our recommendations beyond the budget category, we insist that every lodging we include be sensibly priced. We use every form of media to assist our readers, and are particularly proud of our feisty daily website, the award-winning Frommers.com.

I have high hopes for the future of Frommer's. May these guidebooks, in all the years ahead, continue to reflect the joy of travel and the freedom that travel represents. May they always pursue a cost-conscious path, so that people of all incomes can enjoy the rewards of travel. And may they create, for both the traveler and the persons among whom we travel, a community of friends, where all human beings live in harmony and peace.

Arthur Frommer

THE BEST OF CUBA

Cuba is unlike any other place on earth. What draws people to this fascinating Caribbean island is much more than beaches, sun, and rum cocktails, though there is plenty of all three for those who want them. One of the last Communist-bloc nations left, Cuba doesn't suffer from the drab and desultory demeanor of its faded peers. Cuba's rich culture, unique political history, and continued survival through ongoing economic hardship make it one of the most eye-opening countries that experienced travelers can still discover. Seeing the best of Cuba means dancing to its intoxicating music, admiring how Cubans improvise on a daily basis to make ends meet, and visiting a land that is trying to reconcile its socialist utopia past with its dips into capitalist waters. It's a nation now populated by a significant swath of newly moneyed Cubans who are, wrote Carlos Manuel Alvarez in 2015 in *OnCuba* magazine, "specimens at the midway gallop between Cuba's iron socialist morality and a certain post-realignment Havana consumerism."

CUBA'S best AUTHENTIC EXPERIENCES

- **Patronizing *Paladares* & *Casa Particulares*:** The best way to appreciate Cubans and exchange ideas about Cuba and the outside world is by stepping inside a *paladar* restaurant or a *casa particular*, the Cuban version of a simple bed-and-breakfast. These private initiatives are among the few ways Cubans can earn badly needed hard currency and give travelers a wonderful opportunity to interact with locals.
- **Exploring La Habana Vieja (Old Havana):** The streets and alleys of this colonial-era city center have been immaculately restored. New private restaurants, bars, cafes, and shops have enlivened the colonial core. Wander the plazas, churches, and forts here. See p. 44.

- **Walking along Havana's Malecón:** Your best bet is to start in La Habana Vieja and work your way toward the Hotel Nacional in Vedado. Take time to stop and sit on the sea wall and shoot the breeze with the locals. If you time it right, you will reach the Hotel Nacional in the late afternoon—a good time to grab a cool drink and enjoy the setting sun from the outdoor terrace. The late afternoon light here is also the best for photographers. See p. 75.
- **Celebrating Las Parrandas:** Near the end of the year, the little colonial town of Remedios gears up to host Las Parrandas, one of Cuba's grandest street parties and religious carnivals. Everything culminates on Christmas Eve in an orgy of drums, floats, and fireworks. See p. 264.
- **Going Wild in Baracoa:** The beauty, the legends, the wildlife, the walks, the rivers, the food, and the myths: Cuba's adventure capital is not to be missed. See p. 224.
- **Following in Fidel's Footsteps:** Waging a guerrilla war against the Batista dictatorship, Fidel Castro and his young comrades hid out in the Sierra Maestra mountains in the late 1950s. Their small-scale rebel base camp was never discovered, but visitors today can hike a trail through remote cloud forest up to Comandancia de la Plata, the command post where Fidel turned a country on its head. See p. 221.
- **Joining a Carnival Conga Line:** In the intense heat of summer, Santiago de Cuba explodes with the island's best carnival. Ripe with rumba music, conga processions, booming percussion, fanciful floats, and wild costumes, it's a participatory party. See p. 253.
- **Beach Time:** Lying on one of Cuba's white-sand beaches sipping a *mojito* (Cuban rum cocktail) before dipping into the sparkling waters of the warm turquoise seas is one of the most heavenly things you can do.
- **Dance Like a Cuban:** If you can dance, head to the Casas de la Trova and music venues found in every Cuban town and city. If you can't yet dance, what are you waiting for? Find a dance teacher and your Cuban groove.

CUBA'S best HISTORICAL SIGHTS

- **Catedral de San Cristóbal & Plaza de la Catedral ★★** (Havana): Havana's cathedral and the plaza it sits on are perhaps Old Havana's most distinctive historical sites. The twin towers and undulating Cuban baroque facade of this ancient church are beautiful by both day and night. See p. 71.
- **Museo de la Ciudad ★★** (Havana): Old Havana's preeminent museum displays colonial-era artifacts. Stroll the rooms, courtyards, and interior veranda of the former Cuban baroque Palacio de los Capitanes Generales (Palace of the Captains General), which houses the museum. See p. 72.
- **Parque Histórico Morro y Cabaña ★★** (Havana): Across the harbor from Old Havana, the Morro & Cabaña Historic Park complex is comprised of

two major forts charged with protecting Havana's narrow harbor entrance. It has a lighthouse, several museums, restored barracks, and batteries of cannons. See p. 78.

- **Cementerio de Colón ★★★** (Havana): Columbus Cemetery is an impressive collection of mausoleums, crypts, family chapels and vaults, soaring sculptures, and ornate gravestones. All of the dead are laid to rest above ground, and you'll be awed by the surfeit of marble and alabaster. See p. 75.
- **Complejo Escultórico Comandante Ernesto "Che" Guevara ★** (Santa Clara): Featuring a huge sculpture of the revolutionary hero overlooking a vast plaza, this place is deeply revered by Cubans. Underneath the statue is a museum with exhibits detailing the life and exploits of "El Che," as well as a mausoleum holding his remains. See p. 146.
- **Trinidad ★★★:** The entire town of Trinidad qualifies as a historical site. The impeccably preserved relic—several blocks square of perfect pastel-colored mansions, churches, and cobblestone streets—is one of the greatest collections of colonial architecture in the Americas. See p. 161.
- **Plaza San Juan de Dios ★★★** (Camagüey): This dignified square is the highlight of Camagüey's colonial quarter, one of the largest in Cuba with more than a dozen 16th-, 17th-, and 18th-century colonial churches. Marked by cobblestones and colonial houses with red-tile roofs and iron window grilles, the understated plaza is home to a 17th-century baroque church and hospital of the order of San Juan de Dios. See p. 194.
- **Museo El Chorro de Maíta ★** (Guardalavaca): This small museum site is a Taíno burial ground from the late-15th and early-16th centuries, the biggest and finest American Indian cemetery discovered in Cuba. The well-preserved remains of more than 100 members of the community reveal important clues about native groups after the arrival of the Spanish conquistadors. See p. 205.
- **Casa Velázquez (Museo de Ambiente Historico Cubano) ★★** (Santiago de Cuba): Diego Velázquez founded the original seven *villas* (towns/settlements) in Cuba, and his 1515 mansion in Santiago de Cuba, the oldest house in the country and one of the oldest in the Americas, is still standing. Today it's a museum of colonial furnishings from the 16th to the 19th century. See p. 241.
- **Castillo El Morro ★★** (Santiago de Cuba): Although nowhere near as expansive as its sister fort in Havana, this massive fortress is nonetheless impressive. You almost feel as if you're part of the history here while walking the mazelike alleyways. See p. 256.

CUBA'S best NATURAL AREAS

- **The Viñales Valley ★★★:** This broad, flat valley is punctuated by a series of rounded limestone karst hills, or *mogotes*. The area provides great opportunities for hiking, mountain biking, horseback-riding, bird-watching, and rock climbing, and there are plenty of caves to explore. See p. 97.

- **Las Terrazas ★:** This planned ecotourism project is set amid the Sierra del Rosario Biosphere Reserve. It has a host of trails and attractions, including swimming holes, a zipline canopy tour, and Cuba's only authentic vegetarian restaurant. See p. 104.
- **Parque Nacional Ciénaga de Zapata ★:** The Zapata Swamp National Park is a massive expanse of mangroves, swamp, and wetlands housing an abundant variety of flora and fauna, including flamingos and Cuban crocodiles. The area is a mecca for bird-watchers, naturalists, and anglers. The diving is also superb. See p. 137.
- **Parque Nacional Topes de Collantes ★★:** The dense pine-covered mountains of the Sierra del Escambray lurk on the outskirts of Trinidad, and the Topes de Collantes National Park is a lovely, cool refuge from the town's stone streets. It's great for hiking, with several well-established trails, the best of which culminate in refreshing waterfalls. See p. 173.
- **Baracoa ★★★:** Cuba's first settlement, overlooking a beautiful oyster-shaped bay, remains a natural paradise, with thick tropical vegetation, 10 rivers, and a distinctive flat-topped mountain called El Yunque, a UNESCO Biosphere Reserve. Travelers into rafting, beaches, and boating will also find ample opportunities to explore this isolated area. The Parque Nacional Alejandro de Humboldt around the Río Toa is rich in diversity. See p. 224.
- **Sierra Maestra ★:** The highest and longest mountain range in Cuba, the Sierra Maestra is full of lore for Cubans—it's where Fidel Castro and his band of rebels hid out and waged guerilla warfare against the Batista government in the 1950s. Stretching across three provinces, its peaks are almost on top of the rocky southern coastline. The Gran Parque Nacional Sierra Maestra and Parque Nacional de Turquino are perfect for hikers and nature lovers. See p. 212.

CUBA'S best OUTDOOR ADVENTURES

- **Landing a Marlin, Tarpon, or Bonefish ★★★:** If you really want to emulate Ernest Hemingway, you'll head out to sea to fish. The waters off Cuba's coast are excellent for sportfishing year-round. Big-game fish are best sought off the northern coast, while bonefish and tarpon are better stalked off the southern coast. **Náutica Marlin** (www.nauticamarlin.com) and **Gaviota** (www.gaviota-grupo.com) run a string of marinas with modern, well-equipped sport-fishing fleets all around Cuba's coastline.
- **Rock Climbing the Mogotes of the Viñales Valley ★★:** Although in its infancy, rock climbing is a rapidly developing sport in Cuba, and Viñales Valley is the place to come and climb. More than 250 routes and 300 pitches have been marked and climbed, and more climbs are constantly being uncovered. See p. 97.

- **Scuba Diving at Jardines de la Reina ★★★:** Cuba has good diving at La Isla de la Juventud, María la Gorda, and Cayo Largo, but the Jardines de la Reina (Gardens of the Queen) are considered the last pristine reef environment in the Caribbean. The protected vibrant coral reefs teem with goliath grouper, turtles, and dozens of silky, reef, Caribbean, lemon, and nurse sharks. Liveaboard diving or fishing is the only way to go. See p. 188.
- **Bird-Watching in the Zapata Peninsula ★★★:** A dedicated (and lucky) bird-watcher might be able to spot 18 of Cuba's 25 endemic species in the swamps, mangroves, and wetlands of the Zapata Peninsula. In addition to the endemic species, ornithologists and lay bird-watchers can spot more than 100 other varieties of shore birds, transients, and waterfowl in this rich, wild region. See p. 140. Other top bird-watching destinations include **La Güira National Park** (p. 107), as well as the areas around **Cayo Coco** and **Cayo Guillermo** (p. 180) and **Baracoa** (p. 224).
- **Hiking and Rafting in Baracoa ★★:** Baracoa, long isolated by impenetrable tropical vegetation, steep mountains, and rushing rivers, is an adventurer's dream. El Yunque, a curiously flat-topped limestone mountain, is home to dozens of bird species, orchids, and unique tropical plants and forest; it's also great for climbing. The Río Toa, the widest river in Cuba, is one of the few spots in Cuba for rafting, and Parque Humboldt offers opportunities for walking and boating. See p. 227.
- **Hiking Pico Turquino ★★:** Pico Turquino, tucked within the celebrated Sierra Maestra National Park, is the highest peak in Cuba at just under 2,000m (6,562 ft.). The trail to the summit is swathed in cloud forest and tropical flora. Mountaineers in good physical condition can do the 15km (9-mile) round-trip journey in a day, but most camp overnight below the summit. The panoramic views of the coast and Caribbean Sea are breathtaking. See p. 220.

CUBA'S best BEACHES

- **Playa Paraíso & Playa Sirena, Cayo Largo del Sur ★★★:** These two connected beaches are the most outstanding of the uniformly spectacular stretches of sand along the length of Cayo Largo del Sur. Located on the more protected western end of the island, these are broad expanses of glistening, fine white sand, bordering the clear Caribbean Sea. There's a simple beachside restaurant on Playa Paraíso, and not much else—and that's a large part of their charm. See p. 118.
- **Varadero ★★:** This is Cuba's premier beach-resort destination, ranking right up there with the best in the Caribbean. I personally prefer some of the island's less-developed stretches of sand. But if you're looking for a well-run all-inclusive resort loaded with amenities and activities, Varadero is a good choice. The 21km (13 miles) of nearly uninterrupted beach here is fabulous. See p. 128.

- **Playa Ensenachos & Playa Mégano, Cayo Santa María ★★★:** Located on the tiny islet of Cayo Ensenachos, which is part of la Cayerías del Norte, these protected crescents of sand drop off very gently, allowing bathers to wade 90m (295 ft.) or more out into the calm, crystal-clear waters. You'll have to shell out big bucks to visit these beaches, as they belong to the Iberostar Ensenachos. Both beaches are astoundingly beautiful, but I slightly prefer Playa Mégano. See p. 151.
- **Playa Maguana ★:** The name for a series of about five wild coves scooped out of the coastline, north of Baracoa. The creamy sands and teal green waters are overshadowed by royal palms, and you can even get fish cooked on the sands. See p. 232.
- **Cayos Coco & Guillermo, Jardines del Rey ★★:** These tiny cays off the north coast, separated from the Cuban mainland by a long man-made causeway, are tucked into shallow waters that flow into the Atlantic. There's barely a sign of the "real Cuba," but what you do get is stunning, unspoiled beaches, and a full contingent of watersports. The most beautiful beaches here are Playa Las Colorados and Playa El Paso. The gorgeous Playa Pilar at the western tip of Guillermo is being built up, so loses its "best virgin beach in Cuba" status. See p. 180.
- **Cayo Jutías, Western Cuba ★:** Beyond the tourist section, walk for miles along virginal sands backed by beautiful driftwood sculptures before reaching what's known as Playa de las Estrellas del Mar (Starfish Beach), where enormous burnt-orange starfish dwell in the shallows. See p. 110.
- **Guardalavaca, Oriente ★★:** Cuba's prettiest resort area, Guardalavaca is a hot spot, but not overheated like Varadero. The area, a prime archaeological zone of pre-Columbian Cuba, is one of lush tropical vegetation, brilliant white sands, and clear turquoise waters. Long stretches of coastline are interrupted by charming little cove beaches, and some of Cuba's finest resort hotels are here. See p. 199.

CUBA'S best HOTELS

- **Hotel Saratoga ★★★** (Havana): Set right on the Paseo del Prado, with stunning views of El Capitolio from many of its rooms, this hotel has the most luxurious rooms of any hotel in Havana. Add to that a wonderful rooftop pool and bar, and this hotel is the number-one luxe address in the city. See p. 53.
- **Hotel Moka ★★** (Las Terrazas): Run by the eco-community of Las Terrazas, deep in the heart of the Sierra del Rosario mountains, this hilltop retreat has a family-run feel. After bird-watching from your balcony, and a few leisurely laps in the alfresco pool, lounge in your bath with views overlooking the precious-wood forests. See p. 106.
- **Paradisus Princesa del Mar ★★★** (Varadero): The sleek new Royal Service complex at the Paradisus Princesa del Mar has good-looking butler

service, free Wi-Fi, a fancy new restaurant, and a gorgeous slice of beach. There's no need to look any further. See p. 133.

- **Meliá Buenavista ★★★** (Cayo Santa María): An intimate and stylish Royal Service resort with beautiful rooms, butler service, great food, and a couple of slices of pure white Caribbean sand. The on-site spa and the free Wi-Fi complete the appealing picture. See p. 151.
- **Iberostar Grand Hotel Trinidad ★** (Trinidad): A grand city-center hotel that ticks all the right boxes for professional service; smart, spacious, and comfortable rooms; and a good in-house restaurant. See p. 167.
- **Meliá Cayo Coco ★★★** (Cayo Coco): Of the several fine hotels on Cayo Coco, Meliá's top property on the cays is the most sophisticated and stylish, with cool bungalows overlooking a natural lagoon, elegant decor throughout, good restaurants, a beautiful pool area, and a great stretch of beach on a natural cove. See p. 186.
- **Paradisus Río de Oro ★★★** (Playa Esmeralda, Guardalavaca): This sprawling Meliá property hugs a rocky cliff and has some of the most luxuriously designed grounds you'll find anywhere. Rooms are large, refined, and private. Sunbathers will have a hard time deciding between the supremely handsome Esmeralda beach and the small, secluded cove beaches near the spa. For the ultimate in luxury beach living, opt for the Royal Service rooms. See p. 207.
- **Villa Las Brujas ★** (Cayo Santa Maria): Perched on a rocky outcrop over the turquoise Caribbean, the reasonably priced, stylish, and comfortable villas here are connected by a raised, rugged wooden walkway through scrub and mangrove and face a long stretch of beautiful white-sand beach. Staff members are very friendly, too. See p. 152.
- **Villa Maguana ★★** (Playa Maguana): An attractive set of wooden beach cabanas fronting a private, pretty cove next to a 2km (1¼-mile) white-sand beach. This kind of rustic (but well-equipped) cabin accommodation is a rarity in Cuba. See p. 230.
- **Hotel El Castillo ★★** (Baracoa): This hotel has history, charm, and a location to die for. Inside the walls of one of the town's oldest fortresses, up on a hill where the pool comes with splendid panoramic views of Baracoa and the bay, this is the kind of place you won't want to leave. Relaxed and unpretentious, it suits Baracoa perfectly. See p. 230.

CUBA'S best RESTAURANTS & PALADARES

- **La Cocina de Lilliam ★★★** (Havana): Lilliam Domínguez has raised the bar for *paladares* around Havana. Her delicious *criolla* cooking always makes the most of whatever ingredients are locally available, and her softly lit garden setting is stunning. See p. 68.

- **La Terraza ★★★** (Havana): A smorgasbord of char-grilled seafood and meats on the third floor of the Centro Asturiano building overlooking Havana's busy Prado promenade. See p. 64.
- **Santy's ★★★** (Havana): Santy's restaurant is an off-the-beaten-track fisherman's shack hinged to the edge of the River Jaimanitas. It specializes in wonderful sushi eaten right next to the water's edge. See p. 67.
- **Finca Agroecológica El Paraíso (Finca Wilfredo's) ★★★** (Viñales): An organic farm perched on a hilltop serving up what is probably the biggest banquet in Cuba. The suckling pig is exquisite. See p. 103.
- **Salsa Suárez ★★** (Varadero): This elegant, smart roadside restaurant is a game changer in Cuba. The professional uniformed staff is on hand to advise on a seasonally changing menu that includes seafood, meats, and Italian dishes. See p. 134.
- **Restaurante San José ★★** (Trinidad): Inside this supremely elegant dining room, huge grilled seafood platters come with sweet potatoes and vegetables. See p. 170.
- **El Palenquito ★★★** (Santiago de Cuba): El Palenquito serves up tantalizingly delicious barbecued food to its regular customers and those visitors who trek to its flower-filled garden on the city's outskirts. See p. 249.
- **St Pauli ★★** (Santiago de Cuba): A welcome addition to the Santiago de Cuba dining scene. The seasonal menu is chalked up on the blackboard, but expect fresh seafood dishes daily. See p. 249.

SUGGESTED CUBA ITINERARIES

2

Cuba is a big island—the largest in the Caribbean—and its attractions and charms run the gamut from the hustle and bustle of Havana to the colonial grandeur of Trinidad and a host of other small and well-preserved old cities and towns to the steamy, vibrant streets of Santiago and the sparkling seas and white sand of a half-dozen or more topnotch beach destinations. So you'll want to plot an itinerary that meshes with your interests and passions.

Use the following itineraries as rough outlines. Other options include specialized itineraries focused on a particular interest or activity. Bird-watchers could design an itinerary that visits a series of prime bird-watching sites. Dance or art enthusiasts could arrange a specialized trip devoted to Latin culture. And history buffs could build a complete trip around visits to the Moncada barracks in Santiago, the Che Guevara Memorial in Santa Clara, and the Bay of Pigs (Playa Girón). Feel free to pick and choose—combine a bit of one with a smidgen of another, or build something entirely your own.

THE REGIONS IN BRIEF

Cuba is probably the most intensely diverse island destination in the Caribbean, with everything from standard fun-in-the-sun beach resort getaways to colonial city circuits, myriad land and sea adventure opportunities, tobacco and classic-car theme tours, and a wide array of cultural and artistic offerings. There's a lot to see and do in Cuba, and most travelers will have to carefully pick and choose. This chapter provides you with descriptions of the country's regions, along with itineraries that will help you get the most from your visit.

Cuba is the westernmost and largest of the entire chain of Caribbean islands, located at the convergence of the Caribbean Sea, the Gulf of Mexico, and the Atlantic Ocean just 145km (90 miles) south of Florida. They say that if you use your imagination, Cuba looks something like a crocodile: The head is in the east, a line of

The Regions in Brief

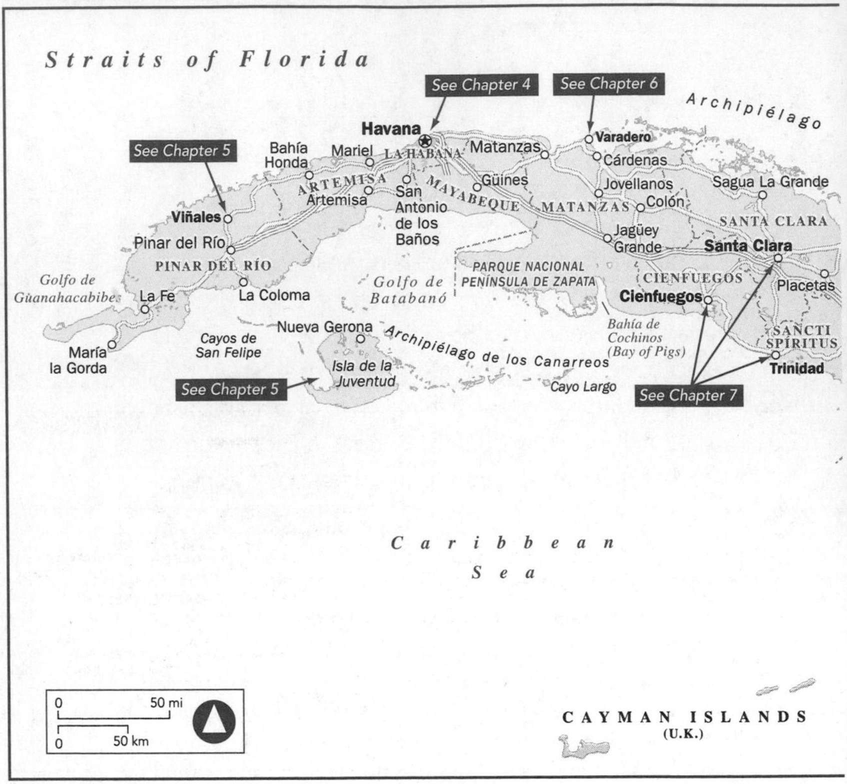

small islands forms the ridges along its back, the Sierra Maestra national park forms the front legs, the Zapata Peninsula forms the rear legs, and Pinar del Río province is the tail. Cuba is in fact a closely linked string of archipelagos, made up of more than 4,000 separate little islands and cays.

Cuba's two major cities, Havana and Santiago de Cuba, are port cities with large, protected harbors. Most of the island's other principal cities lie along its centerline, either right on or just off the Autopista Nacional (National Hwy.), the country's principal trade and transportation route.

HAVANA & PLAYAS DEL ESTE **Havana** is Cuba's capital and the country's most important cultural, political, and economic hub. With a wealth of museums, antique buildings, old forts, the Malecón seaside promenade, and modern restaurants, clubs, and music venues, Havana is one of the liveliest and most engaging cities in Latin America. Just east of the city center are some 15km (9 miles) of very respectable white-sand beach, the **Playas del Este.** While nowhere near as stunning as some of Cuba's more celebrated beach destinations, the Playas del Este are certainly a suitable alternative,

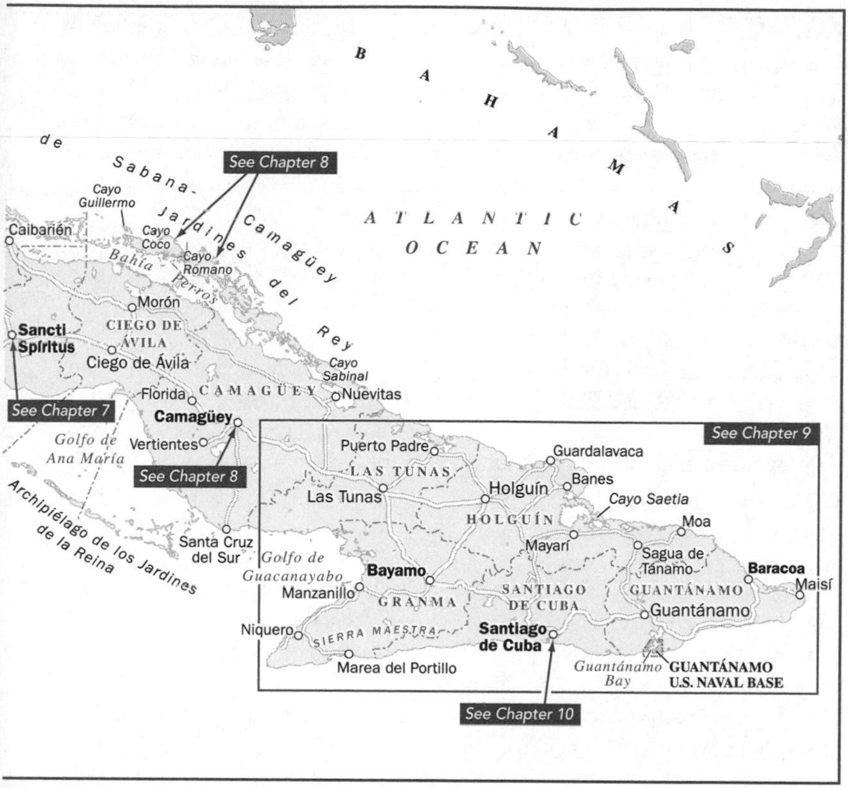

either as a base for exploring Havana or as an easily accessible place for sun, sand, and sea.

VIÑALES & WESTERN CUBA Comprising the new province of Artemisa and the most western province of Pinar del Río, western Cuba is a wonderfully rustic region of farms and forests, flanked by some beautiful and relatively underpopulated beaches. The only real city in the province, **Pinar del Río,** is of limited interest on its own but serves as a gateway to **Viñales** and the **Vuelta Abajo,** Cuba's premiere tobacco-growing and cigar-manufacturing region. Just north of Pinar del Río, Viñales is a pretty little hamlet in an even prettier valley, surrounded by stunning karst hill formations. Viñales is Cuba's prime ecotourist destination, with great opportunities for hiking, bird-watching, mountain biking, and cave exploration. On the far western tip of the island sits the tiny resort of **María la Gorda,** home to some of the best scuba diving in Cuba. Lying off the southern coast of this region in the Caribbean Sea are the island destinations of **Isla de la Juventud,** one of Cuba's premier scuba-diving destinations, and **Cayo Largo del Sur,** another long stretch of dazzling and isolated white sand. Closer to Havana is the ecotourism community of **Las Terrazas.**

VARADERO & MATANZAS PROVINCE Matanzas is Cuba's second-largest province and home to its most important beach destination, **Varadero.** Boasting some 21km (13 miles) of nearly uninterrupted white-sand beach, Varadero is Cuba's quintessential sun-and-fun destination, with a host of luxurious all-inclusive resorts strung along the length of this narrow peninsula. In addition to Varadero, Matanzas province is home to the colonial-era cities of **Matanzas** and **Cárdenas.**

In the southern section of the province is the **Ciénaga de Zapata,** a vast wetlands area of mangrove and swamp, renowned for its wildlife-viewing, bird-watching, diving and fishing opportunities. This is also where you'll find the **Bahía de Cochinos (Bay of Pigs),** where the nascent Cuban revolutionary state defeated an invasion force trained, supplied, and abetted by the United States. The beaches of **Playa Girón** and **Playa Larga** serve as a base for access to some of Cuba's best scuba diving. Playa Girón also possesses, arguably, the most stunning colorful waters in Cuba.

TRINIDAD & CENTRAL CUBA Beginning with the provinces of Villa Clara and Cienfuegos, and including the neighboring province of Sancti Spíritus, central Cuba is the start of the country's rural heartland. Vast regions of sugarcane, tobacco, and cattle ranges are spread out on either side of the Autopista Nacional, which more or less bisects this region as it heads east.

Trinidad is perhaps Cuba's quintessential colonial-era city, with beautifully maintained and restored buildings set on winding cobblestone streets. The cities of **Santa Clara, Cienfuegos,** and **Sancti Spíritus** are considered lesser lights on the tourism circuit, but all have ample charms of their own. A lively university town, Santa Clara is considered the "City of Che Guevara," with its massive memorial to the fallen revolutionary leader. To the north of Santa Clara lie the tiny and utterly charming colonial city of **Remedios** and the beautiful beaches of **la Cayerías del Norte (Cayo Santa María).** Cienfuegos is a charming port town with the country's second-longest seaside promenade. Sancti Spíritus is one of the original seven *villas* of Cuba, with some wonderful old historic churches and buildings, and a more natural feel than you'll find in other more touristy towns.

CAMAGÜEY & NORTHEASTERN CUBA This section of mainland Cuba is little more than a string of rural towns and small cities, anchored by two colonial-era cities. This is Cuba at its quietest, stuck in time and in no rush to break free. However, off the northern coast here lie a series of modern beach resorts built on stretches of soft and silvery white sand, connected to the mainland by a long, narrow causeway that seems to barely skirt the surface of the sea. The sister resort islands of **Cayo Coco** and **Cayo Guillermo** are two of the finest and most popular resort destinations in Cuba. Several less-developed beach resorts stretch east along the coast on the string of islands making up the Archipiélago de Sabana, better known as the **Jardines**

del Rey (King's Gardens). The cities of **Ciego de Avila** and **Camagüey** are under-explored colonial-era cities. The latter, in particular, has loads of charm and attractions and is being restored to highlight much of its former glory. North of Camagüey is the tiny but growing beach resort of **Santa Lucía**. It's best known for the opportunity to dive with bull sharks. On the opposite side of the island the pristine coral reefs and shark life of the **Jardines de la Reina (Gardens of the Queen)** comprise Cuba's premier dive site.

EL ORIENTE For most of the country's history, the whole eastern end of Cuba was known as El Oriente. Today, it is comprised of four separate provinces: **Holguín, Granma, Santiago de Cuba,** and **Guantánamo**. This is a large region with a host of gorgeous natural attractions, highlighted by the mountains of the **Sierra Maestra**—a mecca for naturalists and adventure travelers as well as those looking to follow in the revolutionary footsteps of Fidel and Che—and the very beautiful beaches of **Guardalavaca,** yet another of Cuba's premier beach destinations, with unimaginably fine white sand and turquoise waters. Of the cities here, **Santiago de Cuba** and **Baracoa** are tourist draws in their own right, although visitors to **Holguín** and **Bayamo** will experience Cuba at its most authentic.

SANTIAGO DE CUBA This is Cuba's second largest city. Set between the Sierra Maestra mountains and the sea, Santiago is a vibrant city with a rich artistic, musical, and cultural heritage. Santiago is considered the heart of Cuba's Afro-Cuban and Afro-Caribbean heritage, which is expressed in the music, dance, and religion you'll find here. Santiago's Carnival celebrations are by far the best in Cuba, and some of the best in the entire Caribbean.

The city itself has a fascinating colonial-era center and a host of interesting museums and attractions, including José Martí's tomb and mausoleum, the original Bacardí rum factory, and the impressive Castillo del Morro protecting the city's harbor. Nearby sites worth visiting include the El Cobre shrine to the island's patron saint, La Virgin de la Caridad, and the Gran Piedra, a massive rock outcropping allowing for great hiking and views.

CUBA IN 1 WEEK

This is a tough one. Many visitors are content to spend an entire week soaking up the rays and lying in the sand at an all-inclusive beach resort. I often devote an entire week to Havana. The following itinerary seeks to pack a handful of Cuba's top attractions into a concise, yet doable, weeklong visit. You'll get a taste of the country's best big city and its top colonial-era town, as well as some time on the beach.

Day 1: Arrive & Settle into Havana

Arrive and check in to your hotel. Take an afternoon walk along the **Malecón** and sip a sunset cocktail at the **Hotel Nacional de Cuba ★★** (p. 57). For dinner, head to either **La Guarida ★★** (p. 65) or **La Cocina**

Cuba in 1 & 2 Weeks

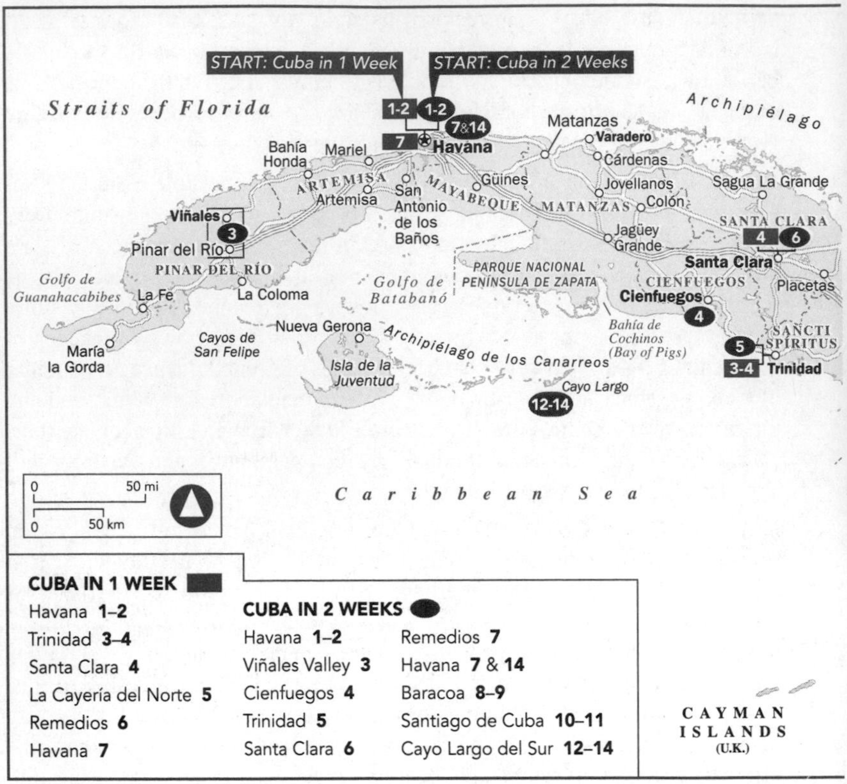

de Lilliam ★★ (p. 68), two of the city's best *paladares.* Be sure to make a reservation as soon as you get to your hotel, because these places book up fast. After dinner, catch some jazz at **Café Miramar** ★★ (p. 88) if you're not jet-lagged, or have a drink at **Madrigal** (p. 91) or **El Cocinero** (p. 90).

Day 2: Step Back in Time in Havana

Start the morning off in **La Habana Vieja** (p. 44). Visit the **Plaza de la Catedral, the Plaza de Armas, Plaza Vieja,** and **Plaza de San Francisco.** Be sure to tour the **Museo de la Ciudad** ★★ (p. 72), the **Castillo de la Real Fuerza** ★ (p. 69), and any other attractions that catch your attention. Have lunch at **Dona Eutimia** ★ (p. 63). After lunch, head toward **Parque Central** and visit either the **Museo Nacional de las Bellas Artes** ★★ (p. 72), or the **Museo de la Revolución** ★ (p. 72). Finish up your afternoon strolling along the **Malecón** (p. 75). If you have a spare half-hour, drive by the **Plaza de la Revolución** ★ to see the José Martí memorial and the iconic iron sculpture of the face of Che Guevara

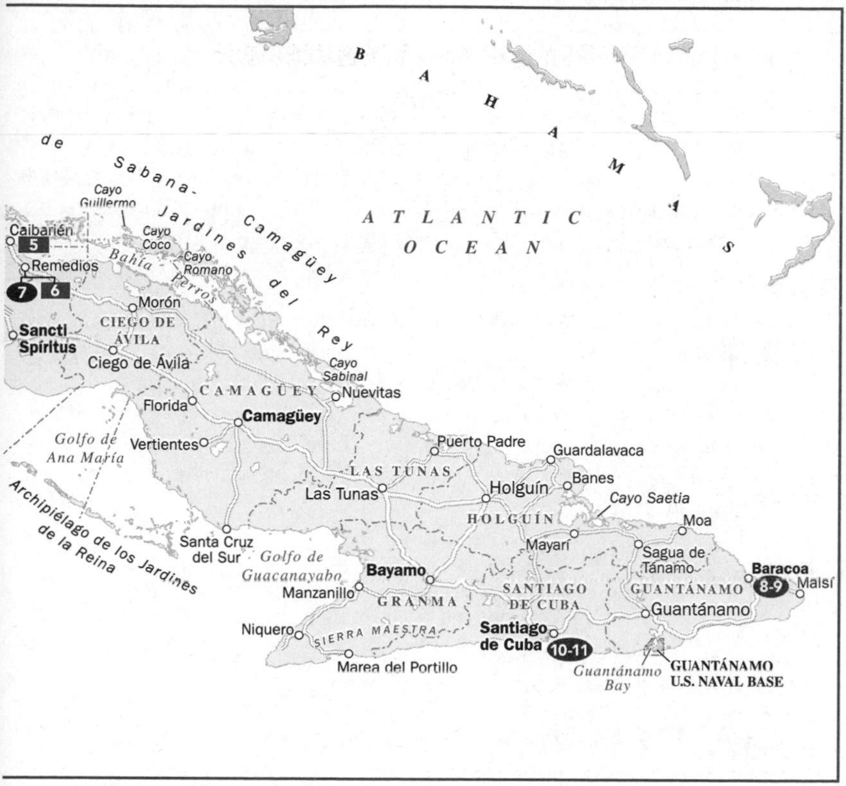

on the Ministry of the Interior building. Before dinner, head for a drink at **La Floridita** or **304 O'Reilly** (p. 63). In the evening, head to the **Fábrica de Arte Cubano** (p. 89) or take in dinner and a show at the **Tropicana ★★★** (p. 90).

Day 3: Trinidad

Head for Trinidad. Stay in one of the many glorious *casas particulares* right in the colonial center of this classic little city. Spend the afternoon touring Trinidad's colonial-era landmarks, including the **Plaza Mayor ★★,** the **Plazuela El Jigüe,** the **Iglesia de la Santísima Trinidad,** and the **Museo Romántico ★★** (p. 165). Take tea or coffee in the cute patio of **Café Don Pepe** (p. 170). For dinner, make a reservation at **Restaurante San José ★★** (p. 170) or **Taberna La Botija** (p. 170). After dinner, stroll around the Plaza Mayor and listen for where the action is. It might be a salsa or *son* band playing on the steps below the **Casa de la Música ★** (p. 171), or it might be in any one of several clubs nearby, including the excellent **Palenque de los Congos Reales ★★**.

Day 4: Checking in with Che

Spend the morning strolling the streets of Trinidad and browsing the various little street markets, shops, and artists' studios around town. From Trinidad, head north to **Santa Clara** ★, Che Guevara's city. Your first and most important stop here is the massive and impressive **Monumento Ernesto Che Guevara** ★ (p. 146), set on the Plaza de la Revolución. In the early evening, head to **Parque Vidal,** the downtown heart and soul of Santa Clara. Stop in to tour the **Teatro La Caridad** (p. 146), and then head to **Restaurant Auténtica Pérgola** ★ (p. 149) for dinner. After dinner, see if there's anything happening at **Club Mejunje** ★★ (p. 149).

Days 5 & 6: Hit the Beach

From Santa Clara, head to **La Cayerías del Norte (Cayo Santa María)** ★★★ (p. 151), which boasts several large and luxurious resorts on some of the finest beaches in Cuba. Be sure to stop for a bit in the tiny, colonial-era town of **Remedios** ★★★ (p. 149) on your way. And then settle in for some serious relaxation. There's excellent snorkeling, as well as numerous opportunities to indulge in other watersports. Or you can just chill.

Day 7: Going Home

Return to **Havana** in time for your international connection. If you have extra time, head to the secondhand book market in the Plaza de Armas and the **Almacenes San José** market (p. 84) to do some last-minute shopping before you go.

CUBA IN 2 WEEKS

If you've got 2 weeks, you'll be able to hit all the highlights mentioned above, plus some others, including Cuba's second city Santiago, a side trip to the gorgeous *mogotes* (limestone formations) and tobacco farms of the Viñales valley, and visits to Cienfuegos and Baracoa. Plus, the extra time lets you do all this at a slightly more relaxed pace. This itinerary starts off very similar to the 1-week version above, but soon diverges.

Day 1: Arrive & Settle into Havana

Arrive and settle in to your hotel. Spend the afternoon walking along the **Malecón** ★★★ and have a sunset cocktail at the **Hotel Nacional** ★★ (p. 57). After sunset, head over for dinner at **La Divina Pastora** (p. 68) in the **Parque Histórico Morro y Cabaña** ★★ (p. 78). Stick around for the ***cañonazo*** (cannon-firing) ceremony.

Day 2: Step Back in Time

Start the morning off in **La Habana Vieja** ★★★. Visit the **Plaza de la Catedral,** the **Plaza de Armas, Plaza Vieja,** and **Plaza de San Francisco.**

Be sure to tour the **Museo de la Ciudad** ★★ (p. 72), the **Castillo de la Real Fuerza** ★ (p. 69), and any other attractions that catch your attention. Have lunch at **Mama Inés** (p. 64). After lunch, head toward **Parque Central** and visit either the **Museo Nacional del Bellas Artes** ★★ (p. 72) or the **Museo de la Revolución** ★ (p. 72). Finish up your afternoon strolling past El Capitolio, down the Prado promenade and out to the Malecón. If you have a spare half-hour, take a short tour of the **Cementerio de Colón** (p. 75) and drive by the **Plaza de la Revolución** ★ to see the José Martí memorial and the iconic iron sculpture of the face of Che Guevara on the Ministry of the Interior building. In the evening, head to **Café Miramar, Fábrica de Arte Cubano,** or the **Tropicana** ★★★ (p. 90) for a show.

Day 3: The Viñales Valley by Day, Jazz at Night

Sign on for an organized day tour of the **Viñales valley** ★★★. You'll get to take in some of Cuba's best natural scenery, and also visit a tobacco farm and cigar-rolling facility. You'll probably also visit the Guayabitas liquor factory in **Pinar del Río** (p. 92), and take a quick tour through **La Cueva del Indio** (p. 98). This jam-packed day tour should still get you back to Havana in time for a dinner at one of the city's standout *paladares* (private home restaurants), followed by some hot jazz at **Café Miramar** or **La Zorra y El Cuervo** ★★ (p. 91) or some subterranean sounds at **Café Teatro Brecht** (p. 88).

Day 4: Cienfuegos, la Perla del Sur

Pick up a rental car and head for **Cienfuegos** ★, a bustling port city on the southern coast, with a compact, yet very attractive colonial-era core. Get to know the old center around **Parque José Martí,** visiting the **Catedral de la Purísima Concepción** (p. 156) and the **Teatro Tomás Terry** ★ (p. 156). In the afternoon, head out to the Punta Gorda district and have a sunset drink on the roof of the **Palacio del Valle** (p. 156) or at the bar in the garden on the point. For dinner, walk to the end of Punta Gorda to **Villa Lagarto** (p. 160).

Day 5: Trinidad

From Cienfuegos, it's a short hop to **Trinidad** ★★★, with some beautiful scenery along the coast. Stay in one of the glorious *casas particulares* right in the colonial center of this classic little city. Spend the afternoon touring Trinidad's colonial-era landmarks, including the **Plaza Mayor,** the **Iglesia de la Santísima Trinidad,** and the **Museo Romántico** ★★ (p. 165). For dinner, make a reservation at **Restaurante San José** ★★ (p. 170) or **La Botija** ★★. After dinner, stroll the area around the Plaza Mayor and listen for where the action is. It might be a salsa or *son* band playing on the steps below the **Casa de la Música** ★ (p. 171), or it might be in any one of several clubs nearby, including the excellent **Palenque de los Congos Reales** ★★, or the classic **Casa de la Trova** (p. 171).

Day 6: Checking in with Che

Spend the morning strolling the streets of Trinidad and browsing the various shops, street markets, and artists' studios around town. From Trinidad, head north to **Santa Clara ★**, Che Guevara's city. Your first and most important stop here is the massive and impressive **Monumento Ernesto Che Guevara ★** (p. 146), set on the Plaza de la Revolución. In the early evening, head to **Parque Vidal,** the downtown heart and soul of Santa Clara. Stop in to tour the **Teatro La Caridad** (p. 146), and then head to **Restaurant Autentica Pergola ★★** (p. 149) for dinner. After dinner, see if there's anything happening at **Club Mejunje ★★** (p. 149).

Day 7: Remedios and Back to Havana

In the morning, drive to the charming nearby town of **Remedios ★★★** (p. 149). This is one of Cuba's smallest and best-preserved old colonial-era towns. Tour the **Iglesia de San Juan Bautista ★★** (p. 149), with its intricately carved and ornate baroque altar, and stop for a cool drink or light lunch at the open-air **Café El Louvre ★** (p. 150) right on the town's central plaza. Allow yourself a little over 4 hours to drive from Remedios back to Havana, where you'll turn in your rental car before taking a flight for the rest of your trip.

Days 8 & 9: Head East to Baracoa

From Havana, take a flight (booked well in advance) to **Baracoa ★★★** (p. 224), the oldest city in Cuba and the city with the most beautiful setting. You'll definitely want to stay in the **Hotel El Castillo ★★** (p. 230), with its commanding setting on a hillside over the city or in one of the city's excellent *casas particulares*. Spend a day exploring the architecture and old-world charms of the city, and another day hiking the lush forests around **El Yunque ★★** and swimming at **Playa Maguana,** or take a boat tour of the World Heritage Site the **Parque Nacional Alejandro de Humboldt ★★** (p. 229). Despite its diminutive size, Baracoa is a bustling little burg with excellent nightlife.

Days 10 & 11: Sweltering Santiago

In Baracoa, you can arrange for a transfer, Víazul bus, or private taxi to **Santiago de Cuba ★★★**, the island's second-largest city. If you want to be in the heart of downtown, choose the **Hotel Casa Granda ★★** (p. 255); if you're looking for more comfort, amenities, and facilities, you should book a room in the **Meliá Santiago de Cuba ★★** (p. 247) or stay in one of the city's lovely *casas particulares*. You'll need 2 days to fully explore this colonial-era port city, with its host of historical and architectural attractions. Be sure to schedule at least 1 night at Santiago's fabulous **Casa de la Trova ★★** (p. 254) or **Casa de las Tradiciones ★★★** (p. 254).

Days 12, 13 & 14: Hot Sun, Cool Sands, Clear Water

Finish your trip with some downtime at an all-inclusive resort on **Cayo Largo del Sur ★★★** (p. 117). You'll have to fly here from Havana, and you're best off just buying a 3-day/2-night package from any of the tour desks in Havana or Santiago. You should easily be able to arrange a flight from Santiago to Havana that connects with a flight to Cayo Largo (although you would have to transfer from José Martí airport to the Playa Baracoa, Havana airfield); be sure your flight back from Cayo Largo gets you into Havana in time for your international connection and flight home. If you have time pressures, opt for one of the top-end all-inclusives at **Varadero ★★**. Or head north to the stunning beaches of **Guardalavaca ★★**, a 4-hour drive from Santiago.

CUBA FOR FAMILIES

Most of Cuba's principal attractions—its art, architecture, history, music, cigars, and so on—are geared toward adults. There are, in fact, few attractions or activities geared for the very young. This is why I recommend families base themselves in a town that has a large, all-inclusive resort with a well-developed children's program. For my money, Varadero is the best bet, although a case can be made for Guardalavaca as well. Both have a host of excellent all-inclusive resorts. If your children are worldly and inquisitive, feel free to swap out some resort days for the more cultural side trips to cities, destinations, and attractions described in some of the other itineraries in this chapter.

Day 1: Arrive in Varadero

Fly directly into **Varadero.** I recommend the **Meliá Península Varadero ★★★** (p. 134), which has an excellent children's program and tons of activity and tour options. After settling into your room, check out the **children's program** and any **activities** or **tours** scheduled for the coming days. Feel free to adapt the following days' suggestions accordingly. Spend some time on the beach or at the pool.

Day 2: Take in an Attraction or Two

Varadero is chock-full of attractions geared toward the whole family. You can head to see the dolphin show at the local **Delfinario** (p. 127) or take a cruise up the main strip in a gleaming candy-pink classic American convertible (p. 130). If your family is adventurous, try the **Boat Adventure ★**, a fast and furious trip through the mangroves aboard sit-on-top motorized watercraft.

Day 3: A Trip to Trinidad

All of the hotel tour desks offer day trips to **Trinidad ★★★**. This immaculately preserved colonial city has a very compact central core that shouldn't tire or bore your children. In fact, they should get a kick out of the rough cobblestone streets, ancient architecture, vibrant street markets, and real glimpse into everyday Cuban life.

Day 4: Parents' Day Off

Drop the kids off with the **children's program** for at least 1 full day and treat yourselves to some time alone. If you play golf, schedule a round at the **Varadero Golf Club ★** (p. 128), or, if you want to try something new, learn to kite-surf. Or simply pamper yourself with the excellent **spa services** right at the **Meliá Península Varadero** (p. 134). Pick up the kids and treat them to dinner off the resort grounds. I recommend **Paladar Nonna Tina** (p. 135) for its family-pleasing Italian dishes. If your kids are more grown-up, take them to dinner at swish **Salsa Suárez** (p. 134).

Day 5: Head for the High Seas

Sign up for a **day cruise** on one of the many sailboats operating out of Varadero. These cruises head out to nearby cays and include some snorkeling time, as well as lunch either on the boat or on some private little island beach.

Day 6: Parents' Night Off

This is your last day, so take advantage of the resort's in-house facilities and activities, but be sure to reserve a babysitter for the evening and make reservations for dinner and a show at the **Tropicana Matanzas ★★** (p. 90). Feeling active? Organize a dance class with Paradiso's **academia de arte y cultura** (p. 130) and then head for a cocktail at the **Casa Blanca bar** (p. 136), atop the Mansión Xanadú.

Day 7: Heading Home

Use any spare time you have before your flight out of **Varadero** to buy last-minute souvenirs and gifts, or just laze on the beach or by the pool. The Centro Comercial de Hicacos has a children's **toy shop** (p. 130) and various stores sell Havaiana flip-flops at about a quarter of the price seen outside the country.

HAVANA IN 3 DAYS

Havana is an amazing—at times, overwhelming—city, overflowing with history, art, architecture, culture, nightlife, and more. Three days will allow you to take in its most important attractions, and maybe even discover some of its lesser-known charms.

Day 1: Start in the Old City

Start your day in La Habana Vieja. Visit the **Plaza de la Catedral,** the **Plaza de Armas, Plaza Vieja,** and **Plaza de San Francisco.** Be sure to tour the **Museo de la Ciudad ★★** (p. 72), the **Castillo de la Real**

Fuerza ★ (p. 69), and any other attractions that catch your attention. Have lunch at **La Terraza** ★ (p. 64). Spend the afternoon exploring the area around Parque Central, which includes **El Capitolio** ★ (p. 74), the **Museo Nacional de las Bellas Artes** ★★ (p. 72), and the **Museo de la Revolución** ★ (p. 72). Make a reservation in advance for the last tour of the **Partagás cigar factory** (p. 75) and take a taxi through Chinatown to get there. You will not have time to visit four attractions in one afternoon, so prioritize them beforehand.

As the day cools down, take a stroll on the **Malecón** ★★★ (p. 75). If you've got the energy, take the 30-minute walk to the **Hotel Nacional** ★★ (p. 57) in time for a sunset *mojito* at its outdoor bar.

La Guarida or San Cristóbal

For dinner, either visit the film-set paladar La Guarida or the eclectic interior surrounds of the excellent paladar San Cristóbal in Centro Habana.

Day 2: Vedado & Miramar

Start the morning with a stroll among the beautiful tombs and mausoleums of **Cementerio de Colón** ★★ (p. 75). From here, head in a classic car to the **José Martí Memorial** (p. 76), and enjoy the panoramic view from the highest spot in Havana. Then, imagine the Plaza de la Revolución fit to bursting during a political rally and admire the iconic **image of Che Guevara cast in iron** ★ on the Ministry of the Interior building and the new **image of Camilio Cienfugos** on the Ministry of Communications building opposite the memorial. After lunch, take your classic car through the grand avenues of the Vedado district and head over to the outdoor art exhibit that is the **Callejón de Hamel** ★★★ (p. 73), or take a half-day art tour with curator Sussette Martínez. After that you should have worked up enough of a sweat for a refreshing bowl of ice cream at **Coppelia** ★ (p. 76).

Have dinner at **La Cocina de Lilliam** ★★★ (p. 68), on the one hand because it's an excellent restaurant renowned for its homemade cuisine, and on the other, because it's close to the Tropicana. If the Tropicana doesn't float your boat, the new and hopping **Fábrica de Arte Cubano** (p. 89) is a must-visit.

Tropicana

It's time to pull out all the stops and head to the Tropicana (p. 90) for a show. This place is the original and still the best cabaret show in Cuba. Stick around after the show for some serious salsa dancing.

Day 3: More La Habana Vieja

Give yourself another day in **La Habana Vieja**—there's just no way you've seen it all in one day. Be sure to visit some of the art galleries and spend some time shopping at the **Almacenes San José** indoor market (p. 84), the Plaza de Armas, and the new breed of shops in town such as **Piscolabis** (p. 84) and **Clandestina** (p. 84). Have lunch on one of the ancient plazas here. I recommend **Dona Eutimia, Mama Inés,** or **Paladar los Mercaderes** (p. 64), or, for a light lunch, **Dulcería Bianchini** (p. 62). In the late afternoon, head over to the **Parque Histórico Morro y Cabaña** ★★ (p. 78) and explore the forts and museums at this complex.

La Divina Pastora ★

After touring the Parque Histórico Morro y Cabaña complex, grab an outdoor table near sunset at La Divina Pastora (p. 68), and enjoy the view of Havana across the harbor from the restaurant balcony. Be sure to finish your dinner in time for the *cañonazo* ceremony.

After dinner and the *cañonazo,* head to **Café Miramar** or **La Zorra y El Cuervo** ★★ (p. 91) for a late-night jazz concert, or to the **FAC** (p. 89), or simply to one of Havana's late-night bars such as **Espacios** (p. 90) or **Madrigal** (p. 91).

CUBA IN CONTEXT

3

Cuba is an ongoing and enduring enigma. By any conventional measure, this Caribbean island should be a mere speck in the global geopolitical ocean. Yet for more than half a century, this nation of 11.3 million people has commanded the world stage in a manner wholly incommensurate with its small size and economic significance. A former colony of Spain and playground of American high rollers, Cuba struck out on its own in the late 1950s, and the nation remains a hot topic in the corridors of the world's power brokers. Fiercely independent but rarely free, and the unlikeliest of major players, Cuba arouses passions like perhaps no other nation.

For decades, those inflamed feelings have focused on the Communist regime that one man, Fidel Castro, brazenly engineered. Hated and worshiped in almost equal measure, Fidel Castro defied critics, confounded pundits, and frustrated his own followers. His brother, Raúl Castro, who became president in February 2008, walks a similar walk with Cuba's unique brand of homegrown communism. However, Raúl inherited a crumbling economy during a global recession that forced him—and the government—to review and "update" some of Cuba's socialist policies. U.S. President Obama's rapprochement with the nation—initiated after some 54 years of political stalemate—was a hopeful move for Cubans as the thaw began in 2015.

Slowly, though, the world is learning that Cuba is more than a coveted property in a high-stakes game of Risk. Wider exposure to Cuban culture (especially its music and dance), the island's colonial treasures, and the Cuban people has given rise to a love affair that transcends international politics.

CUBA TODAY

Cuba was one of the major stories of the 20th century, from the stunning overthrow of the dictator Fulgencio Batista in 1959 by a ragtag revolutionary army to Fidel Castro's tenacious hold on power. And although virtually everything about Cuba is filtered through an ideological lens, Cuba is a fascinating living laboratory of social and political experimentation, and a test case for a people's perseverance. A defiant Fidel Castro weathered the fierce opposition of the U.S. government and the hostility of Cuban exiles in Miami, just 145km (90 miles) to the north. While some of his radical reform goals have been achieved, Cubans have also been greatly disheartened by the regime's abject failures. The Cuban people have been forced to make unfathomable sacrifices in the face of a poorly planned (and worse performing) economy and the American trade embargo.

Cuba was once the dazzling iconoclast, held in awe by much of Latin America for its willingness to stand up to the United States. In recent years, though, Fidel Castro found himself increasingly isolated, and few are those who don't believe that Cuba is a Communist dinosaur. Although the Castros have promoted foreign investment and joint ventures in oil, mining, and tourism, Cuba remains willfully individualistic and nationalistic.

The country's uniqueness is also the source of its phenomenal appeal. Cuba is a puzzling anachronism, a creaky and sputtering country caught in a tortuous time warp. Many of Havana's crumbling colonial buildings are little more than facades, propped up like a movie set. While most of the planet plunges ahead at a dizzying digital pace, Cuba crawls along in slow motion. Homes have only the most rudimentary appliances—if they have any at all. Vintage Chevy and Cadillac jalopies from the '40s and '50s, their chrome fenders pock-marked and their engines patched together with a hodgepodge of parts, lumber down the streets of dimly lit cities. In rural areas, even antique cars are a luxury; transportation is more commonly by oxen-led cart, and horse carriages.

To many visitors, Cuba offers a mystifying if welcome retreat from the whiz-bang of technology and convenience to which most of us have become accustomed. Groups of underemployed men while away the hours playing dominoes on card tables set up in the street. Septets of octogenarian musicians play traditional Cuban *son,* music with roots in the 19th century and whose rhythms are largely unaffected by outside influence and changing global tastes. Neighbors gather on doorsteps in the wilting heat of the late afternoon to chat and fan themselves, and form friendly networks working together to solve problems of accommodations, transportation, plumbing, and electricity.

Many travelers, convinced that Cuba cannot forever remain a Communist bastion, hasten to experience the country before it gets reeled in by a ravenous capitalistic Western world. Cuba's tourist potential is almost unlimited, and the government has embraced tourism as its best and perhaps only hope to bring in hard currency and employ large numbers of people. The largest island in the Caribbean, Cuba is abundantly blessed with palm trees, sultry temperatures, hip-swiveling rhythms, stunning beaches, warm people, a surfeit of rum, and the world's finest hand-rolled cigars. In the mid-1980s, only about 250,000 visitors traveled to Cuba annually; in 2014, there were 3 million visitors. Tourism has now surpassed the source of Cuba's original wealth, the sugar industry, to become one of the country's top three revenue earners (US$2.5bn) along with US$2.7 billion of remittances sent from exiles, and the medical export of Cuban personnel to Socialist-friendly countries (CUS$10bn). If all Americans were allowed to travel legally, politicians and hoteliers reason, Cuba might receive as many as 10 million visitors annually. Yet massive tourism is still a dream in Cuba. Many travelers still cling to package tours and tourist resorts clustered on beaches, and U.S. visitors (as of mid-2015) remain restricted in their travel to Cuba by the U.S. trade embargo.

Modern Cuba is a tangle of contradictions. The centralized economy is dependent upon capitalistic joint ventures with foreign investors from Canada, Great Britain, Germany, Italy, China, and Spain. Plenty of Cubans survive only with the assistance of political and religious opponents of the regime who've fled the country and send millions of dollars in hard currency each year to relatives. Until the change of head of state in February 2008, the socialist regime, ostensibly founded upon an egalitarian revolution, didn't allow its own citizens to step foot into certain tourist enclaves, including many resorts, hotels, and restaurants, and a long list of goods and services readily available to foreigners could not be enjoyed by nationals. Many of these goods still cannot be enjoyed by Cubans. Although they're now allowed to own mobile phones and computers, for example, for the vast majority of Cubans these consumer goods are far beyond the reach of their pitiful state wages. Start-up mobile-phone contracts cost CUC$40, but with average salaries around CUC$20 a month, owning a mobile phone is a pipe dream for most Cubans.

Raúl Castro's late 2010 reforms opened the door to some much-needed private enterprise. Around 201 (nonprofessional) jobs were permitted by the state—including accountant, dog groomer, palm trimmer, photographer, and florist—and rules were relaxed for private restaurant and B&B owners. In 2011, Cubans were permitted to buy and sell property, in 2014 to buy and sell new and used cars, and in 2013 to leave the country for travel without an exit visa and without forfeiting their homes. But Cubans are still chomping at the bit for more economic and business freedoms.

Cubans often fall back on an all-purpose national refrain to describe what their lives are like: *No es fácil.* It isn't easy. Cubans are specialists in what might be called the *arte de inventar,* the art of inventing solutions where there are none. That means fighting to make ends meet through odd jobs and hustling. Setting up neighborhood networks that distribute contraband goods, such as cigars nicked from the tobacco factory. Running illicit *paladares* in living rooms and backyards, serving black-market lobster or beef. Cuba is an entire nation jimmy-rigged and bandaged with duct tape.

Unless you're ensconced in a gleaming, all-inclusive beach resort, where the realities of Cuban life are whitewashed for the benefit of tourists, the grinding deficiencies of the Cuban economy and bottomless needs of the Cuban people are hard to ignore. Talk to almost any Cuban and he'll tell you about appallingly overcrowded housing and transport conditions, state rations that don't cover basic needs, the scarcity of basic commodities, and the CUC$15-to-CUC$20 monthly salaries paid in Cuban currency, the national peso, which then must be converted to the convertible peso (CUC) often at an unfavorable exchange rate. Workers trained by the state as engineers and doctors instead scramble for more lucrative positions as bellboys, while others cobble together a few dollars worth of hard currency from occasional, often extralegal, odd jobs. Ration booklets (*libretas*) allow Cuban citizens to buy a certain amount of basic goods at highly subsidized prices in Cuban pesos. However, the rations allotted do not suffice: just 10kg of rice, 6kg of white sugar, 2kg of dark sugar, 1 packet of coffee, 250ml of oil, and 5 eggs; meat is distributed about every 2 weeks. Rations have been cut back year after year, and supplies like cigarettes, beans, and chicken are difficult to get. A few other goods are available on an irregular basis, such as fish, ham, and toothpaste. Anything beyond those miserly provisions must be purchased on the black market or in hard-currency-only stores.

The much-touted talk of doing away with Cuba's double currency (p. 33), has yet to materialize.

Yet Cuba is remarkably free of the crushing poverty sadly common in Africa, India, and even other parts of Latin America and the Caribbean. Housing is provided by the state—homeless people sleeping on the streets are nowhere to be seen in Cuba—and all citizens receive regular food rations. Many appear surprisingly well dressed, no doubt a privilege of possessing a job that earns a few dollars or having family members outside of Cuba who send money and clothes that help ease the pain.

Fidel Castro took power in 1959 with a commitment to remake the nation by overhauling its economy, land ownership, education system, and healthcare. On a social agenda, Cuba has been remarkably successful. All Cubans receive free healthcare. However, most hospitals and pharmacies lack the most basic supplies, like aspirin and X-ray plates. Some hospital interiors are appallingly outdated, and back-up-electricity generators for *apagónes* (power cuts) have been known to fail while operating theaters are in use. Compulsory state education through high school is free, and the national university system has produced some extremely accomplished professionals in medicine and the sciences. Average life expectancy rose from 57 years in 1958 to 79 in 2012—the same as that of the U.S. and the second-highest in Latin America. Infant mortality, just 4.7 per 1,000 births, is the lowest in the region and equal to or better than many developed countries, including in the U.S. Literacy rates are above 95 percent (the government claims to have erased illiteracy entirely), violent crime is rare, and the pervasive sexism and racism of pre-Revolutionary Cuba have given way to a more equitable landscape.

Those achievements receive less attention, though, than Cuba's strangled economy and continued political repression. Opponents of the socialist regime, both outside of Cuba and increasingly within the country, make the case that Cuba is a nation with no semblance of democracy. A single political party dominates all Cuban life. Cubans cannot speak freely, the media are state-owned and closely orchestrated by the Communist Party, and doctors and military personnel, among others, have no rights to travel freely beyond Cuba.

Hundreds of thousands of Fidel Castro's early opponents fled Cuba in the early days of the Revolution, when the state was busy expropriating private property, land, and businesses. Since then, thousands more have tried, only a few successfully, to make it to U.S. shores, often in rickety *balseros* (rafts). The less daring, but equally hopeful form daily queues at the U.S. Embassy in Havana and other foreign embassies, desperately hoping for visas. On three major occasions, including the Mariel Boatlift in 1980, Fidel Castro sought to relieve pressure by allowing large groups, many of them deemed "undesirables," to emigrate.

Although the U.S. trade embargo and travel restrictions are still in place, there has been much focus on U.S. President Barack Obama's December 2014 detente policy towards Cuba. Obama's early promise to close the U.S. prison at Guantánamo Bay in eastern Cuba (p. 223) has not been met, but in early 2015 he relaxed rules on Cuban Americans visiting their families in Cuba (p. 23) and on licensed travel for U.S. citizen. In 2009 he also removed certain restrictions on food and medicines and offered to open a dialogue with Raúl Castro. It took 5 years—an effort brokered by Pope Francis—for the diplomatic thaw to begin. The U.S. announced it would reestablish political relations with Cuba, reopen its embassy, and relax—but not withdraw—travel restrictions. At the same time, imprisoned USAID contractor Alan Gross was released after 5 years, and the remaining three of the "Cuban Five" were released back to Cuba. As of mid-2015, political talks were ongoing as Cuba demanded that the topics of the U.S. trade embargo and the U.S. naval base at Guantánamo Bay be brought to the table.

Diplomatic overtures aside, the Castros' regime rolls on. Despite years of difficulty and isolation, *La Revolución,* now 56 years old, continues to be the nation's rallying cry and raison d'être. Schoolchildren don't become Boy or Girl Scouts, but Young Communist Pioneers. Local chapters of the Committee for the Defense of the Revolution (CDR) keep tabs on dissenters and those not upholding the party line. Throughout the country, giant billboards function like government pep talks to convince a population more worried about shoes and food than ideology to stay on the path. Billboards proclaim quaint notions like VICTORIA DE IDEAS (A Victory of Ideas), VIVIMOS EN UN PAIS LIBRE (We Live in a Free Country), LA REVOLUCION SOMOS NOSOTROS (We Are the Revolution), and even the melancholy rationalization SOMOS FELICES AQUI (We're Happy Here). Larger-than-life portraits of heroes and martyrs like Che Guevara (the roguish icon of revolution the world over), José Martí, Camilo Cienfuegos, and now, anachronistically, "Los Cinco" (five suspected spies convicted and imprisoned in the United States, with the last three released in December 2014) guard the entrances to towns and are plastered on the walls of shops, offices, and homes. Perhaps fittingly, most of these billboards and portraits are now worn and faded.

Amid the extraordinary dilapidation of Havana and other decaying towns, it's near impossible for travelers not to wonder: What must this place once have looked like? Formerly grand, and now just badly faded and deteriorated buildings stand—if barely so—as harsh evidence of 5½ decades of frustration, empty state coffers, and bankrupt promises of an idealistic, battle-hardened regime. Cubans are exhorted to fight on to bring the Revolution to fruition, but many Cubans, especially the young who've known nothing but Fidel, are weary of waiting. *Un año más*—one more year, they say.

Still, Cuba is as exhilarating as it is perplexing. One of the most exciting, mind-bending, and sensation-tingling countries you can visit, Cuba is a flood of indelible images. Many are inspiring, others heartbreaking. An open-air cafe with a smiling band of preternaturally cool musicians locked in a perfect groove. Huge crowds of hitchhiking Cubans gathered on the side of the road, desperate for a lift. Noisy Carnival rumbas and conga groups piercing the heat with Afro-Caribbean rhythms. Sexy couples with well-oiled hips gliding across dance floors. Those combative billboards forlornly pitched along the side of empty highways. Crowded *camellos,* crazy people-hauler flatbed trucks that look like urban transportation in a post-apocalyptic world. Mile-long lines for ice cream at Coppelia shops and bread at the state-run bakery. Kids playing *pelota,* the national pastime of baseball, with a stick in the hollows of a ruined building.

But perhaps the truest picture of Cuba comes from the people themselves. Resilient and eternally patient Cubans somehow find the will to rise above devastating poverty, shortages, dense bureaucracy, and political authoritarianism. (And the late 2010 economic reforms have shown how entrepreneurial will can overcome all manner of obstacles.) With wonderful senses of humor and hospitality like few others, they invite visitors into their cramped homes even if they've nothing to offer. Schoolchildren, like a UN ad in identical maroon-and-mustard-hued uniforms, smile sweetly for photographs.

Cuba remains a quandary and a country full of potential. Hope can be seen in the painstaking restoration of landmark colonial buildings in La Habana Vieja, whose decrepitude only a few years ago was the perfect metaphor for Cuba. Now that the ailing Fidel Castro is in the background, all eyes are firmly on Raúl Castro, the widening of his economic reforms, and the game-changing political talks with the U.S. (see also "Cuba Under Raúl Castro," later in this chapter).

LOOKING BACK AT CUBA

In the first half of the 20th century, the United States, the primary purchaser of Cuba's sugar, dominated the island's economy and to a considerable extent controlled its political processes. Until the 1950s, Cuba was besieged by political corruption and violence. Fulgencio Batista, though only a sergeant in the army, managed to dictate Cuba's internal affairs through a series of puppet presidents for nearly a decade before winning the presidency outright in 1940. Though Batista retired in 1944, he staged a military coup and returned to power in 1952. Batista's corrupt dictatorship, supported by the United States, overlooked growing poverty across the country while Batista fattened his overseas bank accounts.

Havana was effectively ruled by a group of millionaires more powerful than anywhere else in Latin America, a distortion that allowed Cuban officials to claim that Cuba had the second-highest per capita income in the region. The capital was overrun by brothels, casinos, and gangsters, with high rollers in zoot suits transforming the city into their personal playground. Meanwhile, most of the country was mired in poverty, and more than half of all Cubans were undernourished in 1950. The nascent republic's unequivocal dependence on the United States, corruption, and absence of social equality reinforced the seeds of discontent that had been planted as far back as the 1920s.

Guerrilla Warfare & Revolution

By the 1950s, the climate was ripe for revolution, though it would come in fits and starts. A band of young rebels attacked the Moncada Barracks, the country's second-most-important military base, in Santiago de Cuba on July 26, 1953 (the rebels would later take the date of the attack as the name for their movement, calling it the "Movimiento 26 de Julio"). The effort failed miserably, and many of the rebels were killed or later captured and tortured by the military. But the attack gave its young leader, a lawyer named Fidel Castro Ruz, the bully pulpit he needed. Jailed and tried for offenses against the nation, Castro's legendary 2-hour defense—presaging an uncanny ability to speak for hours at length about Cuba and the Revolution—included the now-famous words, "History will absolve me" (the title of Castro's revolutionary manifesto). Castro was imprisoned offshore on the Isla de la Juventud until May 1955, when Batista granted an amnesty to political prisoners.

Castro fled to Mexico, where he spent a year in exile planning his return to Cuba and the resumption of his plans to overthrow the government. The following year, Castro sneaked back to the southeastern coast of Cuba, along with a force of 81 guerrillas, including Ernesto "Che" Guevara and Castro's brother Raúl, aboard a small yacht, the *Granma.* The journey was beset by myriad problems and delays, including unfortunate weather, and Batista's forces were tipped off to the rebels' imminent arrival. Only 15 rebels reached their planned destination, the Sierra Maestra mountains. From such unlikely beginnings, the rebel forces evolved into a formidable guerrilla army, largely through the assistance of peasants who were promised land reforms in exchange for their support.

Following 2 years of dramatic fighting in the mountains and strategic points, Castro's insurrection gained strength and legitimacy among a broad swath of the Cuban population. Batista saw the end in sight, and on January 1, 1959, he fled the country for the Dominican Republic. The combat-weary but triumphant rebels, known as the *barbudos* (the bearded ones), declared victory in Santiago de Cuba and then entered Havana a week later.

Cuba Under Fidel Castro

The new government immediately set about restructuring Cuban society: It reduced rents, instituted agrarian reform, and limited estates to 400 hectares

(1,000 acres). As part of a comprehensive nationalization program, the government expropriated utilities, factories, and private lands. The fledgling government also embarked upon wide-ranging programs designed to eradicate illiteracy and provide universal healthcare and free schooling.

The Revolution's lofty aims were mitigated by cruder attempts to consolidate state power. The transition to a centralized, all-powerful state antagonized many Cubans, mostly elites. Castro placed the media under state control, as it remains today, and he promised elections that were never held. Local Committees for the Defense of the Revolution (CDRs) kept tabs on dissenters. In the early years of Castro's reign, many thousands of people suspected of opposing the Revolution were interrogated, imprisoned, or sent to labor camps, along with other social "undesirables," such as homosexuals and priests.

In just 3 years after the triumph of the Revolution, nearly a quarter of a million Cubans—mostly professionals and wealthy landowners—fled the country. They settled in nearby Florida and established a colony of conservative Cuban Americans, which, in the coming decades, achieved not only economic success but also a level of political clout that was disproportionate to its size.

Washington, opposed to Cuba's political evolution and spurred on by politically active Cubans living in Miami, continued to try to isolate Castro in Latin America. Just 1 year after Castro took power, in 1960, the U.S. government launched a trade embargo against Cuba in retaliation for Cuba's state appropriations and seizures of the assets of U.S. businesses. The trade embargo, which Cuba terms a blockade (*bloqueo*), and travel restrictions later imposed on most U.S. citizens, continue to this day. In 1961, the United States broke diplomatic relations with Cuba, and CIA-trained Cuban exiles launched an attempt to overthrow the Castro government. The Bay of Pigs mission was an utter fiasco and a severe black mark against the Kennedy administration. Cuba's resistance strengthened Castro's resolve to stand up to the United States.

Castro had not revealed any Communist leanings in the decade since coming to power, but soon after the Bay of Pigs, Castro declared himself a Marxist-Leninist. Some historians have argued that the aggressive ploys of the U.S. government were fundamental in pushing the Cuban government into the arms of the American enemy in the Cold War, the Soviet Union and its Eastern bloc of potential trading partners. The USSR was only too eager to develop a strategic relationship with an ideological opponent of Washington in the backyard of the United States. By the end of the 1980s, the USSR dominated Cuban trade and provided Cuba with subsidies worth an estimated $5 billion annually.

In the fall of 1962, the Soviet Union under Nikita Khrushchev installed 42 medium-range nuclear missiles in Cuba. A tense standoff ensued when President Kennedy ordered a naval blockade on the island and demanded that the existing missiles be dismantled. The world waited anxiously for 6 days until

Khrushchev finally caved to U.S. demands to turn back his ships. The possibility of a nuclear war was averted in return for a U.S. promise never to invade Cuba.

Another 200,000 people abandoned Cuba as part of the Freedom Flights Program between 1965 and 1971. In 1980, Castro lifted travel restrictions and opened the port of Mariel (west of Havana); during the Mariel Boatlift, at least 125,000 Cubans—many of whom Washington charged were criminals and drug addicts—made it to U.S. shores before President Carter forced Castro to close the floodgates.

The Special Period

Soviet trade and subsidies propped up Cuba's heavily centralized and poorly performing economy until the end of the 1980s. But the fall of the Berlin Wall and dismantling of the Soviet Union suddenly left Cuba in an untenable position, as supplies of food, oil, and hard currency were cut off while the U.S. trade embargo continued.

The Cuban government initiated a "Special Period" in 1990—a euphemism for harsh new austerity measures and hardship to be borne by the large majority of Cubans. Rationing of basic goods had existed for most of Castro's years in power, but limited government distribution now included many more necessities. During the Special Period and years since, most Cubans found it virtually impossible to subsist on rations alone.

Complicating the delicate situation was the 1992 Cuba Democracy Act, which broadened the U.S. embargo to cover a ban on trade with Cuba for foreign subsidiaries of U.S. companies. Though the U.S. government denies that its trade embargo can be blamed for the shortcomings in the Cuban economy and resulting shortages of food and medicine, many analysts believe that the embargo has greatly exacerbated the difficulties experienced by ordinary Cubans. Meanwhile, Castro held onto power and made few concessions, even using the U.S. trade restrictions to his advantage: They have given him something and someone to blame for Cuba's grinding poverty and lack of goods.

With the economy in shambles, the Cuban government was forced to introduce a limited number of capitalist measures. Foreign investment, which has taken the form of joint ventures primarily in the fields of tourism and mineral and oil exploration, has been openly encouraged (and strengthened in 2014 with further laws and the opening of the free trade zone in the port of Mariel). Castro, with inescapable irony, legalized the U.S. dollar in 1993—even establishing state-owned, dollar-only stores, small-scale private enterprises like *casas particulares* and *paladares* (private homestays and restaurants), and the introduction of private farmers' markets. While these capitalist initiatives benefited some Cubans, giving them access to hard currency (through jobs in tourism or relatives sending remittances from abroad), the dual economy has ultimately turned many other Cubans into have-nots, unequals in a socialist society.

In August 1994, in a frantic safety-valve measure designed to alleviate some of the economic pressure on the state, Castro lifted restrictions on those wishing to leave. More than 30,000 Cubans accepted the invitation and set out across dangerous waters to Florida on *balseros* (homemade rafts). Faced with the political embarrassment of an influx of poor Cubans, President Clinton abolished the standing U.S. policy granting automatic asylum to Cuban refugees. Instead, they were returned to the Guantánamo Bay Naval Base to await repatriation.

After Castro visited the Vatican in 1996, Pope John Paul II returned the favor. His visit to Cuba in 1998 prompted a relaxation of the government's harsh views of the Catholic Church in Cuba. In late 1999, 6-year-old Elián González became the latest face of political animosity between the United States and Cuba. González survived for 2 days alone on a raft after his mother and other escapees had perished, only to become the object of an international tug-of-war. Castro and most Cubans, in huge demonstrations, demanded the boy's return to be with his father in northern Cuba. Castro's opponents in the United States sought to allow the boy to stay with distant relatives in Miami. After weeks of wrangling, the Immigration and Naturalization Service returned Elián to his father and Cuba, where he received a hero's welcome.

Former President Jimmy Carter made a historic visit to Cuba in the spring of 2002, voicing support for Castro's call for an end to the trade embargo and travel restrictions while also criticizing the Cuban government's lack of democracy. Carter met with dissidents and gave an uncensored and at times harshly critical speech in front of Castro that was broadcast on Cuban television.

Carter's visit had little lasting effect, however. In 2003, Castro jailed some 75 prominent dissidents and government critics, imposing stiff sentences following abbreviated trials (most of those imprisoned were released in 2010 following a deal brokered by Pope Benedict). In early 2004 and again in 2006, the Bush administration tightened the screws on U.S. citizens' right to travel to Cuba, virtually eliminating all educational and humanitarian licenses and severely reducing the amount of time and money that Cuban Americans can spend in Cuba.

The U.S. naval base at Guantánamo Bay has been in the news in recent years after Al Qaeda prisoners from the wars in Afghanistan and Iraq were taken to the base for interrogation and detention (116 detainees remained in mid 2015).

In July 2006, Fidel Castro fell ill and withdrew from public life. His younger brother Raúl became acting president. Fidel Castro relinquished power in February 2008 and Raúl was unanimously elected as Cuba's new president by the country's National Assembly.

Cuba Under Raúl Castro

One of the first reforms that Raúl instituted following his election as Cuba's new president was the lifting of restrictions on Cubans owning TVs, DVD players, computers, and other electrical appliances. This was followed by a move to decentralize the state-run agricultural economy, including allowing farmers to till fallow land and to buy their own equipment. In June 2008, Raúl abolished the egalitarian wage system, allowing hard-working employees to earn a better salary, and raised the state pension. In July 2008, Raúl authorized land grants for private farming. This move was aimed at boosting agricultural production and reducing the amount of food that Cuba imports. Then Raúl lifted the restrictions on cellphone ownership and the prohibition preventing Cubans from staying in tourist hotels.

Like much of the world, Cuba suffered from the effects of the global recession: Tourism was down and oil imports were limited because of a lack of cash. At the same time, Cuba was still reeling from spending millions of dollars to restore parts of the country battered by three hurricanes in autumn 2008. Cuba's economy became so strained that in a rare nod to private property development, Cuba signaled that it would allow foreign companies to develop golf and leisure developments with 99-year leases on condominium complexes. The first development of its kind (around 12 are in the pipeline) was given the green light in 2015.

It seems that Cuba's crumbling economy has forced Raúl to review some of Cuba's socialist policies. Raúl has said that "We have to end forever the notion that Cuba is the only country in the world where you can live without working," and he instituted some fairly radical reforms. On January 1, 2009, Cuba celebrated the 50th anniversary of the Revolution, and after this low-key celebration, government officials announced that Cubans with the financial means could build their own homes—a huge advance. Later that year, Castro leased millions of acres of uncultivated fertile state land to private farmers; this was followed, in April 2010, with news that barber shops and beauty salons could trade privately, joining private restaurants *(paladares)* and bed-and-breakfasts *(casas particulares)* as means of self-employment. In fall 2010, Cubans were permitted to sell home-grown products from their homes and kiosks. That same year, the Cuban government announced it would lay off more than a million state workers in the next few years. Some Cubans hoped that these unemployed state workers would be allowed to run small, private businesses—and indeed, the government soon after announced proposals to allow 178 forms (later increased to 201) of self-employment (*cuenta propia*), including *casa particulares*, *paladares*, some forms of transportation, and nonprofessional jobs. The Communist Party's media, *Granma* (www.granma.cubaweb.cu), is the best source of up-to-date information on this issue.

Cuba watchers are still keen to see where the new Mariel port development, the 2010 domestic economic reforms, the 2014 foreign investment law, and the proposed dismantling of the dual currency takes the country as it enters a new economic relationship with its own citizens and a new political relationship with the U.S. As for domestic politics, Raúl Castro has said he will step down from the presidency in 2018. The Castros' nominated successor is Miguel Díaz-Canel, First Vice President of the Cuban Council of State.

CUBA'S ART & ARCHITECTURE

Architecture

Before the arrival of the Spaniards in 1492, Cuban aboriginals, such as the Siboney and Taíno, lived in *bohios* (thatched huts). After Cuba was conquered by the Spaniards, the *conquistadors* imported Spanish and Moorish styles. From 1511, conquistador Diego Velázquez de Cuéllar founded the seven *villas* (towns) of Cuba. Fortresses, homes, and buildings centered around courtyards in *Mudéjar* style, and, in later years, Baroque-influenced and neoclassical architecture bloomed. Havana's Old City is the Spanish colonial prize and a UNESCO World Heritage Site. For example, in La Havana Vieja, the Castillo de la Real Fuerza, built between 1558 and 1577, was the first fortress in the New World. The rest of La Habana Vieja (p. 44) is a treasure trove of Spanish colonial architectural excellence. Outside of La Habana Vieja, the historic core of Trinidad is an architectural gem and also a UNESCO World Heritage Site. Parts of Santiago de Cuba and Camagüey (whose historic core is also a UNESCO site) also preserve remarkable examples of Spanish architectural styles with the 16th-century Casa de Diego Velázquez in Santiago, named the oldest house in Cuba.

Wonderful examples of **Art Nouveau** structures can be found in the Vista Alegre suburb of Santiago (p. 238) and the Havana suburb of Vedado (p. 44). An **Art Deco** highlight in Havana is the outstanding **Edificio Bacardí,** built by Esteban Rodríguez Castells and Rafael Fernández Ruenes in 1930 on the edge of La Habana Vieja, topped by the trademark bat symbol. Other highlights are

A GUIDE TO CUBA'S architectural DETAILS

While you're traveling through Cuba, keep an eye out for these architectural and decorative details that adorn the interiors and exteriors of Cuba's buildings:

- ***Mediopunto*** are stained-glass half-moon windows positioned above wooden doors, introduced in the mid-18th century. Some of the best examples are found on the facade of the Casa del Conde de Bayona and the Hotel Santa Isabel in La Habana Vieja (p. 44).
- ***Mamparas*** are half-door screens inlaid with plain or decorative glass that were installed in the houses of the rich.
- ***Barrotes*** are window grilles made of turned wood that date back to the 18th century.
- ***Guardevecinos*** are plain or decorative wrought-iron grilles that date back to the 19th century; these grilles served to divide neighbors' balconies.
- **Stone balustrades** (small posts that line the upper rail of a railing) line the roofs of many mansions; this became common in the 19th century.
- **Ornamental urns** line the roofs of many mansions; this became a popular feature in the 19th century. An example that has this feature is the Palacio Junco in Matanzas.

art IN CUBA

The history of *artes plásticas* (plastic arts) in Cuba dates back to 1818, with the foundation of the **San Alejandro Academy** (www.sanalejandro.cult.cu) in Havana. The Academy was created by French painter Juan Bautista Vermay (who painted the frescoes in el Templete in La Habana Vieja; see p. 71) to promote Fine Arts and work made by the black and mulata community. Thus begun a century of academic painting—mostly of landscapes and portraits—influenced by European models.

The 19th century brought new developments for Cuba: a national hymn, a national flag, and nationalistic sentiment; during this time, there was a backlash against academic national art, which gave way to modern art. In the 1930s, Cuban artists began to focus their attention on Cuban roots and the search for national values, resulting in a characteristically Cuban art. Some of these first-generation artists are Víctor Manuel (1897–1969), Carlos Enríquez (1900–1957), Eduardo Abela (1889–1965), Fidelio Ponce (1895–1949) and Wifredo Lam (1902–1982). Subsequently, the 1940s and 1950s brought abstract and expressionist art to Cuba.

Following the 1959 Revolution, art began to promote the ideals of the Revolution. For this reason, the 1960s witnessed an intense movement expressed through painting, poster art, and documentary photography that was attuned to the climate of enthusiasm that prevailed in Cuban society. During the 1970s, many artists born in the far-flung corners of the island began to graduate from new schools of art—like the National Art School founded in 1962 and the School for Art Instructors founded in 1961. Some of the artists that graduated during this era today are grand masters of Cuban art, such as Tomás Sánchez, Nelson Domínguez, Flora Fong, Flavio Garciandía, and Eduardo Roca (better known as CHOCO). They worked at a time when new artistic genres such as Pop Art, kinetic art, and photorealism began to enrich the island's art scene. The 1980s marked a period of thriving growth of the visual arts in Cuba. This was the first time that Cuban artists began to use diverse mediums such as art installations and performance and group art; it was also a time when artists portrayed subjects of political satire, which had previously been taboo.

Cuban modern art has continued to develop and has won both national and international acclaim. The variety of themes and styles of Cuban art today reveal a richness not reached in previous years. For more information on galleries, exhibitions, and artists, consult **www.galeriascubanas.com, www.opushabana.cu,** and **www.cubarte.cult.cu/en.**

—Sussette Martínez Montero, art curator

the 1941 **Teatro América** building on Galiano in Centro and the ziggurat-topped **Edificio López Serrano,** designed by Ricardo Mira and Miguel Rosich in 1932 in Vedado. Other noteworthy buildings in Havana are the 1952 **Tropicana cabaret,** by Max Borges Jr., and the 1957 **Hotel Habana Riviera,** by Igor Polevitzky and Philip Johnson, which was commissioned by Meyer Lansky.

The 1959 Revolution brought not only a change in the country's ideals and policies, but also a change in architectural styles. A crush of Brutalist Soviet blocks were erected, mainly in the form of residential buildings and hotels.

Some of these structures evoke the style of the famous Swiss architect Le Corbusier, with impersonal, open-plan buildings. Highlights of the post-Revolution period include Ricardo Porro's 1961 sensual and erotic **Instituto Superior de Atte** (continued until 1965 by Roberto Gottardi and Vittorio Garatti) and Mario Girona's 1966 **Coppelia** ice cream parlor.

THE LAY OF THE LAND

Cuba is the largest island in the Caribbean and is some 1,200km (745 miles) long; its greatest width is 210km (130 miles). It has about 6,073km (3,774 miles) of coastline and 345km (214 miles) of beach sheltering sea water that's an inviting 24°C (75°F) year-round.

Some 4,000 islands and islets offshore in both the north and south create an area of 110,992 sq. km (4,2854 sq. miles). There are two principal islands—both off the southern coast—the **Isla de la Juventud** and the tourist enclave of **Cayo Largo del Sur.** Most of the northern coast of the mainland is fringed by white sand beaches and palm trees with coral reefs just offshore; on the southern coast, black sand beaches can be found.

The interior of the island is dominated by three mountain ranges. In the west, stretching down the spine of the Pinar del Río province is the **Cordillera de Guaniguanico;** in central Cuba is the **Sierra del Escambray** and in Oriente, the **Sierra Maestra,** with Cuba's highest mountain, Pico Turquino at 1,974m (6,476 ft.). Waterfalls, such as **Salto del Caburní** in the Escambray and **El Nicho** near Cienfuegos, abound. Limestone geology has meant that there are extensive cave networks in the country; those near Viñales, Santo Tomás, and the Cuevas del Bellamar near Matanzas are the most famous. In the World Heritage Site of the **Viñales Valley,** erosion left limestone stumps in its wake. These limestone round-topped mountains covered in clambering vegetation are scattered on the floor of the Valley, and are known as ***mogotes.***

Cuba's landscapes are diverse and verdant (some 55 inches of rain fall a year) and include rolling sugar cane fields, tobacco plantations, coffee bushes, rivers, Royal Palms, river canyons, and forests bursting with bird life and orchids; across the country more than 300 protected areas have been established.

Cuba has six UNESCO Biosphere reserves: Guanahacabibes Peninsula and Sierra del Rosario in the west; Parque Nacional Ciénaga de Zapata in the south at the Bay of Pigs; Buenavivista in the north central area; Parque Nacional Baconao, east of Santiago; and Cuchillas del Toa near Baracoa.

Cuba is also rich in flora and fauna. Some 374 species of bird exist in Cuba (of which 25 are endemic). The most famous bird species is the **tocororo,** a trogon *(Priotelus temnurus)* and Cuba's national bird (it sports the colors of the national flag—red, white and blue). **Flamingos** *(phoenicopterus ruber)* stalk the marshlands of the Zapata peninsula and the saline flats along the north coast from Cayo Coco to Playa Santa Lucía. The smallest bird in the world, the **zunzuncito** *(Mellisuga helenae),* a hummingbird; the world's smallest frog *(Eleutherodactylus iberia);* and the world's smallest bat *(Natalidae lepidus)* all live in Cuba, along with the **Cuban crocodile** *(Crocodylus rhombifer)* and a rare creature called the **Cuban solenodon** *(Solenodon cubanus).* Another unusual Cuban animal is the **jutía,** a tree-loving giant tree rat. The most endearing of Cuba's fauna is the ***polymita picta* snail,** shaded in swirls of yellow, green, black, brown, and white; this rare snail is found near Baracoa.

Cuba is home to about 6,700 species of flora, including 74 endemic plants. A common sight is the **royal poinciana** *(flamboyán),* known for its starburst of red flowers; the **mariposa,** the white fragrant national flower; the **ceiba tree;** and voluptuous **hibiscus** flowers. The national tree is the **royal palm** (*Roystonea regia*).

CUBA IN POPULAR CULTURE

Cuban Music

Perhaps no other nation—certainly no other nation of its size—is as spectacularly endowed musically as is Cuba. The seductive sounds of richly percussive Cuban music are, in many people's minds, Cuba's greatest export. In the late 1990s, a series of records and a documentary film brought a group of aging Cuban musicians to the world's attention. The unexpected popularity abroad of the *Buena Vista Social Club* and its individual artists—Ibrahim Ferrer, Compay Segundo, Rubén González, Eliades Ochoa, and Omara Portuondo—made traditional Cuban sounds very much in demand throughout Cuba and internationally. Buena Vista and company, though, is only the latest round of Cuban music to circle the globe, echoing the earlier mambo and cha-cha-chá crazes that took the United States and Europe by storm in the 1950s.

Within Cuba, music is a daily presence across the island, from rural areas and dusty provincial towns to the capital. It seeps out of cafes and *casas de la trova* (music clubs) in the midafternoon and thunders out of dance halls as the sun rises over the Malecón (promenade). The musical diet is a dizzying menu of styles with uncommon appeal, so emphatically tropical that you can almost hear the humidity in the vocals, chords, and percussion.

Cuba's musical heritage, an onomatopoeic stew of salsa, rumba, mambo, *son, danzón,* and cha-cha-chá, stems from the country's rich mix of African, Spanish, French, and Haitian cultures. The roots of contemporary Cuban popular music lie in the 19th century's combination of African drums and rhythms along with Spanish guitar and melody. Most forms of Cuban music feature Latin stringed instruments, African bongos, congas, and claves (wooden percussion sticks), and auxiliary instruments such as maracas and güiros.

The heartbeat of Cuban music is the clave, which refers to a distinctive rhythm and the instrument used to play it. While the actual instrument is not necessarily played in every song, all Cuban rhythms are built up from the simple concept of the clave. The perennial form of Cuban traditional music is *son* (literally, "sound"; pronounced *sohn*), a style of popular dance music that originated in the eastern, poorer half of the country known as El Oriente in the early 1900s.

You can and will hear live music anywhere you go in Cuba, but the best places for authentic traditional *son* and more modern styles are Havana, Trinidad, Santiago de Cuba, and Baracoa. The last three possess the best *casas de la trova* (music clubs) in the country, spots thick with sultry air, slowly rotating ceiling fans, and grinning octogenarians plunking away on weathered guitars and stand-up basses. Cubans seem only too happy to share the dance floor with tentative foreigners.

Books on Cuba

There's a wealth of books on Cuba's history and politics. For a good historical overview, try Jaime Suchlicki's ***Cuba: From Columbus to Castro and Beyond*** (Brasseys, 2002), or Richard Gott's ***Cuba: A New History*** (Yale University Press, 2005). More than 1,800 pages, Hugh Thomas's ***Cuba, or The Pursuit of Freedom*** (Da Capo Press, 1998) is far more comprehensive and fascinating, but it takes a while to read.

A unique account of post-revolutionary Cuba comes from a well-known Latin American journalist, Alma Guillermoprieto, who writes of the 6 months she spent in Cuba in the early '70s teaching dance. ***Dancing with Cuba: A Memoir of the Revolution*** (Vintage, 2005) is a portrait of the artistic world of Cuba in the '70s and a self-reflective memoir of the author's political awakening.

No reading list for Cuba would be complete without a biography or two of Fidel Castro and Che Guevara. The best are Leycester Coltman's ***The Real Fidel Castro*** (Yale University Press, 2005), Tad Szulc's ***Fidel: A Critical Portrait*** (Avon Books, 2000), and Jon Lee Anderson's ***Che Guevara: A Revolutionary Life*** (Grove, 1997). (Jon Lee Anderson has also written a book about Fidel that is awaiting publication) Another Fidel biography is ***Fidel Castro: My Life*** (Penguin, 2007) by journalist Ignacio Ramonet. Also worth a read are ***Guerilla Prince: The Untold Story of Fidel Castro*** (Little, Brown, 2002) by Georgie Anne Geyer, and ***The Life and Death of Che Guevara*** (Vintage, 1998) by Jorge Castañeda. There are also several volumes of writings worth looking into by both Fidel and Che. Che's own ***The Motorcycle Diaries: Notes on a Latin American Journey*** (Ocean Press, 2003) provides an interesting glimpse into the social and psychological genesis of this great revolutionary figure, although it deals with the period in Che's life prior to meeting Fidel and going to Cuba. The book was made into a very successful film (*The Motorcycle Diaries*) by director Walter Salles.

Another compelling perspective on the Revolution is offered by Enrique Oltuski, a former Shell Oil engineer and a leader in the 26th of July movement, in ***Vida Clandestina: My Life in the Cuban Revolution*** (Jossey-Bass, 2002).

For contemporary accounts, ***Cuban Revelations: Behind the Scenes in Havana*** (University Press of Florida, 2015) by Marc Frank provides a comprehensive summary of Cuba changes since 2006. Julia Cooke's ***The Other Side of Paradise: Life in the New Cuba*** (Seal Press, 2014) details multiple portraits of 21st-century Cuban lives through up-close-and-personal vignettes.

Any exploration into Cuban literature should include the works of poets José Martí and Nicolás Guillén, as well as the novels and prose writings of Alejo Carpentier and José Lezama Lima. Prominent works that exist in English include Guillermo Cabrera Infante's ***Three Trapped Tigers*** (Marlow, 1997), and several of Reinaldo Arenas's novels and his best-selling autobiography ***Before Night Falls*** (Penguin, 1994), made into a stunning film by Julian Schnabel.

Of contemporary output, the gritty writing of ***Dirty Havana Trilogy*** by Pedro Juan Gutiérrez (Faber and Faber, 2001) portrays life in the underbelly of Havana, and the **detective novels** of Leonardo Padura have a great following.

Also worth reading is Cristina García's novel, ***Dreaming in Cuban*** (Ballantine, 1993), which chronicles the lives of three Cuban women after the Revolution. If you like García's book, you might also enjoy Ana Menéndez's ***Loving Che*** (Atlantic Monthly Press, 2003), the story of one woman's quest to uncover the mysteries and romance of her mother's past.

The Sugar King of Havana: The Rise and Fall of Julio Lobo, Cuba's Last Tycoon (Penguin Press, 2010) by John Paul Rathbone is a gripping read.

Of course, it goes without saying that you've already read Hemingway's ***The Old Man and the Sea*** (Scribner, 1952) and Graham Greene's ***Our Man in Havana*** (Heinemann, 1958).

Cuban Films

In addition to the poignant *Before Night Falls* and the excellent *The Motorcycle Diaries,* mentioned above, there are a host of wonderful films that can be rented prior to any trip to Cuba or bought while you are there from ARTex stores (www.cubacine.cu). One true classic film available on DVD is ***Soy Cuba (I Am Cuba)*** by the great Russian director Mikhail Kalatozov, who shot this Communist-era piece of social-realist propaganda in Cuba shortly after the Revolution. The film features a screenplay by Russian poet Yevgeny Yevtushenko and the Cuban writer and filmmaker Enrique Piñeda Barnet.

Cuba's own film industry has produced several fine films, including the celebrated *Fresa y Chocolate* (Strawberry and Chocolate), *Memorias del Subdesarrollo* (Memories of Underdevelopment), and *Muerte de un Burócrata* (Death of a Bureaucrat), all by Tomás Gutiérrez Alea. The animated comedy *Vampiros de la Habana* (Vampires of Havana) by Juan Padrón proved popular. Three of my favorite Cuban films are *Guantanamera* by Tomás Gutiérrez Alea and Juan Carlos Tabío, *Lista de Espera* by Juan Carlos Tabío, and *El Benny* by Jorge Luis Sánchez. Also look out for *Suite Habana* by Fernando Pérez. More recent successes have included *Habanastation* by Ian Padrón, and *Conducta* by Ernesto Darnas.

For a good look into the conflict between Cubans in Cuba and their relatives and friends in the United States, check out *Azucar Amarga* (Bitter Sugar) by Leon Ichaso, or *Quién Diablos es Julieta* (Who the Hell Is Juliette?) by Carlos Marcovich. The movie *Buena Vista Social Club* documents the rediscovery and newfound fame of some of Cuba's great traditional musicians. The accompanying Grammy Award–winning CD *Buena Vista Social Club* is as good a place as any to start listening to Cuban music.

Santería & Afro-Cuban Culture

Cuba's prominent African-influenced culture is one of the nation's defining characteristics. African culture brought by slaves and developed within the context of the Spanish colony has had a profound impact on religion, music, and indeed, virtually all of Cuban society.

One of the most salient aspects of Afro-Cuban culture is Santeria (also called *Regla de Ocha*). Frequently misunderstood and misinterpreted as a religious cult or form of voodoo, Santería is in fact a major syncretic and animistic religion that, by most estimates, has a greater following in Cuba than does Roman Catholicism. Its practice is not restricted to Afro-Cubans or a certain socioeconomic class.

Havana's **Casa de Africa** museum, Obrapía 157, between San Ignacio and Mercaderes in La Habana Vieja (✆ **7861-5798**), has exhibits on Santería and other African-origin religions for those interested in learning more. The museum is open Tuesday through Saturday 9am to 5pm and Sunday 9am to 1pm. The **Museo de los Orishas**, Prado 615 between Monte and Dragones (✆ **7863-5953**), uses mannequins and performance to explain the Santería saints and practices.

HAVANA

It's hard to convey the wonder, sensuality, and alluring beauty of Havana. It's hard to imagine a city with such rhythm and verve, a city at once so tremendously vibrant and at the same time laid-back—that is, until you've taken a lazy stroll along the Malecón, gotten lost in the time warp of La Habana Vieja's colonial cobblestone streets, taken a ride in a 1940 Dodge taxi through crumbling Centro Habana, danced salsa until dawn, or witnessed Afro-Cuban religious rituals on the street.

Originally established in 1514 on Cuba's southern coast, by 1519 San Cristóbal de la Habana had been moved to its present-day location on the island's north coast, at the mouth of a deep and spacious harbor with a narrow, protected harbor channel. Before long, Havana had become the most important port in the Spanish colonial empire, a natural final gathering place for the resupply and embarkation of the Spanish fleet before returning to the Old Country laden with bounty. By 1607, Havana had been declared the capital of colonial Cuba, and by the early 1700s, it was the third-largest city in the Spanish empire, behind Mexico City and Lima.

Subsequent centuries saw Havana grow steadily in wealth, size, and prominence. Havana was luckily spared the bulk of the violence and fighting that occurred in Cuba's Wars of Independence, and later revolutionary war. Following the sinking of the USS *Maine* in Havana harbor in 1898, a long period of direct U.S. control and indirect U.S. influence followed. This period saw the first indications of suburban sprawl and the growing importance of the western neighborhoods of Vedado and Miramar. This era was also marked by a strong presence of mob activity, with the likes of Al Capone, Meyer Lansky, and Lucky Luciano setting up shop in Havana.

Havana has been largely frozen in time in the wake of the 1959 Revolution. Decades of economic crisis and shortages have left much of Havana in severe decay and decomposition. The great exception to this rule is La Habana Vieja, much of which has been meticulously restored to its colonial glory, using a percentage of tourism receipts from the Old City hotels and restaurants. Although the situation in Havana is beginning to change, with the recent boom in tourism and tourism-related growth, what new construction has occurred over the past 40 years has largely borne the drab architectural stamp of the former Soviet Union and its central state planning. Luckily, most of this has taken place outside the boundaries of the city center. Today, Havana, with some 2.5 million inhabitants, is the largest city in the Caribbean and Cuba's undisputed political, business, and cultural center.

ESSENTIALS

Getting There

BY PLANE

Arriving international passengers clear Customs on the ground level of Terminal 3 at the **José Martí International Airport** (© **7266-4133;** airport code HAV). All of the major car-rental agencies have kiosks or booths just outside of Customs. There's also an **Infotur** kiosk (www.infotur.cu; © **7/266-4094**), where you can buy a map and pick up some brochures.

The airport has a few ATMs inside and outside and two CADECAS on either side of the main exit doors on the ground floor. Outside on the ground floor is an **Etecsa** office where you can purchase temporary and permanent SIM cards (p. 294). Terminal 3 has Nauta Wi-Fi. Yellow taxis wait in a long line just outside the ground-floor exit. The fixed rate to any destination in Vedado is CUC$20, to La Habana Vieja CUC$25.

Some charter flights and all national flights arrive at either Terminal 1 or 2. Both terminals also have Infotur offices or kiosks, an ATM, CADECA, telephones, Etecsa office, and taxis.

If you're driving from the airport, the main artery into Havana is Avenida de Rancho Boyeros. This will bring you to the Plaza de la Revolución and the towering José Martí Memorial. In general terms, if you continue straight, or roughly north toward the sea, you will hit the University of Havana and Vedado. Miramar and Playa will be to the left (west) and are best reached via the Malecón, while Centro Habana and La Habana Vieja are to the right (east).

BY CAR

Entering Havana by car is a confusing mess. Almost none of the major arteries into downtown are marked. This is especially true of the Autopista Nacional coming in from the east, which dumps you unceremoniously into the midst of the urban mess of some of the city's outer neighborhoods. Similarly, while there is ostensibly a beltway, or *Circunvalación,* around the downtown area, it and its various exits are virtually unmarked.

One good tactic for navigating Havana is to somehow find your way to the Malecón; from there, the entire city is relatively easy to access. The main thoroughfare through Miramar and Playa is Avenida 5.

> **Leaving Havana**
>
> International flights leave from **Terminal 3.** Charter flights and a few international flights leave from **Terminal 2;** domestic flights leave from **Terminal 1.** A taxi to the airport costs CUC$20 to CUC$25. The Departure Tax was abolished in 2015.

BY TRAIN

The principal train station, or **Estación Central,** is located in La Habana Vieja at Calle Egido and Calle Arsenal (✆ **7861-4259**). Taxis are always waiting.

BY BUS

The main **Víazul** bus station (www.viazul.com; ✆ **7881-1413** or 7881-5652) is located at Avenida 26 and Zoológico in Nuevo Vedado, on the outskirts of downtown. From here, it is a CUC$5 taxi ride to Vedado and CUC$5 to CUC$7 to La Habana Vieja. There are always taxis available at the station. The ticket office is open daily from 7am to 6pm and 7pm to midnight.

BY BOAT

Marlin's Marina Hemingway, Avenida 5 and Calle 248, Santa Fe, Playa (✆ **7204-5088**; www.nauticamarlin.com), is the principal port of call and official point of entry for clearing Customs and Immigration. When arriving by sea, contact the marina before entering Cuban waters (19km/12 miles offshore) on VHF channels 16 or 77. Commercial cruise ships dock at the **Sierra Maestra Terminal** in La Habana Vieja, just off the Plaza de San Francisco (✆ **7862-7434**).

Visitor Information

Infotur (www.infotur.cu; ✆ **7866-3333**), Calle Obispo, corner of Bernaza, the official state-run tourist information agency, has offices or kiosks in several strategic spots around Havana and in each of the three terminals at the airport. It can provide you with some brochures and information. Most of the kiosks also have a small selection of maps and local tourist guides and books for sale. It should not be confused with tourism information as Westerners would understand it.

A handful of large, state-run tour agencies have desks at most hotels around town that are actually more useful than Infotur in general; these include **Havanatur** (www.havanatur.cu; ✆ **7838-4384**), **Cubanacán** (www.cubanacan.cu; ✆ **7208-6044**), and **Cubatur** (www.cubatur.cu; ✆ **7833-3569**). These are your best bets for information and tour bookings around the country. In Havana, the **San Cristóbal** agency, part of Habaguanex, Calle Oficios between Calles Lamparilla and Obrapía (www.viajessancristobal.cu; ✆ **7864 2338**), also provides city tours that include some interesting sociocultural tours not offered by other agencies.

City Layout

Havana is a major city built around its ample and protected harbor. The oldest colonial-era buildings are closest to the harbor, and the bulk of the expansion heads out west from there. The city is bordered along its northern edge by the Atlantic Ocean. The majority of Havana's denizens live in large, densely populated working-class neighborhoods to the south of the principal downtown business and tourist neighborhoods. While there are communities on the eastern side of the harbor, the most important neighborhoods and developments are all found on the western side. These communities are generally laid out in a series of abutting grids, although they often abut at odd angles.

While the streets in Vedado and Playa tend to be numbered or carry a letter designation, the neighborhoods of La Habana Vieja and Centro Habana have only named streets. To make matters more confusing, most of the streets in La Habana Vieja and Centro Habana have two or more names—those that appear on maps and street signs are often different from their common names. Wherever possible, we try to give the most common and popularly used name.

In La Habana Vieja and Centro Habana, street names are generally displayed on little plaques or signs attached to the sides of corner buildings at street intersections. The plaques tend to be hung relatively high, at about 3m (10 ft.) or so. In Vedado and Playa, you'll want to look lower, as most intersections feature a .5m-high (1½-ft.) concrete block in a sort of pyramid shape, with the street name engraved on it.

Street addresses are usually given as follows: Prado no. 22, e/ Tejadillo y Empedrado; or 23 e/ L y M. In the case of the first example, the address is for building 22 on Paseo del Prado, located between the cross streets Calle Tejadillo and Calle Empedrado. In the second case, the address is for an unnumbered building on Calle 23 between Calles L and M. Note that Cuban addresses frequently omit the word "Calle" or "Avenida." Also, Cubans usually refer to Avenida 5 as "Quinta Avenida," "5ta Avenida," or—most commonly—simply "5ta."

Neighborhoods in Brief

La Habana Vieja La Habana Vieja (Old Havana) is the historic colonial heart of Havana. Situated at the eastern edge of the city, in the area beginning around the Paseo del Prado and the Parque Central, and extending to the Harbor Channel, it is a dense collection of colonial-era and neocolonial houses, mansions, churches, seminaries, and apartment buildings punctuated by a few picturesque plazas and parks. UNESCO declared La Habana Vieja a World Heritage Site in 1982, and today it is one of the most beautiful colonial cities in the world. You will find the city's greatest collection of museums and attractions here, as well as a broad selection of restaurants and beautifully restored palaces that are now hotels. This is an area best explored on foot.

Centro Habana In many ways, Central Havana is little more than the necessary and neglected area connecting La Habana Vieja with Vedado. It is defined on its northern edge by the Malecón, the seaside pedestrian walkway that stretches from La Habana Vieja to the end of Vedado. The stretch of the Malecón (and everything inland from it) between the Hotel Nacional and La Habana Vieja is a study in decay and decomposition. Still, it is quite picturesque and charming in its own way. Centro Habana is primarily a residential area, although it does have a high concentration of *casas particulares* (private rooms for rent). ***Beware:*** We cannot stress enough the level of decay here. Balconies, crown molding, and other large chunks of brick, mortar, and stone regularly drop off buildings here, sometimes injuring passersby below.

Vedado & the Plaza de la Revolución Beginning more or less at the Hotel Nacional and extending west to the Almendares River and south to the Plaza de la Revolución, Vedado is a an elegant mix of middle- to upper-class houses and businesses. As the older sections of La Habana Vieja and Centro Habana began to overflow, residential and business growth centered on Vedado. Calle 23, or La Rampa, is the principal avenue

La Habana Vieja & Centro Habana

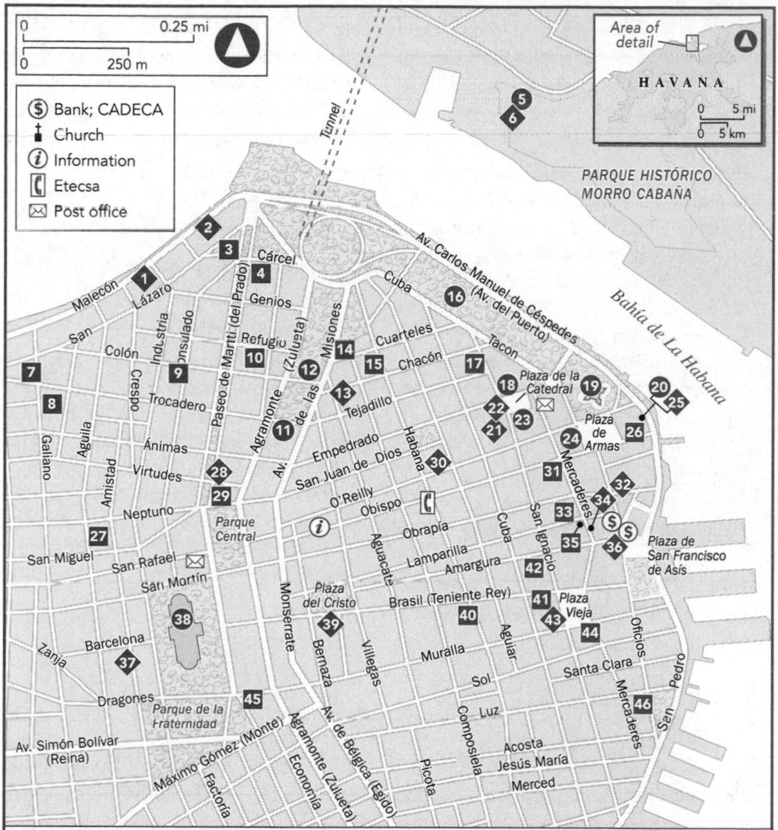

0.25 mi
250 m

Area of detail

HAVANA
0 5 mi
0 5 km

($) Bank; CADECA
✝ Church
(i) Information
[C Etecsa
⊠ Post office

PARQUE HISTÓRICO
MORRO CABAÑA

Bahía de La Habana

HOTELS ■

Bohemia apartments **43**
Casa Arrate **44**
Casa Eduardo Canciano **10**
Casa Esther Cardoso **27**
Casa Federico and Yamelis Llanes **3**
Casa Mary **4**
Casa Melba and Alberto **8**
Casa Vitrales **15**
Chez Nous **41**
Hostal Balcones **9**
Hostal El Angel **14**

Hotel Ambos Mundos **31**
Hotel Conde de Villanueva **35**
Hotel Habana 612 **40**
Hotel Raquel **42**
Hotel Santa Isabel **26**
Hotel Saratoga **45**
Hotel del Tejadillo **17**
Iberostar Parque Central **29**
Loft Habana **46**
Suite Havana **33**
Tropicana Penthouse **7**

RESTAURANTS ◆

Café del Oriente **36**
Café O'Reilly 304 **30**
Castropol **1**
Doña Eutimia **21**
El Chanchullero **39**
El Templete **25**
Ivan Chefs Justo **13**
La Bodeguita del Medio **22**
La Divina Pastora **6**
La Terraza **28**
Los Mercaderes **34**
Mama Inés **32**
Nazradovie **2**
SiáKará Café **37**

ATTRACTIONS ●

Castillo de la Real Fuerza **19**
Catedral de San Cristóbal **18**
El Capitolio **38**
El Templete **20**
Museo de Arte Colonial **23**
Museo de la Ciudad **24**
Museo de la Revolución y Memorial Granma **12**
Museo Nacional de Bellas Artes **11**
Parque Histórico Morro Cabaña **5**
Parque La Maestranza **16**

defining Vedado, and it's where you'll find Coppelia, the Habana Libre (former Havana Hilton), and the Hotel Nacional. The broad Plaza de la Revolución sits on high ground on the southern edge of Vedado and houses several government agencies, in addition to the towering José Martí Memorial, the National Theater, and the National Library.

Playa This upscale residential district is located just west of Vedado, past the Almendares River. The most important neighborhood here is **Miramar,** home to many prominent businesses and most of the resident foreign community in Cuba. Almost all of the various embassies and diplomatic missions have set up shop in the Batista-era mansions that make up this neighborhood. You'll find several large and luxurious business-class hotels here, as well as many private rooms for rent in wonderfully maintained neocolonial mansions.

Habana del Este & Playas del Este On the eastern banks of the harbor is Habana del Este, and about 11km (6¾ miles) farther east along the coast are the Playas del Este, or eastern beaches, which stretch on for about 15km (9 miles) of their own. Habana del Este and Playas del Este are connected to the rest of Havana by a tunnel running between La Habana Vieja and the area around the Morro Castle. Little passenger ferries run between La Habana Vieja and the neighborhoods of Regla and Casablanca. The towns that comprise Habana del Este, Alamar, Cojímar, and Ciudad Panamericana are working-class and industrial. The beaches of Playas del Este, on the other hand, are beautiful stretches of white sand fronting the sea. These beaches are popular with both Cubans and travelers alike.

Near the Airport The area near and around the airport is an industrial wasteland. There are no hotels or facilities for tourists here. Playa and Miramar, about a 15- to 20-minute drive away, are the closest neighborhoods for travelers looking for quick access to the airport; however, the extra time and distance to hotels in Vedado or La Habana Vieja is negligible.

Getting Around

BY TAXI

The vast majority of drivers who work for **Cubataxi** are now self-employed. Cubataxis can be called on a central number (✆ **7855-5555/59**) or easily found in the street or in front of hotels. All tourist taxis have meters, which are rarely used. Rates vary somewhat, but most of the meters start at CUC$1 for the first kilometer and then charge between CUC$.50 and CUC$.85 for each additional kilometer. In practice, you will need to agree on a fare *before* you get in, and, regrettably, as a visitor you will be overcharged. Note that Lada taxis (see below) tend to *aprovechar* (take advantage of the foreign visitor situation) less than the more modern yellow Cubataxi fleet. You will fare better if you speak Spanish. Generally speaking, a taxi driver won't budge for less than CUC$3 these days, and fares within Old Havana should never be more than CUC$5. From Old Havana to Vedado, fares should be CUC$3 to CUC$7; from Old Havana to Miramar, CUC$7 to CUC$15. A taxi to Santa María del Mar costs from CUC$15. Always bargain; tips are not expected. If you hire a taxi driver for the day, the rate is calculated by kilometers; waiting time is generally not charged, although this is now being factored in by some taxi drivers.

The most economical cabs are the yellow Lada Panataxis without air-conditioning, followed by the new yellow models with air-conditioning.

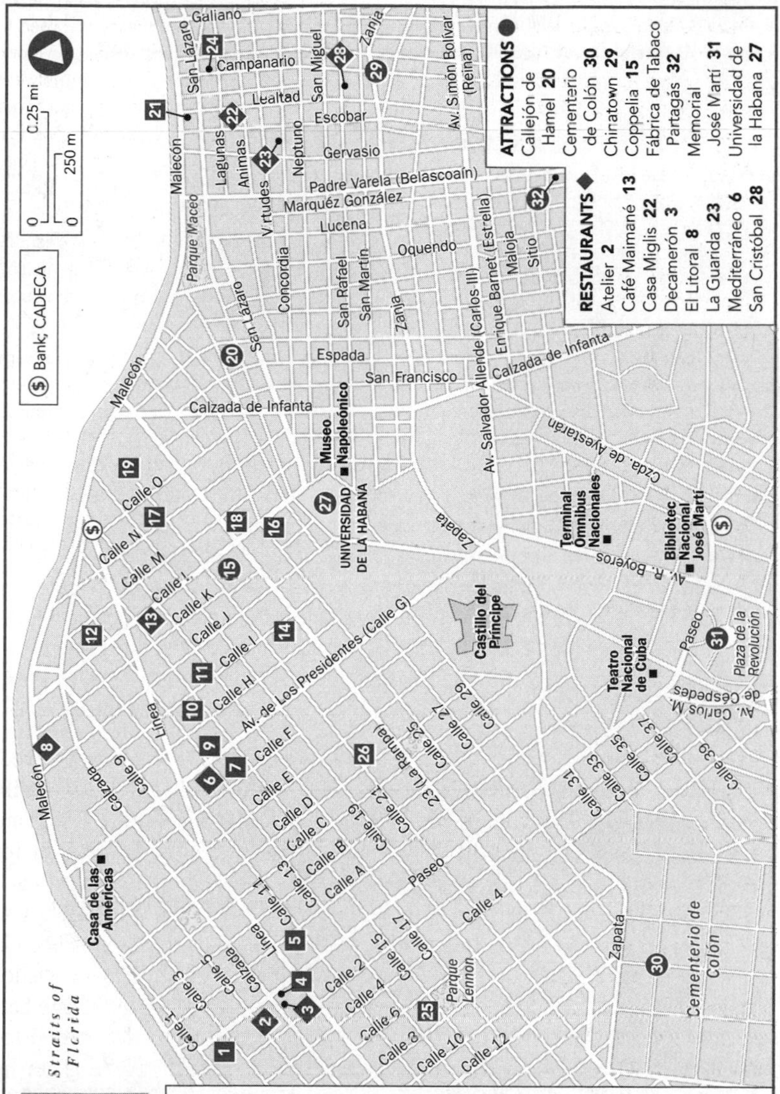
$ Bank; CADECA
0 0.25 mi
0 250 m
Area of detail
HAVANA
0 5 mi
0 5 km
Straits of Florida
HOTELS ■
Artedel Luxury Penthouse 11
Casa Carlos Peña Avila 7
Casa Delta Torres Pagán 26
Casa Jorge Coalla Potts 14
Casa Lilly 9
Casa Luis Alberto Gómez Garcés 10
Casa María Elena Matos Fernández 12
Casa 1932 24
Casa Norma Alvarez Bustio 16
Casa Teresita 4
Hotel Capri 17
Hotel Meliá Cohiba 1
Hotel Nacional de Cuba 19
Hotel Terral 21
Hotel Tryp Habana Libre 18
Vedado House Cultural 5
Villa Celia 25
RESTAURANTS ◆
Atelier 2
Café Maimané 13
Casa Miglis 22
Decamerón 3
El Litoral 8
La Guarida 23
Mediterráneo 6
San Cristóbal 28
ATTRACTIONS ●
Callejón de Hamel 20
Cementerio de Colón 30
Chinatown 29
Coppelia 15
Fábrica de Tabaco Partagás 32
Memorial José Martí 31
Universidad de la Habana 27
Malecón
Galiano
San Lázaro
Campanario
Lealtad
San Miguel
Zanja
Escobar
Lagunas
Animas
Virtudes
Neptuno
Gervasio
Padre Varela (Belascoaín)
Marquéz González
Lucena
Oquendo
Av. Simón Bolívar (Reina)
Parque Maceo
Concordia
San Rafael
San Martín
Espada
San Francisco
Calzada de Infanta
Av. Salvador Allende (Carlos III)
Enrique Barnet (Estrella)
Maloja
Sitio
Museo Napoleónico
UNIVERSIDAD DE LA HABANA
Czda. de Ayestarán
Zapata
Terminal Ómnibus Nacionales
Av. R. Boyeros
Biblioteca Nacional José Martí
Castillo del Príncipe
Calle O
Calle N
Calle M
Calle L
Calle K
Calle J
Calle I
Calle H
Av. de Los Presidentes (Calle G)
Calle F
Calle E
Calle D
Calle C
Calle B
Calle A
Línea
Calzada
Calle 9
Calle 11
Calle 13
Calle 19
Calle 21
23 (La Rampa)
Calle 25
Calle 27
Calle 29
Teatro Nacional de Cuba
Paseo
Plaza de la Revolución
Av. Carlos M. de Céspedes
Calle 31
Calle 33
Calle 35
Calle 37
Calle 39
Casa de las Américas
Calle 1
Calle 3
Calle 5
Calle 2
Calle 4
Calle 6
Calle 8
Calle 10
Calle 12
Calle 15
Calle 17
Parque Lennon
Cementerio de Colón

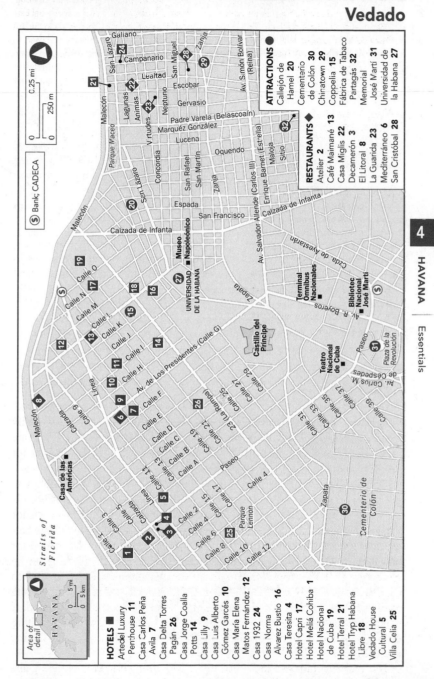

Other options include **horse-drawn carriages;** the so-called **Coco Taxis** (✆ **7873-1411**/7878-8784), yellow, round, open-air two-seaters powered by a motorcycle; and **antique cars** that range from a Model T Ford to a '57 Chevy. Both the horse-drawn carriages and Coco Taxis cost from CUC$5 to CUC$10 per hour. **Gran Car** (✆ **7878-8784**) is the only state agent for antique-car rentals. Gran Car rates, with a driver, run CUC$25 or CUC$30 per hour. However, hundreds of licensed taxi drivers now rent classic cars at slightly cheaper rates. Our recommendation is **Yenima Rodríguez Roque** (✆ **7682-0024**/5295-5376), who has a fleet of chrome-festooned convertibles.

Peso collective taxis, known as *almendrónes*, ply set routes in the city for between 10CUP and 20CUP per journey. If you pay for your 10CUP journey with 1CUC, you will receive between 13 and 15 CUPs in change. These are flagged down on the sides of the road.

Bicitaxis (bicycle taxis) charge from a couple of CUC for short journeys up to an inflated CUC$20 per hour for a city tour. Bargain very hard.

BY FOOT

Havana is a great town to walk around. It's almost entirely flat (although you need to keep an eye on the rough pavements) and safe (although there have been reports of muggings and pickpocketing). Early morning, late afternoon, and early evening are the prime times to walk. High heat and heavy humidity can make long walks, particularly around midday, a little uncomfortable. La Habana Vieja is best explored on foot, and a walk along the Malecón is obligatory. Attractions in Vedado and Miramar are a little spread out, making them less desirable to explore on foot, although the walking is pleasant as they are leafier districts. A walk along La Rampa in Vedado, or Quinta Avenida (Av. 5) in Miramar, are both rewarding.

BY CAR

There's really no reason for tourists to rent a car to explore Havana. Taxis are plentiful and relatively inexpensive. Moreover, streets are poorly marked and Havana is a confusing city to navigate.

One exception is to rent an antique car and its driver from **Gran Car** (✆ **7878-8784**) or a private classic car and its convivial driver (see above). Gran Car's fleet runs from restored 1930s open-air Ford cruisers to classic 1950s Chevys, Buicks, De Sotos, and Studebakers.

If you do want to rent a modern car while in Havana, the options include **Cubacar** (✆ **7272-5986;** cubacar@transtur.cu), **Havanautos** (✆ **7273-2277;** havanautos@transtur.cu), and **Rex** (✆ **7835-6830** or 7835-6832; www.rex.cu). All three are run by **Transtur** (www.transtur.cu; ✆ **7838-3995**). **Vía Rent a Car** (www.gaviota-grupo.com; ✆ **7207-9502**) is also an option. All of the above companies have desks at the airport and at all major hotels in Havana. See "Getting Around" in chapter 11 for more information.

In general, traffic is much lighter than you'd find in most major urban areas. However, you do have to pay more attention to a wide range of obstacles, from pedestrians to bicyclists to horse-drawn carriages. While most roads in

HOTELS ■
Casa de Cleo y
 Alejandro **5**
Casa de Gertrudis
 Martorell **4**

RESTAURANTS ◆
El Aljibe **7**
Esperanza **3**
La Cocina de Lilliam **6**
La Fontana **2**
Otramanera **8**

ATTRACTIONS ●
Acuario Nacional **1**

Area of detail

HAVANA

0 5 mi
0 5 km

0 0.25 mi
0 250 m

Teatro
Karl Marx ■

Straits of
Florida

MIRAMAR

Parque
Miramar

Santa Rita
de Cassia

LA SIERRA

KOHLY

ALMENDARES

AMPLIACION DE
ALMENDARES

4

HAVANA | Essentials

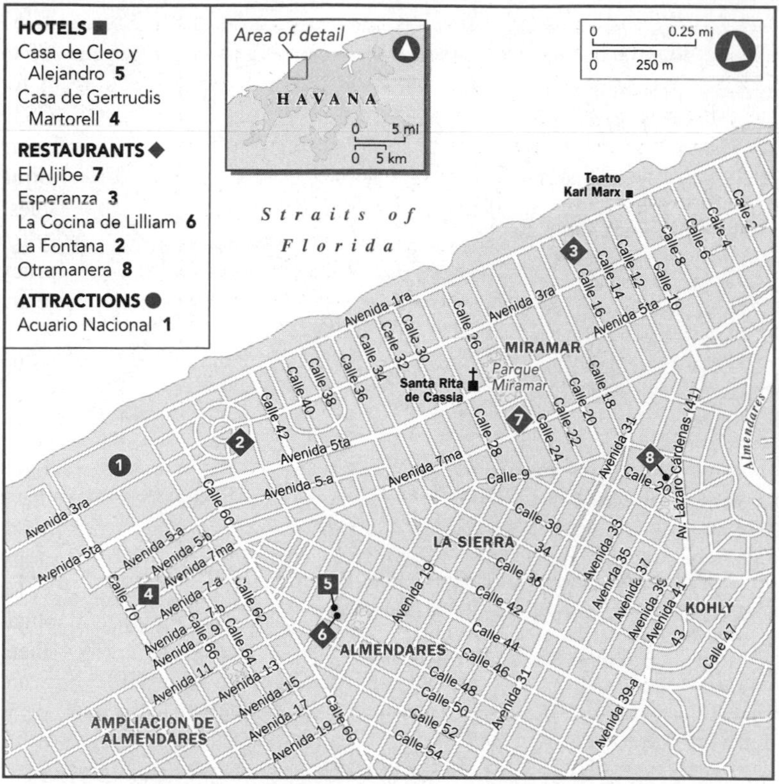

Havana are in pretty decent shape, it's not uncommon to come across huge potholes or torn-up sections of road with no markings or warnings. Moreover, street markings and signs are minimal, making navigation challenging.

BY BUS

For all intents and purposes, Havana's woefully overburdened urban bus system is not a viable option for tourists. Routes are overcrowded, and there are no readily available route maps and schedules.

Transtur runs the red **HabanaBusTour** coaches (www.transtur.cu; ✆ **7838-3991**) on two routes with a hop-on/hop-off service. Route T1 starts at Almacenes San José in La Habana Vieja and terminates at Restaurant La Cecilia (5th Avenida between Calles 110 and 112). T3 runs from Parque Central to Playas del Este. One ticket is valid for the whole day. Both buses costs CUC$5. Children 5 and under travel free (one child per adult). Buses run daily from 9am to 7pm. The last departure from Santa María del Mar to Havana is at 6pm. All schedules are marked at the bright red bus stops.

[Fast FACTS] HAVANA

Car Rentals See "Getting Around," above.

Currency Exchange Currency exchange offices are ubiquitous around Havana. There are branches of the state-run *casa de cambio* **CADECA** (✆ **7855-5701**) throughout Havana, as well as at the airport and in the lobbies of most major hotels (although many of these will only change money for hotel guests; the Hotel Cohiba is an exception to this rule). Most banks also exchange money.

Dentists **Hospital Cira García,** Calle 20 no. 4101, Playa (www.cirag.cu; ✆ **7204-2811**), and other major medical centers also provide dental care. If you want a specific recommendation, contact your embassy, or ask at your hotel's front desk. Alternately, you can contact **Asistur** (www.asistur.cu; ✆ **7866-4499**), which can help you with dental emergencies.

Doctors Cuba has a surfeit of doctors, and many hotels catering to tourists have one or two on staff. If not, your hotel is still probably your best bet for a recommendation. You can also contact your embassy or **Asistur** (www.asistur.cu; ✆ **7866-4499**), which specializes in emergency medical care and insurance.

Drugstores Well-stocked drugstores are few and far between in Havana. There's a 24-hour pharmacy at the international terminal of the José Martí airport (✆ **7266-4105**). The pharmacies at the **Hotel Sevilla** (✆ **7861-5703**) in La Habana Vieja, and **Tryp Havana Libre** (✆ **7838-4593**) in Vedado, are usually decently stocked. In Miramar, you can try the **Farmacia Internacional,** Avenida 41 and Calle 20 (✆ **7204-4350**), also at Avenida 3 between Calle 78 and 80 (✆ **7204-4515**) and Avenida 7 and Calle 26 (✆ **7204-7980**).

Embassies & Consulates See "Fast Facts: Cuba," p. 290.

Emergencies Dial ✆ **106** for **police;** ✆ **104, 7838-1185,** or 7838-2185 for an **ambulance;** and ✆ **105** for the **fire department.** At none of these numbers can you assume you will find an English-speaking person on the other end. You can also try contacting **Asistur** (✆ **7866-4499**), which specializes in emergency medical care for travelers.

Express Mail Services The main office of **DHL,** Calle 26 and Avenida 1, Miramar (www.dhl.com; ✆ **7204-1578/7204-1876**), offers a collection service from its HQ.

Eyeglasses Look for the word *óptica*. **Optica Miramar,** Avenida 7 and Calle 24, Miramar (✆ **7204-2269**), is one of the better *ópticas* catering to foreign residents and visitors. It has a branch in downtown Havana at Calle Neptuno 411, between San Nicolás and Manrique (✆ **7863-2161**), and another at Obispo 364 between Habana and Compostela. For contact lenses, try the **Centro de Contactología,** Obispo 359 between Habana and Compostela (✆ **7860-8262**). Service is quick at Obispo 364.

Hospitals Your best bet is **Hospital Cira García,** Calle 20 no. 4101, Playa (www.cirag.cu; ✆ **7204-2811**), which provides emergency services and long-term care. Another possibility is the **Hospital Hermanos Ameijeiras,** Calles San Lázaro and Belascoaín, Centro Habana (✆ **7876-1000**).

Internet Access Internet access is more common and available in Havana, but it can still be a frustrating experience. Your best options are the various hotels with Wi-Fi and Internet terminals using the Nauta disposable card system, which most of the country uses. The official price is CUC$2 per hour (July 2015). Alternately, you can go to any **Etecsa** office. These offices also sell disposable Nauta access, which are good at any Internet-equipped Etecsa office in the country for 30 days after first usage. There's **Telepunto de Obispo,** Calle Habana 406 btw. Obispo and Obrapia, La Habana

Vieja; **Telepunto del Focsa,** Calle 17 and M, Edificio Focsa, Vedado; and **Oficina Comercial,** Calle 17 between B and C, Vedado. Note that some hotels (such as the Melia Cohiba, Melia Habana, and the Nacional) have their own Wi-Fi systems that cost more. Some hotels offer Nauta but like to overcharge CUC$8/hr.

Maps The various Infotur booths and kiosks around town sell a pretty decent map of Havana for CUC$1; sometimes they'll even give you a copy for free. Most rental-car agencies and hotels can also give you a copy of the same, or a similar, map. The Cuban Geographic and Cartographic Institute publishes a couple of much more detailed maps of Havana, including the *Ciudad de la Habana Mapa Turistica,* which you can get at most tourist gift shops and Infotur kiosks.

Police Dial ✆ **106.** Although it's possible for someone who speaks English to be rounded up, do not expect to find an English-speaking person on the other end. In the event of serious danger, you are probably better off contacting your embassy (nonlicensed U.S. citizens should contact the U.S. Interests Section only as a last resort).

Post Office Most major hotels either have small post-office branches or will sell you stamps and post letters. This is generally your best bet, as the *correos* (public post-office branches) are often crowded and inefficient. In La Habana Vieja, there's a *correo* on the west end of the Plaza de San Francisco and another at Calle San Juan de Díos y Calle Aguacate. Both are open Monday through Saturday 8am to 6pm.

Safety Havana is a very safe city. It has a strong police presence, and street crime is uncommon, especially in tourist areas. But because streetlights are virtually nonexistent, it's wise to avoid the dark alleys and side streets of Havana after dark. There have been recent reports of muggings and pickpocketing in Havana, so be aware of your surroundings. Solo female travelers should not walk alone through Centro Habana late at night, unless you're walking through Galiano or the pedestrian section of San Rafael. Popular tourist spots are relatively safe at night. Still, given the vast economic gap between Cubans and tourists, you should be careful about where you walk and with whom you engage. It is best not to wear much jewelry or make other showy signs of wealth.

WHERE TO STAY

Havana offers a wide range of **hotel options,** mostly divvied up among the large state-run chains. **Habaguanex** has monopoly control over the hotel scene in La Habana Vieja, and **Gaviota, Cubanacán,** and **Gran Caribe** own the remainder of the midrange to upper-end hotels around Havana. Of the international hotel chains, the major player in town is the Spanish-owned **Sol Meliá**, which manages three large, high-end properties in Havana. Given the fact that hotel chains control so much of the market, one major problem is a generalized lax attitude toward overbooking.

Havana has hundreds of ***casas particulares*** (private rooms) for rent. In general, the rooms and homes are kept very clean, while the furnishings and amenities can be quite simple. Rates average between CUC$20 and CUC$40 (and up) per room, and meals are often available at very reasonable prices, with breakfast starting at CUC$3. In addition to the recommendations below, check out **www.cubacasas.net**. ***Note:*** Rates for any *casa* in Havana in the CUC$20–CUC$40 range are not supplied, because those rates fluctuate so much in low and high season. You'll see fixed-rate prices for high-end *casas* or private apartments.

Given the compact nature of Havana, the proximity of its major attractions, and the wide availability of relatively inexpensive taxis, the neighborhood you choose is not a limiting factor. In general, most visitors will want to spend most of their time exploring La Habana Vieja, so the hotels there or nearby in Centro Habana are best for direct walking access. Large group and package tourists, as well as business travelers, are usually funneled toward hotels in Vedado and Playa, about a 10- to 15-minute ride away from most of the action, although the area is also home to some of the better dining and nightlife spots.

La Habana Vieja (Old Havana)

La Habana Viejano is one of the best locations in Havana. With one exception, all of the hotels in Old Havana are owned and run by the Cuban chain **Habaguanex.** These are intimate, boutique-style hotels in beautifully refurbished old buildings. We've listed favorite Habaguanex hotels below, but for others that are also nice, check **www.habaguanex.ohc.cu/hotels/** for complete listings. The much-anticipated Kempinski-managed Hotel Manzana de Gómez, on the Parque Central, is scheduled to open in 2016.

EXPENSIVE

Hotel Ambos Mundos ★ The "Hemingway Hotel" was undergoing a much-needed revamp in mid-2015. While the rooms here are pretty standard, most visitors come for the location, the Hemingway connection, and the hotel's two bars. The pleasant rooftop terrace bar, with great views of Havana and its harbor, has been remodeled with smarter furniture, and breakfast here is a great start to the day. At the other end of the day, the lobby bar is a relaxing spot when tinkling piano music pours out into the humid night. Although Hemingway didn't show a propensity toward these hotels bars, he claimed the Ambos Mundos was "a good place to write." Today, the room where he penned parts of *For Whom the Bell Tolls* has been turned into a small **museum,** featuring his typewriter and photocopies of drafts and notes (room no. 511; daily 10am–5pm; CUC$2). The hotel's other draw is the ancient iron-grated elevator, which serves all floors and is manned by a uniformed attendant.

Calle Obispo 153 (corner of Calle Mercaderes). www.habaguanex.ohc.cu. ✆ **7860-9530.** 52 units. CUC$135–CUC$240 double; CUC$185–CUC$290 junior suite; CUC$235–CUC$240 suite. Rates include breakfast. MC, V. Street parking nearby. **Amenities:** Restaurant; 2 bars.

Hotel Conde de Villanueva ★ Known as the cigar lover's hotel, and with good reason, this hotel hides a wonderful Olde Worlde–style cigar store and lounge up a tiny wooden staircase that leads to a mezzanine hideaway. The cigar sommelier and cigar roller have 49 years of experience between them. The nine rooms—all on a first floor beautifully illuminated by stunning *mediopunto* (fan-shaped stained-glass windows)—are arrayed around a central courtyard pecked by a pet peacock and a chicken! The choice room in this 1864 mansion is the vast master suite, which comes with its own humidor. Some rooms could use an updating. Smoking is allowed anywhere on the premises.

Calle Mercaderes 102 (btw. Calles Lamparilla and Amargura). www.habaguanex.ohc.cu. ✆ **7862-9293.** 9 units. CUC$150–CUC$240 double; CUC$250–CUC$340 suite. Rates include breakfast. MC, V. Parking. **Amenities:** Restaurant; bar; room service; Internet.

Hotel Raquel ★★ The Art Nouveau Hotel Raquel is an Old Havana treat. The glorious baroque façade—it was once an elegant fabric company—gives way to a forest of pale pink Corinthian marble columns and a huge, stunning mandarin-and-white decorated glass skylight by artist Rosa María de la Terga. De la Terga also created the Jewish-style glass decoration of the *mamparas* (half-doors) in the restaurant. Ensuite rooms arrayed off the porticoed three-story gallery are vast, with mostly twin beds and enough space to hold a party. The staff, some of whom are drawn from the Jewish community, are lovely. The only drawback is the somewhat desultory breakfast, which, at this price, is unacceptable.

Calle Amargura, at the corner of San Ignacio. www.habaguanex.ohc.cu. ✆ **7860-8280.** 25 units. CUC$150–CUC$240 double; CUC$200–CUC$290 junior suite. Rates include breakfast. MC, V. Parking. **Amenities:** Restaurant; bar; gym; room service.

Hotel Santa Isabel ★ The honey-hued palace of the Count of Santovenia, now the extraordinarily good-looking Hotel Santa Isabel, flanks almost the entire eastern edge of the Plaza de Armas. While it's touted as one of the top Habaguanex hotels, it's limited on amenities, and some front-desk staff are snooty. While the facade is striking, with its multiple columned arches and *mediopunto* windows, the rooms are somewhat understated for the hotel's five-star billing. The Santovenia suite features a lovely, draped four-poster bed. Aside from the palatial suite, the top rooms here are nos. 304–314, which feature rooftop terraces facing the plaza. The rooftop bar has gone, but the **sidewalk café** is a pleasant (if expensive) spot for a mojito.

Calle Baratillo 9 (btw. Calles Obispo and Narciso López), Plaza de Armas. www.habaguanex.ohc.cu. ✆ **7860-8201.** 27 units. CUC$230–CUC$330 double; CUC$290–CUC$390 junior suite; CUC$350–CUC$450 Santovenia suite. Rates include breakfast. MC, V. Parking. **Amenities:** Restaurant; 2 bars; room service; smoke-free rooms; Wi-Fi.

Hotel Saratoga ★★★ The forest-green Saratoga, which straddles Old Havana and Centro, offers the most luxurious rooms in Havana. A tall hotel with a wonderful alfresco rooftop pool and winning views from the rooftop bar, this is the most elegant address in town. The suites are the top rooms here. Our favorite, the Prado Suite (no. 315), has a grand four-poster bed and huge bathroom on a mezzanine level. The Habana Suite is also a top choice, but even the interior rooms, with guaranteed silence, are plush with soft furnishings and lovely mosaic-tiled bathrooms. The Cuban Passport—listing attractions and restaurants around town—is a nice touch. The excellent breakfast at the **Anacaona** restaurant will power you through the day. The mezzanine-level, palm-filled, 24-hour bar is a chic spot for an evening tipple.

Paseo del Prado 603. www.hotel-saratoga.com. ✆ **7868-1000.** 96 units. CUC$246–CUC$470 double; CUC$294–CUC$532 junior suite; CUC$424–CUC$650 Prado suite; CUC$516–CUC$772 Capitolio suite; CUC$714–CUC$1032 Habana suite. Rates do not include breakfast (CUC$25 + 10% tax). MC, V. Free parking. **Amenities:** 2 restaurants; 3 bars; small gym; rooftop pool; room service; smoke-free rooms; Wi-Fi (free).

Iberostar Parque Central ★ The Parque Central encompasses two buildings: the older but modern building facing Parque Central, and the glassy tower across a road, behind it. The original building houses the large, buzzy lobby bar under the atrium and the principal services of the hotel. The alfresco rooftop pool in this section is also more attractive, with outstanding rooftop views. The breakfast buffet here can get mobbed around 8am, however, with a line forming. The rooms in the newer Torre section, reached by an underground tunnel from the original section, are smarter and more stylish although a little smaller, but the advantage here is there's no line for the breakfast. While the Torre rooftop bar is great for a drink, the alfresco rooftop pool is a little exposed. This hotel unfortunately suffers from a pendulum swing in service: It's generally very good but has moments of terrible; and rooms are rarely available at the 4pm check-in time.

Calle Neptuno (btw. Calles Prado and Zulueta). www.iberostar.com. ✆ **7860-6627.** 427 units. CUC$280–CUC$370 standard double; CUC$340–CUC$430 junior suite; CUC$400–CUC$490 suite. Rates include breakfast. MC, V. Free valet parking. **Amenities:** 3 restaurants; 3 bars; health club; Jacuzzi; two rooftop pools; room service; smoke-free rooms; Wi-Fi.

MODERATE

Hotel del Tejadillo ★ This is the best-located hotel in Old Havana for sightseers. Its bar tables spill out into the street down the side of the cathedral, and it's just a short hop to the Cathedral Square, Centro Wifredo Lam, and Hemingway's watering hole, La Bodeguita del Medio. The mansion is centered around two courtyards, one of which hosts the less-than-impressive breakfast. The best rooms face the quiet Tejadillo street on the first floor and are vast and supremely comfortable, complete with small kitchenettes.

Calle Tejadillo 12 (corner of Calle San Ignacio). www.habaguanex.ohc.cu. ✆ **7863-7283.** 32 units. CUC$135–CUC$240 double; CUC$185–CUC$290 junior suite. Rates include breakfast. MC, V. Street parking nearby. **Amenities:** Restaurant; bar.

INEXPENSIVE

Thanks to Habaguanex's complete control of the area, La Habana Viejano has no truly budget hotel options. However, the new **Habana 612** (www.habaguanex.ohc.cu/hoteles/habana-612-hotelhotel-habana-612hotel-habana-612/attachment/02) is fairly priced, has ultra-contemporary rooms and a restaurant with a breezy bistro feel, and is in a great location.

The presence of *casas particulares* (private rooms, apartments, or homes) in Havana is a game changer; in the last 2 years, some super-stylish holiday pads have come on the market. The following are recommended.

- **Bohemia apartments** A collection of small urban hideaways inside the lofty mansion of the Count of Lombillo. All are comfortable and minimalist in style, wrapped in the gorgeous signature shade of Havana blue. Breakfast can be taken in the (pricey) deli/café below (Calle San Ignacio 364 btw. Muralla and Brasil; www.havanabohemia.com; ✆ **7860-3722;** doubles from CUC$60).
- **Casa Arrate** This cute two-bedroom apartment with antique furniture and mamparas has a cozy feel. It straddles a handsome corner of Plaza Vieja. Breakfast is made for you on the premises but those keen to cook can use the small kitchen (Calle Muralla 101, Apt. 2, btw. Inquisidor and San Ignacio, Plaza Vieja; www.casaarrate.com; ✆ **7867-2644;** apartment CUC$100 per night including breakfast).
- **Casa Eduardo Canciano** This first-floor flat is run by a friendly family and has a wonderful Sevillana patio and Spanish colonial wooden windows. The large bedroom equipped with air-conditioning and a fan has an adjoining original jet-black-and-yellow bathroom. The dining room is next to the sweet balcony overlooking the street (Calle Refugio 103 btw. Calles Prado and Morro; www.winpict.com/cuba/eduardo/eduardo_canciano.htm; ✆ **7863-0523;** eduardo.canciano@infomed.sld.cu).
- **Casa Mary** This flat has an enormous terrace overlooking El Morro. It's next door to the Spanish Embassy in a quiet location. The two small rooms both have doors leading out onto the terrace, where you can lounge on painted iron chairs (Calle Cárcel-Capdevila No. 59, 2nd floor, btw. Calles Morro and Zulueta; http://casacolonialmary.feelcuba.com; ✆ **7861-5911**).
- **Casa Vitrales** A very funky place to stay. The nine bedrooms ramble around a colonial home in the northern part of Havana where new bars and restaurants are opening all the time. The ultra-stylish, light, and white bedrooms are comfortable and accented by antique furniture; the rooftop terrace is perfect for breakfast. This property may be rented as a whole, too (Calle Habana 106 btw. Cuarteles and Chacón; www.cvitrales.com; ✆ **7866-2607;** rooms CUC$20–CUC$40, CUC$450 whole house).
- **Chez Nous** This friendly house is a stone's throw from Plaza Vieja. Two rooms, furnished with colonial antiques, share a smart bathroom, and another room has an ensuite bathroom and a great terrace where you can take in the sun (Calle Teniente Rey 115, btw. Calles Cuba and San Ignacio; ✆ **7862-6287;** hostalcheznous@gmail.com).
- **Hostal El Angel** This is a lovely and friendly place to stay overlooking the Plazuela de Santo Angel. The rooms are big (save the cute little hideaway up the spiral staircase); breakfast is filling, and the staff is most helpful. The lovely living room with its plush antique furniture overlooks the Church of Santo Angel Custodio (Calle Cuarteles no.118, 2nd floor, btw. Missiones and Habana; www.pradocolonial.com; ✆ **7860-0771**).
- **Loft Habana** Fashioned out of a monumental colonial building facing the harbor, these architect-designed, mezzanine-level contemporary apartments have huge windows and balconies. The sleek superior duplex suite

even has a small kitchenette. Both superior and standard duplexes have sofa-beds to accommodate children. Breakfast is taken on the rooftop terrace with outstanding views of the bay (Calle Oficios, No. 402, btw. Luz and Acosta; www.cubarealtours.eu; rooms from CUC$150 including breakfast).

- **Suite Havana** Sitting pretty on one of Old Havana's manicured streets, this ultra-stylish, two-bed apartment is decorated with the works of Cuba's contemporary artists. It boasts a loft-style kitchen and a roof terrace where you can pluck your own mint for a mojito at sundown (Calle Lamparilla no 62 (altos) btw. Mercaderes and San Ignacio; www.suitehavana.com; ✆ **5829-6524;** apartment 200€ including breakfast).

Centro Habana

Centro Habana is devoid of significant sights but has some great *paladares* (see p. 62). It's a slice of residential Havana that most visitors love to explore because it's completely unmanicured and home to a vast number of Habaneros.

EXPENSIVE

Hotel Terral ★★★ A small, attractive, and stylish hotel set right on the Malecón sea road with show-stopping views of the Florida Straits, this hotel protects itself from the inclement weather with louvered shutters. The standout rooms are the two penthouses with beds positioned to face the sea. All rooms are decorated in a nautical theme with a preponderance of navy blues and silvers. The a la carte breakfast is one of the best in the city. Guests can enjoy theirs in bed at no extra cost, while nonguests can indulge in the all-you-can eat morning banquet for CUC$10.

Malecón, corner of Lealtad. www.habaguanex.ohc.cu. ✆ **7860-2100.** 14 rooms. CUC$150–CUC$240 double; CUC$200–CUC$290 penthouse rooms. Rates include breakfast. MC, V. **Amenities:** Restaurant; bar; room service; Internet.

Tropicana Penthouse A bijoux boutique sky-high penthouse with winning views of Havana and the ocean. This rooftop bolthole, in updated 1950s style, is perfect for couples wanting to escape the maelstrom below. Breakfast is delivered to your door in a basket, but an extra caffeine boost can be made in the small kitchenette. The penthouse sits right on Galiano and lies in the heart of Centro action.

Calle Galiano no. 60, Penthouse Apt., 9th floor (btw. San Lázaro and Trocadero). www.tropicanapenthouse.com. CUC$149–CUC$199.

INEXPENSIVE

There are literally hundreds of official and unofficial rooms for rent in private homes throughout Centro Habana. The modern apartment of a superfriendly young couple, **Federico and Yamelis Llanes,** has two ensuite rooms and a balcony that overlooks Prado, at Calle Cárcel 156 between Calles San Lázaro and Prado (✆ **7861-7817;** fllanes@gmail.com). Another great option with ensuite rooms, incredible balcony views, and a communal living room is the apartment of **Melba and Alberto,** Calle Galiano 115, Apto 81, between

Calles Animas and Trocadero (✆) **7863-5178;** barracuda1752@yahoo.es). **Casa 1932** ★, Calle Campanario 63 (bajos) between San Lázaro and Lagunas (www.casahabana.net; ✆ **7863-6203**), is an elegant, beautifully furnished colonial home run by the friendly Luís Miguel; Cuba's first jazz band, Orquesta Hermanos Castro, once resided here. The lovely **Casa Esther Cardoso,** Calle Aguila 367 between Calles San Miguel and Neptuno (✆ **7862-0401;** esthercv2551@cubarte.cult.cu), has a great terrace and interesting furniture and prints on the walls. **Hostal Balcones,** Consulado 152 (altos) between Colón and Trocadero (✆ **7860-1843;** isabelgomezhabana@gmail.com), owned by Isabel Gómez Durán, is a renovated property with three rooms, beautiful floor tiles, louvered shutters, and modern bathrooms.

Vedado & The Plaza de la Revolución Area

Leafy, chic Vedado offers plenty of accommodations and excellent dining and drinking choices, easy access to the rest of the city's attractions, and quite a few natural charms of its own.

EXPENSIVE

Hotel Capri ★ The Capri has risen from the ashes. This Mob-built hotel, which opened in 1956, has been restored and sits in a prime location in the nightlife district of Vedado. The famous rooftop swimming pool, dubbed the "Cabana in the Sky" in the '50s, has been altered, but it's still a great sky-high swim and the views are magnificent, although the tall glass windows detract. The standard rooms are spartan but comfortable with 1950s-style furniture. Here, you'll want the junior suites, which are more jaunty in style and furnished with repro '50s furniture; try to secure the one that's a towel's throw from the pool. The on-site **Anacaprí** restaurant does a delicious pizza.

Calle 21 (btw. N and O). www.nh-hotels.com. ✆ **7839-7200.** 220 units. CUC$150–CUC$230 double; CUC$250–CUC$310 junior suite. Rates include breakfast. MC. V. **Amenities:** 2 restaurants; 2 snack bars; 2 bars; gym; parking; rooftop pool; sauna; Wi-Fi.

Hotel Nacional de Cuba ★ Havana's iconic hotel has the potential to be a stunner, but unfortunately it's not the great hotel it could be. It's wonderfully atmospheric: The royal-palm-tree lined entrance is emblematic; the lobby carpeted in Moorish tiles is impressive, and the cooling drink on the alfresco terrace overlooking the sea is a must. The hotel could do with an upgrade, and the entire breakfast offering needs a complete revamp. Your best bet is to opt for the smart executive rooms on the 6th floor. Some standard rooms on other floors have been upgraded and are attractive. Don't miss the daily history tours that take you past the rooms the Mafia stayed in and the trenches in the gardens used during the 1962 missile crisis. The Mob held their 1946 Christmas conference here and dined on roast flamingo and roast manatee.

Calle O (corner of Calle 21). www.hotelnacionaldecuba.com. ✆ **7836-3564.** 426 units. CUC$175–CUC$230 double; CUC$252–CUC$270 junior suite; CUC$1,000 presidential suite. Rates include breakfast buffet. MC, V. Free valet parking. **Amenities:** 3 restaurants; 6 bars; business center; 24-hr. cafe; babysitting; cabaret; hairdressers; 2 outdoor pools; room service; lit outdoor tennis court; Wi-Fi.

Meliá Cohiba ★★ The ugly modern facade hides an excellent, well-run hotel with a full range of services. It sits just off the Malecón and is close to some of the city's top private restaurants and bars. The junior suites on the Royal Service floor are the top rooms here, with a warm contemporary feel and Jacuzzi baths with outstanding city views. The hotel pool is one of the loveliest in the city. It has a host of restaurants, the Habana Café, and a free shuttle service six times a day into Old Havana.

Av. Paseo (btw. Avs. 1 and 3). www.meliacuba.com. ✆ **7833-3636.** 462 units. From CUC$220 double; from CUC$245 junior suite; from CUC$260 royal service double; from CUC$314 royal service junior suite. MC, V. Valet parking. **Amenities:** 6 restaurants; 7 bars; 2 lounges; business center; health club; Jacuzzi; large outdoor pool; room service; sauna; smoke-free rooms; Wi-Fi.

Tryp Habana Libre ★ Sections of the former Havana Hilton have undergone a revamp including some rooms and the swimming pool area, but other rooms are looking very dated, with antiquated furniture. This is a shame, since the rooms are super-spacious and views are outstanding. A stay here is really more about the address and the enviable location. When Fidel Castro marched into Havana on January 8, 1959, he used the Hilton as his headquarters. His room can now be visited (with an advance reservation). The Habana Libre has a good stable of eating and drinking options. The **Polinesio,** virtually unaltered since its 1958 opening as an original Trader Vic's tiki restaurant and a piece of hotel heritage in its own right, is good fun; and the 24-hour **La Rampa** snack bar is a reliable and fairly priced central option.

Calles L and 23. www.meliacuba.com. ✆ **7834-6100.** 532 units. CUC$157–CUC$294 double. Rates include buffet breakfast. MC, V. Valet parking. **Amenities:** 4 restaurants; 2 bars; 2 lounges; 3 snack bars; dance club; outdoor pool; room service; smoke-free rooms; Wi-Fi.

INEXPENSIVE

Given that this is one of Havana's prime middle-class neighborhoods, there's a glut of *casas particulares,* many in wonderful old neoclassical and Art Deco homes and apartment buildings. You'll also find a handful of great private apartments to rent. The following are all recommended.

- **Artedel Luxury Penthouse** Run by art collector Ydalgo Martínez, this penthouse pad in the heart of the artsy Vedado district boasts three rooms, a wraparound terrace, and a plunge pool. It's a stylish place to stay, with contemporary art on the walls and 1950s accents. All the rooms are supremely comfortable, but the suite has three terraces (Penthouse, Calle 17, no. 260, btw. Calles I and J (http://cubaguesthouse.com; ✆ **7830-8727;** CUC$75–CUC$120 including breakfast).
- **Casa Cachita Abrantes** This beautiful house, owned by the founder of Havana's La Maison fashion house, offers three rooms surrounding a central living room decorated with the works of René Portocarrero and Pablo Oliva. This leads out to a lovely garden anchored by a great pool (Calle 43 no. 1120 btw. Calle 36 and Ave Kholy, Nuevo Vedado; ✆ **7881-4303;** cachitaaf@yahoo.com; house from CUC$250).

- **Casa Carlos Peña Avila** Owned by a very polite man, this *casa* has two bedrooms furnished with antiques and modern bathrooms (Calle F 305, Apt. 3, btw. Calles 13 and 15; www.carlosyneida.com; ✆ **7833-5992**).
- **Casa Delta Torres Pagán** This grand corner house is full of antiques. The front room is embellished with French chandeliers, a beautiful 18th-century grandfather clock, and huge 1930s-era glass lamps that were destined for the Hotel Nacional. Of the two rooms here (one with an independent entrance), you'll want the larger interior room with the 18th-century bed. Delta is a great conversationalist, and this is a fascinating place to stay (Calle D No. 501, btw. Calles 21 and 23, Vedado; ✆ **7832-9078;** CUC$30 double).
- **Casa Jorge Coalla Potts** Managed by Jorge and Marisel, helpful and very hospitable hosts, this ground-floor apartment in a handsome, modern white apartment building is in an excellent location (Calle I btw. Calles 21 and 23, no. 456, Apt. 11; www.havanaroomrental.net; ✆ **7832-9032**).
- **Casa Lilly** On the 13th floor of a 1950s block building, this enormous flat affords spectacular views of Vedado and the Malecón. Rooms are spacious and attractively decorated, and guests share a large, minimally decorated living room enhanced by Asian influences. Breakfast is served at the elegant dining table or on the wraparound terrace. Run by Lilly and her family, it's a gorgeous place to stay. Guarded parking available beneath the flats (Calle G, no. 301, corner of Calle 13, 13th floor; www.casalilly.com; ✆ **5268-9737**).
- **Casa Luis Alberto Gómez Garcés** This quirky house with a Spanish turret has one large room with a small kitchenette and an independent entrance. The room is next to a small patio. The interior décor in the main house is shabby-chic, with a chandelier, some choice pieces of furniture, and lovely hallway tiling (Calle 15, no. 305 [*bajos*], btw. Calles H and I (✆ **7836-3954;** mroche@infomed.sld.cu).
- **Casa María Elena Matos Fernández** A huge, smart flat with elegant proportions in an Art Deco building close to the Malecón. The one room has two beds and pretty floor tiles and an adjoining large 1950s bubble-gum-pink bathroom (Calle 13 no. 106, btw. Calles L and M, Apt. 5 (✆ **7832-4346;** ernesto.mato@infomed.sld.cu).
- **Casa Norma Alvarez Bustio** One lovely ensuite room in an excellent location. Norma is most welcoming (Calle 25 359, Apt. D, btw. K and L (✆ **7832-2207;** hugovaldes@cubarte.cult.cu).
- **Casa Teresita** This handsome green mansion sits right on Paseo. The two rooms share a glorious bathroom with a stained-glass window. Breakfasts are taken at the communal dining table served by Teresita's charming sister, Cachita. This is a lively household and a good spot in which to meet other travelers (Paseo no. 208 btw. Línea and 11; ✆ **7830-2649**).
- **Vedado House Cultural** José Camilo used to work for the Ministry of Culture and is a mine of information on events worth seeing in Havana. His flat has one ensuite room and an excellent Vedado location (Apt 4,

Calle 11, corner of A; www.facebook.com/vedadocultural.renthouse; ✆ **5243-3686;** milovalls2014@gmail.com).

- **Villa Celia** Celia's beautiful 1940s villa has two spacious bedrooms in a secure patio facing leafy John Lennon Park. The rooms enjoy a shared kitchen and living room; Celia is a wonderfully friendly host (Calle 15 910 btw. 6 and 8; ✆ **7833-6832;** celiagonzalezn@gmail.com).

Playa

INEXPENSIVE

Playa has scores of *casas particulares* and private rooms for rent. Given the fact that this was a popular upper-class residential neighborhood prior to the Revolution, most are housed in large, comfortable homes and apartments.

Casa de Cleo y Alejandro, Calle 48 no. 1307, between 13 and 15 (✆ **7209-6514;** cleo.dominguez@gmail.com; CUC$70 per night), has an intimate cottage appeal, with wrought-iron bedsteads, floral spreads, plenty of cabinets stacked with china, and a small kitchen. This two-bedroom home has a shared bathroom and is next door to the outstanding paladar Cocina de Lilliam (p. 68). After comfort, its biggest appeal is that breakfast is served by the *paladar* and a discount is offered on meals there. A very handsome home inside an architect-designed 1955 building, **Casa de Gertrudis Martorell,** 7ma Avenida, no. 6610, between 66 and 70 (www.habitacionhabana.com; ✆ **7202-6563;** CUC$370 per night), offers an upstairs independent apartment with a tiny kitchenette, four large rooms, and original 1950s bathrooms—plus a vast terrace with TV and barbecue. Downstairs, amid the work of some of Cuba's most famous contemporary artists, are two more rooms.

Habana del Este & Playas del Este

Some of the beaches of Playas del Este are quite beautiful. Moreover, the four long, consecutive beaches here are just a 15- to 25-minute taxi or car ride from La Habana Vieja, making it a good choice for combining your fun in the sun with some city pleasures. Of the most significant beaches, the farthest east is **Guanabo,** where Habaneros decamp during weekends and the summer months. Closer to Havana, **Santa María del Mar** is essentially a strip of hotels and villas. The hotel choices here are limited, however. Several all-inclusive resorts offer a range of entertainment and activities, but the majority of lodging options here are far less polished and attractive than similar offerings in Varadero or other prime all-inclusive destinations. In fact, if you want a beautiful beach resort just a little bit farther east of Playas del Este, head to **Memories Jibacoa** (see below). Both Santa María del Mar and Guanabo have *casas particulares.*

MODERATE

Hotel Atlántico The only hotel on the sands at Santa María has rooms found in accommodation blocks dating back to 1959 and 1992. You'll want the "newer" rooms, which are more spacious, even though a no-frills policy pervades the locale. None of the rooms actually face the sea, so all have partial views. There are better hotels elsewhere; this is only really for travelers who don't have the time to explore further. However, for a quick getaway from Havana, with an all-inclusive deal, the beach here is quite attractive. The day pass at CUC$25 is not a good deal—you'll find better food at the beach.

Av. Las Terrazas 10, Santa María del Mar. www.gran-caribe.com. © **7797-1085.** 92 units. CUC$70–CUC$100 double. Rates are all-inclusive. MC, V. Free parking. **Amenities:** Restaurant; snack bar; 3 bars; outdoor pool; outdoor tennis court; free watersports equipment; Internet.

Villas Los Pinos ★ These independent villas are a little dated, but if you can snag one of the six actually on the beach at Santa María, you could be in for a good weekend. Each comes with a fully equipped kitchen, and all but six have private swimming pools. Nos. 44 and 45 have great views, while no. 36 has its own tennis court. This place gets super-busy; try to book 2 months in advance from May to September, and give at least 2 weeks' notice for the rest of the year. For CUC$25 per day, you can hire your own personal housekeeper.

Av. Las Terrazas 21 (btw. Calles 4 and 5), Santa María del Mar, Playas del Este. www.gran-caribe.com. © **7797-1361/1269.** reservas@complejo.gca.tur.cu. 26 villas. CUC$110–CUC$150 2-bedroom villa; CUC$150–CUC$190 3-bedroom villa; CUC$180–CUC$225 4-bedroom villa. MC, V. Free parking. **Amenities:** 2 restaurants; 2 bars; 20 outdoor pools; 2 outdoor tennis courts; watersports equipment rentals.

INEXPENSIVE

Santa María has just one *casa particular,* but there are a host of casas up the hill behind the beach. **Casa Adnan y Laura**, Av Sur 51, corner of 5ta (© **7797-1250;** cubacolors@gmail.com), is just behind the Villa Los Pinos reception building, a short walk from the beach. It has two rooms, a patio, and a pool; the larger room can accommodate two adults and a child. Curiously, it also has a call button for service in the smaller room. Breakfast in bed? Yes, please. A modest-looking 1956 house, **Cabañas del Sol Santa María,** Calle 3ra, no. 54, btw. 5ta and Vía Blanca, Reparto Los Pinos (© **7798-1443**/5826-7397; josueplaya@nauta.cu, sales75@cabanasdelsol.com; whole house CUC$160), is home to four rooms and a swish, fully equipped kitchen. All the rooms have TVs and huge beds, apart from the fourth room, which is small. The friendly housekeeper comes in to make breakfast if required.

A Little Farther East

Memories Jibacoa ★★ This is, without doubt, the loveliest all-inclusive spot on the coast that is close to Havana. It's a low-key, intimate resort anchored around a large, inviting pool, a handsome avenue of palms leading to the sea, and an arc of low-slung buildings scattered around a handsome curve of beach backed by gently sloping hills. The offshore snorkeling is excellent, and diving is possible. The standard rooms are very spacious, the food is good, and the staff is warm and friendly, plus it's only a 50-minute drive from Havana.

Memories Jibacoa. www.memoriesresorts.com. ✆ **47/29-5123.** 250 units. CUC$135–CUC$150 standard room; CUC$184–CUC$204 suite. Rates are all-inclusive. MC, V. No children under 16 allowed. **Amenities:** 4 restaurants; 5 bars; cabaret; small, well-equipped gym; large outdoor pool; 2 tennis courts; free non-motorized watersports equipment.

WHERE TO DINE

Havana used to be a bit of a culinary desert but, since autumn 2010 when President Raúl Castro permitted greater self-employment, dozens of private restaurants have opened. A number of them are outstanding, and eating well in Havana is now a joyful possibility. With few exceptions, it's best to avoid state restaurants: The food is mediocre, service is substandard, and overcharging is attempted with disheartening frequency. (It is wise to review all bills when eating out.) For the best *paladares* (private restaurants), an evening reservation is now a must. Your hotel concierge or *casa particular* should be able to help. Only cash is accepted.

Paladares are now widespread in Havana. No longer limited to 12 seats, *paladares* are restricted from selling lobster, but many do. If you want cheaper (Cuban) sparkling mineral water, you will need to expressly request *agua con gas nacional* as many *paladares* have an unacceptable habit of bringing out more expensive bottled water already opened unless you have expressed your preference. Ice served in restaurants is safe to drink. Many *paladares* now automatically add a 10% service charge to the bill.

Note: It is best to avoid being taken to a restaurant by a *jinetero* (street hassler). If you do, you will be paying his or her commission, and you likely won't even know it. Most restaurants have two menus: one standard and one "with commission"—the latter showing inflated prices to cover the cost of the *jinetero*'s commission.

COFFEE, LIGHT BITES & SWEETS For a coffee-and-cake pit stop, try the very cute **Bianchini**, Calle San Ignacio 68, tucked off the Plaza de la Catedral (and at a cubbyhole in Calle Sol no. 12 between Oficios and Av del Puerto (www.dulceria-bianchini.com; ✆ **7862-8477**). At the attractive, partially alfresco **Café el Escorial**, Mercaderes 317, corner of Muralla (✆ **7868-3545**), on Plaza Vieja, you can sit under the lemon-yellow arches and sample coffee, ice cream with amaretto, sandwiches, and cookies. **El Dandy Brasil,** corner of Calle Villegas (✆ **7867-6463**) is adorned with cool knick-knacks and the striking photos of the Swiss photographer owner Anders Rising on a corner of the increasingly hip Plaza el Cristo area.

La Habana Vieja

In addition to those restaurants reviewed below, we also recommend **Ivan Chefs Justo ★★**, Calle Aguacate 9, corner of Calle Chacón (✆ **7863-9697**), for its seafood dishes in a lovely old colonial home. A funky cubbyhole on the Plaza del Cristo, **El Chanchullero**, Calle Brasil no. 457A (*bajos*) between Bernaza and el El Cristo (✆ **7862-8227**), serves bargain-priced shrimp in garlic in earthenware dishes. Hugely popular and hip gin bar and restaurant **Café O'Reilly 304**, Calle O'Reilly between Habana and Aguiar (✆ **5264-4725**), offers divine, tangy ceviche.

Café del Oriente ★ INTERNATIONAL An elegant state-run restaurant in a corner of the Plaza San Francisco, where, when the weather permits, you can sit at one of the sprinkling of outdoor tables. Inside is a sumptuous interior with marble and malachite floors, a long bar, and a player tinkling the ivories of the handsome piano. The menu is a little extravagant and pricey for Havana, however. We recommend the simple but tasty grilled snapper in garlic, tomato, and basil. Not ready for a meal? A lemonade in the air-conditioned calm makes a cool respite from sightseeing.

Calle Oficios 112 (btw. Calle Armargura and Lamparilla). ✆ **7860-6686.** Main courses CUC$12.50–CUC$30. MC, V. Daily noon–midnight.

Doña Eutimia ★★ CRIOLLO Tucked in a tiny home at the end of the Callejón del Chorro in a corner of the Cathedral Plaza, Doña Eutimia is rightly lauded, and its sensible pricing means it's always full. A couple of tables on the cobblestones are available for walk-ins, but if you want an interior spot you'll need to reserve. Ever since the famous city historian Eusebio Leal hung his shirt in the restaurant to promote the *paladar* (so the story goes), it seems to have held onto its crown as one of the top restaurants in the city. The *ropa vieja*—here made with shredded lamb—is always tasty, as is the Cuban flan. We also recommend the beef and pork meatballs in sauce.

Callejón del Chorro 60C, Plaza de la Catedral. ✆ **7861-1332.** d.eutimia@yahoo.es. Main courses CUC$7–CUC$10. Reservations recommended for lunch and dinner. Daily noon–10:30pm.

El Templete ★★★ INTERNATIONAL/SEAFOOD This attractive state restaurant offers fine dining portside on tables spilling out under the blue awnings or inside the air-conditioned cool. It's still a grand dining spot despite the excellent competition from the private sector. Thanks to its mix of Malagueño and Basque chefs, El Templete remains a hotspot for government officials, expats, and visitors. Its longstanding sesame-wrapped tuna with *piquillo coulis* has always been a favorite, as is the cod accompanied by large prawns bathed in garlic and orange. This has always been a place where you need to make room for the chocolate desserts, and, if you are so inclined, a bottle of wine (from 170 to choose from) and a cigar from the cigar menu, with a helpful guide to the time it takes to smoke each *puro*.

Avenida del Puerto (corner of Narciso López). ✆ **7866-8807.** Main courses CUC$13.50–CUC$30. MC, V. Daily noon–midnight.

La Bodeguita del Medio CRIOLLAN An overcrowded, badly serviced, touristy rip-off. The only reason we mention it in this guide is that it's on the Hemingway trail, and first-time visitors always like to swing by "La Bodeguita" and hang out at the decibel-challenged in-house bar. There are better places to sample mojitos—available here overpriced (CUC$5) and subpar—and if you want to drink in a Hemingway haunt, we recommend the more atmospheric El Floridita. If you're inclined to eat, you'll be shown to the graffiti-clad back rooms; the breezy upstairs terrace is for drinking only. The food is pretty good, however. We like the *ropa vieja,* and the slices of roast leg of pork in a mojo. The service is bad, however, and a drink came in a can with a straw, and the side dishes (included in the price) include rice and beans, except there were no beans (*frijoles*). We requested a proper serving of frijoles and when they came, they were delicious. Frankly, there are much better places nearby to dine, and La Bodeguita feels very Cuba culinary scene, circa 2000.

Calle Empedrado 207 (btw. Calles San Ignacio and Cuba). ✆ **7867-1374.** Reservations recommended. Main courses CUC$9–CUC$22. MC, V. Daily noon–midnight.

La Terraza ★★★ GRILL La Terraza used to be a bit of a secret. No longer. Enormous portions of freshly charcoal-grilled seafood and meats are served on the third-floor terrace under citric-yellow ceramic shades overlooking Prado. You'll want the handful of peacock-shaped wicker chairs plus tables with a view. It's all delicious, from the octopus carpaccio to the divine tuna in sesame sauce accompanied by chargrilled vegetables to the tasty, rosemary-infused pork skewers with cherry tomatoes and fried garlic. If you've got the room, the mango cheesecake makes a delicate finish. While you're there, take the time to visit the **Restaurant El Gijones** in the same Centro Asturiano building. It's housed in the old American Club: The lofty, wood-paneled dining room features all the shields of the United States minus Alaska and Hawaii.

Prado 309, corner of Virtudes. www.havana-gourmet.com. ✆ **7864-1447**. Main courses CUC$10–CUC$15. Daily noon–midnight.

Mama Inés ★★ CRIOLLO/SEAFOOD This modest and laidback little restaurant is all bare brick walls, white lace cloths, glassware, bronze chandeliers—and famous chef. Fidel Castro's former personal chef, Tomás Erasmo Hernández, opened this *paladar* on a quiet cobblestoned Old Havana street under a coffered Cuban blue ceiling in a vintage colonial home. We recommend the marlin bathed in a rich garlic sauce served with aromatic herb rice accompanied by a white bean and tomato salad. The sturdy dome of Cuban flan sprinkled with cinnamon is the perfect ending to a delicious meal. The menu is chalked up on a board daily.

Calle Obrapía 60 (btw. Oficios and Baratillo). ✆ **7862-2669.** Main courses CUC$12.50–CUC$14. Mon–Sat 1pm–9pm.

Paladar Los Mercaderes ★★ CRIOLLO/SEAFOOD This handsome old Havana home, adorned with Cuba's iconic film posters and with two protruding balconies overlooking pretty Calle Mercaderes, is an Old Havana standout. The food is always abundant, and the service is faultless. We recommend the *pescado infiesta,* snapper served in a fish-shaped glass dish and bathed in a tasty lemon sauce, accompanied by chunky sweet potato fries. The *ropa vieja* (shredded meat), using pulled lamb, is also recommended. This is also one of the few restaurants in Havana that properly caters to vegetarians. Prices are a little inflated, and one bathroom for such a popular restaurant is highly inconvenient.

Calle Mercaderes 207 (altos) (btw. Lamparilla and Amargura). ✆ **7861-2437.** Mains CUC$6.50–CUC$19.50. Daily 11:30am–11:30pm.

Centro Habana

In addition to the restaurants reviewed below, we also recommend the stylish Russian *paladar* with outstanding Malecón views, **Nazradovie,** Malecón 25, 2nd floor, between Prado and Cárcel (www.nazradovie-havana.com; ✆ **7860-2947**). For Swedish and Cuban dishes with style, head to hip **Casa Miglis**, Calle Lealtad 120 between Anímas y Lagunas (www.casamiglis.com; ✆ **7864-1486**). The excellent, unfailingly reliable **Castropol**, Malecón 107 between Genios and Crespo (✆ **7861-4864**), is run by the Asturias Society and has great Malecón and sea views.

La Guarida ★★ CRIOLLAN/INTERNATIONAL La Guarida is famous for its starring role in the iconic movie *Fresa y Chocolate,* about the friendship between a young straight revolutionary and a rebellious gay artist. The building is exceptionally beautiful, and the statues fashioned by Cuban artist Esterio Segura for the film still adorn the premises. The new rooftop bar—where you can lounge in a giant picture frame—has given it a wow factor, and the one-of-a-kind communal bathroom is a must-visit in itself. We have eaten here plenty of times, especially since it was a culinary beacon in the years before things changed in late 2010. We have recently had mixed experiences, however, with both food and service—it can be excellent one time and mediocre the next. We recommend the outstanding tender suckling pig in orange honey reduction; skip the overpriced baked chicken in honey and lemon sauce.

Calle Concordia, no. 418 (btw. Gervasio and Escobar). www.laguarida.com. ✆ **7866-9047.** Main courses CUC$14–CUC$20. Daily noon–4pm and 7pm–midnight. Bar 6pm–2am.

San Cristóbal ★★★ CRIOLLAN/SEAFOOD This fantastically glorious 1914 colonial home in Centro Habana, adorned with the private collection of photographs and record sleeves of the chef, has remained a top Havana dining experience ever since it opened in December 2010. From the maitre d' Leo to the highly professional waiters and the personal welcome from Chef Carlos Cristóbal Márquez Valdés (who has worked in Brazil, Mexico, Italy, and the UN), you are made to feel special every time you dine. It's no wonder that Nancy Pelosi dined here in spring 2015. Choose the assortment of petite starters before embarking on the seafood or the highly recommended steaks. Try the hogfish bathed in butter with lemon wedges and served with a huge dollop of creamy mashed potatoes. San Cristóbal is popular, and you'll want to dine in the interior rooms rather than the patio, so reservations are recommended.

Calle San Rafael, no. 469 (btw. Lealtad and Campanario). ✆ **7867-9109.** sancristobal-paladar@gmail.com. Main courses CUC$7–CUC$20. Reservations required for dinner. Mon–Sat noon–midnight. Closed Aug.

SiáKará Café ★★ CRIOLLAN/INTERNATIONAL Hip SíaKará is mostly known as a place to get a good drink, ordered from a menu backed by the old colorful *chapas* (Cuban license plates). Hidden behind the Capitolio, a little off the tourist path, it's artfully decorated with antiques, books, and a curtain of men's ties. It has two cozy Marrakech-style nooks (one hidden away on a mezzanine) for drinks or coffee, set to the soundtrack of the likes of Descemer Bueno, and a small dining area that is a little awkwardly arranged—a minor complaint considering the tasty, excellent-value food it offers in the heart of the tourist district. The snapper filet accompanied by a malanga and pumpkin mash is winningly delicious and appealingly priced at CUC$7.50, when main-course costs all around in 2015 appear to have reached the price of the average Cuban monthly salary. If you're eating and drinking at 10pm, you'll be treated to the pianist's repertoire. In case you're wondering, that's a portrait of Fernando VII behind the bar.

Calle Industria 502 (corner of Calle Barcelona). www.siakaracafe.com. ✆ **7867-4084.** Main courses CUC$4.50–CUC$7.50. Daily 1pm–2am.

Vedado & the Plaza de la Revolución Area

In addition to the reviews below, we also recommend **Café Maimané,** Calle L, no. 206, between 15 and 17), an arty café set over a couple of levels that offers good-value nourishment in an increasingly expensive district. We're sold on the coconut ice-cream shake. It's open Sunday to Thursday from 8am to midnight and Friday and Saturday from 8am to 3am, making it a cozy day-to-night pit stop. **Atelier,** Calle 5ta, no. 511 (altos), between Paseo and 2, Vedado (✆ **7836-2025**) is also a swanky spot for a meal amid the artwork and antique accents in the restored home of the 1920s President of the Cuban Senate, Clemente Vazquez Bello. The alfresco terrace is a beautiful spot for a cocktail. The family-run **La Casa**, Calle 30, no. 865, between 26 and 41, Nuevo Vedado (www.restaurantelacasacuba.com; ✆ **7881-7000**), offers the consummate dining experience with great food, attention to detail, and warm welcome.

Bar-Restaurante Mediterráneo ★★ MEDITERRANEAN Mediterráneo has gained currency for its fresh dishes cooked up with produce from its own organic countryside farm. Whether you want pizza (we recommend the 4 stagioni), pasta, fresh goat's cheese prepared by Sardinian chef Luigi Fiori, or something more substantial (the grilled fish filet or mixed grilled seafood), Mediterráneo succeeds every time. The alfresco second-floor terrace is the perfect spot at night; the first-floor air-conditioned dining room is a boon during hot days. Mediterráneo also thoughtfully offers a children's menu.

Calle 13, no. 406 (btw. F and G). www.medhavana.com. ✆ **7832-4894**. Main courses CUC$7–CUC$23. Daily noon–midnight.

Decamerón ★ CRIOLLAN/SEAFOOD/ITALIAN Decamerón, with its extraordinary collection of hanging clocks, is a frequent favorite. It's an intimate, unassuming affair, the staff is most welcoming, and you can eat well at reasonable prices. The menu is wide-ranging: Our favorite dish is the *ropa vieja* accompanied by chunky sweet potato chips. It's in an excellent Vedado location just off the main Línea and Paseo intersection.

Línea 753 (btw. Paseo and Calle 2). ✆ **7832-2444**. Daily noon–midnight.

El Litoral ★★★ SEAFOOD/INTERNATIONAL This elegant ocean-road restaurant has remained on top of its game since opening in December 2013. The garlic shrimp, served with pasta doused in squid ink and sun-dried tomatoes, is a popular dish, but we opt for the supremely tender shoulder of lamb each time. El Litoral is also a vegetarian's dream, with a whole roster of plump salads; it also offers a fulsome salad bar that is a top lunchtime favorite for American diplomats (posted down the road), artists, and those in the know.

Malecón 161 (btw. K and L). www.ellitoralhabana.com. ✆ **7830-2201**. Main courses CUC$10–18. Salad bar small dish CUC$7.50; large plate CUC$15. MC, V. Daily noon–11pm.

Playa

In addition to the recommendations below, we also recommend **Otramanera,** Avenida 35 between 20 and 41 (www.otramanera.com; ✆ **7203-8315**), for its ultra-contemporary garden setting and wonderful perky Cuban cuisine at reasonable prices (closed Sun & Mon). **Santy's ★★★,** a fishermen's shack on the River Jaimanitas, 240A, corner of 3ra. Calle, Jaimanitas (✆ **5286-7039**), serves up Havana's best sushi. Head to the leafy patio at **La Fontana,** Avenida 3A, no. 305 and 46 (www.lafontanahavana.info; ✆ **7202-8337**), for first-class grilled food. **Elite,** Calle 38, no. 705 between 42 and 7ma (www.elitehabana.com; ✆ **7209-3260**), offers up exquisite veal and professional service in monochrome surrounds. **Esperanza,** Calle 16, no. 105, between Avenidas 1 and 3 (✆ **7202-4361**), is an old-style *paladar* in the living room of a sprawling home in Miramar.

El Aljibe ★ CRIOLLAN This popular state-run tourist restaurant is a pleasant surprise. The fixed-price *pollo asado El Aljibe* is one of the best dishes in Havanam and the *frijoles* (black beans) are some of the softest and silkiest you will taste anywhere. The slow-roasted chicken is served up with white rice, the famous frijoles, fried plantain, and salad under a vast thatched-roof restaurant on one of Miramar's main avenues. It's touristy, sure, but the food is always excellent. The secret of the mojo that accompanies the chicken is a state secret. Someone has even written a novel hinging on the elusive ingredients (Phillippe Diedrich's *Sofrito*).

Av. 7 (btw. Calles 24 and 26). ✆ **7204-1583**. Reservations recommended at lunchtime. Main courses CUC$10–CUC$25. MC, V. Daily noon–midnight.

La Cocina de Lilliam ★★★ SEAFOOD/CRIOLLAN One of Havana's top dining experiences, the longstanding La Cocina de Lilliam continues to stave off much of the new wave of competition. Lilliam Domínguez was a fashion designer in the special period before turning professional in the kitchen. Her beautiful garden restaurant is full of Cuba's elite and visitors in the know—and for good reason. The culinary experience here is outstanding: Every dish, from the melt-in-the-mouth home-baked herb bread to the homemade ginger or basil ice cream, is a delight. Try the *pescado al papillote*, snapper infused with an abundance of herbs baked in a paper parcel. La Cocina is a short drive from Tropicana.

Calle 48 no. 1311 (btw. Calles 13 and 15). www.lacocinadelilliam.com. ✆ **7209-6514.** Reservations highly recommended. Main courses CUC$9.50–CUC$15. Tues–Sat noon–3pm and 7–11pm.

Habana del Este & Playas del Este

La Divina Pastora ★ SEAFOOD/CRIOLLAN There's no better view to be had of Old Havana while dining than that from the "Balcony of Havana" at the La Divina Pastora restaurant beneath the La Cabana fortress. This used to be a state restaurant but has happily segued into a cooperative-run place, and the food and service are, unsurprisingly, improved. We recommend the huge plate of baby octopus immersed in garlic and the very tasty *picadillo a la Habanaera*. This place is perfect for a meal and/or a drink before or after the Canonazo.

Parque Histórico Morro y Cabaña, Carretera de La Cabaña. ✆ **7793-7807.** Reservations recommended for dinner. Main courses CUC$5–CUC$20. MC, V. Daily noon–11pm.

La Terraza de Cojímar ★ SEAFOOD/CRIOLLAN This seaside restaurant is a de rigueur lunch stop for any visitor following the Hemingway trail. Cojímar was one of Papa's favorite spots, and his fishing friend Gregorio Fuentes, said to be the inspiration for the protagonist in the prize-winning novel *The Old Man and the Sea*, lived in the seaside community. La Terraza cooks up great soups, and its paella is recommended, too.

Calle Real no. 161, corner of Candelaria, Cojímar. ✆ **7766-5151**; comercial@terrazas.palmares.cu. Reservations recommended. Main courses CUC$7–CUC$25. MC, V. Daily noon–11pm; bar open from 10am.

Paladar Il Piccolo ★ ITALIAN All the dishes are delicious at this off-the-beaten-track pizzeria, but we recommend the Diablo pizza with its ají and chili sauce. Enter through the swinging green doors to a leafy patio and ceramic tables before heading inside to the pizza parlor, adorned with paper money and knick-knacks and the hard-working pizza oven. Service is very friendly.

5th Avenue (btw. Calles 502 and 504), Guanabo. ✆ **7796-4300.** Main courses CUC$4.25–CUC$10. Daily noon–midnight.

WHAT TO SEE & DO

Havana is a city with a rich historical and architectural legacy. It has scores of sights and attractions, ranging from museums and churches to city squares and colonial forts—and more. There's easily a week's worth of worthy attractions, with the most important sights below.

All the major tour agencies offer **city tours.** These affairs generally take in as many attractions as can be fitted into the allotted time period. The most common tours include stops at the José Martí Memorial, a ride along the Malecón, and a walk around La Habana Vieja (including stops at a handful of churches and attractions, and, of course, La Bodeguita del Medio). Some include tours of any number of the attractions listed below, with perhaps a visit to El Morro or the Hemingway Museum thrown in, while others are theme based—castles and forts, churches, tobacco, art, or Hemingway, for example. Different tour agencies mix and match the various attractions at their discretion. If you want to see something specific, be sure it's on the tour you sign up for. The tours can range from 4 to 8 hours in length and cost between CUC$15 and CUC$50 per person. Private classic-car taxi drivers also offer citywide tours for from CUC$20 an hour.

Note: You may occasionally find a museum closed in Cuba despite the stated opening hours. In case of a temporarily closure for anti-mosquito fumigation, you should return later in the day.

The Top Attractions

LA HABANA VIEJA

In addition to the places mentioned below, the neighborhood has scores of other interesting little museums and attractions. Moreover, many of the hotels and restaurants mentioned above (including El Floridita, Hotel Santa Isabel, and Hotel Ambos Mundos, to name just a few) are practically attractions in their own right, and worth a quick visit on any walking tour.

Castillo de la Real Fuerza ★ This well-preserved 16th-century fort sits within a broad cloverleaf moat. It's the oldest surviving fort in the hemisphere. It was actually pretty much a failure, built too small and too far from the harbor entrance to be of much use. Still, crossing over the old drawbridge and walking around the ancient stone battlements gives you a great sense of history. The most distinctive feature of this compact fort is the weathervane, La Giraldilla, which has come to be the city's defining symbol. The original 1634 bronze sculpture is now on display in the entrance; a copy adorns the top of the fort's bell tower. Today, the fort also contains exhibits featuring items salvaged from shipwrecks, as well as replicas of Spanish colonial boats. Kids will love the chests stuffed with treasure, but the standout exhibit is a huge 4-meter-long (13-foot) model (with accompanying film explanations) of the *Santísima Trinidad,* the largest naval ship of its time; it sank after the Battle of Trafalgar.

Calle O'Reilly 2 (at Av. del Puerto). ✆ **7864-4488.** Admission CUC$3 adults, free for children under 12; camera use CUC$5. Tues–Sun 9:30am–5pm.

A QUICK KEY TO HAVANA'S PARKS AND PLAZAS

Any tour of La Habana Vieja will be oriented around the several colonial plazas or squares, and the Parque Central (Central Park). Although relatively close together, each is almost a world of its own. The principal attractions of each are described in greater detail below, but here's a general overview.

The smallest, **Plaza de la Catedral,** is probably the most visited. Named for the cathedral that defines its northern boundary, this compact cobblestone square is surrounded by a series of stunning, colonial-era buildings and former palaces. With the cathedral's bell towers lit up each night, this is a great plaza to visit after dark. Within a 1-block radius in any direction, you will find La Bodeguita del Medio, the Centro Wifredo Lam, and the Museo de Arte Colonial.

The **Plaza de Armas** probably has the densest concentration of historic buildings and attractions. Surrounding the shady urban park that now takes up the plaza, you'll find the Palacio de los Capitanes Generales and Museo de la Ciudad, the Castillo de la Real Fuerza, El Templete, and the Hotel Santa Isabel, housed in the former palace of the Count of Santovenia. Most days, the square is lined with stands set up by scores of used-book sellers (although these are scheduled to be moved to the Almacenes San José).

The oldest plaza, **Plaza Vieja,** was first laid out in 1599 and was dubbed "Plaza Nueva" (New Square). It soon lost prominence to the better-located Plaza de Armas and Plaza de la Catedral. In fact, for most of the last half of the 20th century, it served simply as a parking lot. It has been meticulously restored, however. At the center of the broad open square is a replica of an 18th-century fountain. Surrounding it are historic buildings representing 4 centuries of construction.

Near the waterfront, you'll find the **Plaza de San Francisco.** Asymmetrical in shape, this is the most open and uncluttered plaza in La Habana Vieja. Facing the Sierra Maestra cruise-ship terminal, it is anchored by the Fuente de los Leones (Lion's Fountain), which was carved in 1836 by Italian sculptor Giuseppe Gaggini, modeled after a sister fountain in the Alhambra in Granada, Spain. The area's former importance as a business center is quickly noted in the imposing facades of the Lonja de Comercio (Stock Exchange) and a couple of large banks and money exchange houses that dominate the northern side of the plaza. The southern edge is defined by the lovely, 16th-century Basílica Menor de San Francisco de Asís. Be sure to climb the bell tower here, the tallest church tower in Havana, for a wonderful view of La Habana Vieja and its harbor.

Parque Central marks the western boundary of La Habana Vieja. This is a popular local gathering spot, particularly known for its heated conversations about baseball. It is bordered on the west by the Prado, featuring El Capitolio and the Gran Teatro de la Habana. On the eastern edge, you'll find the Palacio del Centro Asturiano, which now holds the international collection of the Museo Nacional de Bellas Artes. Classic hotels that ring the park include the Hotel Inglaterra, Hotel Plaza, and the Hotel Telégrafo, as well as the modern Hotel Parque Central. A short stroll down the Prado will soon bring you to the Museo Nacional de Bellas Artes, Museo de la Revolución, and the Memorial *Granma;* while just 1 block in the other direction, heading toward La Habana Vieja on Calle Obispo, you'll hit El Floridita.

Catedral de San Cristóbal ★★ This is Old Havana's classic cathedral. The plaza fronting the cathedral and the church's baroque facade, with its asymmetrical towers, are the most visited attractions in La Habana Vieja. Inside, the cathedral is simple, almost to the point of austerity, thanks to a radical, 19th-century neoclassical makeover. Still, the vaulted ceilings, massive stone pillars, and modest collection of art and antiquities certainly make it worth a visit. Of these, the 17th-century wooden sculpture of Saint Christopher is interesting—note the shortened legs, which were cut in order to get the piece into place. Despite the official visiting hours listed below, the church is frequently closed tight. If you're lucky, you might be able to attend Mass here at 9am on Sunday.

Calle Empedrado 156, Plaza de la Catedral. ✆ **7861-7771.** Free admission. Tower climb CUC$1. Mon–Sat 9am–5pm.

El Templete A tall (and still growing) ceiba tree stands in front of this neoclassical Doric temple. The tree is the younger cousin of a fallen giant that stood here, on the site where local citizens celebrated the town's first Mass and town meetings in the early 1500s. Behind the tree stands the "little temple," which was built between 1754 and 1828. Inside, you'll find three large canvases by Jean-Baptiste Vermay depicting the inauguration of the temple, as well as depictions of those town meetings and masses. You'll also find a bust of the artist beside an urn containing his ashes.

Calles Baratillo and O'Reilly, Plaza de Armas. Admission CUC$1 adults, free for children under 12. Tues–Sun 9:30am–4:30pm.

Museo de Arte Colonial ★★ This museum is often overlooked, but it's a hidden gem. The first-floor antiques, Baccarat crystal chandeliers, Cuban smoking chairs, and artwork are impressive, and the views of the cathedral and surrounding square are unbeatable. A renovation of the museum introduced two new interesting elements: an exhibition of salvaged beautiful *mediopunto* and *mamaparas,* and a new ground-floor exhibition of beautiful fans from Cuba and Spain made from bone and feather—some with exquisitely carved decoration.

Calle San Ignacio 61 (btw. O'Reilly and Callejón del Chorro). ✆ **7866-4458.** Admission CUC$3; tour guide CUC$5. Tues–Sat 9am–5pm, Sun 9am–5pm.

Strolling Calle Obispo

Calle Obispo, Old Havana's main shopping street, is one of the most distinctive streets in La Habana Vieja. This bustling pedestrian-only boulevard conveniently connects Parque Central and the nearby Capitolio with the Plaza de Armas and its many surrounding attractions, making it a classic route for any walking tour of La Habana Vieja.

Museo de la Ciudad ★★ Parts of the city museum, housed in the 18th-century baroque Palacio de los Capitanes Generales (Palace of the Captain Generals), were undergoing restoration in 2015. The highlights of this grand palace, seat of Cuba's government for more than 100 years, is the porticoed courtyard dominated by a marble statue of Christopher Columbus flanked by two towering royal palms; the Throne Room built for Spain's monarchs; and the long flag room, which contains historic hanging flags and personal objects belonging to Cuba's heroes-of-independence wars, such as swords and other weaponry.

Calle Tacón (btw. Calles O'Reilly and Obispo), Plaza de Armas. ✆ **7869-7358.** Admission CUC$3 adults, or CUC$5 with guide or audio tour in English, French, German, and Spanish, free for children under 12. Tues–Sun 9:30am–5pm.

Museo de la Revolución y Memorial Granma ★ The Museum of the Revolution is undergoing a restoration, and some of the exhibition rooms relating to the Wars of Independence are closed. What remains starts at the 26th of July 1953 Moncada barracks attack in Santiago and continues through Fidel Castro's 1959 Revolution. The exhibits are dense and intense and poorly organized. The highlights are the replica of Versailles' Hall of Mirrors; ornate bas-relief work and interior decorations by Tiffany; the life-size montage of Che Guevara and Camilo Cienfuegos in the Sierra Maestra; the Hall of Cretins (caricatures of U.S. presidents, mainly); and the principal exhibit the glass-enclosed *Granma,* the 18-meter (59-foot) motor launch that carried Fidel Castro, Che Guevara, and 80 other fighters to the island in 1956, and the surrounding military memorabilia. Improvements are ongoing.

Calle Refugio 1 (btw. Calles Monserrate and Zulueta). ✆ **7862-4098.** Admission CUC$8 adults, CUC$4 children 6–12. Guided tours in Spanish only are given throughout the day and cost an additional CUC$2. Daily 9am–5pm; last ticket entry 4pm. Café on premises.

Museo Nacional de Bellas Artes (Cuban section) ★★★ One of Havana's finest museums has a modern-art section that showcases 5 centuries of Cuban art. The collection stretches across three floors, but the layout is confusing, so it's best to grab one of the leaflets with a floor map at the entrance. Here you'll find the Cuban greats—Wifredo Lam, Raúl Martínez, Amelia Peláez, and René Portocarrero—before moving on to contemporary artists such as Lázaro Saavedra, Esterio Segura, Tonel, Manuel Mendive, and Alexander Arrechea. The international collection is based in the grand Centro Asturiano building, where you'll find classical European works and a Canaletto dating to 1751 that features Chelsea College and the River Thames. Both buildings offer shops and cafes. The no-frills cafe in the modern section is one of the cheapest places in the historic core to get a drink (ask for the drinks' menu, though), while the cafe in the universal section is a little-known decorative delight.

Calle Trocadero (btw. Calles Zulueta and Monserrate) and Calle San Rafael (btw. Calles Zulueta and Monserrate). www.museonacional.cult.cu. ✆ **7863-9484.** Admission CUC$5 adults, free for children under 12. Combined museum entrance CUC$8. Tues–Sat 9am–5pm; Sun 10am–2pm. Café on both premises. No bags or cameras allowed.

LUIS POSADA carriles

On October 6, 1976, Cubana de Aviación flight 455 was blown up by plastic explosives, killing all 73 people aboard. The victims included Cuba's entire Olympic fencing team. The man implicated in the bombing, Luis Posada Carriles, is emblematic of the confusing and contradictory nature of U.S./Cuba relations, and relevant in terms of the latter-day War on Terror.

A former CIA operative and U.S. Army officer, the 82-year-old Posada Carriles took part in the failed Bay of Pigs invasion and later worked with the Nicaraguan contras to destabilize the Sandinista government. He has bragged, and later denied, that he was responsible for the Cubana airplane bombing, as well as a string of bombings at hotels and tourism facilities in Cuba in which several civilians and tourists were killed. Along with Orlando Bosch, he is implicated in the 1976 car bombing in Washington, D.C., that killed Chilean ambassador Orlando Letelier.

Posada Carriles has been jailed in both Venezuela and Panama. He broke out of jail in Venezuela in the mid-1980s, but was later arrested on charges of attempting to assassinate Fidel Castro at a 2000 regional summit in Panama. In July 2005, Posada Carriles was pardoned by outgoing President Mireya Moscoso. Between 2005 and May 2007, he was held in an Immigration detention center for illegally entering the United States, after his requests for political asylum were denied. Charges were then dropped and he remains a free man. In June 2008, however, the Panamanian Supreme Court overturned the presidential pardon. This has opened up the possibility of extradition to Panama.

Posada Carilles represents an embarrassment to the United States. A self-proclaimed and proud "terrorist," he was seen as being coddled by the Bush administration, which refused to prosecute him under any terrorist statutes or grant extradition officially requested by both Cuba and Venezuela. In 2010, he stood trial in Texas not for any alleged acts of terrorism but for lying to immigration authorities; he was ultimately acquitted.

Parque La Maestranza Located on the edge of La Habana Vieja, this 2-block stretch of city park is dedicated to the little ones, with a little train ride, inflatable rooms for romping around in, and more rides. It's decidedly low-key and low-tech by Western standards, but the mix of mostly Cuban and some foreign kids don't seem to mind. Popcorn and drinks are for sale.

Calle Cuba (btw. Calle Tacón and Cuarteles). Admission CUP$3. Wed–Fri 10am–5pm, Sat and Sun 9am–6pm.

CENTRO HABANA

Callejón de Hamel ★★ Nearly every inch of this narrow, two-block-long alleyway is painted in bright colors, the work of painter Salvador González. Most are mural-size depictions of Afro-Cuban deities. There are also sculptures made from scrap and old bike parts, as well as a *Nganga,* a sacred place for the celebration of Palo Monte rituals centered on a giant cauldron. This open-air bazaar offers crafts and food for sale and a handful of *paladares;* González also has a small gallery here. Between noon and 3pm

Son et Lumière: Maqueta del Centro Histórico

Tucked in behind the doors of an anonymous-looking building is a handcrafted city model. Stand behind the black curtain to witness this absolutely delightful sound, music, and light show, which covers the rising of the sun in the east over the city model with all the noises, birds, music and tinkering of the day through to nightfall. We won't say more, so as not to spoil the magic (Maqueta del Centro Histórico, Calle Mercaderes 114 btw. Obispo and Obrapía; ✆ **7866-4425;** Tues–Sat 9:30am–5:15pm, Sun 9:30am–1pm; CUC$2).

each Sunday, it's the site of a weekly rumba show. (To locate this alleyway, see the "Vedado" map on p. 47.)

Callejón de Hamel (btw. Calles Hospital and Aramburu). Free admission. Daily 9:30am–6pm. Rumba noon–3pm.

Chinatown You'll see Havana's Chinatown touted in local literature, tour offerings, and other guidebooks. Occupying a small section of Centro Habana, it has few distinguishing features, a very small population of residents of Chinese descent, and none of the vibrancy of Chinatowns in cities like New York, San Francisco, or Toronto. A block-long pedestrian-only street, **El Cuchillo de Zanja** is packed with nondescript and unimpressive Chinese restaurants and shops. The biggest attraction here is the large, pagoda-style Dragon's Gate at the corner of Calle Dragones and Calle Amistad. One of the most interesting aspects, though, is the former site of the city's most notorious 1950s live-sex theatre, Teatro Shanghai (Zanja btw. Manrique and Campanario), haunt of British novelist Graham Greene. It's now a rather awkward park site, and the addition of a statue of Confucius seems a conscious effort to blot what was considered the most public witness of moral decline. (To locate this area, see the "Vedado" map on p. 47.)

In the area bordered by Calles Dragones, Zanja, Rayo, and San Nicolás. Free admission. Daily 24 hr.

El Capitolio ★ Modeled after its U.S. cousin, the Cuban Capitol is a stunning architectural work of grand scale—it's actually a tiny bit taller and longer than the Washington, D.C., version. Its large scale and intricately inlaid marble floors are impressive. The entrance hall has a replica of a 25-carat diamond embedded in the floor, from which all highway distances radiating out from Havana are measured. There's also the *Statue of the Republic,* a 17m-tall (56-ft.), 49-ton Roman goddess covered in gold leaf, which some claim is Jupiter. The monumental building has been closed for restoration since 2010 and is currently being transformed into the new seat of the National Assembly; it should be operational by the end of 2015, and some parts of the building will be open to the public.

Calle Prado (btw. Calles San José and Dragones). ✆ **7861-5519.**

El Malecón ★★★ This oceanside pedestrian walkway stretches all the way from the Castillo de San Salvador de la Punta in La Habana Vieja to the Almendares River, which separates Vedado from Miramar (about 7km/4¼ miles in total). No trip to Havana is complete without at least some time spent strolling and lingering along the Malecón, the social center for a wide range of Cubans. Throughout the day, you'll see children swimming and men fishing off the coral outcroppings that border the walkway, and at night, you're sure to see lovers entwined on cozy perches and groups of revelers all along the seawall.

The section fronting Centro Habana is perhaps the most picturesque, with the crumbling facades and faded paint of neoclassical and neo-Moorish buildings and apartments lining the avenue that separates the Malecón from the city. If you've got the legs and time, a walk from the Hotel Nacional to La Habana Vieja (or vice-versa) should only take you about 35 minutes. On blustery days, you may have to time your steps—or cross the street—as waves break furiously over the seawall. Alternatively, you can hire a horse-drawn carriage or Coco Taxi for the trip.

Free admission. Daily 24 hr.

Fábrica de Tabaco Partagás ★ The cigar factory in the original building has closed and the 460 workers transferred to the Pollack building in Centro Habana where, over several floors, they roll cigars for Montecristo, Romeo and Juliet, and Cohiba. The workers are read Granma in the morning, listen to reggaeton over lunchtime, and are read a novel in the afternoon while they work. The tour is fairly informative but not comprehensive. You can stop in and buy cigars (and rum) from the well-stocked shop, **La Casa del Habano,** around the corner from the Pollack building in the Romeo y Julieta factory shop (✆ **7870-4797;** Mon–Sat 9am–5pm; Sun 9am–1pm).

Calle San Carlos y Peñalver. ✆ **7873 0656.** 25-min. guided tour CUC$10. Tickets must be bought at the hotel desks of nearby hotels. Mon–Fri 9am–1pm every 15 min. No photography allowed.

VEDADO

Cementerio de Colón ★★★ A miniature city of mausoleums, crypts, family chapels and vaults, soaring sculptures, and ornate gravestones, Columbus Cemetery covers 55 hectares (136 acres). Designed by Spanish architect Calixto de Loira in the mid-1800s, it was laid out in grids around a central chapel. The main entrance features a large sculpture of Faith, Hope, and Charity in Carrara marble. There's also a large monument to fallen soldiers of the Revolutionary Armed Forces, and an impressive stainless-steel sculpture capping a memorial to the martyrs of the 1957 attack on Batista's Presidential Palace. One of the most popular graves is that of La Milagrosa (The Miraculous One). The story goes that when Amelia Goyri de la Hoz died in childbirth in 1901, she was buried with her stillborn daughter placed at her feet. When the tomb was opened a few years later, the baby was found in her arms. Amelia is now considered the protector of pregnant women and newborn children. Pilgrims paying homage must not turn their backs to the tomb upon leaving. Don't miss the doors engraved with angels on the Art Deco Catalina-Lasa Baró Lalique-glass-decorated mausoleum, or the exquisite gold mural by René Portocarrero deep inside the tomb of the Raúl de Zárraga family (Avenida Obispo Fray Jacinto and Calle 5). Brief guided tours are available (for free, but a tip is generally expected), or you can buy a little guidebook with a detailed map (CUC$1) at the entrance.

Calles Zapata and 12. ✆ **7832-1050.** Admission CUC$5 adults, free for children under 12. Daily 8am–5pm.

Coppelia ★ Made famous in Tomás Gutiérez Alea's hit film *Fresa y Chocolate* (Strawberry and Chocolate), this is the main branch of the Cuban national ice-cream company, named by Celia Sánchez, Fidel Castro's secretary, after her favorite ballet. At the center of the block-long complex is a postmodern building of curving concrete and glass designed by Mario Girona in 1966, surrounded by a series of open courtyards with wrought-iron tables, where customers are served bowls of the frozen nectar. There are actually a dozen or so small booths selling cones and bowls spread around the park. Cubans form long lines to wait their turn at a table or stand to purchase ice cream in *moneda nacional*. Tourists who don't want to wait in line can pay in hard currency and are shown to two 24-hour kiosks or an air-conditioned salon, "*las Cuatro Joyas,*" inside the park. On any given day, five flavors are available, and the ice cream is sold by the gram.

Calles 23 and L. ✆ **7832-3450.** Sept–June Tues–Sun 10am–10pm; July–Aug daily 10am–10pm.

Memorial José Martí The 109m (358-ft.) marble tower here is the highest point in Havana. At the base of the tower is a massive statue of the poet and national independence hero José Martí. Inside the base is a small museum dedicated to Martí featuring manuscripts, memorabilia, portraits, and other informative displays (with explanations in Spanish only). An elevator takes visitors up to a series of lookout rooms atop the tower, providing far-reaching panoramic views of Havana. The lookout is by far the most interesting and popular attraction here, although there's also a little theater where concerts and poetry readings are sometimes held. The memorial sits in the Plaza de la

Imagine

Beatles fans will want to stop by the little **Parque Lennon (Lennon Park)** at Calles 17 and 6 in Vedado, where you'll find a life-size statue of John Lennon seated on a park bench. Lennon is quite revered here, and an annual open-air concert in this park every December 8 features a wide range of prominent Cuban musicians singing his songs and commemorating his assassination on that day.

Revolución, host to all political rallies, and faces the Ministry of Interior building with the iconic image of **Che Guevara's face cast in iron ★** as well as the Ministry of Communications, which depicts the face of Camilo Cienfuegos, also cast in iron.

Plaza de la Revolución, Nuevo Vedado. ✆ **7859-2347**. Admission museum CUC$3 adults; museum and mirador CUC$5; mirador CUC$3 adults. Mon–Sat 9am–4:30pm.

Universidad de la Habana The compact campus of Havana's main university sits on a patch of high ground in Vedado close to the former Havana Hilton. The broad staircase leading up to the school, with its signature *Alma Mater* statue of a seated woman with outstretched arms, is a popular gathering spot for students, and you can sometimes catch impromptu concerts here. The campus has a couple of small museums—**Natural History** (its collection similar to a Victorian cabinet of curiosities) and **Montane Anthropology** (with an original Taíno tobacco idol)—as well as the nearby and intriguing **Museo Napoleónico ★**, Calle San Miguel 1159, at the corner of La Ronda (✆ **7879-1460**; Tues–Sat 9:30am–5pm, Sun 9:30am–12:30pm; CUC$3), with the largest collection of Napoleonic-era memorabilia outside of Europe (including a death mask) housed in a restored Florentine mansion.

Universidad de la Habana, Colina Universitaria, Edificio Felipe Poey, Calles L and 27, La Ronda. ✆ **7877 4221** and **7879-3488.** Free admission to the university and museums. Mon–Fri 9am–4pm.

PLAYA

Acuario Nacional Cuba's National Aquarium is not SeaWorld or Baltimore's National Aquarium, but it's a pretty spiffy attempt for Cuba. A variety of tanks and pools re-create all the major water habitats of Cuba, and sea lion and dolphin shows are presented throughout the day. It has a couple of simple cafeteria-style restaurants and one pseudo-fancy option, the **Gran Azul Restaurant,** with a huge Plexiglas wall opening onto a large tank where the dolphins swim. This place is very popular with Cuban families and school groups, so it's a great spot to mingle.

Av. 3 and Calle 62, Miramar. www.acuarionacional.cu. ✆ **7202-5872** or 7202-5871. Admission CUC$10 adults, CUC$7 children 2–14, free children under 2. Tues–Sun 10am–6pm. July, Aug, and school holidays Tues–Sun 10am–10pm. Dolphin shows noon and 5pm; July and Aug and school holidays noon, 5pm, 7:30pm, and 9:20pm. Sea lion shows 11am and 4pm; July and Aug and school holidays 11am, 4pm, and 8:30pm.

OUTSIDE DOWNTOWN

Museo Ernest Hemingway ★ Unfortunately, visitors cannot enter Ernest Hemingway's Cuban villa but must peer in from windows and doors. Everything is as Hemingway left it, an array of books, hunting trophies, clothes, and prized possessions. The tower, which was built so he could write in peace, can be climbed, and the panoramic views of Havana are extraordinary. In the lush gardens, filled with birds, you can see the empty swimming pool, Papa's pet cemetery, and his beloved fishing boat, the *Pilar,* which is dry-docked.

Finca la Vigía, San Francisco de Paula, Carretera Central Km 12.5. ✆ **7691-0809.** Admission CUC$5 adults, free for children under 12; CUC$5 for a guide; CUC$50/hr to take video. Mon–Sat 10am–5pm. Note that the property closes if it is raining. Piña colada stand and stalls and shops on the premises.

Parque Histórico Morro Cabaña ★★ Located across the harbor channel from La Habana Vieja, this historic park of forts, battlements, and barracks was responsible for the protection of Havana for centuries. The complex is actually made up of two separate forts, or attractions: the Castillo del Morro and La Fortaleza de San Carlos de la Cabaña.

The Morro Castle, or "El Morro," as it is most commonly known, is the first fort you come to after crossing under the harbor channel tunnel. Sitting on the point overlooking Havana's narrow harbor channel, it was built between 1589 and 1630 and served as an important line of defense against pirate attacks and naval invasions. In addition to its ramparts, barracks, and banks of cannons, El Morro has a series of exhibition rooms (including one commemorating the Taking of Havana by the English in 1762) and mini-museums. You can walk the fort's ancient streets and even climb the still-functioning, 19th-century lighthouse here. El Morro affords excellent views of Havana and the curve of the Malecón.

About a kilometer (½-mile) away, and separated by a deep ravine, is the larger **La Fortaleza de San Carlos de la Cabaña,** more popularly referred to as simply "la Cabaña." Built between 1764 and 1774 in response to the 1762 British invasion, the long fort is a miniature city, with a high perch overlooking the harbor channel and La Habana Vieja. As at El Morro, it has several exhibition halls and a handful of restaurants, cafés, and a shop. One of the more popular exhibition halls is the **Comandancia de Che Guevara** (undergoing restoration in mid-2015), a room where the revolutionary leader briefly set up a command post after storming the fort in January 1959. Be sure to stop in at the cigar shop, where *torcedor*-in-residence José Cueto Castelar created an 81m (268-ft.) stogie duly registered in the Guinness Book of World Records as the largest in the world. At the extreme southern end of the complex is a display of military hardware relating to the 1962 Cuban missile crisis, the Casa del Che exhibiting artifacts from the guerilla's Bolivian campaign, and beyond, the statue El Cristo. The **views of Havana ★★★** from here are outstanding.

A taxi to the complex from Havana costs between CUC$5 and CUC$7. You can walk between the two forts—it's about a 15-minute walk that's only moderately strenuous if you stick to the high ground—or you can take a taxi between the two for CUC$3 to CUC$5.

Carretera de La Cabaña, Habana del Este. ✆ **7862-0617** for El Morro and La Cabaña. Admission El Morro CUC$6 adults, free for children under 12; La Cabaña CUC$6 adults before 6pm, CUC$8 adults after 6pm, free for children under 12. El Morro daily 8am–8pm; La Cabaña daily 10am–10pm.

The Cañonazo

The **cañonazo (cannon blast)** ★ is a picturesque ritual that takes place at La Fortaleza de San Carlos de la Cabaña every night. An honor guard in 18th-century military garb emerges from the barracks at about 8:40pm and conducts a small parade to a bank of cannons overlooking Havana's harbor channel. With pomp and circumstance, the cannon is loaded and fired precisely at 9pm. Arrive early if you want a good vantage point. The blast itself is quite loud—you can hear it in most parts of Havana—so protect your ears. You can combine the ceremony with a meal at **La Divina Pastora** (p. 68).

OUTDOOR PURSUITS

BASEBALL Baseball is Cuba's national sport. The country's amateur players are considered some of the best in the world, and the premier players are aggressively scouted and courted by the Major Leagues. The regular season runs November through March, and playoffs and the final championship usually carry the season on into May. **Industriales,** the main Havana team, plays at the **Estadio Latinoamericano,** Calle Zequeira 312, Cerro (✆ **7870-8175**). It's usually easy to buy tickets at the box office for less than 5 Cuban pesos, or ask at your hotel and perhaps they can get tickets for you in advance—although for these, you'll probably end up paying CUC$1 to CUC$2.

GOLF While the only regulation 18-hole course in the country is located in Varadero (see chapter 7), the Club de Golf Habana, Carretera Vento, Km 8, Capdevila, Rancho Boyeros (✆ **7649-8918**), has a decent little 9-hole course for true golf junkies. A round of 9 holes will run you CUC$20. Each hole actually has two sets of tees, so you can really play 18 holes and fake the impression that it's a regulation course. A round of 18 holes costs CUC$30. Club rental is an extra CUC$10 and a caddy costs you CUC$5. It's open daily 9:30am–6:30pm.

GYMS Havana has no chains of modern gyms. Visitors looking for a regular workout on modern gym equipment should stick to the larger hotels with well-equipped facilities (see "Where to Stay," earlier in this chapter). If you're not staying at one of these hotels, you can use the facilities at the Meliá Habana or Meliá Cohiba for a fee. The Hotel Raquel has a small basement gym with a great-value day pass.

Club Habana, Avenida 5, between Calles 188 and 192, Reparto Flores, Playa (✆ **7204-5700**), has a decent gym. Guests may use the facilities for CUC$20 a day (Mon–Fri) and CUC$30 a day at weekends.

The new **O2 Spa**, Calle 26, corner of 26B, Nuevo Vedado (www.02habana.com; ✆ **7883-1663**), offers gym equipment as well as a hair salon, massage parlor, and café.

KITE-SURFING & SURFING Kite-surfing and surfing are emerging watersports in Cuba. The **Havana Kite & Surf Club** (www.hkckite.com) has two bases at Tarará and Santa María del Mar offering courses and equipment for rent.

JOGGING The Malecón is a fabulous place to jog. Early mornings and early evenings, when the heat has somewhat abated, are best. You'll have to watch your step in certain sections where the sidewalk is torn up or deteriorated, but overall this is the choice route for jogging.

SCUBA DIVING While the diving is nowhere near as good as you'll find in more dedicated dive destinations in Cuba, it's certainly possible to do some underwater exploring out of Havana. Your best bet is to head over to **Club Acuario,** Avenida 5 and Calle 248, Santa Fe, Playa (© **7204-1150**), La Aguja; **Marlin Diving Centre,** Marina Hemingway, corner Avenida 5 and 248, Playa (www.nauticamarlin.com; © **7204-6848**); **Centro Internacional de Buceo,** Club Habana, Avenida 5, between Calles 188 and 192, Playa (© **7275-0100**); or **Marina Tarará,** Vía Blanca Km 18, Playa Tarará, Habana del Este (© **7796-0242**), located 18km (11 miles) east of the city. It costs CUC$40 for a one-tank dive and CUC$70 for two-tank dives, including equipment, instructor, and boat.

SPORTFISHING It's easy to follow in Hemingway's wake and try your luck at landing a big one. As with diving, your best bet is to head over to **Club Acuario,** Avenida 5 and Calle 248, Santa Fe, Playa (© **7204-1150**), or **Marina Tarará,** Vía Blanca Km 18, Playa Tarará, Habana del Este (© **7796-0242**). Deep-sea sportfishing costs CUC$200 for one to four people including gear and Cuban drinks. Fly-fishing costs CUC$280 for 3 hours, and CUC$550 for 7 hours including boat, equipment, and Cuban drinks.

SWIMMING If your hotel does not have a swimming pool, most of the larger hotels, except for Melia and Iberostar, allow nonguests to use their pool facilities for a price with a *consumo mínimo* attached. Rates generally range between CUC$5 and CUC$25 per person. Although it's possible to use the small beach at the Club Habana, the nearby Playas del Este is your best bet for some beach time. Most tour agencies and hotel tour desks offer a day trip to Playa Santa María del Mar for CUC$25 to CUC$40, including round-trip transportation, lunch, and often free run of the facilities at one of the all-inclusive hotels out there. However, you can also get there on your own steam using the HabanaBusTour (see p. 49).

Note: Do not be tempted to join the locals you see swimming off the coral outcroppings just below the Malecón. The coral is jagged and sharp, and the seas can get suddenly rough. Moreover, in recent years there have been complaints that the water is very polluted.

TENNIS Unless you're staying at one of the few Havana hotels with a court, your options are limited. Your best bet is the Club Habana, Avenida 5, between Calles 188 and 192, Reparto Flores, Playa (© **7275-0300**).

SHOPPING

The Shopping Scene

Havana is by no means a great shopping city (although it is the best in Cuba), but the recent economic opportunities have spawned a couple of excellent private shops. Given the reality of the Cuban economy, all shops selling any goods above and beyond the basic necessities are by default geared entirely toward tourists, a small community of foreign diplomats and workers, and a growing community of Cubans earning enough hard currency, or being in possession of hard currency, to afford such luxuries. Hence, it's a challenge to find interesting shops with unique local items at good prices.

Shops selling to tourists operate with Cuban convertible pesos and in *moneda nacional* (CUP) equivalent. Most are run by big, state-owned enterprises. The most common stores belong to the **Caracol** chain, which is geared primarily to tourists, while the **Tiendas Panamericanas** chain specializes in household and domestic items. In recent years, modern malls have begun popping up.

In general, stores throughout Havana are open from 9am to 5pm, Monday through Saturday and until around 1pm on Sundays.

Shopping A to Z

ART GALLERIES

The sleek modern space of **Galería Habana ★★★**, Calle Línea 460 between E and F (www.galerihabana.com; ✆ **7832-7101**), is the leading art gallery for contemporary art in Cuba. **Galería Artis**, Calle 7ma and 18, Miramar (✆ **7204-7768**), is a brand-new space staging innovative exhibitions. **Galería Acacia,** Calle 18 No. 512 between 5ta and 7ma, Miramar (www.galeriascubanas.com)**,** is the place to go for high-end contemporary Cuban art. **Galería Villa Manuela**, Calle H, No. 406, between 17 and 19, Vedado (www.galeriavillamanuela.com; ✆ **7832-2391,** ext 260), is also a gallery worth seeking out for its temporary exhibitions. In Old Havana, head to **Factoría Habana**, Calle O'Reilly 308 between Habana and Aguiar (www.facebook.com/FactoriaHabana; ✆ **7864-9518**), which has held some of the most exciting shows in Havana in recent years in this finely restored paper factory space.

Arts, Crafts & Music: ARTex Stores

ARTex ★ (✆ **7204-0813**) is the state-run company in charge of managing Cuba's artistic export products. Its job runs the gamut from promoting Cuban musicians and artists abroad to marketing their goods and negotiating contracts. Its stores usually carry a good selection of Cuban music, Cuban films, tourist T-shirts, and kitschy arts and crafts. The better outlets have decent quality drums and percussion instruments, as well as art prints and posters. In Vedado, check out **Habana Sí,** Calle 23 and L (✆ **7838-3162**), across from the Tryp Habana Libre.

The ground-breaking **Kcho Estudio** (www.kchoestudio.com), a huge arts and library complex, has opened in the marginal barrio of El Romerillo, close to the ISA. The **ISA ★★★**, Cuba's Instituto Superior de Arte (www.isa.cult.cu), is Cuba's leading art school, based in the grounds of an old country club. The architect-designed buildings are some of the most beautiful in the world; Cuban Royal Ballet dancer Carlos Acosta plans to turn the stunning ballet school into a **Dance Foundation** (http://carlosacostafoundation.org).

For a very handy guide to Cuban art and studios in Havana, pick up artempo's new *Cutting Edge Art Havana.* The Cuban-produced *Arte Cubano Contemporáneo* is also insightful.

Art Havana ★★★ A half-day or 1-day tour with curator Sussette Martínez is a fascinating and compelling experience that takes in visits to the studios of contemporary artists and/or photographers in Cuba. The tour is geared to people who are interested in collecting Latin American art and for those wanting to learn more about contemporary art in a wider sociocultural context. ✆ **7267-7989**. Tour costs CUC$40–CUC$60 excluding transport.

Emerging Artists' Tour ★ Art historian and young art curator **Elizabeth Pozo** (✆ **5817-0791;** eliza24p@gmail.com) offers a new tour that showcases the best of Havana's young emerging contemporary artists, including many newly graduated artists from the ISA—such as Lisandra Isabel García and her extraordinary glasswork, and the already hot-selling Miguel Alejandro Machado Suárez. Tour from CUC$70 per two people, excluding transport.

BOOKS/CURIOS/MEMORABILIA

Plaza de Armas has multiple stalls ★★★ selling secondhand and antiquarian books, including many with revolutionary and political themes. (You can also find coins, stamps, and other Revolution memorabilia.) Bargain very hard. The book stalls were due to move to the Almacenes San José (p. 84) so you will know where the books have gone if you find the Plaza de Armas empty.

La Casa de Carlos, Calle Villegas 101, corner Calle San Juan de Díos (✆ **7863-9329**), is run by the affable Carlos and is stuffed full of antiques, bottles, costume jewelry, and historic memorabilia. Carlos's son runs a super *casa particular* upstairs.

The lovely shop **Memorias ★★**, Calle Animas 57, between Prado and Zulueta (www.memoriashabana.com; www.cubamuseo.com; ✆ **7862-5133**), has maps, pictures, and postcards and could easily keep you browsing a while. Owner Luis is a mine of information.

CERAMICS

Terracota 4, Calle Mercaderes, between. Obrapía and Lamparilla, La Habana Vieja (✆ **7866-9417**), a working studio-cum-gallery, features the works of Amelia Carballo and Angel Norniella. The pieces show a wide range of influences and utilize a variety of techniques. One or more artists are usually on hand, and sometimes you get a chance to see them working. Serious ceramic fans should head out to the **Santacana Estudio,** Calle 66, no. 104, between 5ta and 1ra, Flores, Playa, for Beatriz Santacana's intriguing ceramic and metal angel sculptures and Joan Miró–inspired work (www.beatrizsantacana.com; ✆ **7271-4392**).

CIGARS

Cigars are Cuba's most prized luxury product. The word *Cubans* is synonymous with the highest-quality cigars on the planet. Locally, they are called *puros* or *habanos;* the latter is the name of the country's official cigar company. All of the various brands—Partagás, Cohiba, Romeo y Julieta, Punch, and so on—are marketed by **Habanos S.A.** Cigars not officially sold by Habanos fall into the various categories of black- and gray-market stogies. Habanos markets its product through a series of storefronts, usually called **La Casa del Habano.** Official sales are also held at shops at most cigar factories, as well as at many higher-end hotels, restaurants, and attractions around town. ***Beware:*** Black- and gray-market cigars sold on the street or by *jineteros* (hustlers) are falsely marked, lower-quality cigars.

Cuban cigars range widely in size and shape. Prices range from around CUC$30 to CUC$50 per box for the smallest, lowest-quality *puros* to over CUC$400 per box for the more coveted cigars. Most shops sell only complete boxes, although certain cigars are available individually or in boxes of five.

The best **La Casa del Habano** shops are those in the Hostal Conde de Villanueva at Calle Mercaderes 202, La Habana Vieja (✆ **7862-9293**); the Partagás cigar factory at Calle Industria 520, between Dragones y Barcelona, behind El Capitolio (✆ **7866-8060**); and in the Quinta y 16 shopping minicomplex at Avenida 5 and the corner of Calle 16, Miramar (✆ **7204-7973**). Another nice one in La Habana Vieja is the **Casa del Ron y Tabaco Cubana,** Calle Obispo and Calle Bernaza (✆ **7866-8911**), where you can combine two of Cuba's greater pleasures—smoking cigars and drinking rum.

FASHIONS, ACCESSORIES & DESIGN

Perhaps the most distinctive clothing items a traveler can buy include T-shirts with the image of Che Guevara on the front and the revolutionary's signature green *boina* (beret) with a little red star in front.

Men might want to pick up a *guayabera* or two. This cool, pleated, embroidered tropical shirt comes in a variety of (mostly) solid colors and in both long- and short-sleeve versions. As a rational alternative to heavy suits and ties in a tropical clime, *guayaberas* are appropriate for everything from informal occasions to high-level government and business meetings (in Cuba, at least). You'll find *guayaberas* for sale all over; some of the typically touristy gift shops even carry them. One good place to shop for a *guayabera* is **El Quitirín,** Calle Obispo and San Ignacio (✆ **7862-0810**). For a more upscale selection of imported clothes, head over to Miramar and shop at **Le Select,** Avenida 5 and Calle 28 (✆ **7207-9681**).

For clothes, try **Galería Comercial Comodoro,** Avenida 3 between Calles 80 and 84, Playa (✆ **7204-6177**), which houses Mango, Adidas, Converse, Benetton, and Clarks stores, or **Paul and Shark, Lacoste,** and **Benetton** on Plaza Vieja, La Habana Vieja.

Hilda Zulueta Sardiñas is crafting beautiful leather bags out of her shop, **Zulu**, on Calle Amargura 104 e/ San Ignacio and Cuba, La Habana Vieja (http://communacuba.es/zulu; ✆ **7621-1145**).

The hip new design store **Clandestina** (www.clandestinacuba.com), Calle Villegas 403 between Brasil and Muralla, La Habana Vieja, is owned and run by designer Idania del Río, who sells T-shirts, silk prints, toys, and hats.

Piscolabis (http://piscolabishabana.com), Calle San Ignacio 75 between Callejón del Chorro and O'Reilly, opened by a designer and an architect, sells handcrafted, mainly recycled products, such as patchwork cushions fashioned from jeans, funky lamp stands from old bottles, and baskets woven from metal and cassette tape. The lovely store also has a small café and is a stone's throw from the cathedral.

HANDICRAFTS

Cuba doesn't have a particularly strong tradition in producing handicrafts, but the rise in tourism has seen local artisans quickly making up for lost time. Tourist gift shops as well as the street markets discussed below are well stocked with locally produced handicrafts. The best buys are woodcarvings and statues, papier-mâché masks and religious figures, and simple jewelry made from shells and seeds. You'll also find a host of Afro-Cuban percussion instruments for sale. Drums you'll find include the two-headed, hourglass-shaped *bata* drums; paired bongos, carved African-style religious drums; and congas, the modern salsa backbone. *Shékeres* (gourd shakers) and *claves* (two wooden sticks used to play the fundamental rhythm in various Cuban genres) are also available.

Most visitors head to Havana´s largest craft market, **Almacenes San José,** Calle Desamparados (Avenida del Puerto), between Damas and San Isidro, for clothing, paintings, tourist souvenirs, ceramics, baseball bats, jewelry, and a multitude of other products. A CADECA is on-site. It's open daily 9am to 6pm.

MUSIC

Music is one of Cuba's greatest exports. Many CDs available in Cuba are also widely available abroad or via the Internet. Most CDs in Cuba sell for between CUC$8 and CUC$15. Be careful, however: Unless you are shopping at one of the official state-run stores, the CDs you buy may be low-quality bootlegs.

If you're looking for **salsa,** pick up a disc or two by Los Van Van, NG La Banda, or Havana d'Primera. Fans of **Cuban folk music** should definitely stock up on recordings by Silvio Rodriguez and Pablo Milanes. **Jazz** fans will want some Chucho Valdés with Irakere, Ernán Lopéz-Nussa, Roberto Fonseca, Aldo López-Gavilán, and Gonzalo Rubalcaba, while those looking to groove to some **Afro-Cuban sounds** should check out Síntesis, Los Muñequitos de Matanzas, Yoruba Andabo, and Clavé y Guaguanco. For ***son*** and **mambo,** pick up discs by Adalberto Alvarez y su Son, or the classic re-releases of Beny Moré and Peréz Prado. Since you've probably already got a copy of ***Buena Vista Social Club,*** you might stock up on solo albums by its various members: Compay Segundo, Rubén Gonzales, Eliades Ochoa, and Omara Portuondo. If you enjoy **Reggaeton,** Eddy-K or Gente de Zona is your group; and current **singing sensations** are Diana Fuentes, Descemer Bueno, and Buena Fe.

Egrem (www.egrem.com.cu) is the national recording industry's signature label, the home of many prominent Cuban musicians. Egrem has a series of storefronts around the country called **Casa de la Música Egrem.** You can also buy discs at one of the many **ARTex** shops around Havana, or you can shop the ARTex catalog online at **www.mallcubano.com**.

Casa de la Música Habana Housed in a classic old apartment building in Centro Habana, this is the nicest and best stocked of the Egrem storefronts. Calle Galiano (btw. Calles Concordia and Neptuno), Centro Habana. ✆ **7860-8296.**

La Habana Si This modern store, opposite the Hotel Habana Libre, sells musical instruments, CDs, DVDs, and souvenirs. The staff is quite helpful. Calle 23 (corner of L), Vedado. ✆ **7838-3162.**

Longina Música This ARTex shop has an excellent selection of CDs and cassettes, as well as sheet music, magazines, and one of the better stocks of Afro-Cuban drums, shakers, and claves you'll find. Calle Obispo 360, La Habana Vieja. ✆ **7862-8371**.

PERFUME

Habana 1791 This attractive shop in Old Havana sells traditional perfumes and aromatherapy distillations in faux-vintage glass jars and vials. It also now offers aromatherapy massages—but be warned: If you're overweight, you get charged more (prices from CUC$16–CUC$30). Calle Mercaderes 156 (corner of Calle Obrapía), La Habana Vieja. ✆ **7861-3525**.

RUM

After cigars, **rum** is one of Cuba's signature products. Cuba produces several fine rums. The most commonly sold brand, Havana Club, comes in white and dark varieties of various vintages and ages. The premier rum in Cuba is Havana Club's Máximo Extra Anejo. This limited edition of 1,000 bottles a year sells for anywhere from CUC$1,700 per bottle. The new Selección de Maestros has a burnt amber hue and is highly palatable. It costs CUC$40 a bottle. The 7-year-old Havana Club is also a fine rum at around CUC$12 per bottle. Other good rums include Ron Caney, Ron Santiago, Ron Varadero, Matusalém, and Ron Mulata.

Don't Run to Buy *Ron*

Your best bet for buying rum is the duty-free shop at the airport. The prices and selection are as good here as you'll find anywhere on the island, and you'll save yourself the hassle of hauling heavy bottles around with you while traveling.

STREET MARKETS

A **small street market** is held daily in Vedado in a small open area on the south side of La Rampa, at Calle 23 between Calles M and N. The market, open daily from 9am to 5pm, has fewer artworks than the market at **Almacenes San**

José (see "Handicrafts," above), but it has plenty of woodcarvings and simple jewelry for sale. The **crafts-market patio** on Calle Obispo 411 (btw. Compostela and Aguacate) is open Thursday to Tuesday from 10am to 6pm.

Note: Cubans don't really have a firm grasp on this capitalism thing. Moreover, given the huge gap between the peso and hard currency economies, Cubans often have a hard time understanding the true value of the convertible peso. Prices are often grossly inflated for tourists, on the principle that they "must all be rich." Although **bargaining** is possible at street markets, it's not necessarily a fluid or enjoyable process. Still, if you think something is overpriced, definitely feel free to offer whatever you believe to be fair or whatever you are prepared to pay.

HAVANA AFTER DARK

Some would say Havana only really gets going after dark, when the slow pace and heat-induced stupor of the day finally wears off. This is a vibrant and truly cosmopolitan city with scores of bars, dance clubs, and theaters to choose from. Consult the monthly "What's On" download at **Cuba Absolutely** (www.cubaabsolutely.com/lahabana.com) or the weekly **Egrem** (http://promociones.egrem.co.cu) lowdown. **Suenacubano** (http://suenacubano.com/cartelera) is also useful.

Finding out what's on in the musical scene can be extremely tricky. British musician and composer **Sue Herrod**, who has lived and worked with Cuban musicians and artists in Havana for the last 16 years, is available to personally guide music fans on performances/rehearsals/meeting musicians and help discover the best of Havana's trova, rumba, folkloric, rock, jazz, classical, choral, and contemporary music scenes (✆ **5297-1982;** suelahabana@gmail.com).

The Performing Arts

Cuba has a strong tradition in the performing arts. Cuban musicians, playing in a range of styles, are world-renowned. The **Cuban National Ballet ★** (www.balletcuba.cult.cu; ✆ **7835-2945**) has been garnering international accolades for decades, under the direction of Alicia Alonso. There's an active theater scene (and plenty of movie theaters), both of which are popular with locals, given the scant offerings of Cuban television. The major venues for the classical performing arts are the **Teatro Nacional de Cuba,** Paseo and Calle 39, Vedado (✆ **7879-3558**), which specializes in theater performances by local and visiting companies; the **Gran Teatro de La Habana,** Paseo de Martí and Calle San Rafael, Centro Habana (✆ **7861-3077,** ext. 115), home to the Cuban National Ballet, as well as a prime venue for concerts and dance performances (it is currently closed for restoration with no official reopening date); and the **Teatro Amadeo Roldán,** Calle Calzada, between Calles D and E, Vedado (✆ **7832-1168**), home to the National Symphony Orchestra. Other important and working theaters include the **Teatro Mella**, Línea 657, between A and B (✆ **7833-5651**), Vedado, **Teatro Karl Marx**, Avenida 1ra, between 8 and 10, Miramar (✆ **7203-0801**), and the **Café Teatro Brecht**, Calle 13, corner of I (✆ **7832-9359**). The exquisitely restored **Teatro Martí,** Calle Zulueta, corner of Dragones, La Habana Vieja (✆ **7866-7152**), is a venue for music and piano festivals.

Visit **www.cubaescena.cult.cu** and **www.paradiso.cu** for a rundown of annual festivals and events. **Paradiso** (✆ **7833-3921**), the tourism arm of the Ministry of Culture, publishes the highly elusive ***Cartelera*** magazine (✆ **7204-5493**), a free periodic bilingual magazine with listings for movies, theaters, bars, and live music, which is sometimes available at the front desk of hotels in Havana. For good, up-to-date information in English, consult ***Cuba Absolutely*** (www.cubaabsolutely.com/lahabana.com).

Your best bet for any advance planning is to go online or call the venue when you are in Havana. You can call any of the theaters listed above directly for performance schedules and ticket information.

The Cabaret, Club & Dance Scene

I'll bet Havana has more floor shows per capita than Las Vegas. In addition to the clubs and cabarets listed below, you'll find nightly and entirely respectable shows at the Habana Riviera's **Copa Room,** Paseo and Malecón, Vedado (✆ **7836-4051**) where the dance show **Havana Queens** (www.havanaqueens.ch) is now based.

There's also a vibrant flamenco show at the **Hotel Mesón de la Flota,** Mercaderes 257 between Amargura and Teniente Rey, La Habana Vieja (✆ **7863-3838;** shows at 12:30pm–3pm and 8–10pm).

The **Cabaret Las Vegas,** Calle Infanta no. 104, corner of 25 (✆ **7836-7939**), draws crowds for its transvestite cabarets.

Habaneros love to dance and party, and you'll find a wild dance and club scene here. In fact, dance aficionados come to Havana from all over to learn

Feel the Rumba Beat

The **Conjunto Folklórico Nacional de Cuba (Cuban National Folklore Group)** hosts the weekly **Sábado de la Rumba,** a mesmerizing show of Afro-Cuban religious and secular dance and drumming. The 2-hour shows (CUC$5) are presented every Saturday at 3pm, at **El Gran Palenque,** Calle 4, between Calzada and Avenida 5, in Vedado. Call ✆ **7830-3060** or 7830-3939 for more information.

Two of Cuba's best rumba groups include **Clave y Guaguancó**, one of Havana's longest-standing and best outfits for rumba, folkloric, and spiritual dance, who perform on the first and third Wednesday of the month (5pm–7pm) in the garden patio at UNEAC (Calle 17, no. 354, btw. G and H, Vedado; ✆ **7832-4551;** CUC$5), where there is more of a mix of Cubans than tourists. **Yoruba Andabo** is really worth keeping an eye out for. Check the schedules at the **Palacio de la Rumba** (Calle San Miguel, no. 860, btw. Hospital and Arambaru; ✆ **7873-0990**), at the **Casa de Africa** in Old Havana, or at **http://promociones.egrem.co.cu**.

the basic steps, fine-tune their moves, and watch the locals strut their stuff. Most clubs don't get going until after 10pm, and most stay pretty vibrant until the wee hours of the morning. While salsa is king in Cuba, most of the popular dance clubs catering to travelers have been putting some house, techno, Reggaeton, and other modern sounds into the mix. Dress codes are somewhat casual, but locals still like to put on the ritz as much as possible before a night of dancing, so bring some finery if you plan to hit any of the more popular clubs.

For a schedule of events at Havana's **Casas de la Música,** visit **http://promociones.egrem.co.cu**. If you'd like to learn to dance, contact **Salsa en Casa** (www.salsaencasa.com), where you are taught by the greats, who have revealed their secrets to none other than the British Ambassador in Havana and a former BBC correspondent.

Café Cantante Mi Habana Top acts often perform at this popular club, but it also has a much more informal dance scene happening every afternoon between 5 and 8pm. This is a place where locals come to mix it up with foreigners in town specifically to learn how to salsa. Cuba's alternative rock band, Qva Libre, plays here weekly. Teatro Nacional, Paseo and Calle 39, Plaza de la Revolución. ✆ **7878-4275**. Cover CUC$5–CUC$10.

Café Miramar ★★★ As highly talented pianist Ernan López-Nussa said as he played Café Miramar in June 2015, this is "the new jazz venue in Havana." Look no further: This is definitely the most atmospheric of the capital's jazz venues, and multigenerational Cuban jazz fans, artists, and a trickle of tourists flock here for the top talents. 5ta, corner of 94, Miramar. ✆ **7203-7676**. Tues–Sun 6pm–2am. Cover 50.00 MN or CUC$2; occasionally CUC$5.

Café Teatro Brecht (No sé las digas a nadie) ★★ A very cool basement club played by a roster of singer-songwriters. The subterranean 1950s red bar is even more cool—untouched since the adjacent synagogue built the place in 1953 as a religious and community center. Teatro Brecht, Calle 13, corner of I. ✆ **7832-9359**.

Casa de la Música Centro Habana ★ A cavernous place with a massive dance floor and concert space in the heart of Centro Habana, Casa de la Música offers a roster of changing bands. Look for such headline bands as Charanga Habanera. The crowd is a mix of Cubans, tourists who can seriously dance salsa, those that cannot, and *jineteros* who can dance and those who

A Way In

Cuban women (and to a lesser extent Cuban men) tend to hang out at the entrance to popular clubs looking for an unattached foreigner to pay their admission. Their pleadings can be quite earnest. You are by no means obligated to do so, but it's likely they have no other means to get in. Keep in mind that you may also be expected to buy their drinks as well.

cannot. It's a pretty intense place, and it takes a brave female traveler to go it alone here for evening entertainment. The matinees are worth searching out, though. Watch your bag like a hawk, and leave your cellphone at home. Calle Galianao 225 (btw. Neptuno and Concordia). ✆ **7860-8296**. Cover CUC$10–CUC$30. Matinee Tues–Sun 5–9pm. Daily 11pm–3am.

Casa de la Música Miramar Housed in a beautiful former Masonic Lodge Hall, this place heaves with *jineteros* for nightly concerts that range from bolero to salsa to jazz. The matinees are more palatable. The in-house club, **Diablo Tun Tun ★★**, is the place to be for the extended matinee of *novísima trova* on Thursdays with Ray Fernández. Calle 20 (corner of Calle 35), Miramar. ✆ **7204-0447**. Cover from CUC$5. Tun Tun 5pm–9pm and 11pm–3am. La Casa 5pm–9pm and 11pm–6am.

1830 Club One of the premier salsa dancing spots in Havana. This alfresco spot is always popular and full. As a solo female traveler, if you are without dancing companions, it's easier to find one here than other Havana hotspots. Malecón y Túnel, Vedado. ✆ **7838-3090/1/2**. Cover varies.

Fábrica de Arte Cubano ★★★ The brainchild of rock musician X Alfonso, the Cuban Arts Factory is a game-changer: a powerhouse for music, theater, dance, cinema, arts, and photography in Havana. The vast industrial setting is also a very cool design feat, a showcase for some great Cuban art such as Esterio Segura's "Goodbye My Love" and a dazzling light-and-thread woven sculpture by Duvier del Dago. Set across the multileveled platforms of an old electricity station, this hotspot opened in February 2014 and is still the place to frequent on a weekend night, with its alfresco bars and exciting roster of events. Entry is via a card, and when drinks are bought the card is stamped; revelers pay on exit. In 2015, a small restaurant opened on the ground floor run by Chef Liset Rodríguez, who used to run the excellent former *paladar* Calle Diez. Calle 26, corner of 11, Vedado. www.fac.cu. ✆ **7838-2260**. Thurs–Sun 8pm–4am. Programming at https://es-la.facebook.com/fabricadeartecubano.cu. Cover 2CUC or 50CUP.

Habana Café This place, right next to the Meliá Cohiba, has quite a funky interior, with an old propeller fighter dangling from the ceiling and a vintage 1957 Chevy dominating the bar. In addition to traditional dance offerings, this venue is home to a Buena Vista Social Club cover band. Note that the official Buena Vista Social Club band disbanded in 2015; the club's advertising can be a little misleading. Meliá Cohiba, Paseo (btw. Avs. 1 and 3), Vedado. www.cohiba-habanacafe.com. ✆ **7833-3636**, ext. 2710. Covers from CUC$20. Daily 9pm–midnight for the show. Recorded music for dancing midnight–2am.

La Gruta The weekly salsa night held here in this vast "cavern" is popular. We don't recommend that solo female travelers come here to dance alone, not because it's unsafe, but because the attention may be unmanageable! Calle 23 (La Rampa) no. 111, corner of O, Vedado (beneath Cine La Rampa). ✆ **7836-9320**. Cover CUC$3.

Tropicana ★★ Accept no substitutes. This is the real deal. It's expensive—in fact, overpriced—but if you're going to see a cabaret show in Havana, it should only be at the Tropicana; the other offerings are desultory in comparison. First opened in 1939, this open-air dinner theater is still the defining cabaret show in Cuba, if not the world. You enter the lush garden theater after passing the club's signature sculpted *Fountain of the Muses*. The show itself begins around 10:30pm (dinner here is not recommended). Once the show begins, the stage and verdant surroundings become an orgy of light, color, spectacular sparkly costumes, and pulsating movement. Scores of scantily clad showgirls and dancers seamlessly weave together a series of different numbers. The 2-hour-long spectacle covers most of the bases of popular Cuban show and dance music, from *son* to bolero to *danzón* to salsa, with a bit of Afro-Cuban religious music thrown into the mix. After the show, you can continue the celebration by dancing the night away at the adjoining **Salón Arcos de Cristal.**

Every hotel and tour agency in Havana can book you a night at the Tropicana (although you can now book online); book the top-tier tickets so you get the tables closest to the stage and uninterrupted views. If it rains, the show is moved into the Salón Arcos de Cristal. Calle 72 no. 4504 (btw. Calles 41 and 45), Marianao. www.cabaret-tropicana.com. ✆ **7267-1010**. reserves@tropicana.gca.tur.cu; Show 10pm–midnight; dancing to recorded music midnight–1am. Cover CUC$75, CUC$85, and CUC$95, which includes (per person) a quarter of a bottle of rum, 1 mixer, & 1 salad. No shorts or children under 16 admitted.

The Bar Scene

In addition to the bars listed below, **La Bodeguita del Medio** (p. 63) and **El Floridita** are two famous watering holes. Try the rooftop bar at the **Hotel Ambos Mundos** (p. 52). Havana's new private bars are all the rage—except technically they're not legal. But instead of going speakeasy-style, they've all opened under the umbrella of a private restaurant license, and some serve meals and tapas on the side to meet the regulations.

Bar El Cocinero On the rooftop of a converted peanut-oil factory is this desirable bar next to the Fábrica de Arte Cubano. Nab a spot on one of the sofas lining the back wall for prime comfort and people-watching views. One of the stars of the show is Damian Aquiles's metal sculpture, which covers the bathroom facade. Calle 26 (corner of 11), Vedado. ✆ **7832-2355**. Daily 4pm–midnight.

Espacios ★★ A new Havana hotspot tucked into the four walls and garden patio of a private Havana mansion in Calle 10. The leafy garden, with tables and chairs under the branches, is a popular drinking hole with Havana hipsters and Cubans from the worlds of art, film, and music—and it keeps serving until 6am. Calle 10, no. 513 (btw. 5ta and 7ma), Miramar, www.espacioshavana.com. ✆ **7202-2921**.

La Torre La Torre has zero ambience—it's essentially a glass box in the sky—but it boasts extraordinary views of Havana from its perch on the top of the modern Focsa building. Photographers will want to come in the hours before sunset to capture the stunning tropical light. Calle M (corner of 17), Vedado. ✆ **7832-7306**. Daily noon–11:30pm.

La Zorra y El Cuervo ★★ This cozy basement bar plays host to a nightly roster of musical talent. Enter through a British red telephone box and down the stairs to the simple bar below. The program is posted outside. Look for young musician Harold López Nussa and his trio, and the well-known Roberto Fonseca and his band Temperamento. La Rampa, Calle 23 no. 155 (btw. Calles N and O), Vedado. ✆ **7833-2402**. Daily 10pm–2am. Cover CUC$10 (with 2 drinks included).

Lluvia de Oro A jolly and rowdy bar in the heart of Old Havana on Calle Obispo. Live music from 12:30 to 4pm and 6:30 to 11pm and a lively mix of tourists and locals keep the place buoyant. Calle Obispo no. 316 (corner of Habana), La Habana Vieja. ✆ **7862-9870**. Daily 9am–midnight.

Madrigal An intimate, subdued light infuses this 2nd-floor bar in a classical mansion in Vedado. The walls are hung with the artwork of Javier Guerra, and tables and chairs are scattered around. Skip the tapas and enjoy the cocktails, and be sure to snag one of the few tables on the alfresco terrace. This was the first of Havana's private bars to open, and its popularity remains undimmed. Calle 17, no. 809 (altos; btw. 2 and 4), Vedado. ✆ **7831-2433**. Fri–Sat 6pm–4am; Tues–Thurs and Sun 6pm–midnight.

VIÑALES & WESTERN CUBA

5

When folks talk about western Cuba, they mean Pinar del Río, the country's prime ecotourism destination, and the new province of Artemisa. A pastoral and underdeveloped region, western Cuba has been inhabited continuously for over 4,000 years, beginning with the Guanahatabey, Ciboney, and Taíno indigenous tribes. In addition to the province of Pinar del Río, the general geographic area of western Cuba also includes the Archipiélago de los Canarreos (the Canary Archipelago) and the two largest islands of the chain, Isla de la Juventud and Cayo Largo, with lovely, uncrowded beaches. The small hamlet of Viñales is widely considered one of the country's most beautiful places.

Rock climbing, spelunking, mountain biking, hiking, and birdwatching are all excellent in the **Pinar del Río** province. **La Güira National Park,** the **Guanacahabibes Peninsula,** and the **Sierra del Rosario Biosphere Reserve** make this one of Cuba's richest and wildest areas. **Viñales** is rapidly becoming the region's center for nature and adventure tourism. At the far western tip of the island, **María la Gorda** is one of Cuba's signature scuba-diving destinations. And the diving at **Cayo Levisa, Isla de la Juventud,** and **Cayo Largo** isn't too shabby either. To top it all off, Cayo Largo has some of the most beautiful and least-crowded beaches in Cuba.

Pinar del Río province is also Cuba's most heralded tobacco-growing region. Cigars made from tobacco grown in the **Vuelta Abajo** area, just west of the city of Pinar del Río, are coveted the world over.

PINAR DEL RÍO

174km (108 miles) SW of Havana

Pinar del Río, the provincial capital, is named for the pine trees that grow along the banks of the Río Guamá, where the city is set. Originally founded as Nueva Filipina (New Philippine), it was rechristened Pinar del Río in 1774 and is one of the last major cities founded by the Spanish in Cuba. Pinar del Río is an animated little city of around 150,000, with a university, several hospitals, and some industries. The city's architecture is a mix of colonial and neoclassical, with buildings in varying states from finely restored to post-revolutionary decay. The major attractions can easily be visited in a day, and you'd be better off giving more time and attention to the province's less urban destinations. Still, Pinar del Río provides a glimpse of a town unfettered by major tourism.

Essentials

GETTING THERE

BY BUS The **bus station** (✆ **48/75-5255**) is located at Calle Adela Azcuy between Avenidas Colón and Comandante Pinares. **Víazul** (www.viazul.com; ✆ **48/75-2572** in Pinar del Río) has buses at 8:40am, 11:25am, and 2pm from Havana to Pinar del Río; journey time is 2 hours and 40 minutes (CUC$11). This bus continues on to Viñales. If you pick the bus up here, it costs CUC$6 to Viñales. Buses to Havana leave Pinar del Río at 10am and 2:50pm daily.

BY CAR Take the Autopista Nacional (A4) west to Pinar del Río. It's a straight shot, and the Autopista actually ends as it enters Pinar del Río. To get on the Autopista Nactional from Havana, drive south out of Havana on Av. Independencia. At the spaghetti junction at Alturas de la Habana, turn right on Av. San Francisco (Calle 100). At a second spaghetti junction, turn left (west) onto the unsigned Autopista (A4) for Viñales. (Just before Pinar del Río, there's a sign marked Las Ovas to the east/right; this is the western route, a winding cross-country shortcut to Viñales.) Two alternative routes are the old Carretera Central, which runs roughly parallel to the newer Autopista and connects Havana with Pinar del Río, and the Circuito Norte, or "northern circuit," a road that runs from Havana to Mariel to Bahía Honda. At La Palma, you'll want to head south on the Viñales highway and then on to Pinar del Río. Both of these routes are two-lane affairs that are slower and more picturesque than the Autopista. On either of these, slow-moving ox carts and trucks combine with bicycle traffic, pedestrians, and potholes to slow you down—not a bad thing if you want to take in some of the scenery. I recommend integrating the Circuito Norte route into an itinerary that encompasses Pinar del Río, Viñales, and either Cayo Levisa or Cayo Jutías.

GETTING AROUND

You can easily walk to most places in Pinar del Río. Taxis are also readily available all around town, and are either at hand, or can be called, at most hotels and *casas particulares.* Call **Cubataxi** (✆ **48/75-8080**) for a cab ride. If you want to rent a car, contact **Havanautos** (✆ **48/77-8015**), which has an office at the Hotel Pinar del Río, or **Cubacar** (✆ **48/77-8278**).

ORIENTATION

The Autopista Nacional ends and turns into Calle Martí as it enters Pinar del Río from the east. As you enter town, you'll see the Hotel Pinar del Río on your right. The heart of downtown is straight ahead. At the western end of downtown, you'll find the small, triangular-shaped Plaza de la Independencia.

The main north-south byway, Calle Isabel Rubio, is also the old Carretera Central, and bisects Calle Martí by the post office.

VISITOR INFORMATION

Infotur, inside the Hotel Vueltabajo, keeps irregular hours (✆ **48/72-8616;** infopinr@enet.cu). **Havanatur,** on Calle Osmani Arenado at Martí, is an excellent resource for tourist information.

FAST FACTS

BANKS/ATMS For currency exchange, there's a **CADECA** on Calle Gerardo Medina, and another at Martí 46, virtually opposite the post office.

INTERNET/PHONES You can make local, national, and international calls and connect to the Internet at an **Etecsa** phone office on Gerardo Medina, two blocks east of Coppelia. The Hotel Vueltaabajo has Internet terminals.

MEDICAL The **León Cuervo Rubio hospital** (✆ **48/75-4443**) is at the junction of the Carretera Central and the Viñales highway.

POST OFFICE The main **post office** is located at the corner of Calle Martí and Calle Isabel Rubio (✆ **48/75-5916**); open Mon–Sun 8am–8pm).

Exploring the Area

The principal attraction in town is **Fábrica de Tabacos Francisco Donatién** (✆ **48/77-3069**), Calle Antonio Maceo, just off the Plaza de la Independencia. Several fine brands are rolled at this renowned cigar factory. You can walk through the timeless rolling station, where a caller reads news and short stories to keep the rollers interested. You'll also visit rooms where the final selection and grading, labeling, and boxing take place. You can buy some of the wares here or at the well-stocked **Casa del Habano** across the street. The factory is open Monday through Friday 9am to noon and 1 to 4pm and Saturday 9am to noon. Admission is CUC$5 and includes a guided tour that lasts about 15 to 20 minutes.

The other main attraction in Pinar del Río is the **Casa Garay Fábrica de Guayabitas del Pinar** (✆ **48/75-2966**), Calle Isabel Rubio, 3½ blocks south of Calle Martí. This little factory produces the town's signature Guayabita del Pinar liquor. They produce two types, *dulce* (sweet) and *seco* (dry). Both are cane liquors distilled with the fruit berries of a local bush. I like the *seco* quite a bit. It's a good-quality sipping liquor that, if you stretch your imagination, is almost brandylike. The factory is open during the same hours as Fábrica de Tabacos Francisco Donatién. Admission is free and usually includes a quick guided tour and a stop at the tasting room. Bottles of Guayabita are on sale for around CUC$4.

Aside from the city's two main draws, you can easily spend a few hours walking around town, and perhaps stopping in at either the **Museo Provincial de Historia (Museum of Province History),** at Calle Martí 58 (✆ **48/75-4300**), or the **Museo de Ciencias Naturales (Museum of Natural Sciences),** at Calle Martí and Avenida Pinares (✆ **48/75-3087**). Neither contains exhibits or collections of great interest, although the latter is housed in a wonderful old

smoke 'EM IF YOU GOT 'EM

When Christopher Columbus first visited Cuba, he found the local population smoking a local herb, *cohiba,* through a pipe, or *tobago.* They called the act of smoking *"sikar."* Columbus brought back some samples, and it wasn't long before millions of Europeans were smoking tobacco rolled into cigars and cigarettes. Tobacco was grown commercially in Cuba as early as the 16th century, and by the late 17th century, it was the country's most important export crop. By all accounts, the finest cigars in the world come from Cuba. And of the Cuban cigars available, the crème de la crème are made with tobacco grown in the **Vuelta Abajo,** the low plains spreading west from the city of Pinar del Río.

Most of the tobacco grown in Cuba is grown on small farms. Seeds are planted each year beginning in late October and throughout November to stagger the harvest. In a little over a month, seedlings are transplanted to the fields, or *vegas.* Plants are carefully tended and regularly topped to stimulate leaf growth lower down. The highest-quality wrapper leaves, *capa,* are grown in semishade under protective mesh. Harvesting takes place from January through April. Leaves are classified by plant type, growing region, growing condition (sun or shade), and where they grow on an individual plant. All go through an intensive and carefully monitored process of drying, sorting, preparing, fermenting, aging, and finally, rolling. Real care is taken in handling the prized *capas.* Lesser-quality leaves end up as *capote* (binders) and *tripa* (filler).

Throughout Vuelta Abajo, you'll pass field after field planted with tobacco and see the traditional high-peaked, thatched-roof drying sheds. Tobacco from the Vuelta Abajo region is shipped to various factories in the region and around Cuba. The finest brands—Cohibas, Partagas, Romeo y Julieta, Montecristo, Robaina, H. Upmann, Corona, and Hoyo de Monterey—are all made with tobacco from Vuelta Abajo.

building with ornate Moorish architecture. You could also check out the **Teatro Milanés** (**© 48/75-3871**), Calles Martí and Colón, a striking 19th-century theater that is open for visits during the day and sometimes hosts evening concerts and performances.

La Guille Tienda-Taller, Calle Martí 161 between Comandante Pinares and Ciprián Valdés (**© 48/75-3707**), makes lovely white cotton clothes, textile jewelry, and some very cute oversized, colored bead necklaces. Run by architect Marilyn Laborí Capote and family, it's open Monday through Saturday 9am to 7pm.

Where to Stay

I personally recommend staying in Viñales (see below) and visiting the attractions in Pinar del Río on a day trip.

Most casas charge between CUC$15 and CUC$25 per room and usually offer reasonably priced meal options. **Casa Yusimy,** Calle Martí 164, between Calle Nueva and Comandante Pinares (**© 48/75-2818**), offers a small apartment with two rooms, a kitchen/diner, and a terrace overlooking Martí. **Casa**

El Gallardo, Calle Martí 207 (✆ **48/77-8492;** restaurantgallardo@nauta.cu), offers two rooms, the first brighter than the second, above a ranchón restaurant run by the friendly Roger Domíngue.

MODERATE

Hotel Vueltabajo ★★ It's downtown and within walking distance of all the sights, making this the most appealing hotel option in Pinar del Río. The neoclassical mansion is home to an expansive marble staircase and exquisite colored plasterwork decoration in the restaurant. All the double rooms are compact but comfortable, with attractive Impressionist-style paintings above the beds. Mini suites with balconies (no extra cost) are larger but face the main road, which is very noisy. You'll want an interior room here (nos. 26–38, and 4-19). If you prefer more space, the triples are twice the size of a double.

Calle Martí 103, Pinar del Río. www.islazul.cu. ✆ **48/75-9381.** carpeta@vueltapr.co.cu. 39 units. CUC$53–CUC$60 double. Rates include breakfast. MC, V. **Amenities:** Restaurant; bar; car rental; Internet.

Where to Dine

The most attractive spot for a coffee or a cooling Cristal is the swanky new **Café Ortúzar**, Calle Martí 127 (✆ **48/75-1111**), with a couple of tables streetside. It's open 24 hours. *Malanga* (taro) is found all over Cuba, but it's only in the west that they make malanga chips (crisps), which are not to be missed.

MODERATE/INEXPENSIVE

On the main street, **Las Mil y Una Noche**, Calle Martí 132 (✆ **48/75-6549;** main courses CUC$6.50–CUC$15; Tues–Sun noon–1:30am), is a modest paladar with white wrought-iron furniture serving up delicious snapper with chunky sweet potato and malanga chips. The menu offers plenty of *comida criolla* (Cuban Creole food) and pastas. Its flan is highly recommended, too.

The long-established paladar **El Mesón**, Calle Martí 205 (✆ **48/75-2867;** main courses CUC$1.70–CUC$3; Mon–Sat noon–10pm), is popular (located opposite the Natural Sciences Museum) and understaffed, but the *comida criolla* (priced in *moneda nacional*) is tasty.

Pinar del Rio After Dark

A large outdoor amphitheater space, **Rumayor** (✆ **48/76-3007**) offers up everything from Afro-Cuban dances to reggaeton stars. The Saturday-only show starts at around 11pm and finishes at 1am. Admission is CUC$5, which includes one drink per person.

Alternately, you can also see what's playing at the old **Cine Praga,** Calle Gerardo Medina, next to the Coppelia ice cream parlor. Admission is just a couple of Cuban pesos.

VIÑALES ★★★

200km (124 miles) SW of Havana; 26km (16 miles) N of Pinar del Río

Viñales is an extremely picturesque town in the heart of Cuba's prime tobacco-growing region. The town itself sits in the center of a flat valley surrounded by stunning karst hill formations known locally as *mogotes*. The *mogotes* are irregularly shaped, steep-sided geological formations that rise as high as 300m (984 ft.) and have bases ranging from just a few hundred yards in diameter to as much as a couple of kilometers in length. The *mogotes* are part of the Sierra de los Organos mountain chain, and were formed by eons of erosion. Many consider this to be the most naturally beautiful spot in Cuba, and the view of the Viñales Valley from any of the surrounding hillsides is stunning, particularly at sunrise or sunset. The Viñales Valley is a great spot to bicycle around, and there are good options for bird-watching, hiking, horseback riding, and in particular, rock climbing and spelunking.

Essentials

GETTING THERE

Víazul (www.viazul.com; ✆ **48/79-3112**) has daily buses at 08:40am, 11:25am, and 2pm from Havana to Viñales, via Pinar del Río. The trip takes 3 hours and 15 minutes and costs CUC$12 each way. Víazul buses depart Viñales for Havana daily at 9am, 10am, and 2pm, and pass through Pinar del Río about 40 minutes later, before continuing on to the capital. A bus departs for Trinidad at 06:45am daily (CUC$37; 9.5 hr.). You can hire a taxi to Havana for between CUC$60 and CUC$80 for up to four people, and you can also hire a taxi to Cienfuegos and Trinidad. The **bus stop** (✆ **48/79-3195**) is located at Salvador Cisneros 63, just across the street from the town's main plaza.

To get here **by car,** take the Autopista Nacional (A4) west to Pinar del Río (see above for how to find it). From Pinar del Río, it's another 26km (16 miles) north on the well-marked Carretera Viñales. Entering Pinar del Río from the Autopista, you'll want to turn right at the post office, on Calle Isabel Rubio, and follow the signs for Viñales. Or, alternatively, just before Pinar del Río, there's a sign marked Las Ovas to the right (west). Take the western route, a winding cross-country shortcut to Viñales.

GETTING AROUND

Taxis can be hired in Viñales or called from your hotel. They tend to congregate around the central plaza. A cab to any of the local attractions costs between CUC$2 and CUC$6. You can hire a cab for a full-day trip to anywhere around the region for around CUC$25. A recommended taxi service is provided by **Osviel Echevarría Arteaga** (✆ **48/69-6774** and 5331-1731).

If you'd rather rent a car, **Transtur** (✆ **48/79-6060**) has an office downtown just off the central park, and **Havanautos** (✆ **48/79-6330**) has an office diagonally opposite the Viñales Cupet gas station. Mopeds *(motos)* can now be rented from a place next to the Casa Don Tomás (✆ **48/79-6300**) for CUC$25 a day.

The **Viñales Bus Tour** (no phone) has 18 stops and is a hop-on/hop-off service costing CUC$5 a day. You can pick it up right next to the plaza on the main road.

This is a good region to **bicycle around**. The valley itself is almost perfectly flat, and most of the major attractions can be reached along well-paved roads. You can rent bikes in pretty good shape for CUC$5 to CUC$10 per day from your *casa particular*. Cubanacán also offers a 1-day guided biking tour in the valley for CUC$20 with lunch included.

VISITOR INFORMATION

Infotur can be found opposite the plaza and is open daily from 8:15am to 4:45pm.

FAST FACTS

BANKS/ATMS Viñales has two **banks** with ATMs: the **Banco de Crédito y Comercio,** Salvador Cisneros No 58 (✆ **48/79-3130**); and the **Banco Popular de Ahorro,** Salvador Cisneros No 54 A.

INTERNET **Internet and Wi-Fi** is available at the Etecsa office, just off Calle Cisneros.

Exploring the Area

OUTDOOR ADVENTURES

Caves abound in this area and are one of the major attractions in and around Viñales. **La Cueva del Indio** (the **Indian's Cave;** ✆ **48/79-6280**) is the most popular cave, and as such it's become a real tourist trap. Located about 5km (3 miles) north of Viñales (at Km 33) on the Carretera de Puerto Esperanza, this cave gets its name from the fact that indigenous remains have been found here. Only 1km (½ mile) or so of the extensive cave system here is open to travelers. A well-lit path leads from the entrance through a few small and narrow galleries to a tiny dock on an underground river. Here, you board a small rowboat powered by an outboard engine for a quick trip of about 180m (591 ft.) up and down this river, before exiting the cave at a dock area crowded with souvenir stands and a little snack bar. The entrance fee is CUC$5, and I don't think it's justified. Moreover, when the buses arrive, the line to get in is long and slow. It is open daily from 8am to 5pm.

Those with an interest in more serious spelunking should head to **Las Cuevas de Santo Tomás ★**. With over 45km (28 miles) of connected tunnels, chambers, and galleries, it's the largest explored cave system in Cuba. Some of these chambers and galleries are quite massive, with impressive stalagmite and stalactite formations. Unlike La Cueva del Indio, this cave system has been left in its natural state, and you must visit it with headlamps and flashlights. So far, a relatively simple 1km (½-mile) section has been opened for guided tours, although more adventurous spelunking tours are in the works. Visits here, including a guide and equipment, cost about CUC$10, and are best booked in advance with the **Centro de Visitantes,** located on the highway into Viñales, just beyond the Hotel Los Jazmines (✆ **48/79-6144/43;**

The Viñales Valley

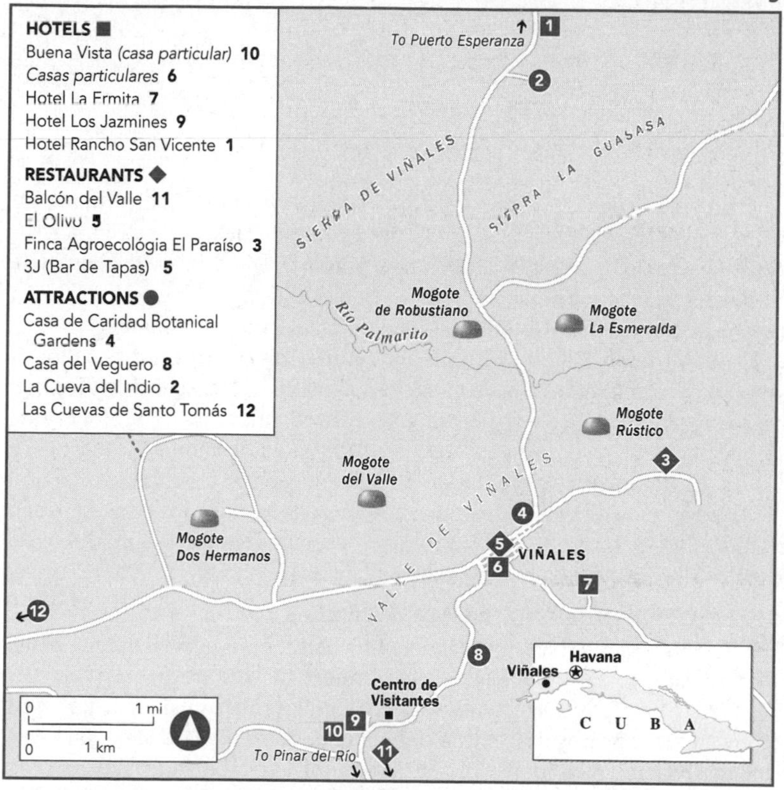

reserva@pnvinales.vega.inf; open 8am–8pm daily). Those with their own transport can pitch up; last departure into the cave is 3pm.

In addition to caving, the limestone mountains and karst formations of Viñales make for excellent **rock climbing** (season: Oct–Apr). Although climbing is still in its infancy as a sport in Cuba, the Viñales Valley is rapidly becoming a mecca for local and visiting climbers. So far, over 300 routes have been identified and climbed in the area. Some carry colorful names, such as "Razor's Edge" and "Friday 13th." A few attest to some of the hazards of the area, such as "Feeding Mosquitoes" and "Poison Oak, Guano, and Spines." For details, check out www.cubaclimbing.com and www.escaladaencuba.com. The Cuban government also plans to open up routes with state guides.

Unless you plan on scaling several *mogotes* (steep geological formations), most of the **hiking** here is on gentle, well-groomed trails. There are several popular trails and routes, but you must hire an official guide to hike most of them. One of the most popular hikes is a simple walk through the *fincas* (farms) of the valley just outside of town (take Calle Adela Azcuy Norte). This provides wonderful views of the surrounding *mogotes,* and allows for encounters with the local farmers and a firsthand view of the tobacco-growing process. Some entrepreneurial farmers have opened up a juice and cocktail bar, **Bar Complaciente,** complete with a domesticated *jutía*, Panchito. More athletic forays into the nearby forests and hills include hikes to and around the valley, hikes up **Coco Solo Mogote** and **el Palmarito,** as well as climbs to the summits of several other *mogotes.* Guided hikes run between CUC$8 and CUC$10 per person, depending on the route and length of the hike. Do-it-yourself hikers can wander the dirt roads and byways of the Viñales Valley but must stay off the marked trails of **Viñales National Park.** For more information on guides and organized hikes, ask at your hotel or check with **Centro de Visitantes** (see above), on the highway into Viñales, just beyond the Hotel Los Jazmines. It offers 14 trails varying in length from 3 to 7 hours.

There are few well-defined trails for serious **mountain biking,** although you'll have plenty of dirt roads to explore all around. **Horseback riding** can be arranged through agencies or official licensed guides for CUC$5 per person per hour. A recommended trek is to the Valle el Palmarito and to the **Cueva El Palmarito**. Some 250m (820 ft.) inside the cave are two natural pools to swim in; on the return you can stop in a tobacco-leaf-drying barn and learn about the cigar process. **Ziplining** is scheduled to start in the Alturas de Pizarras (the area facing the mogotes) in late 2015.

ATTRACTIONS & ORGANIZED TOURS

The Viñales Valley is part of the heart of Cuba's tobacco-growing region and a great place to take a tobacco tour. Typical tours start at the **Casa del Veguero,** a small farm that grows and dries the primary material, followed by a visit to the nearby de-veining station, or *despalilladora.* Here, you'll see workers handle and sort the prized leaves for *capas,* or outer layers. You might also be given a quick tour of a final curing station, where the leaves emit an ammonia gas that will make your eyes tear. Finally, you'll visit a local cigar shop, **El Estanco.** However, you'll have to go into Pinar del Río if you want to visit an actual cigar factory. **Paradiso**, Calle Salvador Cisneros 65 (© **48/79-6258**), can organize this or a trip that ends with lunch at Finca Wilfredo's (p. 103).

Avoid the Crowds

Viñales is an extremely popular destination for day trips out of Havana. If you're staying here, try to visit the various attractions early, before the buses arrive, and then spend the afternoon walking around town, hiking a more remote trail, or lazing around your hotel.

One of the nicer attractions in Viñales is the little **Casa de Caridad Botanical Gardens** ★ at the northeastern end of town. The lush gardens feature a mix of ornamental and medicinal plants and flowers, as well as orchids, bromeliads, palms, and fruit trees. If you're really lucky, you'll be able to munch on some freshly harvested fruit. No admission is charged, but donations are accepted.

Cubanacán and **Paradiso** have offices right off the town's main square and offer a variety of tour options. These jam-packed full-day tours cost CUC$28 per person and usually include a visit to the Casa del Veguero, El Estanco, the Mural de la Prehistoria, the Cueva del Indio, and El Palenque de los Cimarrones, with lunch at one of the latter three places, as well as a sunset cocktail at Hotel Los Jazmines. Other tour options include day trips to Pinar del Río (CUC$36); Cayo Levisa (CUC$29; p. 108); Cayo Jutías (from CUC$15; p. 110); or María la Gorda (CUC$35; p. 110).

Paradiso also offers salsa classes and percussion classes.

Where to Stay

MODERATE

The hotels below do a brisk business with tour groups. It is essential that you have a reservation in advance. Cubanacán is building the Plaza Viñales hotel in town and another one in Valle Ancón.

Hotel La Ermita Set on a hillside behind town, this hotel offers winning views from rooms set around a decent outdoor pool. Only 12 rooms offer the signature valley view; of these, the second-floor end room, at no. 64, boasts uninterrupted views of the valley from its superb balcony. Rooms are comfortably furnished with compact bathrooms and balconies or terraces. The food here is disappointing, but you can always walk to the Fernan-dos paladar down the road. Outside guests can use the pool for CUC$7 (*consumo mínimo* CUC$6 at the poolside *parillada*).

Carretera de La Ermita Km 1.5. www.hotelescubanacan.com. ✆ **48/79-6071.** 62 units. CUC$86–CUC$94 double. Rates include breakfast and dinner. MC, V. **Amenities:** 2 restaurants; 2 bars; outdoor pool; tennis court; Internet (Wi-Fi in the lobby and around the pool).

Hotel Los Jazmines This candy-pink hotel offers winning views of the valley. The most charming rooms are the eight duplex cabins (with terraces) that lead down the hillside behind the pool and overlook the garden and valley with million-dollar views. If these rooms aren't available, opt for room nos. 301 to 316 on the third floor. The rooms are outdated, but the balcony views are stunning. The non-updated pool—plus mojitos at sunset—is a major feature of this hotel. You can easily give the food a miss.

Carretera de Viñales Km 25. www.hotelescubanacan.com. ✆ **48/79-6205.** 70 units. CUC$86–CUC$99 double. Rates include breakfast and dinner. MC, V. **Amenities:** Restaurant; 2 bars; outdoor pool; Internet (Wi-Fi in lobby).

Hotel Rancho San Vicente Located about 270m (886 ft.) north of the Cueva del Indio, this quiet hotel now pivots around two parts: a new tangerine-cream building with smart rooms and an attractive pool on one side of the road, and the older complex with bungalows set amid a garden of pine, mango, and flamboyant trees. If you've not come for the nature, the new 22 rooms in a block are smart and comfortable. In the older section you'll want one of the 20 newer wooden cabins; the six two-story wooden cabins are fun for families. The pool has been given a new lease of life with new sun loungers. Unfortunately the soaking pools fed by sulfuric mineral springs (CUC$5 for 30 min.) could desperately do with an upgrade.

Carretera de Puerto Esperanza Km 33. www.hotelescubanacan.com. ✆ **48/79-6111.** 69 units. CUC$70–CUC$75 double. Rates include breakfast and dinner. MC, V. **Amenities:** 2 restaurants; 3 bars; 2 outdoor pools; Internet (Wi-Fi in lobby).

INEXPENSIVE

Viñales has hundreds of *casas particulares*. Most are on either the main street through town or on the street 1 block southeast and parallel to it. All charge between CUC$15 and CUC$40 per room and offer reasonably priced meal options. I recommend **Casa Oscar Jaime Rodríguez ★,** Adela Azcuy 43 (www.casaoscar.com; ✆ **48/79-3381;** oscar.jaime59@gmail.com), with its friendly family, four rooms, and communal areas. Oscar rents bikes and is well connected to the climbing industry; **Casa Lumino and Heriberto,** Calle Orlando Nodarse 3 (✆ **48/69-6952**), for Lumino's wonderful character and great cooking; **Villa El Cafetal ★**, Adela Azcuy Norte Final s/n (✆ **5331 1752;** elcafetalvinales@nauta.cu), a lovely house run by Marta Martínez that sits at the trail head to the *mogotes* and is surrounded by a garden of coffee and fruit trees (Marta's son, Edgar, is a climbing guide; contact him at ✆ **5266-2787**); and **Casa Déborah Susana, Calle C no.1 Final,** behind the Banco Nacional (✆ **48/79-6207**; deborahsusana7@yahoo.es), with two independent rooms run by Deborah and Juan Carlos.

More recommendations: **Villa Cristal**, 99 Rafael Trejo (www.villacristalcuba.com; ✆ **5270-1284;** villacristalvinales@gmail.com), has two rooms with rain showers, rockers, and a TV/DVD loaded with films (one room has a plunge pool); **Casa Nenita**, Salvador Cisnero Int. No. 1 (✆ **48/79-6004;** emiliadiaz2000@yahoo.es), with five smart rooms around a lovely pool, another four rooms and a Jacuzzi across the road, and a billiards table; the lovely blue and white **Buena Vista**, next to the Hotel de los Jazmines, with two rooms overlooking the valley (only one has a view, though; ✆ **5223-8616;** buenavista@nauta.cu); **Villa Juana**, Calle Rafael Trejo 5 (✆ **48/69-6507;** airyn2009@hotmail.com), with seven rooms between theirs and family members next door; **Casa Leyanis and Jesús Alejandro**, Calle Adela Azcuy Norte 20E (✆ **48/79-6336;** casaleyanis@gmail.com), its four rooms set around an enclosed courtyard and a pool offering magnificent valley views.

Where to Dine

Like Trinidad, Viñales has undergone a private restaurant boom in the village.

El Olivo ★, Calle Salvador Cisneros 89 (✆ **48/69-6654;** open daily noon–10pm), opened in 2012 and still maintains its reputation as the best paladar in town. Huge, fresh salads and delicious meat dishes are served in the dining room, which has doubled in size. The roast lamb with potatoes and caramelized onions is tantalizingly tender.

Perched on a hilltop, the organic farm **Finca Agroecológica El Paraíso (Finca Wilfredo's) ★★★**, Carretera a Cementerio Km 1.5 (**© 5818-8581;** open daily 12:30–4pm and 7–10pm), has in the gorgeous blue-and-white clapboard restaurant one of the best dining options in Cuba. Copious amounts of roast pork, vegetables, soups, rice, frijoles, salads, fish, chicken and other meats are served up in conveyor-belt fashion until you can eat no more. This all-you-can-eat buffet is a bargain for CUC$10 plus coffee. Don't leave without savoring the finca's signature drink, an anti-stress elixir—with or without a splash of rum—a delicious concoction of piña colada, anis, mint, hierba buena, basil, and lemongrass.

With its smart bar and tapas choices, **3J (Bar de Tapas)**, Calle Salvador Cisnero 45 (**© 48/79-3334**) is one of the most happening spots in town. This new kid on the block is run by the experienced Jean-Pierre. Try the green minty Daiquiri 3J and the *jamón serrano* with salted mushrooms. It's open 24 hours.

Balcón del Valle, Carretera a Vinales Km 23, just 120m (130 yards) south of the Centro de Visitantes (**© 48/69-5847**), is a beautiful spot set on wooden balconies built out between the branches of mango trees. It offers set menus of *ropa vieja*, fish, shrimp, pork, and lamb accompanied by all the trimmings for CUC$8. It's open daily 8am to 10pm.

Viñales After Dark

The hugely popular **Patio de Polo Montañez ★**, right on the central plaza, is a good spot for salsa or at the nearby smaller ARTex venue, **Patio del Decimista.** Sol del Valle and its leader, who plays the recorder through his nose, is worth seeking out. The **Discoteca Las Cuevas** is located at the entrance to El Palenque de los Cimarrones. Flashing lights and loud music get an atmospheric boost from the hanging stalactites. There's a cabaret-style show here on Saturday beginning around 9pm; admission is CUC$3.

SIERRA DEL ROSARIO BIOSPHERE RESERVE ★ & SAN DIEGO DE LOS BAÑOS

Soroa: 87km (54 miles) W of Havana; San Diego de los Baños: 120km (75 miles) W of Havana

The mountainous region between Havana and Pinar del Río is another prime destination in the country's budding ecotourism industry. With both the **Sierra del Rosario Biosphere Reserve** and **La Güira National Park,** as well as ecotourism projects in **Soroa** and at **Las Terrazas,** the area offers a wealth of opportunities to explore the flora and fauna of Cuba's inland mountain forests.

Sierra del Rosario Biosphere Reserve

Declared a UNESCO Biosphere Reserve in 1985, the 25,000-hectare (61,776-acre) **Sierra del Rosario** encompasses a mountainous area of rapidly recovering, secondary tropical deciduous forests, cut with numerous rivers and waterfalls. Nearly 100 species of birds can be spotted here, including over half of Cuba's 22 endemic species. Currently, there are few trails and facilities in the reserve, which is not open to individual exploration and trekking. Most activity is confined to two tourism developments: the attractive eco-community of **Las Terrazas** and **Soroa,** which are connected by a loop of paved roads that begins and ends on the Autopista Nacional.

ESSENTIALS

GETTING THERE & GETTING AROUND The only public transportation to Las Terrazas is a once-a-day Víazul bus to Viñales, which can drop off at Las Terrazas. If you want to spend more time, you will either have to rent a car, hire a taxi, or come with an organized tour (which can be booked at any major tour operator or hotel tour desk). Las Terrazas is about 75km (47 miles) west of Havana. Take the Autopista Nacional (A4) west to Km 51. Here you'll see the sign and turnoff for Las Terrazas on your right. The heart of the complex is about 8km (5 miles) from the turnoff. About halfway there, you'll hit the entrance, where you have to sign in and pay an entrance fee of CUC$2 per person, although this is waived for guests at the hotel here.

To get to Soroa, continue through Las Terrazas or on the Autopista until the town of Candelaria at Km 62. The turnoff here is marked, and it's another 8km (5 miles) to Soroa. **Roberto Arodys Miranda** is a reliable Soroa classic-car taxi driver (✆ **5345-7730;** prieto86@nauta.cu).

ORIENTATION The main offices at Las Terrazas are at Rancho Curujey (see below); the community and Hotel Moka are a couple of kilometers away. Everything is well marked and connected by paved roads. If you don't have a reservation at Hotel Moka or its affiliated accommodations, you'll have to check in at Rancho Curujey before undertaking any tours or explorations of the reserve. The reserve gets busy in the high season and on weekends; reservations are recommended, even for day visits.

EXPLORING THE AREA

Las Terrazas ★ (www.lasterrazas.cu; ✆ **7/204-3739** in Havana, or 48/57-8555 on-site) is a wonderful organized project designed around a working community. The community and Hotel Moka are set just above the shores of the diminutive **Lago San Juan.** It has a half-dozen or so trails and swimming holes, along with a smattering of other attractions, including the **Cafetal Buenavista** (which has good bird-watching), an abandoned coffee plantation, and a few artists' and artisans' studios. If you're lucky, you might spot one of the area's endemic lizards or amphibians, including the world's second-smallest frog.

Officially you must have a guide to hike any of the trails here. Guides can be provided either by Hotel Moka or by the offices at Rancho Curujey (✆ **48/57-8555,** ext 221; reservas@terraz.co.cu or reservas@commoka.get.tur.cu). The trails around the **Cafetal Buenavista** make for a good couple of hours of gentle hiking, and the restaurant here makes the whole thing rather convenient. Another popular hike is the slightly more rugged **La Cañada del Infierno (the Gorge of Hell),** which follows a mountain river down beyond the ruins of yet another coffee plantation, ending at the Santa Catalina sulfur springs. A guide costs from CUC$199 per person, depending on the group size and length of your hike.

At the **Baños de San Juan**, where some of the hikes terminate, refresh with a cool beer and swim in the natural terraces of this lovely river.

The zipline **Canopy Tour** adventure features six platforms connected by long steel cables, which you traverse with a climbing-style harness-and-pulley setup. The cables crisscross the little lake here two times. The tour takes about 50 minutes and costs CUC$35 per person for the complete route or CUC$25 for three of the six routes (CUC$20 if you are staying at the hotel).

Fans of the brilliant Polo Montañez can stop off at the **Peña Polo Montañez** (closed Mon), where the singer used to live. The small house overlooking the lake contains dozens of newspaper cuttings, his guitar, and his hat. His brother, Luis Borrego, is usually hanging around talking to visitors.

Shops and artists' studios are growing in Las Terrazas. Stop in at the lakeside studio of Lester Campa and the tiny Ilang shop to buy artisanal mariposa perfume.

Soroa is a small community with one basic mini-resort (see "Where to Stay," below). The area's claims to fame are a lovely 22m (72-ft.) waterfall and a wonderful botanical garden. You reach the base of **Salto de Soroa** after a gentle hike of around 250m (820 ft.). There's a small pool here fit for wading. If you're more adventurous, you can hike or hire a horse for CUC$5 to ride the steep 1.8km (1-mile) trail to the natural lookout, El Mirador. The rainbow that sometimes forms in the mist of this waterfall has earned the whole town the moniker *El Arcoiris de Cuba* (the Rainbow of Cuba). The entrance to the trails is just a few hundred yards from the hotel, on the road to Havana; admission is CUC$3 per person. Another nearby road leads up to a hilltop lookout called **El Castillo de las Nubes,** where you'll find a building built to resemble a small fortress. It's scheduled to open as a fancy six-bed hotel with a pool. There's the **Bar El Castillo** with a small pool (CUC$2 at weekends).

With more than 2,000 species of tropical plants and flowers from around the world, including 500 species of orchids, the **Jardín Botánico Orquideario Soroa** ★ (✆ **48/52-3871**) is a must-see for anyone passing through Soroa. The compact grounds are well tended and pleasant, and at least 20 or so species of orchids are usually in bloom (most flowering blooms are between Nov and May). There's also a good chance of hearing and spotting the national bird, the *tocororo*. Admission is CUC$3; camera use CUC$1; video CUC$5. It's open 8:30am to 4:30pm daily.

A 1-day taxi trip to this area from Havana costs around CUC$80.

WHERE TO STAY

Expensive

Hotel Moka ★★ A lovely eco-lodge nestled in thick woodsy plantation terrain up above Las Terrazas. Stretching across the grounds are three floors with spacious twin rooms with tiled floors and balconies. The marble bathrooms come with tubs next to floor-to-ceiling glass windows (and shutters, of course). The in-room TVs play the catchy songs of Polo Montañez (p. 105), with subtitles for a jolly singalong. The hotel restaurant is mediocre, but the buzzy bar has a great balcony view, and the swimming pool is a most welcome respite after a day's hiking. Alternative accommodations can be found in several **family homes ★** around the lake and in cute, rustic one-roomed cabins on stilts (accessed by a ladder) next to the Río San Juan with breakfast taken at the onsite restaurant, next to the river.

Autopista Nacional Km 51, Las Terrazas. www.lasterrazas.cu. ✆ **48/57-8600.** 47 units, 5 villas and 5 cabins. CUC$90–CUC$120 double; CUC$90–CUC$120 villa; CUC$25 cabin. Rates include breakfast. MC, V. **Amenities:** Restaurant; bar; outdoor pool; tennis court; Internet and Wi-Fi.

Moderate

Hotel & Villas Soroa This complex is made up of an unusual collection of cute brick casitas either dotted around the large figure-eight pool or set up high in the gardens, and a series of three-bedroom concrete apartments with pools (for up to seven adults and three children) in the hills above the resort. The best rooms are those that face the pool (nos. 16–24), but those set behind are quieter, and have more birdlife. Rooms are compact, with simple furnishings that include attractive stained-glass windows, but could do with some improvement. The poolside grill bar does a decent plate of roast chicken and rice, but you're better off eating at the Casa Estudio de Arte (see below). The hotel offers guided walks to nearby attractions and some off-the-beaten-track routes for from CUC$6 per person. The pool can be used by day-trippers for CUC$10 (of that, CUC$7 can be spent on food and drink); in low season it drops to CUC$7 (consumo mínimo CUC$5). The hotel will manage the new luxury hotel at the Castillo de los Nubes when it opens.

Carretera a Soroa Km 8. www.hotelescubanacan.com. ✆ **48/52-3534.** reserva@hvs.tur.cu. 80 units. CUC$35–CUC$72 double. Rates include breakfast buffet. CUC$40–CUC$80 casas. MC and V. **Amenities:** 2 restaurants; 3 bars; outdoor pool; Internet.

Inexpensive

Casa Estudio de Arte ★, Carretera Soroa Km 8½, next to the primary school (✆ **48/59-8116; 5399-5091;** infosoroa@hvs.tur.cu) is run by Spanish teacher Aliuska and her painter husband, Jesús Gastell Soto (www.jesusgastell.com), a graduate of ISA. The two bedrooms with terraces are buried in flourishing gardens. Dine on chicken and fruit on the orchid-festooned terrace and kick back for a few days. Aliuska and Jesús run Spanish and art classes in a taller studio and also teach art to the local schoolkids.

A short distance from the center of Soroa, **Los Sauces**, Carretera a Soroa Km 3 (✆ **5228-9372;** bocourt@af.upr.edu.cu), has three comfortable rooms in a flourishing garden featuring 29 fruit species and dozens of orchids.

WHERE TO DINE

Eco-Restaurante El Romero ★★ VEGETARIAN The brainchild of the passionate Tito Núñez Gudás, this is Cuba's only authentic vegetarian restaurant. Come once, come twice, come as many times as possible. All diners are offered lotus ceviche before a spread that may include herbal breads, pumpkin, and beetroot soup. From the drinks' menu, the anti-hypertension juice with grapefruit, cucumber, and mint is refreshing. The Jinete, a "burger" of beans and yam marinated with onion, garlic, and plants and served with wholemeal rice, is highly recommended.

Las Terrazas. ✆ **48/57-8555.** Reservations recommended. Main courses CUC$3.50–CUC$16. No credit cards. Daily 9am–9pm.

La Fonda de Mercedes ★ CRIOLLAN Doña Mercedes Dache's apartment offers an alfresco terrace for dining and limited main courses, but it's all delicious. There's a Camagüey-style lamb served shredded and cooked in wine, the grilled chicken, or excellent fish. The standout dish, though, is a superlative minestrone soup. After dining, repair to **Café de María** for a Café Las Terrazas, made with coffee, milk, chocolate liqueur, and ice.

Las Terrazas. ✆ **48/57-8647.** Reservations recommended in high season. Set menu CUC$12. No credit cards. Daily 9am–9pm.

San Diego de los Baños & La Güira National Park

Just west of the Sierra de los Rosario, in the foothills of the Sierra de los Organos, you'll find La Güira National Park and San Diego de los Baños. **La Güira** is a small park that is nonetheless a favorite stop for bird-watching tours and general sightseers. **San Diego de los Baños** is a tiny back-of-beyond town built on the edge of a lovely river and some natural mineral springs. The springs, which have been closed for some time, were famed for their medicinal properties for centuries. Today only basic spa and physical therapy treatments are available to Cubans.

GETTING THERE & GETTING AROUND

There is no regular public transportation to San Diego de los Baños. You will either have to rent a car, hire a taxi, or come with an organized tour. San Diego de los Baños is located about 133km (83 miles) southwest of Havana. Take the Autopista Nacional (A4) west to Km 102. You should see the sign and turnoff to your right. From here, it's another 21km (13 miles) to town. A taxi from Havana to San Diego de los Baños costs CUC$70 one way. A few taxis are available in town, charging from CUC$3 to CUC$5 one-way to La Güira.

EXPLORING THE AREA

San Diego de los Baños is a tiny town built on the edge of a lovely river and some natural mineral springs. The **San Diego de los Baños Spa** (✆ **48/54-8812**) is a relatively desultory facility that shows the wear and tear it has borne over the years. It is closed to foreigners. **La Güira National Park** is 5km (3 miles) west of San Diego de los Baños. You enter the park through the grand gates of the former Hacienda Cortina. There are some ruins and tended gardens near the entrance, as well as a restaurant. The park has no marked trails and no signs, but a heavily potholed road leads through it (keep going straight) and up to the **Cueva de Los Portales** (marked by a Campismo sign; ✆ **48/63-6749**), a small cave complex from which Che Guevara coordinated the Cuban defense forces during the Cuban missile crisis. The latter is probably the most interesting site in the area, and a must-see for anyone on the Che trail. Inside, you can tour the compound and see where Che hung his hammock for afternoon siestas, where he and the men took target practice, where they cooked and ate, and where they played chess. You can even peek into the tiny room where the revolutionary icon slept during those troubled times. Admission is CUC$1; it's the same price to take pictures and an extra CUC$2 for a specialized guide. Note that the nearby campsite is not open to international visitors.

CAYO LEVISA ★

113km (70 miles) W of Havana; 53km (33 miles) N of Viñales

Cayo Levisa is an isolated little island accessible only by boat. The island is around 3km (1¾ miles) long and just several hundred yards wide at most points. The entire northern shore of Cayo Levisa is one long stretch of white sand fronting a calm and startlingly turquoise blue sea. The beach is backed alternately by small stands of pine trees and stretches of thick mangrove. There's excellent bird-watching and scuba diving here. Cayo Levisa is part of the Archipiélago de los Colorados, which includes Cayo Paraíso, an even smaller little island reputed to have been a favorite fishing haunt of Ernest Hemingway.

Several Havana, Pinar del Río, and Viñales tour agencies run day tours to Cayo Levisa, so the island's resort and beaches can fill up with 50 to 100 extra visitors between 10:30am and 5pm in high season. If you spend the night, however, you'll feel like you've got the island to yourself.

Getting There

Hotel Cayo Levisa (see "Where to Stay & Dine," below) runs three **boats** daily to Cayo Levisa leaving from the Palma Rubia dock (✆ **48/75-7660**) at 10am, 2pm, and 6pm. The trip takes 30 minutes. If you miss the first two departures and don't want to wait, chartering the boat costs CUC$35 per person. Return boats from Cayo Levisa leave for Palma Rubia at 9am, 2:30pm, and 5pm. If you don't have a prearranged tour to the island, the boat ride will run you CUC$25 per person round-trip and includes lunch and a welcome cocktail.

To get to Palma Rubia from Havana by **car,** drive the northern highway from Mariel to Bahía Honda and continue on for another 40km (25 miles) west to Palma Rubia. If you're coming from Viñales, drive north to La Palma and then another 21km (13 miles) northeast to the embarkation point.

There is no regular or reliable **bus service** to Palma Rubia or Cayo Levisa. You could hire a **taxi** from Havana (CUC$70 each way) or take a tour from Viñales or Pinar del Río (CUC$29; CUC$35 with lunch), but make sure you prearrange a pickup for your return trip if you come by taxi, or you could have trouble getting out of Palma Rubia.

Fun On & Off the Beach

The beach encompasses 450m (1,476 ft.) on either side of the main lodge and is excellent for **sunbathing** and **swimming,** with broad stretches of soft sand and a gentle entry into the sea that allows you to walk out literally hundreds of yards before it gets too deep. The water can get a little rough and the weather cool when cold fronts blow through in the winter months, but this is the exception rather than the rule.

Cayo Levisa is an excellent destination for **diving** and **snorkeling.** It has a good dive operation on-site (cayolevisa@cubanacan.co.cu), and some 22 identified dive sites are within a 45-minute boat ride of the island. Most of the sites are less than 15 minutes away, and some are excellent for snorkeling. Rest stops often include a packed lunch at some deserted little island. Dives cost CUC$40, including equipment. Rental of snorkeling equipment costs CUC$5 per day.

If you're looking to follow in Papa Hemingway's footsteps, take a day trip to **Cayo Paraíso.** This small island is about 10km (6 miles) east of Cayo Levisa. It has a small bust of Papa and a little shack that functions as a bar and grill, where you can buy lunch and drinks. The trip costs CUC$25, including transportation, snorkeling, and refreshments. There have been reports that the dive/excursion boat has been broken on several occasions. Check with Cubanacán before setting off. Catamarans, water bikes, and kayaks can also be hired; sport-fishing is also available.

Where to Stay & Dine

Casa Mario y Antonia, Calle Palma Rubia (✆ **5228-3067;** antonia.felipe@nauta.cu). This cute blue-and-white wooden house offers three rooms and wonderful home-cooked food just 300m (984 ft.) from the Palma Rubia dock.

Hotel Cayo Levisa ★ Hotel Cayo Levisa is evolving and expanding with a new restaurant and bar in the works and the full opening of its bungalow section west of the island. Close to the lobby and restaurant are the newer junior suites and the old oceanfront (tropical) casitas, plus tropical rooms in rustic two-story buildings. Farther west (and much farther away from the sand), reached by a winding wooden walkway, are new compact tropical rooms plus some very spacious bungalows with living rooms and huge bathrooms with double showers. Thee top rooms here, however, are the smart sloped-roof junior suites, which are closer to the sea and the main restaurant, with private balconies and hammocks, alfresco showers, large interior showers, and handsome furnishings. Unfortunately the food at the hotel is abysmal.

Palma Rubia, La Palma, Pinar del Río. ✆ **48/75-6502.** www.hotelescubanacan.com. 54 units. CUC$142–CUC$169 double tropical cabanas; CUC$167–CUC$194 bungalows; CUC$147–CUC$174 junior suites. Rates include all food but no drinks. No credit cards. **Amenities:** 3 restaurants; 3 bars; shop; watersports equipment; Wi-Fi.

Another Nearby Island: Cayo Jutías

A little bit west of Cayo Levisa, you'll find similar attractions and isolated wonder at **Cayo Jutías ★**. Unlike its nearby sister, Cayo Jutías is connected to the mainland by a 8km (5-mile) *pedraplén,* or low-lying causeway. The island is a popular destination for day trips out of Pinar del Río and Viñales. Aside from the 8km (5 miles) of deserted white-sand beach, an open-air beachside restaurant serves standard *criolla* fare at reasonable prices. There's a *náutico* (nautical) center from which excursions can be arranged to **Starfish Beach**—a real highlight, with dozens of enormous starfish—and to **Isla Mégano,** among others, the latter for CUC$15 per person. You can also hike to **Playa de los Estrellas del Mar,** an isolated stretch of beach that will take you past sculpted driftwood; it takes about 2 hours each way to walk along the coastline, but beware that there is no shade and no water. You can also rent pedal boats, kayaks, *tumbonas* (beach chairs), and snorkel gear on the island.

To get to Cayo Jutías from Havana, drive the northern highway from Mariel to Bahía Honda and continue west to Santa Lucía. If you're coming from Viñales, drive north to San Vincente, then continue to San Caetano and Santa Lucía. The *pedraplén* to Cayo Jutías begins about 5km (3 miles) northwest of Santa Lucía (open daily 10am–6pm). All of the major tour agencies offer day trips to Cayo Jutías from Viñales and Pinar del Río (from CUC$15 per person).

MARÍA LA GORDA & GUANACAHABIBES NATIONAL PARK ★

306km (190 miles) SW of Havana

María la Gorda is a tiny beach and dive resort on the eastern end of the Bahía de Corrientes (Current Bay), which is formed by the long, curving Peninsula de Guanacahabibes. If you want to get away from it all, this is a good choice. The one hotel here caters almost exclusively to divers and dive groups, although it's also a good base for naturalists looking to explore the flora and fauna of the **Guanacahabibes Peninsula,** which UNESCO has declared an International Biosphere Reserve. The beach and hotel are named for a legendary Venezuelan beauty who was marooned here by pirates. María allegedly gained quite a reputation for her fleshy charms. She's long gone, but if you're looking to admire raw physical beauty, the sunsets here are some of the best in Cuba.

Essentials

GETTING THERE There is no regular **bus service** to María la Gorda. If you are coming, check with the Gaviota hotel chain, which runs the only hotel here (see "Where to Stay & Dine," below)—they can arrange transportation to and from Havana, leaving at 8am and returning at 11am, for CUC$88 per person one way (for two people; it becomes cheaper the larger the group). Trips can be arranged via Cubanacán in Vinales for CUC$41.

To get here by **car,** take the Autopista Nacional (A4) west to Pinar del Río. From Pinar del Río, it's another 94km (58 miles) to María la Gorda on the old Carretera Central, passing through the prime tobacco-growing towns of San Juan y Martinez and Isabel Rubio and then continuing on to Sandino and La Fe. There are two left turns along the route without signs, so you will need to seek directions. You'll hit the water at Bahía de Corrientes at La Bajada. The road to the left leads 14km (8¾ miles) to María la Gorda. The road to the right heads out the peninsula another 59km (37 miles) to Cabo de San Antonio.

The **Marina María la Gorda Los Morros** (✆ **48/75-0123**) is an official entry and exit port for yachts. When arriving by sea, contact the marina before entering Cuban waters (19km/12 miles offshore) on VHF channels 16 or 19, or HF channel 2760. Theoretically, a Customs and Immigration officer is on 24-hour duty, and water, electricity, and fuel can be had while tying up to the small pier here.

GETTING AROUND **Vía Rentacar** (✆/fax **48/77-8131**) has a car-rental desk here. A four-door compact car with air-conditioning will run you between CUC$55 and CUC$80 daily.

Fun On & Off the Beach

The beach right in front of the hotel quickly hits coral and rock outcroppings as soon as it meets the water. In fact, sand is at a premium here. You'd definitely be wise to bring along a pair of waterproof aquatic shoes or sandals. The best beach for sunbathing and swimming is about 1km (½ mile) southwest of the hotel near an abandoned marina.

Scuba diving ★★★ is the principal activity here—this is one of the top dive destinations in Cuba. The **Club de Buceo** (✆ **48/44-1261**) offers more than 50 dive sites within a 1-hour boat ride of the resort, and many are much, much closer in. You will see fabulous coral and sponge formations, colorful tropical fish, turtles, eels, barracuda, and rays. It costs CUC$35 per dive, with equipment running an additional CU$14. The boat goes out at 8:30am, 11am, and 3pm. Multiday dive packages are available. Snorkelers can reach some decent coral outcroppings in 3 to 7.5m (10–25 ft.) of water within 90 to 180m (295–591 ft.) of the coast.

Depending on boat availability, half-day **fishing** trips can also be arranged for between CUC$100 and CUC$350 with your own equipment only. Possible catches range from tarpon to bonefish to a variety of deepwater fish.

Aside from the watersports mentioned above, the other main attraction here is exploring the nearby **Guanacahabibes National Park ★**. The park has three trails, and you must have a guide to hike any of them. The land here is flat, a mix of lowland scrub, pine forests, and mangrove dotted with numerous little lakes and lagoons. There are quite a few endemic bird, lizard, and mammal species. This was also the last refuge of Cuba's indigenous tribes as the Spaniards completed their conquest, and several small archaeological sites have been uncovered. There's a little lighthouse, **Faro Roncali,** at the point at Cabo San Antonio, wild sandy beaches, and a park ranger station (Centro de Visitantes del Parque Nacional Guanahacabibes); ✆ **48/75-0366;** open daily 9am–5pm) at La Bajada. It costs CUC$6 to CUC$10 per person to hike the trails (starting at 9am; insect repellent required), including a multilingual guide, depending upon which trail you hike. Specialist trips for the same price can be organized for bird-watchers, spelunkers, and photographers. If you just plan on driving your car out the road to Cabo San Antonio and visiting some of the beaches here, you may be able to get away without a guide; however, as a rule, they are averse to foreigners roaming around the park unaccompanied. The road to Cabo San Antonio is bordered by vast plateaus of jagged rock called *dientes del perro* (dog's teeth), and during various crab-breeding seasons you may end up massacring thousands of non-edible red crabs crossing the road. The vegetation is wild; this is only really a trip to be made if you want to stay at the truly remote **Villa Cabo San Antonio** (www.gaviota-grupo.com; ✆/fax **48/75-7655;** CUC$70–CUC$80 double) and are a bird-watcher, diver, or fishermen. The beach is wild but not sufficiently beautiful. You can also book excursions from Villa María La Gorda (see below).

Where to Stay & Dine

Villa María La Gorda This erstwhile no-frills dive camp has undergone a couple of upgrades in the last few years. Just one cute older-style wooden bungalow on the sand, close to the dive center, remains; most of the rooms are in imposing two-story concrete blocks. The standout rooms, set back from the sand behind the reception area, are in a series of large, smart wooden cabanas built above rocks and bush and connected by a rustic wooden walkway. This spot is a favorite for huge iguanas that sun-lounge in the vicinity. Visitors should note that the beach at María La Gorda is not outstanding compared with that of other Cuban beaches, and the quality of food is limited to what's available on-site; this is really more a resort for divers.

Península de Guanacahabibes, Pinar del Río. www.gaviota-grupo.com. ✆ **48/77-8131** or 48/77-8077. 101 units. CUC$50–CUC$60 double. Rates include breakfast. Buffet lunch and dinner CUC$12 per person. CUC$5 extra for oceanview room. MC, V. **Amenities:** 2 restaurants; 2 bars; full-service dive shop; shop; Wi-Fi.

ISLA DE LA JUVENTUD

162km (101 miles) S of Havana

Isla de la Juventud hangs like an apostrophe off the southern coast of Cuba and is the largest and westernmost island in the Archipiélago de los Canarreos. Sometimes referred to as the Island of a Thousand Names, she has been named 11 times and has five popular monikers. She was called variously Siguanea, Guanaja, and Camarco by the early indigenous populations; she was later christened El Evangelista by Columbus, and Isla de Pinos (Isle of Pines) throughout most of the 19th and 20th centuries. Some even call it Treasure Island, claiming Robert Louis Stevenson used it as a model for his book of the same name. Following the Cuban Revolution, it was renamed Isla de la Juventud, or Isle of Youth, after a slew of secondary schools and colleges were built here to educate both Cuban and foreign students.

For travelers, Isla de la Juventud's primary attraction is its stellar scuba diving. Other attractions include some of the most elaborate and best-preserved indigenous cave paintings in the entire Caribbean basin and the eerie prison buildings where Fidel Castro was incarcerated.

Essentials

GETTING THERE

BY PLANE **Aerocaribbean** has two daily flights to **Rafael Cabrera Montelier Airport** (✆ **46/32-2300;** airport code GER) on Isla de la Juventud from José Martí International Airport in Havana. Fares cost CUC$41 each way. Demand is often very high, as the flights are quicker and cheaper than the ferry, so be sure to make your return reservation as far in advance as possible.

Regular public buses connect the airport and Nueva Gerona, 6.5km (4 miles) away. These are marked SERVICIO AEREO. The official fare is 1 peso, but foreigners are usually charged CUC$1. A taxi between the airport and downtown costs around CUC$5 to CUC$6.

BY BUS & FERRY Isla de la Juventud is connected to the mainland by regular ferry service between Nueva Gerona, on the island, and the town of Batabanó, on the coast 71km (44 miles) south of Havana. Several types of ferries make the trip. You'll definitely want to book one of the modern high-speed catamaran ferries. Either of these will make the trip in between 2 and 3 hours, and costs CUC$50 each way. The ferry departs Batabanó daily at 12:30pm, with return trips leaving Nueva Gerona at 11am. The company that books all of the vessels, **Empresa Viamar,** has a desk in the main Astro bus terminal in Havana (✆ **7/870-1841** or 47/588-240 in Batabanó, or 46/32-4415 in Nueva Gerona). Here, you can buy a bus-ferry combination ticket, which I highly recommend. Buses leave the terminal for Batabanó four times a day from 8am and cost $5MN (CUC$0.17). Note that sometimes the connections at the Batabanó end do not work like a fine Swiss watch. In Nueva Gerona, the ferry terminal and dock are approximately four blocks east of Calle José Martí (✆ **46/32-4415**). It is highly recommended that you buy a return ticket at the time of purchase and that you buy tickets at least a day or two in advance—schedules are subject to change and demand is high.

GETTING AROUND

Taxis are available around Nueva Gerona. Rides around town, out to the airport, or to one of the nearby beaches costs between CUC$2 and CUC$7. A trip down to the Hotel El Colony costs CUC$18 to CUC$22. Three or four daily **buses** run between Nueva Gerona and the Hotel El Colony. A full day with a driver costs from CUC$60. You can **rent a car** through **Cubacar,** Calle 32 corner of 39 (✆ **46/32-6666**); rates run from CUC$50 (for a compact vehicle with insurance). **Horse-drawn taxis** generally charge from CUC$1 to CUC$2 for short rides or between CUC$4 and CUC$6 per hour.

ORIENTATION

The main city, **Nueva Gerona,** sits near the northern tip of the island on the banks of the Río Las Casas, while the better beaches and scuba-diving locations are on the southwest and southeastern shores. The **Hotel El Colony** (see "Where to Stay & Dine," below) is located on the shores of Siguanea Bay, on the central western coast of the island. The southern third of the island is an almost entirely uninhabited area of swamp and mangrove.

VISITOR INFORMATION

Ecotur (✆ **46/32-7101**) is your best source of local information and where you should head to book a tour to the attractions listed below. Contact the helpful Sandro Labrada Batista (ecotur@iju.mintur.tur.cu).

FAST FACTS

BANKS/ATMS/EXCHANGES Nueva Gerona has several banks and a **CADECA** office (Calle José Martí, corner of Calle 20).

INTERNET/PHONE **Etecsa Telepunto** phone and Internet center at Calles 41 and 28.

POST OFFICE The **post office** is located at Calle José Martí, corner of Calle 18.

PHARMACY A 24-hour **Farmacia José Martí** is located on Calle José Martí and Calle 24.

What to See & Do

The island's most publicized attraction is the **Presidio Modelo (Model Prison; ✆ 46/32-5112),** located about 5km (3 miles) east of Nueva Gerona. The massive, five-story, circular prison blocks are dire and imposing, the remaining metal brackets whining in the silence, and even brief visits give you an idea of how uncomfortable they must have been. This is the prison where Fidel Castro and other surviving conspirators were sent following the failed Moncada raid. A small museum is located in the block where Fidel and his compadres did time, and you can even visit the Comandante's former cell, no.

3859. The museum is open Tuesday through Saturday 8am to 4pm and Sunday 8am to noon; admission is CUC$2. There's an extra CUC$5 charge for taking photos, and a CUC$15 fee for taking professional video.

If you're spending much time in downtown Nueva Gerona, you might want to stop in at the **Museo Provincial** (✆ **46/32-3791**) on the park. Housed in a circa-1830s building, the museum has a wide range of exhibits illustrating the island's history from pre-Columbian times to the modern era. It's open Tuesday to Saturday 9am to 5pm and Sunday 8am to noon. Admission is CUC$1.

Nueva Gerona's **downtown park,** the Parque Julio Antonio Mella, is a great place to hang out, with some strategically placed benches for sitting and watching the townsfolk stroll by. A pretty little colonial, mission-style church, **Nuestra Señora de los Dolores,** lies on the northern edge of the park, and the snazzy-looking Art Deco **Cine Caribe** is on the eastern edge. Beginning at the park's western edge and running north for five blocks, Calle 39, also known as **Calle José Martí,** is a pedestrian-only street. This is where most of the town's shops, restaurants, and bars are located and is the site of the town's nightlife.

South of Nueva Gerona, beyond the town of La Fe, you'll find the **Criadero de Cocodrilos,** a crocodile-breeding project. The facilities are basic but hold hundreds of these impressive reptiles, ranging in size from little tots to monstrous adults. The facility is open daily from 8am to 5pm, and the CUC$3 entrance fee will get you a brief guided tour.

On the southeastern coast of Isla de la Juventud, 59km (37 miles) from Nueva Gerona is the **Cueva de Punta del Este** ★, a small complex of caves with more than 200 ancient pictographs well preserved on its walls. This cave system has been called the Sistine Chapel of Caribbean indigenous art. The paintings are of abstract and geometric patterns and thought to have both religious and celestial significance. A pretty white-sand beach is here as well, so you can combine a visit to the caves with some beach time. There's no entrance fee to the caves, but you'll need a special permit and guide to enter this military zone; your best bet is to visit as part of an organized tour through **Ecotur** (✆ **46/32-7101**). Ecotur has also opened up a new hiking route, **La Cañada,** in the west. The forlorn American cemetery is also worth a drive by—some 1,000 U.S. farmers emigrated to La Isla in the early 1900s when the U.S. declared the island part of its possessions.

On the Beach & Under the Sea

Isla de la Juventud is one of Cuba's premier **dive destinations** ★★★. The diving here is indeed wonderful: The waters are crystal clear, with undersea walls, corals, caves, and even a few wrecks. The dive center for **Centro de Buceo Colony** (✆ **46/39-8181/8438**), the main dive operator on the island, is located at the small marina a few kilometers beyond the Hotel El Colony (see "Where to Stay & Dine," below).

Most trips head to **Punta Francés** ★★★, a national maritime park, with a stunningly beautiful stretch of sugary white sand fronting a calm and protected sea on the southwestern tip of the island. From here, many of the island's best dive sites are easily accessible. One long pier stretches out into the calm waters. On shore, a small park station has bathroom facilities and some picnic tables, plus the possibility of a fresh seafood lunch. The park station also has several hundred chaise lounges, which are spread out along the beach whenever a cruise ship pulls in for a day tour. When this happens—once or twice a week—this quiet, isolated beach becomes a swarming mass of up to 1,500 sun worshipers. When the cruise ships aren't around, you'll have the joint almost to yourself, and can go in search of pirate Leclerc's hideaway and breeding American crocodiles. Dive trips cost CUC$80 for a two-tank dive, CUC$90 including a full-equipment package, and CUC$100 with equipment and lunch included. If you stay here for any length of time, however, you are best off buying a multiday, multidive package. Day-trippers and snorkelers can take the boat ride out for CUC$33 and CUC$43 with lunch included.

Fishing can also be arranged through **Avalon** (www.avalonfishingcenter.com; ✆ **(+54) 9 261 6721577** in Argentina), which runs packages. Abundant bonefish, tarpon, and permit are among the dozens of fish species encountered here.

The most popular beaches close to Nueva Gerona are the white-sand **Playa Paraíso** and the dark-sand **Playa Bibijagua.** These beaches are 5km (3 miles) and 8km (5 miles) east of town. Oddly, the dark-sand Playa Bibijagua is the more popular spot, although neither is a prime beach destination by any standard.

Where to Stay & Dine

In addition to the hotel listed below, Nueva Gerona has many *casas particulares*. **Villa Peña,** Calle 10 no. 3710, between Calles 37 and 39, Nueva Gerona (✆ **46/32-2345**), offers clean, air-conditioned rooms from CUC$15 per room, as well as reasonably priced meals and rides around the island. **Casa Valsan**, C/43 no. 2004 between C/20 and 22 (✆ **46/32-2774;** janetfc@infomed.sld.cu), offers one central ensuite room with a terrace, as does **Casa Adys and Eduardo**, C/43 between 36 and 38 no. 3604 (first floor; ✆ **46/32-9525;** aineri@correodecuba.cu).

Paladares (private restaurants, often family-run) are few and far between. Try **El Chevere**, C/37 no. 2417 between C/24 and 26 (✆ **46/32-8326**), which offers *comida criolla* in no-frills surrounds from CUC$2.

Hotel El Colony The Colony sits on Red Beach, known for its spectacular sunsets, with most rooms set in a curved block behind the swimming pool. The choice rooms are the overly spacious casitas set close to the beach, with private terraces. Diving can be arranged at the hotel front desk—the hotel has a hotline to the dive center at the marina. The restaurant buffet is mediocre. Most folk congregate nightly in the bar to discuss diving.

Carretera Siguanea Km 42 (49km/30 miles southwest of Nueva Gerona). ✆ **46/39-8181.** reservas@colony.turisla.co.cu. 80 units. CUC$50 double with breakfast; CUC$70 with breakfast and dinner; CUC$90 breakfast, lunch and dinner. MC, V. Taxis to or from Nueva Gerona or the airport CUC$25–CUC$30; public buses make the run 3 times daily for 2 Cuban pesos. **Amenities:** 2 restaurants; 2 bars; outdoor pool; watersports equipment.

Isla de la Juventud After Dark

Start your evening with a stroll and mingle on Calle José Martí, with a lineup of local restaurants and bars. Be on the lookout for places where the local music, *sucu-sucu,* is playing. Or see if there's any live music or performance at the **Casa de la Cultura,** on Calle 24 at the corner of 37.

CAYO LARGO DEL SUR ★★★

177km (110 miles) S of Havana; 120km (75 miles) E of Isla de la Juventud

Cayo Largo del Sur—or more simply, Cayo Largo—is the second-largest island in the Archipiélago de los Canarreos, and the only other island in the chain to support any population or tourism activity. The island's primary attraction is its uninterrupted kilometers of pristine white-sand beach, perhaps the best in Cuba. The island also provides fabulous scuba-diving and snorkeling opportunities, excellent wildlife viewing, and great bonefish, tarpon, and deep-sea fishing.

Cayo Largo has a long and rich history as a stomping and fishing ground for nomadic Caribe and Siboney indigenous populations. It was also visited by Christopher Columbus on his second voyage in 1494, and used as a base and stopover point by pirates and corsairs, including Sir Francis Drake, Henry Morgan, and Jean Lafitte.

Over three-quarters of all visitors to Cayo Largo come direct on charter packages to the island, never even setting foot on mainland Cuba.

Essentials

GETTING THERE Charter flights land at the **Juan Vitalio Acuña Airport** (✆ **45/24-8141;** airport code CYO) from Canada and Europe regularly throughout the year, with greater frequency during the high season. **AeroCaribbean** (✆ **45/24-8364**) has two daily flights here from Havana. These are best booked in Havana with any of the many tour agencies (for contact information, see "Getting Around," in chapter 11) and in advance. Fares are CUC$82 and run around CUC$164 for the day tour. A taxi from the airport to any hotel on the island costs around CUC$5.

The **Marina Internacional Cayo Largo del Sur** (www.nauticamarlin.com; ✆ **45/24-8212**) is an official port of entry to Cuba. If you're arriving by sea, contact the marina before entering Cuban waters (19km/12 miles offshore) on VHF channel 16 or 19.

GETTING AROUND A shuttle periodically runs a route connecting the marina and all the major resort hotels here; fare is CUC$1. Taxis are also readily available on Cayo Largo. A ride anywhere on the island costs between CUC$2 and CUC$10. You can also rent a car or scooter from **Cubacar** (© **45/24-8245**), which has desks at most of the hotels on the island, as well as at the airport. Rates run from CUC$19 for 4 hours to CUC$27 for a full day; it's CUC$60 per day for a small jeep, including your first tank of gas and insurance.

Fun On & Off the Beach

Most visitors to Cayo Largo spend most of their time sprawled out on the 25km (16 miles) of uninterrupted white-sand beach. While the beaches fronting most of the hotels here are some of the finest to be found in the Caribbean, both **Playa Paraíso ★★★** and **Playa Sirena ★★★** on the western end of the island deserve special mention. Protected from the prevailing southeasterly trade winds, these beaches are broad expanses of some of the finest white sand to be found, fronted by calm, clear Caribbean waters of postcard-perfect blue hues. Most of the beaches here are clothing optional, and the large number of European and Canadian visitors to Cayo Largo make topless and nude sunbathing quite common. Shade can be at a premium here, so you'll want to park your towel or beach mat close to a coconut palm or under a beach umbrella or one of the thatched-roof *palapas* that are spread around. Be forewarned, however: Demand usually far exceeds supply. If you have a portable beach umbrella or shade device, I highly recommend you bring it to Cayo Largo. The marina runs a basic restaurant and grill on Playa Sirena, and you can also rent Hobie Cats and windsurfers there. Playa Paraíso is almost entirely undeveloped, with a few thatched-roof A-frame structures on the sand for shade.

Full- and half-day **boat trips,** either on large sailing catamarans or converted fishing boats, are a popular activity here. The trips usually include a stop at Cayo Iguana, a small island with a large population of endemic iguanas, as well as some snorkeling on the barrier reef. These trips often stop at a spot called the *piscina natural* (natural pool). This slightly submerged sandbar is a beautiful and protected spot for a refreshing swim. These trips cost from CUC$69 to CUC$73 per person, including lunch. The excursion to **Cayo Rico ★★★**, a blindingly beautiful spot with orange starfish and rays in the shallows, costs CUC$76 per person including a seafood lunch. The all-day Super Reef excursion costs CUC$89 and includes island visits, snorkeling, lunch, and an open bar. Most of the all-inclusive resorts on the island allow guests unlimited use of small sailboats, catamarans, and windsurfers. Right beside the marina is a small turtle breeding and protection project, **La Granja de las Tortugas.** You can visit the facility and usually see various young turtles in holding tanks or protected nests. The farm is open daily from 9am to 6pm; admission is CUC$1. Between April and September, the folks here occasionally offer nighttime trips to see nesting turtles lay eggs.

The shallow flats and mangroves all around Cayo Largo offer great **bonefishing**. Tarpon, permit, Jack Crevalle, snook, and barracuda are also plentiful. Serious fishermen should contact **Avalon** (www.cubanfishingcenters.com;

© **45/24-8245**) or the **marina** (© **45/24-8212;** nautica.marina@repgc.cls.tur.cu). With rich coral reefs, steep walls, and numerous wrecks, Cayo Largo has excellent **scuba diving** and **snorkeling,** and unlike two of the island's nearby celebrated dive spots, María la Gorda and Isla de la Juventud, you can actually stay in a very comfortable hotel here. Scuba-diving and snorkeling trips are run by the **Dive Center** at the marina (© **45/24-8214;** buceo.marina@repgc.cls.tur.cu) but can be booked by any hotel on the island. A two-tank dive trip costs CUC$80, with a full equipment package costing an additional CUC$10. Whale sharks can be seen around October and November, and it's possible to dive with dolphins at the dive site Cayo Blanco.

Where to Stay & Dine

The hotel listed below is the best choice by far on Cayo Largo, but a second good option is the other Sol Meliá property just next door, the **Sol Pelícano** (www.meliacuba.com; © **45/24-8333**), which is geared more toward families (closed June–Oct). The **Hotel Olé Playa Blanca** (© **45/24-8080)** on Cayo Largo is a nice resort that is now run by **Iberostar.**

Sol Cayo Largo ★★ Both lively and romantic, this leafy, bright, all-inclusive resort is set amid rolling dunes and limestone outcroppings bordering a stretch of Cayo Largo's fabulous Lindamar beach. The spacious rooms are in attractive blocks scattered around the grounds, done in a Cape Cod style, with a faux-distressed paint job that gives the place a lived-in feel. Rooms, painted in sea blue and accessorized in a nautical theme, are quite spacious and comfortable, with either one king- or two queen-size beds and a private balcony or terrace. I think it's worth the CUC$20 supplement for one of the 44 oceanview standard rooms. All of these are located on the second floor and come with a few added amenities, including a little nightstand CD player, stocked minibar, and—my favorite feature—an inviting, siesta-inducing, Yucatán hammock strung on the balcony. The junior suites come with a connecting sitting room and an extra TV.

The huge, long pool is anchored by a pool bar with stools in the water, a great perch from which to sip your piña colada.

Cayo Largo del Sur, Archipiélago de los Canarreos (6km/3¾ miles from the airport). www.meliacuba.com. © **45/24-8260.** 294 units. CUC$219–CUC$338 double. Rates are all-inclusive. **Amenities:** 4 restaurants; 1 snack bar; 5 bars; dance club; health club; large free-form outdoor pool, 2 lit outdoor tennis courts, nonmotorized watersports equipment; Internet.

6

VARADERO & MATANZAS PROVINCE

Matanzas is Cuba's second-largest province and the site of its principal beach destination: Varadero. An easy drive from Havana, the province is also home to the colonial-era cities of Matanzas and Cárdenas, as well as the Ciénaga de Zapata, a vast wetlands area of mangrove and swamp. The southern section of Matanzas province holds great historical and sentimental value to modern Cubans; it was here, in the Bahía de Cochinos (Bay of Pigs), that the nascent Cuban revolutionary state defeated an invasion force trained, supplied, and abetted by the United States. Today the area draws divers for the stunning clear waters and colorful coral.

MATANZAS

98km (61 miles) E of Havana; 40km (25 miles) SW of Varadero

Matanzas is a city of many names: City of Bridges, City of Rivers, and the Venice of Cuba. All refer to the fact that the city is divided by two major rivers, and connected back by a series of pedestrian, auto, and rail bridges. Thanks to its slow pace and laidback nature, Matanzas is also sometimes called Cuba's Sleeping Beauty. But the moniker the city is probably most proud of is the Athens of Cuba, a name reflecting Matanzas's important cultural tradition and history. The first *danzón,* a languid and lyrical original dance and musical form, was originally composed and played in Matanzas in 1879 by native son Miguel Faílde, and Matanzas has a rich legacy of prominent poets, writers, painters, and musicians. Today, Matanzas competes with Varadero for visitors, but this off-the-beaten-track city is well worth a stop.

Essentials

GETTING THERE

BY PLANE The nearest airport is Varadero's **Juan Gualberto Gómez International Airport** (**© 45/24-7015;** airport code VRA), located more or less midway between Varadero and Matanzas. See "Varadero," below, for more information.

BY BUS The **bus station** is located at the corner of Calzada de Esteban and Calle Terry. **Víazul** (© **45/29-1473** in Matanzas) has four buses daily for Varadero, stopping in Matanzas (2 hr.; CUC$7). From Varadero, there are five departures daily (1 hr.; CUC$6).

BY TRAIN One interesting alternative means of reaching Matanzas is the **Hershey Train ★**, a legacy of the famous chocolate company's formerly vast network of sugar plantations in Cuba. This slow-moving electric train leaves from Havana's **Casablanca Station** (© **7/862-4805**). The Hershey Train station in Matanzas is located at Calle 67, in Reparto Versalles, just north of the Río Yumurí (© **45/24-4805**). This scenic trip takes between 3 and 4 hours, making numerous stops, and costs CUC$3. There are three departures daily in each direction, leaving more or less simultaneously from each terminal station at roughly 4:39am, 12:09pm, and 4:20pm. However, the train rarely departs on time because of deteriorated service; call ahead for the schedule.

BY CAR Matanzas is connected to Havana by a modern coastal highway, the Vía Blanca, which begins as you exit the tunnel connecting La Habana Vieja with Habana del Este. It's a straight shot and scenic drive that generally takes around 90 minutes. A taxi from Varadero to Matanzas costs CUC$30; from Varadero airport, CUC$25.

GETTING AROUND

You can easily visit all the principal sites in downtown Matanzas on foot. **Taxis** are readily available and can be found gathered around the Plaza de la Vigía and Plaza de la Libertad.

ORIENTATION

Matanzas is divided into three distinct sections by the Yumurí and San Juan rivers. All let out onto the broad bay, Bahía de Matanzas. The northern section and the first you'll reach coming in on the Vía Blanca from Havana is **Reparto Versalles.** The central section, **Reparto Matanzas,** is where you'll find the city center and most of the local attractions. Heading south and out of town toward Varadero is **Pueblo Nuevo.**

FAST FACTS

BANKS/ATMS A CADECA branch is located on Jovellanes and Milanés (© **45/25-3558**).

INTERNET There's an **Etecsa** center at Calles 28 and 83 (© **45/24-3123**). Wi-Fi is available at the Hotel Velasco.

POST OFFICE The main **post office** is located at the corner on Calle 85 between Calles 288 and 290.

Exploring the Area

Matanzas has a very compact city center. Two small plazas anchor the social and cultural life of Matanzas, the **Plaza de la Vigía** and the **Plaza de la**

Libertad. Both are within 5 blocks of each other in the historic center. **Ediciones Vigía ★★,** Plaza de la Vigía (✆ **45/24-4845**), is a publishing house that fashions exquisite handcrafted, hand-painted books from recycled waste. Alongside are two art galleries.

Probably the most visited site in Matanzas is the stunning neoclassical **Teatro Sauto ★★**, on the Plaza de la Vigía (✆ **45/24-2721**). The theater, which was finished in 1863, is the design of Italian architect and artist Daniel Dal'Aglio, who also painted the beautiful frescoes that adorn the ceiling. Dance, theater, and classical music performances are still regularly held here, and it's worth checking to see if there's anything playing while you're in town. Otherwise, you may be able to take a guided tour of the theater (CUC$2 daily 9am–5pm). ***Note:*** The theater was undergoing restoration in 2015.

The other main attraction in town is the **Museo Farmacéutico ★★**, Calle 83 no. 4951, Plaza de la Libertad (✆ **45/24-3179**). Seemingly little has changed here since its founding in 1882 by the French pharmacist Ernesto Troilet. Porcelain jars of potions and elixirs are stacked high in beautiful floor-to-ceiling wood cabinets. The museum is open daily from Monday to Saturday 10am to 6pm and Sunday from 10am to 4pm; admission is CUC$3; CUC$5 camera use.

The **Sala Conciertos José White,** Calle 79 between 288 and 290, has been magnificently restored and is scheduled to reopen in late 2015 for orchestral concerts.

Out on the northern edge of the bay is the **Castillo de San Severino,** Avenida del Muelle. Built in 1734, this small fort served as a line of defense, slave-trading post, and long-standing prison. It's been restored, with a new museum of slave history, and is definitely worth a visit, if for nothing other than the great view of Matanzas Bay. The Castillo is open Tuesday through Saturday from 9:30am to 4pm and Monday and Sunday 9:30am to noon; admission is CUC$2; CUC$5 camera use.

On the outskirts of the city, you'll find the **Cuevas de Bellamar ★**, Finca La Alcancia (✆ **45/26-1683**), a cave complex of nearly 3km (1¾ miles) of galleries and passageways, with intricate stalactite and stalagmite formations, indigenous pictographs, and several underground rivers. You can tour the first kilometer or so of caves for CUC$5 per person, including a guide (camera use CUC$5). This section is lit, so no equipment or flashlights are needed. The caves are located 5km (3 miles) southeast of Matanzas, off a well-marked access road. Entrances are scheduled at 9:30am, 10:30am, 11:30am, 1:15pm, 2:15pm, 3:15pm, and 4:15pm daily.

Where to Stay & Dine

The restored **Hotel Velasco,** Plaza de la Libertad (www.hotelescubanacan.com; ✆ **45/25-3880**) is the only hotel in town. Founded in 1902, the handsomely restored hotel offers 17 rooms and a large dining hall serving up surprisingly good food (CUC$63–CUC$73 double).

A handful of *casas particulares* are congregated around the downtown center. **Hostal Alma,** Calle Milanés (C/83) 29008 between 290 and 292 (✆ **45/29-0857;** hostalalma63@gmail.com), is a lovely colonial home with well-preserved *mediopuntos* (semi-circular stained glass windows positioned above wooden doors). The most attractive spot in town for a daytime tipple or coffee is the historic **Taberna La Vigía,** Plaza de la Vigía (open 11am–11pm daily).

Paladar San Severino (✆ **45/28-1573**), in a beautiful tiled building overlooking Plaza de La Libertad, serves up good *comida criolla,* tasty seafood, pizzas, and paellas (main courses CUC$4.50–CUC$14). It's open Thursday to Tuesday noon to 10:30pm.

Bistro Kuba Bar-Café, Calle 18 9014 between 290 and 292 (✆ **5342-9865**), is a swish new bar with a monochrome palette, staging live music on weekends (open 11am–2am daily).

Matanzas After Dark

Matanzas is a quiet city with few nightlife options, with one notable exception. The younger sister to the venerable Tropicana in Havana, **Tropicana Matanzas ★**, Autopista del Sur Km 4.5 (✆ **45/26-5380**), seeks to provide the classic Tropicana cabaret experience to the thousands of tourists who come to Cuba and never venture far from Varadero. Like its famous sibling, this is a large open-air theater with extravagant performances, held here on Tuesday and Thursday nights. The artistic direction is shared between the two venues, and the show here is quite up to snuff. The 90-minute show starts around 9:30pm. After the show, you can continue the celebration by dancing the night away at the adjoining dance club.

Virtually every tour agency in Varadero can book you a night at the Tropicana Matanzas; packages include a complimentary *cuba libre* (rum and Coke cocktail). All include round-trip transportation. Tickets for the show are CUC$35. Since it's open-air, rain cancels the function. You'll get your money back on a rainout, but there are no guaranteed reservations for a makeup show.

VARADERO ★★

140km (87 miles) E of Havana; 40km (25 miles) NE of Matanzas

Varadero is Cuba's most renowned and popular beach destination. Varadero is the common name for the entire length of the Hicacos Peninsula. The peninsula, which takes its name from a local spiny cactus, is 21km (13 miles) long, with a nearly continuous broad band of fine white sand fronting a clear blue sea. Backed by mangroves and the calm waters of Cárdenas Bay, it is less than a mile at its widest point. Large resort hotels take up a large percentage of the entire length of this peninsula.

There are three distinct parts of the peninsula. The far eastern end is home to the most expensive, remote upscale resorts where the beaches are quieter. Downtown, from Calles 10 to 64, is part of Varadero town; this is dominated

HOTELS ■

Beny's House **12**
Casa de Tammy **8**
Casa García Dihigo **3**
Casa Lola **5**
Casa Menocal **4**
Ely House **6**
Hotel Los Delfines **10**
Mansión Xanadú **15**
Meliá Las Americas **16**
Meliá Marina
 Varadero **23**
Meliá Peninsula
 Varadero **21**
Meliá Varadero **17**
Paradisus Princesa
 del Mar **22**

ATTRACTIONS ●

Delfinario **19**
Marina Chapelín **18**
Marina Dársena **1**
Marina Varadero **24**
Museo Municipal
 Varadero **11**
Parque Ecológico
 Varahicacos **20**
Parque Josone **13**
Varadero Golf Club **14**

$ Bank; CADECA
Etecsa
ⓘ Information
✚ International
 Clinic

RESTAURANTS ◆

Casa de Al **2**
Paladar Nonna Tina **9**
Paladar Salsa Suárez **7**

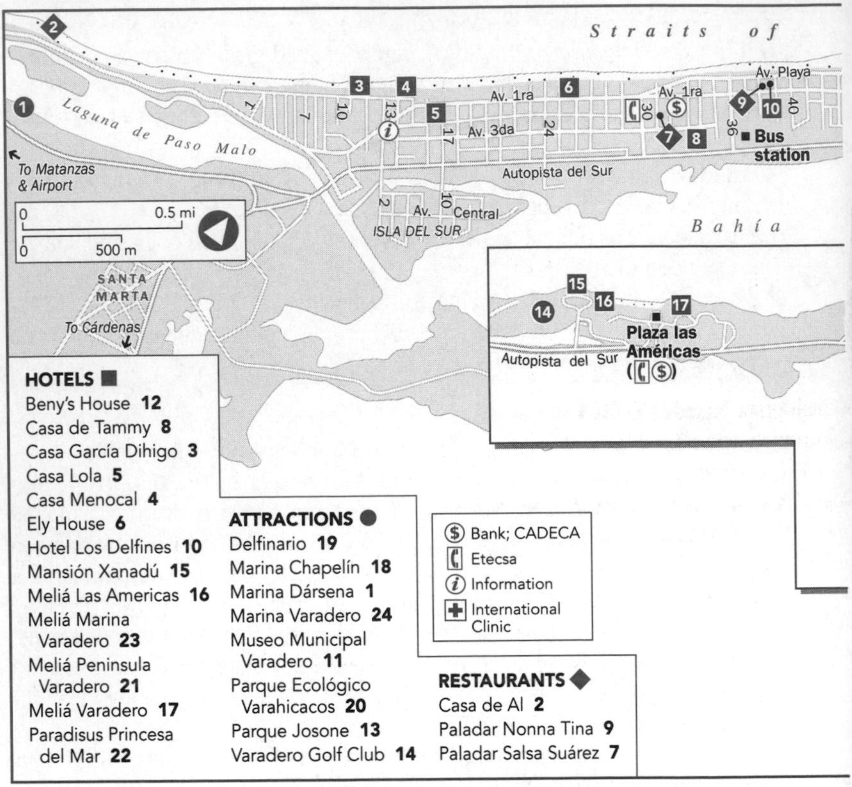

by a cluster of mostly cheaper hotels that are on and off the beach and, since 2011, a growing industry of *casas particulares*. (This is also the most popular area with the majority of Cuban visitors.) During the summer months, this beach is extremely busy. At the far western end are a handful of medium-size and moderately priced hotels; the beach here is lovely and remarkably empty even in the height of summer.

Home to indigenous populations and a base camp for itinerant Taíno and Carib fishermen, Varadero was largely ignored throughout the Spanish colonial period. While it was first developed as a summer retreat by some 10 families from Cárdenas in 1887, its real potential as a tourist destination was realized relatively late. The first hotel was built here in 1910, and U.S. industrial magnate Irénée Dupont built his Xanadú Mansion here in 1928. A small cadre of celebrities and gangsters followed, including Al Capone. Still, at the time of the Revolution, there were only three hotels in Varadero. Today, there are more than 60—and construction continues. *Note:* Examine your bills and coins carefully to make sure you are not overcharged in all shops, bars, and taxis.

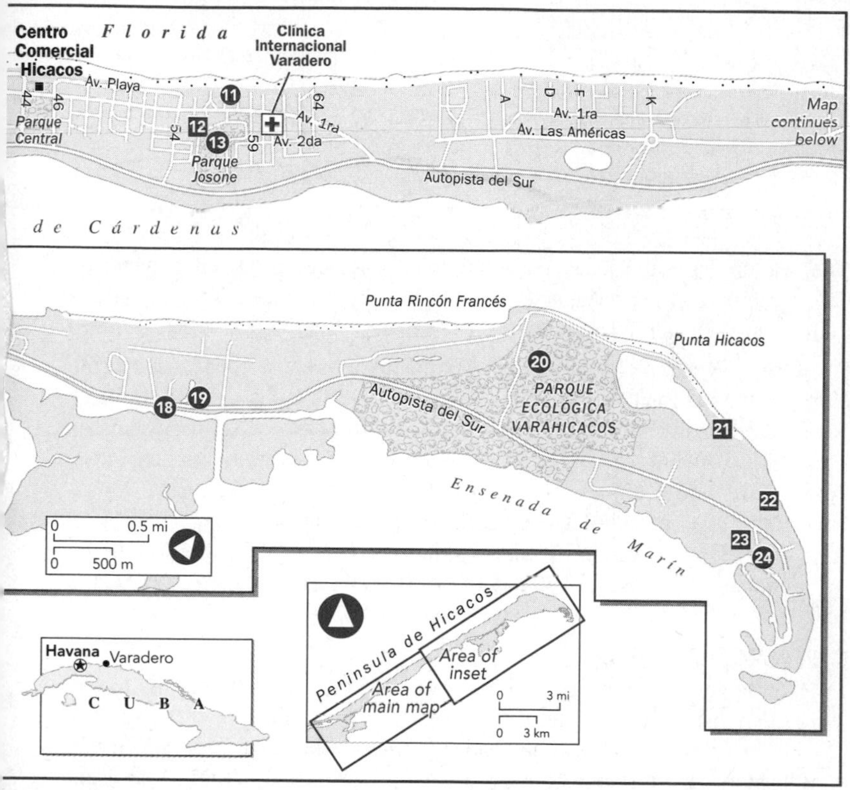

Essentials

GETTING THERE

BY PLANE The **Juan Gualberto Gómez International Airport** (✆ **45/ 24-7015;** airport code VRA) is located 18km (11 miles) west of Varadero, roughly midway between Matanzas and Varadero. Direct charter and scheduled commercial flights arrive in Varadero from Montreal, Toronto, Vancouver, Québec, Halifax, Ottawa, Cancún, Nassau, Montego Bay, and most major European hubs. A taxi between the airport and Varadero costs CUC$36. If you coincide with a Víazul departure, it will cost you CUC$6 to the bus station. **Cubana** (✆ **45/61-1823**) has an office at Av. 1 at Calle 55. **Aerocaribbean** (www.fly-aerocaribbean.com; ✆ **45/61-4723**) is based at the airport.

BY BUS **Víazul** (www.viazul.com; ✆ **45/61-4886** in Varadero) has four buses daily for Varadero (3 hr.; CUC$10). Víazul also has a twice-daily bus from Trinidad via Santa Clara (6 hr.; CUC$20). The bus from Santiago is an overnight departure (15 hr.; CUC$49). A once-daily bus heads to Vinales (CUC$22). The **bus station** is located at Calle 36 and the Autopista del Sur.

Scenic Detour

At 110m (361 ft.), the **Bacuanayagua Bridge ★** is the highest in Cuba. It spans the beautiful Yumurí Valley. Most tourist buses will stop here for a quick break and photo opportunity, and if you are driving, you'll probably want to do so as well. A rugged side road leads off the highway if you want to explore this largely undeveloped valley. The bridge is located 7km (4¼ miles) west of Matanzas, right on the Vía Blanca en route from Havana to Matanzas and Varadero

Note: Return buses to Havana make helpful stops just after the tunnel opposite Café Lucero in Old Havana, and by the University in Vedado, before heading to the Nuevo Vedado bus station.

BY CAR Varadero is connected to Havana by a modern, four-lane, coastal highway, the Vía Blanca, that begins as you exit the tunnel connecting Habana Vieja with Habana del Este. It's a straightforward, scenic drive to Matanzas. The highway then threads its way through Matanzas, generally hugging close to the coast, and continues on the final 40km (25 miles) to Varadero. About 13km (8 miles) outside of Varadero there's a tollbooth (CUC$2 per vehicle each way). The trip generally takes around 2 hours. A taxi from Havana to Varadero costs around CUC$90 to CUC$100; a taxi from Matanzas/Cárdenas costs around CUC$20.

GETTING AROUND

Taxis are plentiful in Varadero. A trip from one end of the peninsula to the other costs from CUC$15, and most trips to other places in the area cost CUC$2 to CUC$10. If by some chance you can't flag one down, or there's none hanging around your hotel, you can call **Cubataxi** (✆ **45/61-4444** or **45/61-1817**). As in Havana, open-air **Coco Taxis** are also available, however prices are exorbitant and they cost way more than a private taxi. A **horse-and-carriage ride** costs CUC$10 for a city tour.

The **VaraderoBeachTour buses** (✆ **45/66-8992**) that ply a loop from one end of Varadero to the other operate a day pass, with unlimited use of the route from 9am–8pm; it costs CUC$5 per day.

One of the best ways to get around Varadero is on a **scooter.** Rental agencies abound. Most rent modern, easy-to-use scooters for CUC$15 for 2 hours, and CUC$24 per day.

There are a host of **car-rental agencies** at the airport and around town. Virtually every hotel either has a car-rental desk, or can easily facilitate renting a car. Contact **Cubacar** (www.transturvaradero.com; ✆ **45/61-1875** or **45/66-7359**) or **Vía Rent a Car** (✆ **45/61-1080** or 45/66-8394) for more information.

VISITOR INFORMATION

Infotur has offices at Calle 13 and Av. 1 (vardirec@enet.cu; ✆ **45/66-2966**) and in the Cento Comercial Hicacos at Av. 1 between Calles 46 and 48

(✆ **45/66-7049**). **Cubatur, Cubanacán,** and **Havanatur** have offices all over Varadero and in the hotels.

FAST FACTS

BANKS/ATMS **CADECA** (✆ **45/66-7870**) is at the airport and Avenida Playa between Calles 41 and 42, and at Avenida 1 corner of Calle 59. **Banco Financiero Internacional** (✆ **45/66-7002**) is at Avenida 1 and Calle 32. The **Banco de Crédito and Comercio** (✆ **45/61-2616**), Avenida 1 (btw. Calles 35 and 36), has a Visa ATM.

INTERNET **Etecsa** has an office with Internet access (open daily) at the corner of Avenida 1 and Calle 30, in Plaza América, and in the Centro Multiservicios de Complejo Hicacos (Av 1ra y 44, Varadero) All hotels have Internet access via terminals or Wi-Fi. A few hotels offer free Wi-Fi.

MEDICAL The **Clínica Internacional Varadero,** Avenida 1 and Calle 61 (✆ **45/66-7711**), is open 24 hours for emergency and routine medical care. It also has a 24-hour pharmacy.

Exploring the Area

This is a beach destination, so aside from lying on the beach and swimming in the clear waters of the Straits of Florida, most of the attractions and activities here are either found or conducted on or under the water. The nicest spot to visit in "downtown" Varadero is the **Parque Josone,** Avenida 1 between Calles 55 and 58 (✆ **45/66-7228**), a beautifully maintained little city park with cool, shady grounds and gardens. There are paths winding around and over little lakes with fountains, several restaurants, and food stands, and the park is dotted with gazebos and park benches. The park is open daily from 9am to 11pm.

Opposite is the **Museo Municipal Varadero,** Calle 57 and Avenida de la Playa (✆ **45/61-3189**), open daily from 10am to 7pm (CUC$1). The exhibits inside are of less interest and appeal than the beautiful old building that houses the collection. The perfectly maintained blue-and-white, two-story wooden building, built by architect Leopoldo Abreus from Cienfuegos, has a gingerbread trim and red-tile roof; it is a tribute to colonial Caribbean architecture but is sadly deteriorating.

Near the Marina Chapelín, on the ocean side of the road, you'll find the **Delfinario,** Autopista Sur Km 12 (✆ **45/66-8031**). Open daily from 9:30am to 5pm, this attraction offers a 40-minute show with trained dolphins at 11am and 3:30pm. Admission is CUC$15; it's CUC$5 extra to take photos and CUC$93 for a 15-minute swimming session with the dolphins if booked through a hotel. While this place is highly touted by tour agencies, I personally find this type of attraction—and this one in particular—depressing and on the cruel side.

If you want a bird's-eye view of things, the **Centro Internacional de Paracaidismo de Varadero,** Vía Blanca Km 1.5, off a little side road across from the Marina Dársena (✆ **45/66-4115**), offers skydiving (www.skydivingvaradero.com; ✆ **45/61-1220**). Tandem parachuting costs CUC$180 per person.

The **Varadero Golf Club ★** (www.varaderogolfclub.com; ✆ **45/66-8482**) features a lovely little resort course, with plenty of water, few trees, and almost no rough. There are beautiful views of Cárdenas Bay from most holes. Greens fees run CUC$70 for a round, plus an extra CUC$30 for a cart. Club rental will cost you CUC$50. You can play a twilight round of 9 holes for CUC$48 after 4pm.

A swath of the eastern end of the peninsula is protected as the **Parque Ecológico Varahicacos (Varadero Ecological Park).** There are some gentle paths through the scrub forests here, and you can visit a series of small caves, some of which contain ancient indigenous pictographs. The park is broken up into two sections, with a small area close to the major hotel district and the larger section farther east. It's open daily from 9am to 4:30pm; admission is CUC$3.

Paradiso's **academeia arte y cultura,** Calle 1ra between 34 and 35 (✆ **45/61-2623**/61-4758; reservas@scva.artex.cu), offers classes in dance, language, and percussion for CUC$20 for 2 hours including transfers from your hotel. Art classes can be arranged, too. Salsa festival **Varadero Baila** (www.varadero baila.com) runs every February.

FUN ON & UNDER THE WATER

If you want to take out a Hobie Cat, windsurfer, paddleboat, or sea kayak, chances are your hotel will have them, either as part of your all-inclusive package or for rent.

Vardara has three main marinas: **Marina Varadero,** at the far eastern end of the Autopista del Sur (✆ **45/66-7755**); **Marina Dársena International,** at the western end of the Autopista del Sur (✆ **45/66-4115**); and **Marina Chapelín,** Autopista del Sur Km 12.5 (✆ **45/66-7550**). You can charter a sailboat or organize a fishing excursion at any of these. Or you can book activities through the tour agencies or your hotel activities desks.

FISHING The waters off Varadero provide the opportunity to go **deep-sea fishing** for marlin, sailfish, tuna, snapper, dolphin, and more. Rates are CUC$395 for a boat for up to four fisherman for 5 hours. Non-fishermen pay CUC$35. However, there are very few rich pickings for deep-sea fishing close to Varadero.

Fishing trips can also be arranged to the **Ciénaga de Zapata** area in southern Matanzas province. See "The Zapata Peninsula & Playa Girón," later in this chapter, for more details.

KITESURFING Kitesurfing has soared in popularity in Cuba and is offered through **Cubakiters** (www.cubakiters.com; ✆ **45/66-8612**). A 3-hour course costs CUC$190; equipment hire from CUC$50. Windsurfing equipment is also for hire.

SAILING Each of the marinas mentioned above offer many charter sailboat options. The most popular outfit, **Seafari ★**, Marina Varadero, has a fleet of broad and comfortable catamarans. A range of cruise options is available, from half-day and full-day cruises to floating sunset sails. Many of the sailing adventures make stops at the small, uninhabited cays off the eastern coast of the peninsula, including Cayo Blanco; these trips can include lunch on one of the cays, as well as snorkeling adventures on close-in coral reefs. Rates are CUC$36 for a half day and CUC$63 for a full day. Those that combine swimming with dolphins cost CUC$109. Many of these boats are outfitted with a bar and carry either a live band or loud, recorded dance music and are essentially booze cruises.

The popular **Boat Adventure ★**, Marina Chapelín (**© 45/66-8440**), is a 2-hour tour on small, motorized two-seater speedboats or aqua-ray Jet Skis, through the canals and mangroves backing the peninsula. A guide leads a caravan of the small craft. This tour runs four times daily; it's CUC$41 per person.

The **Jeep Safari Discover Tour (Jeep & Boat Safari; © 45/66-8000)** involves speedboating up the Rio Canimar, swimming in the Saturno Cave, snorkeling at Playa Coral, visiting Matanzas, and off-roading in Jeeps for CUC$81 (lunch is included).

SCUBA DIVING & SNORKELING Although scuba diving and snorkeling off Varadero is rarely spectacular, most of the large hotels on Varadero either have their own dive operations or can arrange scuba-diving and snorkeling trips around the area. There's an assortment of sites, including a black coral bed, various coral reefs, and wrecks. True aficionados prefer the diving found in southern Matanzas province off the coasts of Playa Larga and Playa Girón. It's about a 90-minute drive from Varadero, and all of the dive operations here offer trips to these dive spots, an especially good choice if a northern wind is blowing and the waters are rough off of Varadero. If your hotel can't arrange this for you, contact **Centro Internacional de Buceo Barracuda,** Calle 1ra (Avenida Kawama; www.nauticamarlin.com; **© 45/61-3481**), or the dive center at **Melia Marina Varadero** (**© 45/66-4121**). Dives are CUC$50, or two immersions for CUC$70 (open water courses CUC$365). There is a recompression chamber at Varadero.

One popular scuba-diving and snorkeling site worth mentioning is the **Cueva de Saturno,** located outside of Matanzas, on the road to the airport. This large cave houses a large deep *cenote* (pool) that can be explored with a mask and snorkel. The cave is open daily from 9am to 6pm; admission is CUC$5, or CUC$10 with lunch and an alcoholic drink. Most agencies and hotels can arrange a half-day trip for CUC$30 per person including snorkeling at **Playa Coral**, where squid can be seen. To really appreciate this cave experience, it pays to not go with an agency. Visit when the large tour groups have gone.

ORGANIZED TOURS

All of the tour agencies in town offer a host of guided excursions to the principal cities and attractions within striking distance of Varadero. Options include half-day tours to Matanzas or Cárdenas and day tours to Havana or Trinidad. Rates run around CUC$15 for half-day tours and from CUC$67 to CUC$90 for full-day excursions. Overnight trips vary widely. Overnight trips to Havana cost between CUC$130 and CUC$180. Your best bet for booking any of these is to check at your hotel, or contact **Cubatur,** Av. 1 at Calle 33 (✆ **45/61-4405**); **Cubanacán,** Calle 24 between Av. 1 and Avenida de la Playa (www.cubanacan.cu; ✆ **45/66-7061**); **Gaviota Tours,** Calle 56 and Avenida de la Playa (✆ **45/61-1844**); or **Havanatur,** Avenida de la Playa, between Calles 33 and 34 (✆ **45/66-7589**).

Paradiso's **academia arte y cultura,** Calle 1ra between 34 y 35 (✆ **45/61-2623/61-4758;** reservas@scva.artex.cu), also offers the interesting **Vive Kuba en familia,** which takes in a visit to Cárdenas, an eco-cultural project, a ceramics workshop with hands-on practice, a salsa class, a mojito class, fishing, and lunch (from CUC$59).

Gran Car (✆ **45/61-0555**) offers various trips, including a day trip spent tooling around Havana in a classic car (CUC$150). The trip includes a tour of La Habana Vieja, with stops at the four major plazas, as well as a visit to a cigar factory, the Plaza de la Revolución, and the Hotel Nacional. Classic car trips start at from CUC$25 to CUC$30 for 1 hour; CUC$30 to CUC$40 for a convertible classic.

Shopping

Varadero has no lack of souvenir stands, T-shirt outlets, and overpriced hotel gift shops, but quality shopping options are limited. For clothes, shoes, beach accessories, and toiletries, head to the **Centro Comercial Hicacos** (Parque del 8000 Taquillas) at Av. 1 between Calles 44 and 46. You'll find several outdoor arts and crafts markets around Varadero: **Artesanía,** Avenida 1 and Calle 12; **Plaza de los Artesanos,** Avenida 1 between Calles 46 and 47; **ARTex** at Avenida 1 and Calle 35, which offers a broad (and standard) collection of trinkets, T-shirts, musical instruments, posters, and CDs.

Taller de Cerámica Artística, Avenida 1 between Calles 59 and 60 (✆ **45/66-7829**), is a working pottery studio and factory with a broad selection of finished goods for sale. The work ranges from abstract and artistic to purely functional. You can usually watch a potter at work while shopping.

For a dense collection and variety of shops, **Plaza las Américas,** Autopista Sur Km 11 (✆ **45/66-8181**), has a modern mini-mall and convention center with clothing boutiques and T-shirt shops, along with an art gallery and a music shop thrown in. There's even a small supermarket here, and several restaurants.

If you want cigars, the best-stocked shop in Varadero is **Casa de los Tabacos,** Avenida 1 and Calle 39 (✆ **45/61-4719**). It usually has one or two rollers making fresh stogies, and there's a comfortable bar for enjoying a cigar while sipping a glass of rum or a strong espresso.

For something different, head to **Reniel's stall** at Avenida 1, corner of Calle 43, where he sells watches, pendants, jewelry, and curios.

Where to Stay

HOTELS

Most of the hotels on Varadero operate as all-inclusive resorts. Still, there are a few options for those who just want a room and breakfast and the freedom to pick and choose where to eat all other times.

Moderate

Mansión Xanadú ★ The impressive mansion of chemical magnate Irénée Dupont de Nemours sits on the only bluff in Varadero, and is now a small hotel. Reached by a beautiful sculpted precious-wood staircase, the six rooms are furnished in 1930s decor with chintzy floral bedspreads, rugs, and heavy furniture. Depending on your point of view, this could be a true retro experience or feel like sleeping in grandma's dated bedroom. Still, the location is unbeatable, and it's a chance to soak up an authentic slice of history in what is still the most luxe address in town. The mansion overlooks the beach and sits right next to the golf course, where guests at the Xanadú enjoy unlimited privileges. Guests can also use the pool at the nearby Las Américas. The Las Américas dining room servicing up international cuisines is a popular spot for a meal; the best seats are out on the veranda with those spectacular views.

Carretera Las Américas Km 8.5, Varadero. www.varaderogolfclub.com. ✆ **45/66-8482.** 6 units. CUC$66 double. Rates include breakfast, dinner, and unlimited greens fees. MC, V. **Amenities:** Restaurant; bar; room service.

Inexpensive

Since 2011, legal ***casas particulares*** have been able to operate in Varadero. Prices are a little higher than elsewhere: from around CUC$25 to CUC$40 a night. These are the casas we recommend:

Casa Menocal ★★, Calle 14 no.1 y Callejón del Mar (www.casavmenocal.com; ✆ **45-61/3164**). A beautiful old wood and Santa Marta stone house built in 1941 right on the sands of Varadero, Casa Menocal can be rented as a whole or per room. The large tiled dining room leads onto a terrace right on the sand. The standout room is the only one with sea views and a private terrace on the first floor. There are four other rooms; two share a bathroom. A great pad for a celebration with the capacity for 12 people.

Casa Lola ★, 1ra Avenida no.1602, corner of Calle 17 (www.livingcuba.com/alojamientos/casa-lola; ✆ **45/61-3383;** omarartemio@nauta.cu). This very cute house is run by Omar Mirabel and Martiza. The four ensuite rooms are compact but smart, bright, and furnished with antiques, and the dining room is all lime green and citrus yellow and adorned with the work of Cuban contemporary artists.

Beny's House, Calle 55 no.124 between 1ra and 2da Avenida (www.benyhouse.com; ✆ **45/61-1700**), is a professionally run, super-smart house with three rooms. The best room is on the ground floor, with a kitchen; the upstairs rooms are brighter, though. Beny and Lourdes helpfully lend sunbeds and umbrellas to guests for the beach. They also run **Villa Sunset**, Calle 13 no.12 between 1ra Av and Playa (facebook.com/villasunset.cu; ✆ **5239-4542;**

adrylopfer@yahoo.es), with four rooms that can be rented separately or as a whole house.

Ely House, 1ra Avenida no.2505 between Calles 25 and 26 (✆ **45/61-3421**). Elida Vázquez Llanes offers three rooms, one of which is an apartment with a small kitchen. The top room choice, though, is a cozy hideaway with its own *ranchón* in the back garden with hammocks, tables, and chairs.

Casa García Dihigo, no.1203 Camino del Mar (✆ **45/61-2369;** raisaalejandra50@gmail.com). Right on the sands of Varadero, with a terrace overlooking the sea, this casa offers five private rooms scattered about the property.

Casa de Tammy, Calle 35 no.112, between 1ra and the Autopista (✆ **45/61-1562**; tnmyp@haanatur.cu). Helpful Tammy offers one small apartment with kitchen and the use of a back patio with chairs, conveniently one block from the Víazul bus station.

ALL-INCLUSIVE RESORTS

There are literally scores of large, all-inclusive resorts in Varadero. The following are my top choices.

Note: Since so much of the market here is European, many of the large resort hotels operate either exclusively on 220-volt electricity or a combination of 110-volt and 220-volt electricity. Regardless, bring the proper adapters with you.

Expensive

Meliá Las Américas ★★ This large but compact resort sits on a beautiful curve of fine sand backed by palm trees and is just a ball's throw from Cuba's only 18-hole golf course. Las Américas boasts views of the ocean, the beach, the golf course, and the handsome Xanadú mansion. Most of the rooms are in the large main building; there are also a series of bungalows spread around the grounds. The standard rooms are done in colorful tangerine and orange tones, while the bungalows' decor is more muted. The lovely Italian restaurant has a great view overlooking the ocean.

Autopista del Sur, Carretera Las Morlas, Varadero. www.melia-lasamericas.com. ✆ **45/66-7600.** 340 units. CUC$387; CUC$477 suite. Rates are all-inclusive. MC, V. Children under 18 not allowed. Amenities: 5 restaurants; snack bar; 6 bars; 18-hole golf course; health club; Jacuzzi; free diving instruction; 4 outdoor pools; room service; sauna; tennis court; nonmotorized watersports equipment; Internet.

Meliá Varadero ★ This popular Melia hotel is centered around an atrium with hanging plants and a water feature. An alfresco bar at the back of the hotel sits on a point overlooking the lovely stretch of the beach; the swimming pool is enormous. Rooms, reached by full glass elevators beneath the atrium, are arrayed off block spokes that extend out from the lobby. Rooms are comfortable and quiet. One floor of the hotel is dedicated to adults-only Royal Service, with upgraded amenities and complimentary food and drink. The best rooms are the snazzy luxury suites with sea views and balconies. There are several a la carte restaurants, but the buffet restaurant offers a fulsome and tasty spread.

Autopista del Sur Km 9, Carretera Las Morlas. www.melia-varadero.com. ✆ **45/66-7013.** 490 units. CUC$327 double; CUC$716 Royal Service suite. Rates are all-inclusive. Children under 2 stay free in parent's room; children 3–12 stay for half-price in parent's room. MC, V. **Amenities:** 6 restaurants; snack bar; 5 bars; babysitting; bikes; children's center and programs; free dive instruction; gym; Jacuzzi; outdoor nightly show; large outdoor pool; room service; lit outdoor tennis court; nonmotorized watersports equipment; Internet & Wi-Fi (free for Royal Service rooms).

Paradisus Princesa del Mar ★★★ The new Royal Service section of this established hotel is one of the standout options in Varadero. Split between the rooms of the older Hilltop Hideaway with their hacienda-style flair and Jacuzzis on the balcony, and the large, modern bright rooms collected around a pool in the newer section, closer to the beach (and with butler service and free Wi-Fi to boot), this is luxury beach living. I prefer the newer brighter apartments, which are closer to the beach and the sleek restaurant, the Miramar. Here's the thing, too, though, the standard part of the hotel is attractive, too, with plantation styling focused around a lovely pool surrounded by white gazebos.

Autopista del Sur, Carretera Las Morlas KM 19.5. ✆ **45/66-7200.** www.paradisus-princesadelmar.com. 630 units. CUC$520 junior suite; CUC$674 Royal Service junior suite. Rates are all-inclusive. MC, V. Children under 18 not allowed. **Amenities:** 9 restaurants; snack bar; 10 bars; dance club; well-equipped health club; Jacuzzi; 3 outdoor pools; room service; sauna; spa; 3 lit outdoor tennis courts; watersports equipment; Internet (free for Royal Service rooms).

Meliá Marina Varadero This new complex needs to be considered as two parts: the hotel and the apartments. The hotel and its main pool are busy and chaotic—rather like Grand Central Station—and thus not terribly conducive to a relaxing holiday (charging extra to lie in a Balinese sunbed next to the main pool is a turnoff, too). The **apartments ★**, on the other hand, set in two sections (the most attractive being farther away from the beach and boasting their own elegant pool), merit attention. Ranging from studios to large three-bedroom apartments, these are stylish and well-equipped, with kitchens, glamorous bathrooms, huge living rooms, and balconies with sunbeds. Residents purchase their own food—including entire pork legs and tuna in the mini-supermarket on the attractive boardwalk next to the marina (readied for 1,200 yachts), which features bars, shops, a bowling alley, and the spa that unites the hotel and the apartments. The principal disadvantage of the whole complex is that sunbathers need to cross a bridge (over a road) to access the beach.

Autopista del sur y Final, Punta Hicacos. www.melia-marinavaradero.com. ✆ **45/66-7330.** 423 units. 348 apartments. CUC$248–CUC$481 double. Apartments CUC$108–CUC$348. Rates are all-inclusive for the hotel rooms. MC. V. **Amenities:** 8 restaurants; 9 bars;

Stake Your Claim

At some resorts, finding a chaise lounge under a shady *palapa* is a cutthroat endeavor. You will either have to stake out your turf early, or find a local worker who, for a small gratuity, will save you a prime spot.

1 snack bar; 5 pools (2 for children); baby club; babysitting; children's club; free dive instruction; gym; Jacuzzi; spa; tennis court; nonmotorized watersports equipment; Internet & Wi-Fi.

Meliá Península Varadero ★★★ This is my first choice for a family resort in Varadero. Spacious family rooms—some with bunk beds—are pitched around the children's pool area and playground with its castle, crocodile slide, galleon, and spouting whale, and the adjacent mini club, baby club, and the thoughtful snack bar for kids. All rooms are in very attractive Key West–style buildings. Most have two twin beds, although a small percentage have king-size beds. Families, of course, may request to stay in family rooms closer to the beach. The resort boasts 300m (985 ft.) of *playa,* so there's room for plenty of sun worshippers.

Autopista del Sur Km 17.5, Punta Hicacos. www.melia-peninsulavaradero.com. ✆ **45/66-8800.** 581 units. CUC$355 double; CUC$459 suite. Rates are all-inclusive. Children 2 and under stay free in parent's room; children 3–12 stay for half price in parent's room. MC, V. **Amenities:** 7 restaurants (1 for children); 1 snack bar; 8 bars; babysitting; children's center and programs; teenage center; disco; health club; Jacuzzi; 3 outdoor pools (2 for children); room service; gym; spa; 2 lit outdoor tennis courts; nonmotorized watersports equipment; free dive instruction; Internet & Wi-Fi.

Moderate

Hotel Los Delfines A budget hotel that sits right on the sand is becoming a bit of a rarity in Varadero as the government proceeds to demolish its stock of cheap hotels on the beach. In fact, some of Hotel los Delfines' buildings are scheduled to be taken down to comply with local environmental laws. This is a low-key resort in the town area with rooms centered around the swimming pool. The uninspiring rooms feature twin beds, floral bedspreads, and balconies and come with pool and sea views or street views. The unappealing food can be bypassed—there are plenty of great private restaurants in the vicinity.

Av. 1 btw. Calle 38 and Calle 39. www.islazul.cu. ✆ **45/66-7720.** 103 units. CUC$100–CUC$120 double, all-inclusive. MC, V. **Amenities:** 2 restaurants; 2 bars; outdoor pool; children's pool.

Where to Dine

Since most hotels in Varadero are all-inclusive, most folks take the majority of their meals at their hotels. However, you may crave some variety when faced with a week or more at one resort, even if it has several dining options.

The restaurants inside **Parque Josone** are dependable, if unspectacular, options; of these, the little lakeside Italian restaurant **Dante** (✆ **45/66-7228**) is my top choice. The cute blue-and-yellow **Ranchón Cielo-Mar,** next to the municipal museum, is a good spot for a drink with a view.

Salsa Suárez ★★ ITALIAN/INTERNATIONAL Owner Joel Suárez has created one of the top restaurants not just in Varadero but in all of Cuba in this swish place with a super-professional staff and chefs who have worked in Varadero's top restaurants. The seasonal menu changes every 2 weeks, mostly to satisfy the palate of the repeat foreign guests who work in Varadero. Salsa

Suárez's menu works across the board, from sushi to risotto to stuffed pasta and pizzas. The chef's suggestions include a delicate roasted red snapper and lobster medallions in a creamy Camembert sauce.

Calle 31 no. 103. www.salsasuarezvaradero.com. ✆ **45/61-4194.** Main courses CUC$7–CUC$20. Wed–Mon 10am–11pm.

Paladar Nonna Tina ITALIAN Run by Davide Moriggi Soa, an Italian from the north of Italy, this popular paladar cheerily offers fresh pastas and pizzas with a glass of house Chilean. Recommended is the spaghetti del Mare, infused with seafood. Reservations are recommended for dinner—the alfresco terrace has limited seating.

Calle 38 no.5 between 1ra and Playa. www.paladar-nonnatina.it. ✆ **45/61-2450**. Main courses CUC$5–CUC$11. Tues–Sun noon–11pm.

Casa de Al CRIOLLAN/SEAFOOD This is a fun place to dine as the place riffs on the legends of Al Capone, who lived here from 1928–29 and ran his bootlegging rum operations from a secret tunnel in the house. Dine in the elegant dining room on terra-cotta tiles under a blue wood ceiling, or on the terrace overlooking the sands and the sea, on the full mafia repertoire: Al Pacino's salad, Al Capone Lobster, Filet Mignon Lucky Luciano, or T-Bone Escape.

Av. Kawama. ✆ **45/66-8018.** MC and V. Main courses CUC$12–CUC$25. Daily 10am–10pm.

Varadero After Dark

Almost every hotel here has some form of nightly entertainment, usually a Broadway theater review or local cabaret-style show. These can vary from sadly comic to totally professional. Most give way to a dance party. By far the biggest and best cabaret show, the **Tropicana Matanzas ★** is located about 20 minutes away on the outskirts of Matanzas; see "Matanzas After Dark," earlier in this chapter for details. Other cabaret options include the **Mambo Club** Carretera Las Morlas Km 14 (✆ **45/66-8565;** cover CUC$10); and the **Palacio de La Rumba** at the Hotel Breezes Bella Costa, Avenida Las Américas (✆ **45/66-8210;** cover CUC$10).

The Egrem-run **Casa de la Música,** Avenida Playa between Calle 42 and 43 (www.cmusicavaradero.com or http://promociones.egrem.co.cu; ✆ **45/66-8918 ext 103**), kicks off at 10:30pm with different shows. Admission is CUC$10. It's open Tuesday to Sunday.

Perhaps my favorite place for a show is the **La Comparsita ★**, Calle 60 and Avenida 3 (✆ **45/66-7415**), which is a lovely open-air space that evokes the feel of a colonial-era courtyard. There are good sightlines from all the tables here and an excellent nightly show from 10:30pm with wide-ranging Cuban music and dance styles. Admission is CUC$3 on Thursdays and Mondays, and CUC$7 on Tuesdays, Wednesdays, Fridays, and Saturdays. The place also has a happening bar upstairs.

Cueva del Pirata, Autopista Sur Km 11 (✆ **45/66-7751**), is a midsize cave that has been converted into a popular cabaret and dance club. Lights create eerie shadows among the stalactites. From Monday to Saturday, the cabaret show begins around 10:30pm and has a pronounced Afro-Cuban emphasis. It's followed by dancing to either a live band or a DJ. Admission is CUC$10.

The **Casa Blanca bar,** atop the **Mansión Xanadú** (✆ **45/66-8482**), is a good spot for a quiet drink with a nice view.

A Side Trip to Cardenas

Located 18km (11 miles) southeast of Varadero, Cárdenas is a small, quiet city with beautiful colonial-era architecture and a timeless quality. Horse-drawn carriages and bicycles far outnumber cars on the streets here. Cárdenas is known as Cuba's "Ciudad Bandera" (Flag City), as it was here, in 1850, that the national flag was first flown. Because it's so close to Varadero, Cárdenas is popular—we'd say almost overrun—with day tours.

The city center is quite compact, and you can easily see most of the sights in a couple of hours while strolling around. Cárdenas has several small squares and parks. The diminutive **Parque Colón,** Avenida Céspedes, between Calles 8 and 9, has an important statue of Christopher Columbus dating from 1862. Fronting it is the beautiful **Catedral de la Concepción Inmaculada** ★, which is famous for its stained glass. In another main park, **Parque Echeverría,** sits the **Museo Casa Natal José Antonio Echeverría,** Calle Jenes 560, between Calzada and Coronel Verdugo (✆ **45/52-4145;** Tues–Sun 8am–5pm; admission CUC$1; CUC$5 for camera use). This beautiful old home has tributes to various independence fighters and revolutionary heroes, including the museum's namesake, a murdered revolutionary student hero who was born here in 1932. The town's main market, **Plaza Molokoff,** Calle 12 and Avenida 3, is housed in an interesting two-story, L-shaped iron building, topped with a large dome. Out by the water's edge is the **Arrechabala Rum Factory,** where the brand Havana Club was born and where present-day Varadero and Buccanero rums are made. Tours of the factory are given daily between 9am and 4pm; admission is CUC$2.

Cárdenas is the birthplace and home of Elián Gonzalez, the little boy who became the center of an international custody dispute in late 1999 when he washed up on the shores of Miami after his mother died at sea. While you're unlikely to see Elián, almost anyone in town will point out his humble home. There's always at least one guard out front. The **Museo Batalla de Ideas (Museum of the Ideological Battle)**, Calle Vives 523 at the corner of Coronel Verdugo (✆ **45/52-1056**), is housed in a beautifully restored old building and features exhibits honoring the child celebrity, alongside numerous other displays documenting Cuba's revolutionary battles. The centerpiece here is a statue of a young Cuban boy, dressed in the uniform of the Young Pioneers, tossing away a Superman doll. The museum is housed in a handsomely restored old firehouse. Admission is CUC$2 (access to the mirador CUC$1); a guided tour is CUC$2. It will cost you an additional CUC$5 to take photos and CUC$15 to take videos. It's open Monday to Saturday 9am to 6pm and Sunday 9am to 1pm.

There's regular public bus service between Varadero and Cárdenas, but it's geared primarily to commuting Cuban workers. A taxi from Varadero to Cárdenas costs from CUC$15 to CUC$20.

THE ZAPATA PENINSULA & PLAYA GIRON ★

202km (126 miles) SE of Havana; 194km (121 miles) S of Varadero

The Zapata Peninsula juts off the southern coast of Matanzas province and is surrounded by stunning colorful waters. The peninsula itself is almost entirely uninhabited; most of it is protected as part of the **Parque Nacional Ciénaga de Zapata (Zapata Swamp National Park) ★**, a haven for bird-watchers and naturalists. The eastern edge of the peninsula is defined by the Bahía de Cochinos (Bay of Pigs), the site of the failed 1961 U.S.–backed invasion of Cuba. The Bay of Pigs, and Playa Girón in particular, is a sort of national shrine to this stunning David-over-Goliath victory. Just off the shore, all along the Bay of Pigs and toward the east, the coast drops off steeply for 305km (1,000 ft.) or more, making this a true haven for scuba divers and snorkelers. The waters near Playa Girón—in rippling shades of sapphire, aquamarine, and lapis lazuli—evoke a picture-perfect postcard of paradise.

Note: Bring plenty of mosquito repellent. Since this is an area of vast swampland, mosquitoes can be fierce, particularly if there's no wind. Also pack lightweight, long-sleeved shirts and pants.

Essentials

GETTING THERE The nearest **airport** is in Varadero; see "Varadero," earlier in this chapter, for complete details. There is no dependable **public transportation** to this area, although most tour agencies in Havana and Varadero offer trips here.

The Zapata Peninsula and the beaches of Playa Larga and Playa Girón are connected to the Autopista Nacional—and each other—by a well-maintained two-lane highway. If you're coming **by car,** get off the highway at the exit for Australia and Jagüey Grande, and head south for 17km (11 miles) to Boca de Guamá. From there, it's another 13km (8 miles) to Playa Larga, and 34km (21 miles) to Playa Girón. Ask to be dropped at Jagüey Grande on the autopista by the Víazul bus, and stop in at the roadside office of the **Cubanacán** travel agency (© **45/91-3224**) at the junction inside the restaurant (open daily 8am–8pm) to arrange a local taxi or coordinate with a passing tour bus for onward transport (CUC$6). A taxi to Playa Larga is CUC$20 and to Playa Girón, CUC$30.

GETTING AROUND Public transportation is very sporadic and unreliable in this area. Most visitors either have their own rental car or come on a guided tour. **Cubacar** is based at both Playa Larga and Playa Girón (© **45/98-4126**), so if you end up here without wheels, you can easily rent some to get around. (There's a gas station at Boca de Guamá and close to Jagüey Grande.) Local taxis also can be hired at either of the hotels listed below. **Cubataxi** (© **45/98-4199**) is based at Playa Girón. The **Guamá Bus Tour** costs CUC$3 and runs between Playa Girón and Boca de Guamá, allegedly departing twice a day in each direction (departs Playa Girón at 9am and 2pm; departs Boca de Guamá at 10:30am and 3:30pm), but service is infrequent and responds to the amount of tourism in the area.

ORIENTATION Heading south from the highway, you come first to Boca de Guamá. Continuing on, the road hits the head of the bay at Playa Larga and then follows the coast, in a southeasterly direction to Playa Girón. There are small communities in both Playa Larga and Playa Girón, but aside from the resorts, restaurants, and few attractions, there's little of interest to travelers along the road. Be on the lookout for the tiny palm-studded island of Cayo Piedra, which can be seen offshore near Playa Girón—it's Fidel's favorite (and private) holiday home.

Exploring the Area

Most organized tours and independent travelers make a stop at **Boca de Guamá** (© **45/91-5551**), a contrived tourist attraction built as a re-creation of a Native American village on a series of small islands at the center of the large **Laguna del Tesoro (Treasure Lake)**. Boat tours of the lake and canals (CUC$12 for 1 hr. between 9am and 4pm) are available. On one small island in the middle of the lake, you'll be able to walk among 32 life-size figures of Taíno Indians sculpted by the late Cuban artist Rita Longa. You can also dine on crocodile meat (CUC$15) at **El Colibrí,** a decent little tourist restaurant here. You can stay at the **Guamá Hotel** (www.hotelescubanacan.com; © **45/95-9100;** CUC$56–CUC$62 double) here (hotel guests need to pay CUC$8 for the round-trip boat ride). The hotel features a series of individual circular bungalows built on stilts over the lagoons. Rooms are spartan, but the setting is pleasant and the hotel has a pool.

Battle Scars: Memorials & Machine-Gun Nests

As you walk along the beaches of Playa Girón and Playa Larga and drive the coastal road connecting them, you will notice tall concrete monuments marking the spots where a Cuban soldier died in the Bay of Pigs fighting. You may also notice many low-lying concrete machine-gun nests, with their open rears for easy entry and thin front slits for wide-angle aiming. Many of these machine-gun nests have been destroyed by hurricanes, but if you spot one, feel free to try it on for size—it makes a unique photo op.

THE bay of pigs

On April 16, 1961, an invasion force of 1,400 Cuban exiles, trained and backed by the United States, landed at several beach points along the Bay of Pigs in an ill-fated attempt to overthrow the Castro regime. They were quickly met by Cuban forces, led by Fidel Castro himself, and soon defeated. Fighting lasted less than 72 hours. Though they were entirely trained and supported—and even escorted—by the U.S. military and the CIA, the invaders were left to fight on their own. President Kennedy was reluctant to commit any direct U.S. forces to the fight. The lack of air support and several serious tactical blunders contributed to the rout. The battle took the lives of some 160 Cubans and around 120 mercenary fighters. Some 1,195 of the invading troops were captured, and most of them were released 20 months later in a bartered exchange with the U.S. government for food, medical supplies, and hospital equipment. Today, the Bay of Pigs continues to be a source of great pride to Cuba's Communist government and supporters, and an equally bitter pill for anti-Castro exiles and opponents.

At the entrance to Boca de Guamá, you'll find a roadside mini-mall of shops and a small zoo with crocodiles, *jutías* (a charming endemic Cuban tree rat), and other animals (open daily 9:30am–5pm; CUC$5). Just down the road from there, you'll find a much more authentic and formidable breeding and conservation crocodile farm: the **Criadero de Cocodrilos** (© **45/91-5656**). If you've never seen a crocodile up close, you will be awed by the size, power, and prehistoric bearing of these impressive reptiles. Admission is CUC$5 (open daily 8am–6pm) and includes a brief guided tour. A series of walkways carry you past numerous pens of around 4,000 crocs of all ages and sizes. You can't exactly pick out your dinner, but it doesn't take much imagination to figure out where all the crocodile meat is coming from—at least you know it's fresh.

If you go to Playa Girón, it's worth taking a quick tour of the little **Museo Playa Girón** (© **45/98-4122**). Two rooms inside this simple building contain a series of photos, relics, and a written history detailing the Bay of Pigs invasion and battles, as well as some local history. A 15-minute documentary video (in Spanish) is shown throughout the day, and outside you can see tanks, heavy artillery, and a U.S. plane. The museum is open daily from 8am to 5pm; admission is CUC$2 for adults. It is an additional CUC$3 for a guide, CUC$1 to see the documentary, CUC$1 to take photos, and CUC$5 to film. Unfortunately, the written explanations are in Spanish only.

Just south of Jagüey Grande is the community of Central Australia where you'll find a decommissioned sugar factory and the **Museo Memorial Comandancia de la FAR** (© **45/91-2504**). This was Fidel Castro's command post during the 1961 Bay of Pigs invasion. It's open Tuesday to Sunday 9am to 5pm, and costs CUC$1.

OUTDOOR ACTIVITIES

You'll need a permit to enter **Zapata Swamp National Park**. The park station and entrance (© **45/98-7249;** usopublico@eficz.co.cu) is located just north of Hotel Playa Larga. It is open daily from 8am to 4pm. The permit costs CUC$10 per person and a guide costs extra, depending on the length and type of excursion. Trips include **Refugio de Fauna Bermejas,** the vast shallows of **Las Salinas ★★★,** the pristine paradise that is the **Río Hatiguanico ★★★, La Turba,** and **Sendero espeleolacustre.** The state-run tour center has naturalist, birding, and fishing guides familiar with this area; English, French, German and Russian is spoken. In addition, all of the hotels and tour agencies in the area can arrange bird-watching excursions and fishing trips with local guides.

BIRD-WATCHING ★★★ The Zapata Peninsula is probably Cuba's richest bird-watching destination. Some 18 of Cuba's 25 endemic bird species can be spotted here, as well as large flocks of resident waterfowl and seasonal migrants. The Zapata wren, Zapata sparrow, and Zapata rail are just some of the endemic species. Hurricane Michelle flattened much of the forest here in 2001, making it harder to spot some species, including the bee hummingbird (the world's smallest bird), that in the past were quite common. Several trails through and around the national park are available to birders. A local guide we recommend is **Orestes Martínez Garcías** (El Chino; © **45/98-7142** or 5253-9004; chino.zapata@gmail.com), who has more than 30 years' experience as an ornithological guide; he charges a minimum of CUC$12 for 2 hours.

FISHING ★★★ Fishing for bass, trout, tilapia, tarpon, permit, bonefish, and the bizarre-looking *manjaurí* (alligator gar, a type of fish) is excellent in this area. Prime fishing sites include the saltwater flats and mangroves of **Las Salinas de Brito** on the eastern edge of the peninsula, particularly for bonefish; the **Hatiguanico River** deep within the national park, particularly for tarpon; and the lagoons of **Boca de Guamá.** Rates range from CUC$240 per day for a boat, guide, tackle, and lunch for one person; an additional fisherman costs CUC$69. Ask at your hotel or any tour agency for details.

SCUBA DIVING & SNORKELING ★★ The waters off the coast between Playa Larga and Playa Girón offer some of Cuba's best scuba diving; the area has 20 immersion points, six cenotes, and four sunken fishing boats to explore. A steep wall, rich in coral and sponges, plunges to depths of over 300m (984 ft.). There are numerous caves to explore, and visibility is typically excellent. In many cases, the drop-off is within 90 to 180m (295–591 ft.) offshore. The dive shops at both of the hotels here typically load people and gear into small buses or trucks and drive to one of numerous put-in points all along the shoreline. The dive shops will also collect guests from the *casas particulares*. Both **Hotel Playa Girón** and **Hotel Playa Larga** have full-service dive facilities on-site and offer a full menu of multiday dive packages. The **Octopus Diving Center** also operates at Playa Larga. Contact Francisco

Veulens at **Naútica** (✆ **45/98-7284**) or Ronel Almeida (✆ **45/98-4129;** micha@infomed.sld.cu) for more diving information. A one-tank dive costs CUC$25, a cenote dive costs CUC$40, and an open-water course costs CUC$365, including equipment and transport. Snorkeling, with transport, costs CUC$10 per day and CUC$3 per 1 hour.

Along the coastal road between Playa Larga and Playa Girón is the **Cueva de los Peces**, a lovely cenote where visitors can dive and snorkel. Near Playa Girón is the **Punta Perdiz,** a small beach area with some good snorkeling and a restaurant. At **Caleta Buena ★**, part of the Hotel Playa Girón, there is very good snorkeling, a dive center, and a beach with chaise lounges; wear sandals because you'll have to cross the *dientes del perro* (dog's teeth rocks) to access the water. Entrance costs CUC$15 adults and CUC7.50 for children, which includes lunch (12:30pm–3pm) and drinks (open from 10am–5pm).

Where to Stay & Dine

The no-frills hotels in this zone are best for hardcore divers, birders, and fishermen. The *casas particulares* offer more comfort and better food at better prices.

Dining is limited to the hotels, a few simple state-run roadside restaurants geared to tourists between Playa Larga and Playa Girón, the growing number of casas particulares, and paladares. The best of the state-run options is the **Cueva de los Peces,** Carretera Playa Larga a Girón Km 18, with good seafood and *criolla* cuisine.

There are a few *casas particulares* in both Playa Larga and Playa Girón. One of the best *casas particulares* in the country, with incredible food, is **Casa Luís and Marley ★★**, Carretera a Cienfuegos at Carretera a Playa Larga, Playa Girón (✆ **45/98-4258;** hostalluis@yahoo.es). Marked by cream-and-blue columns topped with lions, this is a modern *casa* with a front porch, back garden, four comfortable and well-equipped rooms, and ample parking space. The family is very friendly and offers some of the best food and service in the country; Luis also has a classic car for guided tours (recommended). **Casa Enrique Rivas Fente,** Caletón, Playa Larga (✆ **45/98-742**5; enriqueplayalarga@gmail.com), is a very professionally run *casa* with excellent home-cooked food, two rooms that share a bathroom, and a large living room. **Casa Ernesto Delgado Chirino,** Caletón, Playa Larga (✆ **45/98-7278;** ernestodccz@yahoo.es), has a small apartment with a separate entrance at the back of the house with a double and single bed and a kitchenette with fridge. There's no beach in front of this house, but you can watch the little fishing boats bobbing outside.

Hotel Playa Girón The Hotel Playa Girón has a bit more going for it than the Hotel Playa Larga, offering a dash more aesthetic appeal and a more attractive pool. The one- and two-bedroom bungalows are scattered across grassy grounds on either side of the main hotel building. The large breakwater on one section of the hotel beach does the resort no favors.

www.hotelescubanacan.com. ✆ **45/98-4110.** 141 units. CUC$52–CUC$65 double. Rates are all-inclusive. MC, V. **Amenities:** 2 restaurants; snack bar; 2 bars; bikes; dance club; outdoor pool.

Hotel Playa Larga A large, impersonal resort serving up uninspiring food, this resort lacks charm and comfort. The blue-, salmon-, and green-hued casitas are scattered across the grounds and are spartan but adequate. Some offer two bedrooms, useful for friends and family. If you are undecided about choosing between the hotel here and that at Playa Girón, the Hotel Playa Larga has a better stretch of beach.

www.hotelescubanacan.com. ✆/fax **45/98-7294.** 68 units. CUC$64–CUC$68 double. Rates include breakfast. MC, V. **Amenities:** Restaurant; snack bar; 2 bars; dive center; outdoor pool; outdoor tennis court; watersports equipment rental; Internet.

TRINIDAD & CENTRAL CUBA

7

An area rich in both historical and natural attractions, Central Cuba is home to several wonderful colonial-era cities, as well as isolated and pristine beaches. The provincial capital, Santa Clara, a lively university town, is often called Che Guevara's City and features an impressive monument and plaza dedicated to the fallen revolutionary. To the north of Santa Clara lie the small, well-preserved colonial-era city of Remedios and the stunningly beautiful beach resort destination of la Cayerías del Norte (Cayo Santa María).

Heading east from Matanzas into Cuba's central heartland, you first hit the province of **Villa Clara,** which is devoted largely to sugarcane, citrus, tobacco farming, and cattle ranching. Abutting Villa Clara to the south is **Cienfuegos** province. The city of Cienfuegos is affectionately known as *La Perla del Sur* (The Southern Pearl). This busy port city has a pretty colonial-era center and the country's second-longest seaside promenade, or Malecón. Connected to Trinidad by a fetching coastal highway, Cienfuegos is definitely worth a visit on a loop trip around the region.

The province of **Sancti Spíritus** is the only one in Cuba to count two of the original seven *villas* (towns) in Cuba among its offerings. The preserved colonial city **Trinidad,** tucked into the southwest corner of the province, is the highlight of a visit to the central section of the country. The provincial capital, **Sancti Spíritus,** isn't a great deal larger than Trinidad, and though it is more ramshackle and rough around the edges, lacking Trinidad's remarkable collection of perfectly preserved architecture, a sprinkling of colonial highlights makes it worth a visit.

SANTA CLARA ★

270km (168 miles) E of Havana

Heading east from Havana, Santa Clara marks the start of Cuba's central region. The city is strategically set atop the island's spine, right on the main highway, and is the capital of Villa Clara province. Santa Clara was founded in 1689 by settlers from Remedios looking for a site inland that would be less vulnerable to pirate attack. Today Santa Clara is home to one of Cuba's principal colleges, **Las Villas Central University,** and it played an important role in both the independence and revolutionary wars. Thanks to the latter, Santa Clara is known as Che Guevara's City. It is also home to several industrial factories, the legacy of Guevara's tenure as Minister of Industry and his special relationship with this city. In addition to being an interesting destination in its own right, Santa Clara serves as the gateway to the colonial treasure of **Remedios ★★★** and the up-and-coming beaches of **la Cayerías del Norte (the Northern Cays) ★★★**.

Essentials

GETTING THERE

BY PLANE Santa Clara's **Abel Santamaría Airport** (✆ **42/21-4402;** airport code SNU) accepts both national and international charter flights.

BY BUS **Víazul** (www.viazul.com; ✆ **42/22-2524** in Santa Clara) travels daily to Santa Clara on the Havana–Santiago de Cuba route (5 daily from Havana; CUC$18; 4 daily from Santiago; CUC$33), Varadero–Trinidad (1 daily; CUC$11); Trinidad–Varadero (1 daily; CUC$8); Holguín–Havana lines (3 daily; CUC$26); Santiago to Varadero (1 daily; CUC$22). The main **bus station** is on the western edge of town, on the Carretera Central, between Independencia and Oquiendo. Private taxis charge around CUC$3 to $4 to take you into town.

BY CAR Santa Clara sits right on the Carretera Central and lies just off the Autopista Nacional, 270km (168 miles) east of Havana, a 3½ hours' drive.

GETTING AROUND

Taxis are plentiful and inexpensive in Santa Clara. If you can't find one on the street or if your hotel can't hook you up, call **Cubataxi** (✆ **42/22-2555**) or hop on a horse and carriage or *bicitaxi* (bicycle with a carriage).

Car-rental agencies in Santa Clara include **Havanautos** (✆ **42/21-8177**), **Cubacar** (✆ **42/20-2040**), and **Rex** (✆ **42/22-2244**). **VillaCar** (✆ **42/20-1558**) at the airport. Mopeds are available from Havanautos.

AUTOPISTA scam

Many visitors to Cuba rent a car in Havana and set off looking for the Autopista A1. However, the Autopista isn't marked or easily identifiable, leading some visitors to spend hours trying to negotiate their way out of the city, making them easy targets for scam artists. Some wily Cubans flag tourist cars down (identifiable by the T-branded or white license plate) and offer to escort them to the correct turnoff. One report Frommer's received suggested that the Cubans did escort the tourists to the right exit, but then demanded CUC$40 for their troubles. Another report suggested that Cubans returned the travelers to the same (wrong) spot but still demanded CUC$20. To avoid being scammed, drive down the road you believe is the Autopista and then ask somebody if you're on the right road. If you are on the wrong road, it is easy to make a safe U-turn.

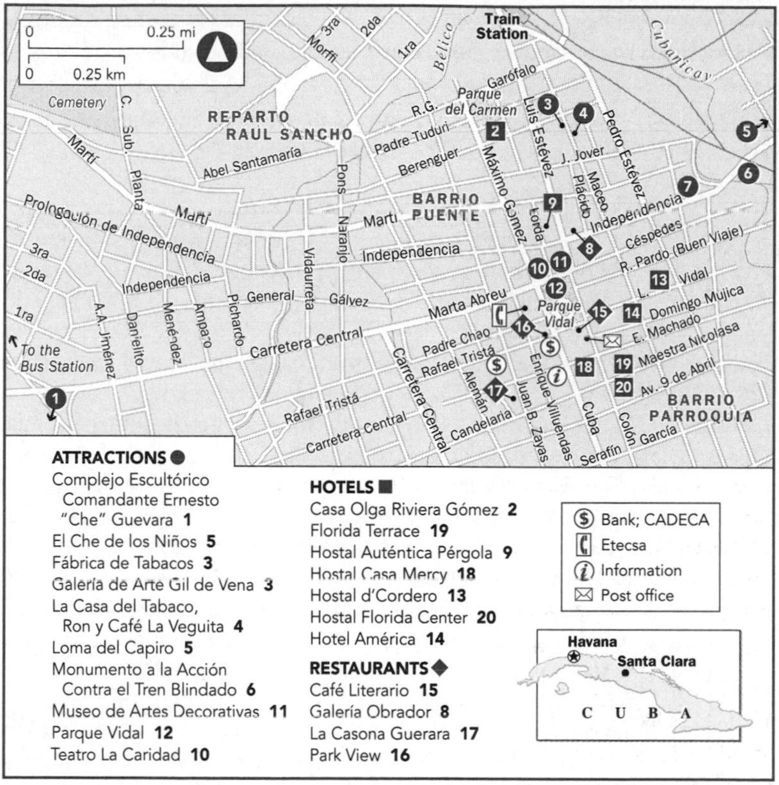

ORIENTATION

Parque Vidal, also called Plaza Mayor, is Santa Clara's center. In addition to having the greatest concentration of colonial-era buildings, most of the city's banks, businesses, and tourism operators are based within a 2-block radius of the park. The city is ringed by a beltway, or *Circunvalación.*

VISITOR INFORMATION

Infotur can be found at Calle Cuba 68 between Candelaria and E. Machado (www.villaclara.cu; ✆ **42/22-7557**). **Cubanacán,** Colón 101 corner of Maestra Nicolasa (✆ **42/20-5189**), **Cubatur,** Marta Abreu 10, between Máximo Gómez y Villuendas (✆ **42/20-8980**), **Havanatur,** Máximo Gómez between Independencia and Alfredo Barreras (✆ **42/20-4001**), and **Paradiso,** Independencia e/ L. Estevez y Plácido (✆ **42/20-1374**), can supply you with information and arrange a wide range of tour and onward-travel options.

FAST FACTS

BANKS/ATMS There are a couple of banks, ATMs, and a **CADECA** branch near the Parque Vidal.

HOSPITAL/EMERGENCIES Head to the **Hospital Arnaldo Milian (Hospital Nuevo, ✆ 42/27-0000)** on Circunvalación and Av 26 de Julio. Ring 104 for emergency.

PHARMACY **Farmacia Internacional** (**✆ 42/20-8069**), Colón 106 between 9 de Abril and M. Nicolasa.

INTERNET The ETECSA building, Martha Abreu and Villuendas and is open daily from 8:30am to 7pm. Wi-Fi is available in the Hotel America.

Exploring the Area

Santa Clara is a great town to walk around. Thanks to the university here, the city has a bit of a typical college-town vibe. The heart of the city is the central **Parque Vidal.** The double-wide streets ringing the park are often crowded with locals and lovers strolling in leisurely circles. A separate five-block-long pedestrian-only mall (the Boulevard), a block behind the **Teatro La Caridad** (**✆ 42/20-5548**), has a series of shops and restaurants aimed at CUC-spending Cubans. The active and ornate 19th-century theater, modeled after the Paris Opera, often features concerts and shows, and is worth a tour (CUC$1), offered Monday to Friday from 9am 4pm; visit the box office for the weekend schedule. Peñas are held on Thursday evenings.

The biggest attraction in town is the **Complejo Escultórico Comandante Ernesto "Che" Guevara ★**, Plaza de la Revolución Che Guevara (**✆ 42/20-5878**), which features a huge sculpture of the revolutionary hero, overlooking a vast plaza where massive gatherings and music concerts are often held. Underneath the statue is a museum with exhibits detailing the life and exploits of "El Che" and a separate mausoleum holding Guevara's remains, as well as tombstones (and some of the remains) of 37 other revolutionary fighters killed alongside Guevara in Bolivia. This place is deeply revered by most Cubans, so don't joke or take it lightly. The monument is located on the western outskirts of the city and is open Tuesday through Sunday from 9:30am to 4:30pm; no cameras, phones, video cameras or bags are allowed.

Another popular revolutionary landmark is the **Monumento a la Acción Contra el Tren Blindado (Armored Train Monument)** at Carretera Camajuani (Av de la Liberación) and the train line. It's a small park built around the spot where Che Guevara and his soldiers derailed an armored train during the critical battles for control of Santa Clara in 1958. In addition to the five cars and some sculptures, there's a tiny museum in this pleasant open-air park. The museum is open Monday to Saturday from 8:30am to 5:30pm; admission is CUC$1; camera use CUC$1. About 450 meters (1,476 feet) northeast past the monument, on Ave. de la Liberación, is **El Che de los Niños,** a bronze statue by Casto Solano located in front of the building that was once Che's barracks during the capture of Santa Clara; today this building is the seat of the Provincial Committee of the Cuban Communist Party. If you continue another 500 meters (1,640 feet) northeast and make a right turn at a gas station, you'll see signs to the **Loma del Capiro,** a group of three small peaks, where the first

THE LIFE & LEGEND OF che guevara

Perhaps no one person, not even Fidel Castro, is so clearly representative of the Latin American revolutionary movement in both image and deed as Ernesto "Che" Guevara. In broad terms, Cubans respect and fear Castro, but they love Che Guevara. Fidel gave the Revolution its brains and brawn, but Che gave it sex appeal.

Born June 14, 1928, in Rosario, Argentina, to a middle-class family, Che set off on a motorcycle trip through the Americas in 1953, having just graduated with a medical degree. (For a good glimpse into this period of his life, see the 2004 film *The Motorcycle Diaries.*) In 1954, he got caught in the crossfire of the CIA-supported overthrow of Guatemala's democratically elected leftist president Jacobo Arbénz. Exiled to Mexico in the aftermath of the coup, he met fellow exile Fidel Alejandro Castro Ruz. The two hit it off immediately, and soon, Guevara was a principal figure in the Cuban revolutionary struggle.

Despite chronic asthma and an overall weak constitution, Guevara was famous for his gritty work ethic and dogged determination. Guevara led the decisive December 1958 battles to seize Santa Clara, and was later rewarded with several high posts in the new revolutionary government, including Minister of Industry and president of the National Bank. As the story goes, Fidel Castro, in need of someone to head up the National Bank, said, "We need a good economist." Hearing him incorrectly, Guevara said, "I'm a good communist." Despite the misunderstanding, he was given the post. However, Guevara soon tired of the bureaucratic life of politics and government, and embarked on a crusade to spread the Revolution and liberate the rest of the world. A falling-out with Castro, never fully clarified, may have also been behind his renewed revolutionary wanderings.

In 1966, after a brief foray in the Congo, Guevara went to Bolivia—namesake of Simón Bolívar, an early Latin American freedom fighter and Pan-American nationalist—and began organizing a guerilla army. However, the United States military and CIA were already on his trail, and on October 8, 1967, Guevara was caught by a unit of the Bolivian army, aided by U.S. "advisors." After consultations with Washington, the injured Guevara was summarily executed in the remote highlands of Bolivia.

skirmish between Che's troops and Batista's troops took place on the December 29, 1958; there is a monument on the summit.

Santa Clara has an excellent **Fábrica de Tabacos** ★ at Calle Maceo 181 (✆ **42/20-2211**). The factory occupies a full city block and produces high-quality Montecristo, Partagas, Romeo y Julieta, Cohiba and Robaina cigars. It's open Monday through Friday from 9 to 11am and 1 to 3pm. A 20-minute guided tour costs CUC$4 per person, but the ticket can only be bought at one of the three principal tour agencies in town (see "Orientation," above). Across the street, there's a well-stocked shop, **La Casa del Tabaco, Ron y Café La Veguita**, Maceo 176-A (✆ **42/20-8952**). It is open Monday to Saturday from 9am to 7pm, Sunday 11am to 4pm.

Galería de Arte Gil de Vena, Calle Independencia no. 313 between M Gutierrez and Pedraza (mgvpallantia@yahoo.es; ✆ **42/21-6145**), is run by Mariano Gil de Vena, a Spanish writer and painter. His store is packed with colonial and 1950s-era memorabilia. He paints recycled tobacco presses and beautiful ceramic English jars with ethereal images of the Santería orishas. (daily 10am–5pm).

The **Museo de Artes Decorativas,** Parque Vidal (✆ **42/20-5368**), is in an 18th-century house whose last owner was named Clara Cartas. The house is stuffed full of Baccarat crystal and chandeliers, including a "spaghetti" chandelier. Its other unusual items include a rocking chair with a carved protruding face at its tip to stop the nanny from falling asleep and a wall plate imprinted with the image of the Crystal Palace in London. It is open Monday to Thursday 9am to 6pm, Friday and Saturday 9am to 10pm, and Sunday 9am to noon and 6 to 10pm. Admission is CUC$2.

Where to Stay

Santa Clara has scores of *casas particulares*. Most are within a block or two of either the Parque Vidal or the Plaza del Carmen. Recommended *casas particulares* include: **Hostal d' Cordero ★★**, Calle Leonicio Vidal (Gloria) 61 between Maceo y Pedro Estevez (Unión; ✆ **42/20-6456;** o_cordero@yahoo.com). A supremely handsome house owned by a 1940s senator, it has four rooms decked out in colonial furniture; breakfast is taken in the fig-tree lined patio. **Hostal Florida Center,** Calle Maestra Nicolasa (Candelaria) 56, between Colón and Maceo (✆ **42/20-8161;** angel.floridacenter@yahoo.com), a gorgeous 1876 colonial house with two rooms, is full of interesting historic furniture and blessed with a flourishing garden and a welcoming host, Angel. Angel has also opened **Florida Terrace ★**, a smart new hostel with six rooms, furnished in Art Deco accents, opposite, at no. 59 (✆ **42/22-1580;** florida.terrace@yahoo.com). **Hostal Casa Mercy,** Calle E Machado 4 (San Cristóbal) between Cuba and Colón (✆ **42/21-6941;** casamercy@gmail.com), is run by the friendly Mercedes and Omelio with two bright rooms, a terrace, a cocktail menu, good food, and a book exchange. **Casa Olga Rivera Gómez,** Calle Evangelista Yanes 20 between Máximo Gómez and Carolina Rodríguez (www.betterhostal.4t.com; ✆ **42/21-1711;** olgamar.rivera@gmail.com), is a lovely house with a roof terrace and beautiful floor tiles, fronting Plaza del Carmen and its church. **★★ Hostal & Restaurant Auténtica Pérgola,** Luis Estévez 61 between Independencia and Martí (✆ **42/20-8686;** carmenrt64@yahoo.es), is a restored 1906 colonial house with beautiful mosaic floors, large ensuite rooms, and a pergola and fountain in the plant-filled interior patio.

MODERATE

Hotel América At last Santa Clara gets a decent city-center hotel—and it boasts an attractive swimming pool surrounded by the shade of canvas umbrellas. Set back from a main thoroughfare, the America has lime-green rooms that are fairly compact, but bathrooms are generously sized. Nine rooms come with balconies facing the Coppelia ice cream parlor, but you may want to opt for an interior room (larger in size) to minimize noise. There's no elevator for the four floors—decorated with the works of local artist Juan Ramón Valdés Gómez (Yiki)—so request a lower-floor room if you have mobility issues. Nonguests can use the pool, the only one in the city center, for CUC$7 (*consumo mínimo* CUC$5).

Mujica 9 between Colón and Maceo. www.hotelescubanacan.com. ✆ **42/201585.** comercial@caneyes.vcl.tur.cu. CUC$74–CUC$81. 27 units. Rates include breakfast. MC. V. **Amenities:** Restaurant, bar, outdoor pool; Internet and Wi-Fi.

Where to Dine

Santa Clara's dining scene used to be a culinary desert, but thankfully things have improved. Stalwart **Café Literario** serves up coffee in CUP on the square; the new **Galería Obrador**, Calle Independencia 109 between Plácido y L Estévez, is a stylish café set amid the works of local artists (daily 2–10pm); and **Park View** is good for a quick sandwich in air-conditioned surrounds.

Restaurant Auténtica Pérgola ★, Calle Luis Estévez 61 between Independencia y Martí (✆ **42/20-8686**), is an elegant rooftop restaurant serving up tasty *comida criolla* (Creole food). We recommend the lamb stew (meals CUC$10–CUC$15 with starter, all the trimmings, and dessert). It's open 7am (for breakfast) until 9:30pm.

At **Hostal Florida Center** (✆ **42/20-8161**), Angel's team serves up enormous platters of delicious seafood and chicken, ropa vieja, plus salads and fruit dishes (dinners CUC$10–CUC$15). The garden is candlelit at night; stop by to reserve in advance. **La Casona Guevara**, Calle Zayas 160 e/ San Cristóbal y Candelaria (www.lacasonaguevara.com; ✆ **42/22-4279**), is another decent *comida criolla* restaurant run by Celia, who helmed one of Santa Clara's long-standing *paladares*, Sabor Latino, for years.

Santa Clara After Dark

The **Bar La Marquesina,** just off the Teatro La Caridad, is open 24 hours daily and usually draws a mix of college students, locals, and tourists; a small group plays nightly. The open-air bar **Europa,** Boulevard and L. Estévez, offers great people-watching opportunities and a shady corner spot. With an artsy bohemian vibe, **Club Mejunje ★★**, Calle Marta Abreu 12 (✆ **42/28-2572;** cover CUP$2), is probably my favorite spot, featuring regular concerts, poetry readings, trova, boleros, gay night on Saturday, and theater pieces put on in their brick-walled, open-air courtyard. Be on the lookout for local singer Roly Berrio. Next-door is the convivial **Sala Margarita Casallas** café and galería, adorned with artworks by Kcho and Zaída del Río.

A Side Trip to Remedios

Celebrating its 500th anniversary in 2015, the tiny old city of **Remedios ★★★** is considered one of Cuba's colonial highlights. It's 45km (28 miles) northeast of Santa Clara. There's not a whole lot to see in Remedios, but that's part of its charm. The small Plaza Martí sits at the colonial center of Remedios, watched over by the beautiful **Iglesia de San Juan Bautista ★★**, with its stunning baroque-style altar covered in 22-karat gold and celebrated pregnant Madonna statue (Mon–Sat 9am–noon and 2–5pm).

For several weeks at the end of each year, the quiet streets of Remedios become the site of one of Cuba's great street parties and religious carnivals, **Las Parrandas.** The infectious revelry keeps things lively throughout the holiday season. Everything culminates on Christmas Eve in an orgy of drums, floats, and fireworks. The whole thing allegedly began in 1820, when the local priest sent some altar boys out to bang on pots and pans and scare some parishioners into the midnight Advent Masses. It later evolved into a sort of battle of the bands and fireworks between two sections of the small town. Today, the festivities drag out over the weeks leading up to Christmas Eve, and have even spread into neighboring hamlets. Still, Plaza Martí in Remedios is the place to be, and the night to be there is December 24. Be prepared to stay up late, and bring some ear protection. If you're not here near year's end, pop in at the **Museo de las Parrandas,** Calle Alejandro del Río 74, where you can get an idea of the pageantry by examining the small display of photos, costumes, and floats. It's open Tuesday through Saturday from 9am to noon and 1 to 6pm and Sunday from 9am to 1pm; admission is CUC$1. And no visit to Remedios would be complete without at stop at the atmospheric **Café El Louvre ★** (✆ **42/39-5639**), set on a corner facing the town's central plaza and church.

For trips to the cayes, contact **Cubacar,** Carretera Caibarien (✆ **42/39-5555**), or your casa particular. Víazul offers a daily service (1 hr.) to and from Santa Clara that continues to the cayes (CUC$7).

In Remedios, the quaint and modest 10-room **Hotel Mascotte,** Máximo Gómez 114, between Calle Margal and Avenida del Río (✆ **42/39-5144;** www.hotelescubanacan.com; CUC$70 double), faces the small central park here. The **Hotel Barcelona**, Calle José Peña between Pastora and Antonio Maceo (www.hotelescubanacan.com; ✆ **42/39-5144**; reerva@granjita.vcl.tur.cu; CUC$70 double; Wi-Fi available), just two blocks away, is more attractive. The **Hotel El Camino del Príncipe**, facing Parque Martí, was scheduled to open at press time. ***Note:*** Hotels in Remedios charge a supplement for stays on December 23 to 25 and June 24.

You'll find various *casas particulares* within a few blocks of the central park. Of these, head first to ★ **Villa Colonial,** Calle Antonio Maceo 43 between Avenida General Carrillo and Fe de Valle (www.casa-villacolonial.com; ✆ **42/39-6274**), which has a gorgeous living room, three guest rooms, and friendly owners who serve tasty meals; the delightful **Hostal el Patio ★**, Calle José Antonio Peña 72, between Antonio Romero and Hermanos García (✆ **42/39-5220;** hostalelpatio@nauta.cu); or to **Hostal El Chalet,** Calle Brigadier González 29, between Independencia and José Antonio Peña (✆ **42/39-6538;** jorgechalet@nauta.cu), a 1950s house with Art Deco ironwork, two rooms, parking and a terrace.

La Cayeria del Norte

About 8km (5 miles) east of Remedios, you'll hit the small coastal town of Caibarién, where Virginia from **Villa Virginia,** Ciudad Pesquera 73 (✆ **42/36-3303;** virginiaspension@gmail.com), will give you a grand welcome and help with transport if necessary. Just outside of Caibarién, you'll come to the toll (CUC$2 each way) for the 50km (31-mile) *pedraplén,* or causeway, that leads out to **la Cayerías del Norte ★★★**, a small string of tiny islands, mangrove swamps, and coral reefs with some of the nicest beaches in Cuba. **AeroCaribbean** operates charter flights from the small **Aeropuerto Las Brujas** (✆ **42/35-0009**), close to the toll.

Víazul offers a daily return service from Santa Clara with stops at Remedios and all the hotels on the cayes; CUC$13. **Taxis** Junior Ramírez Alvarez (✆ 42/271615/5283-4574) and Angel (✆ 42/49-1095/53426788) are authorized to enter and collect from the cayes. A return day trip from Santa Clara is CUC$60; one-way is CUC$50. The day pass at the Villa Las Brujas, the closest resort to the mainland, costs CUC$15 (*consumo mínimo* CUC$12).

A panoramic bus circulates between the hotels on an hourly basis (CUC$1). The Melia bus circulates between the Melia Buenavista and Melia Las Dunas hourly from 10am to 11pm, stopping at the **Pueblo Las Dunas** (www.pueblolasdunas.com), which has shops, restaurants, and a bowling alley. Farther east, the **Pueblo La Estrella** (www.pueblolaestrella.com) offers additional facilities.

While the beaches here are spectacular, perhaps the premier beaches in this area are **Playa Ensenachos ★★★** and **Playa Mégano ★★★**, both on Cayo Ensenachos. The protected waters here are as crystal clear as you can imagine, and you can usually wade out a couple hundred yards without getting in much above your waist. However, these once-public beaches are now the exclusive domain of guests at the **Iberostar Ensenachos** (see "Where to Stay & Dine," below). Aside from premier beaches, the growing number of hotels (nine at the last count) offers a wide range of watersports activities, nature tours, and bird-watching outings into the mangroves here, and organized tours to Remedios, Santa Clara, and beyond. The large **Delfinario** (✆ **42/35-0655**), with shops and a restaurant (entrance CUC$5; children CUC$3), offers swimming with dolphins (CUC$69; children 7–12 CUC$40) at 9am, 11am, 3pm and a show at 10:30am and 4pm.

The **Marina Gaviota Las Brujas** (www.gaviota-grupo.com; ✆ **42/35-0013;** gaviotatourscsm@enet.cu) is next to Villa Las Brujas and offers catamaran cruises and diving. Excursions run by **Gaviota** (✆ **42/35-0670**) include the following: Crucero del Sol (catamaran adventure, snorkeling, short interaction with the dolphins; lobster lunch on beach; CUC$85–CUC$103); swimming with dolphins (CUC$79; children CUC$48); Marine Adventure (speedboating and snorkeling; CUC$39); Sancti Spíritus and Trinidad (CUC$73); Topes de Collantes overnight (CUC$99); Jeep Safari to Caibarién (CUC$70); Santa Clara & Remedios (CUC$75); deep-sea fishing (from CUC$319); sunset cruise (CUC$69); and scooter nature tour (CUC$27).

WHERE TO STAY & DINE

Expensive

Meliá Buenavista ★★★ This sumptuous Royal Service resort is one of the best in Cuba for its accommodations, aesthetics, service, and beaches.

With just 105 rooms in desert-hued buildings with wooden accents, it has an intimate feel. Rooms are smartly decorated in raspberry and white with sitting areas, terraces, and balconies, large bathrooms with walk-in closets, Jacuzzi bathtubs and an additional alfresco rain shower. Resort life focuses around the pretty pool and Balinese sunbeds with the popular pizza oven and poolside-drinks service, and the three beautiful beaches that line the resort. The main beach offers a reef for snorkeling as well as ranch umbrellas and is reached by a rustic wooden walkway. On Sunset Beach, sundowners are offered nightly to guests. The unobtrusive butler service is a big plus. The international restaurant and the a la carte breakfast service are also a draw, as is the on-site spa complex.

Cayo Santa María. www.meliacuba.com. ✆ **42/35-0700.** 105 units. Royal Service CUC$359–CUC$708 double all-inclusive. **Amenities:** 3 restaurants; 3 bars; Jacuzzi; spa; outdoor tennis court; Wi-Fi.

Iberostar Ensenachos ★ This beautiful resort is laid out in handsome gardens with fine rooms and straddles two stunningly beautiful beaches: Playa Ensenachos and Playa Mégano. It's a shame, therefore, that the hotel has major service issues when it comes to restaurant service, bellboy service, and attending to in-room glitches. The hotel is divided into three parts: East Spa, West Park, and Grand Village. The first two sections are closest to the main hotel facilities. East Spa radiates around the spa, pretty gardens with plentiful birdlife, and an attractive pool, while West Park is closer to the beautiful curve of Playa Mégano and centered around a family-friendly pool and a large kids' pool with an aquatic park. The Grand Village is isolated on the long, slender Playa Ensanachos, with grounds so extensive that a buggy service is needed to get around. Rooms here are elegant in olive greens and navy blues with balconies and marble bathrooms, and the food is quite good, with many choices. There is much to appreciate here; here's hoping the service issues get the attention they need.

Cayo Ensenachos. www.iberostar.com. ✆ **42/35-0300.** 506 units. East Spa: CUC$214–CUC$352 double. West Park: CUC$214–CUC$302 double. Grand Village: CUC$361. Rates are all-inclusive. MC, V. **Amenities:** 8 restaurants; 3 snack bars; 6 bars; bikes; fitness center; 2 Jacuzzis; 4 outdoor pools; Kids' Club; room service; smoke-free rooms; spa; 2 outdoor tennis courts; theater; extensive nonmotorized watersports equipment (snorkel equipment not available); Wi-Fi.

Moderate

Villa Las Brujas ★ This is one of the few hotels in Cuba with a boutique beach feel that sits close to the beach. Wooden duplex villas perched on a rocky outcrop overlooking the Caribbean are connected by an attractive, rustic wooden walkway through plants and bushes. All rooms have two beds, a balcony, and a bathtub. You'll want the first-floor rooms; rooms 22, 23, and 24 have access to their own little *playita* (beach) and the marina. The hotel is due for an upgrade and a small Jacuzzi area will be replaced with a pool. At the eastern end of the hotel is a stretch of isolated white-sand beach; at its farthest end, two hotels will be built. Unfortunately, the attractive ranchón restaurant

El Farallón, destroyed by a fire, was replaced by a glass box that serves respectable *criolla* fare and fresh seafood. Staff members are very friendly.

Cayo Las Brujas. www.gaviota-grupo.com. ✆ **42/35-0199.** reservas@villla.lasbrujas.co.cu. 24 units. CUC$84–CUC$95 double sea view; CUC$79–CUC$89 double garden view. MC, V. **Amenities:** Restaurant; bar; 2 outdoor Jacuzzis; Wi-Fi.

CIENFUEGOS ★

256km (159 miles) SE of Havana; 67km (42 miles) S of Santa Clara

Known as *La Perla del Sur* (the Southern Pearl), Cienfuegos is an uncharacteristically calm and inviting port city. Although Columbus visited the deep and protected harbor here on his second voyage, and the Spanish built the Castillo de Jagua in 1745, it wasn't until a group of French colonists settled here in 1819 that Cienfuegos began to grow and develop. The French influence continued through most of the city's history, particularly in the 19th century, when Cienfuegos became a major shipping point for sugar, tobacco, and coffee. As trade with the United States increased, Cienfuegos lost some of its strategic importance to the northern ports of Havana and Matanzas.

Nevertheless, today Cienfuegos remains a busy port, with an assortment of heavy industry and important sugar-producing plantations surrounding it. Yes, the industrial smokestacks, high-tension electrical towers, and abandoned nuclear plant significantly mar the landscape. But the historic center, a UNESCO World Heritage Site since 2005, the beautiful bay and harborfront buildings, the charming wooden homes of Punta Gorda, and the Malecón make it a wonderful city to explore and enjoy.

Essentials

GETTING THERE

BY PLANE Only international flights from Miami and Canada use the small **Jaime González International Airport** (✆ **43/55-2047;** airport code CFG), located 5km (3 miles) northeast of downtown. A taxi from the airport to downtown costs CUC$6.

BY BUS **Víazul** (✆ **43/51-8114** in Cienfuegos at the bus station; Calle 49 between Av 56 and 58; www.viazul.com) has three daily buses to Cienfuegos. Buses return to Havana twice daily. The fare is CUC$20. From Cienfuegos to Trinidad, the fare is just CUC$6, and the ride (six daily) takes around 1½ hours. From Trinidad to Cienfuegos, there are three buses daily. Cienfuegos is also on two other routes from Varadero and Santa Clara.

BY CAR From Havana, take the Autopista Nacional east. (See "Autopista Scam," earlier in this chapter.) Of the several possible turnoffs for Cienfuegos, the first and most popular is at **Aguada de Pasajeros.** This route is marked (at km 170, there is a gas station and cafe) and will bring you through the towns of Rodas and Abreus, before leading you into Cienfuegos. If you continue farther on the Autopista Nacional, your next turnoff will be at Cartagena (km 230). If you are coming from Santa Clara, you can take the turnoff at Ranchuelo (km 255), which is a straight shot into Cienfuegos, passing through the attractive center of Palmira). The trip should take 3½ to 4 hours from Havana.

GETTING AROUND

Taxis are readily available around Cienfuegos. Most rides will cost between CUC$1 and CUC$3. If you can't find one, call **Cubataxi** (✆ **43/51-8454**). Tourists are technically not supposed to use the common **horse-drawn taxis** (they aren't licensed to carry foreigners), though some drivers will let you ride but will only accept CUC$1 or CUC$2. There are also plenty of **bicycle-powered cabs** around town. Car-rental agencies in Cienfuegos include **Havanautos,** Calle 37 at the corner of Avenida 18, Punta Gorda (✆ **43/55-1211**), and **Cubacar** at the Hotel Jagua (✆ **43/55-2014**) and at the Trade Center, Av 50 between Calles 35 and 37 (✆ **43/55-2166**).

ORIENTATION

The two main areas you should concentrate on in Cienfuegos are: the **historic center**, which contains the city's central park, Parque José Martí, and other historic buildings; and **Reparto Punta Gorda,** a slightly newer section that heads out on a narrow strip to the southern point of the city, where you'll find the Hotel Jagua and the Palacio del Valle. Calle 37, or Prado, is the main north-south street and runs all the way to the tip of Punta Gorda. For a long stretch, it runs along the seafront, earning it the moniker the "Malecón" (boardwalk). It is bisected by Avenida 54, an east-west street, also called the "Bulevar," which is pedestrian-only for several blocks between the Parque José Martí and Prado.

VISITOR INFORMATION

The principal tour agencies in town are **Cubanacán,** with two locations on Calle 39 between Avenidas 54 and 56 (✆ **43/55-1242**); and **Havanatur,** Av. 54 between Calles 29 and 31 (✆ **43/55-1639**).

FAST FACTS

BANKS/ATMS There's a **Banco Financiero Internacional** at the corner of the Bulevar and Calle 29 (✆ **43/55-1625**), and the Banco Popular de Ahorro, Avenidas 54 and 33, which has two ATMs; there's a **CADECA** branch on Av. 56 between Calless 37 and 39 (✆ **43/55-2164**).

PHARMACY The **Clínica Internacional,** Av 10 between Calle 37 no. 202, between Avenidas 2 and 0, Punta Gorda (✆ **43/55-1622**), is a small, modern facility that can handle most emergencies and medical needs and has a 24-hour pharmacy.

POST OFFICE The **post office** (✆ **43/51-5622**) is located at Av. 56 between Calles 37 and 35.

INTERNET An **Etecsa** office at Calle 31 between the Bulevar and Av. 56 (✆ **43/51-3046**) has Internet access.

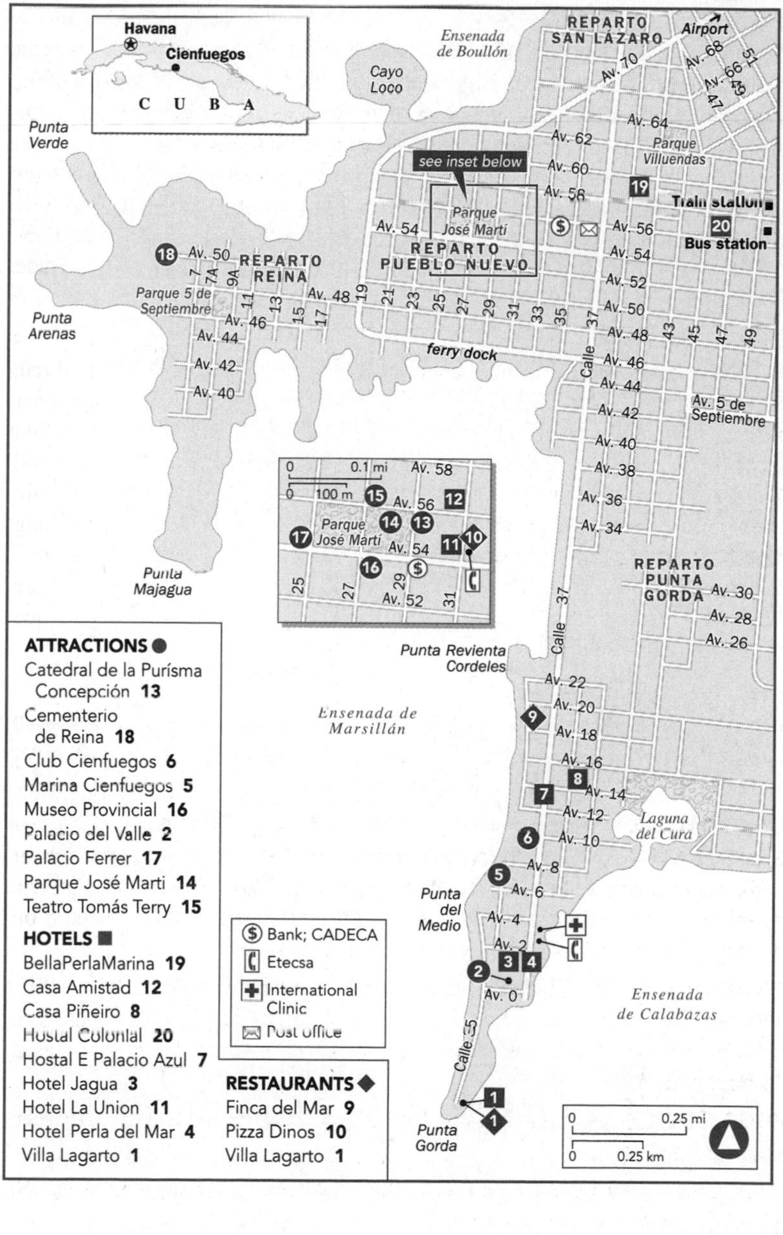
Havana
Cienfuegos
CUBA
Punta Verde
Ensenada de Boullón
Cayo Loco
REPARTO SAN LÁZARO
Airport
Av. 70
Av. 68
Av. 66
Av. 64
Av. 62
Av. 60
Av. 58
Av. 56
Av. 54
Av. 52
Av. 50
Av. 48
Av. 46
Av. 44
Av. 42
Av. 40
Av. 38
Av. 36
Av. 34
Av. 30
Av. 28
Av. 26
Av. 22
Av. 20
Av. 18
Av. 16
Av. 14
Av. 12
Av. 10
Av. 8
Av. 6
Av. 4
Av. 2
Av. 0
Parque Villuendas
see inset below
Parque José Martí
Train station
Bus station
REPARTO PUEBLO NUEVO
REPARTO REINA
Parque 5 de Septiembre
Punta Arenas
ferry dock
Calle 37
Av. 5 de Septiembre
Punta Majagua
REPARTO PUNTA GORDA
Punta Revienta Cordeles
Ensenada de Marsillán
Laguna del Cura
Punta del Medio
Ensenada de Calabazas
Calle 35
Punta Gorda
0 0.1 mi
0 100 m
0 0.25 mi
0 0.25 km
Bank; CADECA
Etecsa
International Clinic
Post office
ATTRACTIONS
Catedral de la Purísma Concepción 13
Cementerio de Reina 18
Club Cienfuegos 6
Marina Cienfuegos 5
Museo Provincial 16
Palacio del Valle 2
Palacio Ferrer 17
Parque José Marti 14
Teatro Tomás Terry 15
HOTELS
BellaPerlaMarina 19
Casa Amistad 12
Casa Piñeiro 8
Hostal Colonial 20
Hostal E Palacio Azul 7
Hotel Jagua 3
Hotel La Union 11
Hotel Perla del Mar 4
Villa Lagarto 1
RESTAURANTS
Finca del Mar 9
Pizza Dinos 10
Villa Lagarto 1

Exploring the Area

IN TOWN

The **Parque José Martí,** formerly the Plaza de Armas, is the historic center's hub. It's a broad city park with a bandstand at its center and a little Arco de Triunfo (Arc of Triumph) dating from 1902 at its western end. Surrounding the park, you'll find Cienfuegos' most interesting historical buildings. The stylish 1918 **Palacio Ferrer** (**© 43/51-6584**), on one corner here, is the city's Casa de la Cultura. This is a good place to find out if any interesting art exhibits or concerts are going on while you're in town. You should also check out the view of the city from the rooftop cupola here; admission is CUC$0.50. On the eastern end of the park, you'll find the **Catedral de la Purísima Concepción,** a beautiful neoclassical church finished in 1870. The church features wonderful stained-glass work imported from France (open daily 8am–3pm). On the north side of the park is the **Teatro Tomás Terry ★** (**© 43/51-3361;** www.azurina.cult.cu). Inaugurated in 1890, the theater has been wonderfully maintained and has been declared a national monument; stars such as Enrico Caruso, Sarah Bernhardt, and Anna Pavlova performed here. Check to see if there will be any performances while you're in town (CUC$5–CUC$10); if not, you can tour the facility during the day. Admission is CUC$2 and includes a quick, guided tour. Across the park, on its south side, is the small **Museo Provincial,** which is only of interest to die-hard museum and local-history buffs.

Out on the end of Punta Gorda, past the Malecón, is the historic old **Palacio del Valle ★★** (**© 43/55-1003 ext. 830**), an eclectic architectural masterpiece, which covers vast stylistic ground in its compact floor plan. The centerpiece here is the Salón Comedor (dining room), which dates to 1917 and tries to imitate the intricate Moorish stucco and tilework of Spain's Alhambra. Other rooms are done variously in baroque, neoclassical, and Gothic styling. The whole thing operates as a restaurant, with a wonderful third-floor rooftop balcony bar and lookout, not to mention a basement tapas bar and wine cellar.

At the very tip of Punta Gorda, there's now **La Punta,** with a small garden, snack bar, and bar open late serving wonderful strong mojitos (open daily 9am–10pm).

Cienfuegos has two picturesque cemeteries, featuring elaborate marble headstones, mausoleums, and aboveground burial crypts. The **Cementerio de Reina ★** is the older of the two and located on the western extreme edge of the city beyond the downtown center (open daily 8am–6:45pm). The **Cementerio Tomás Acea** is in an eastern suburb of the city and features an elaborate entrance modeled after the Parthenon in Greece.

One of the highlights of visiting Cienfuegos is the chance to hear the outstanding local **Cienfuegos Choir ★★★**. Organize in advance (72 hrs.) with **Paradiso,** Av. 54 e/33 y 35 (**© 43/51-1879**/5287/5336; Luisa Fernandez Jiménez: paradiso@sccfg.artex.cu). For groups of from five to nine people, the cost is CUC$48 per person. Paradiso also organizes dance classes and an Afro-Cuban ritual in the interesting town of Palmira.

ON THE OUTSKIRTS OF TOWN

Popular tours from Cienfuegos include visits to the **Castillo de Jagua (© 43/96-5402;** open Tues–Sat 9am–5pm, Sun 9am–1pm; admission CUC$1), which is located on the western flank of the narrow entrance to the harbor. Built between 1738 and 1745, the little fort sits on a hill above the quaint fishing village of Perché. Although the moat is dry, you still enter the castle by crossing the wooden drawbridge. Inside are some basic museum-like exhibits. You reach the castle by driving to the Hotel Pasacaballos, then parking and taking the little ferry across; the cost one-way is CUC$1. More convenient is the thrice-daily ferry from the dock at Avenida 46 between calles 23 and 25. It departs at 8am, 1pm, and 5:30pm, and returns at 6:30am, 10am, and 3pm; cost is CUC$0.50.

The **Jardín Botánico Soledad ★**, Calle Central 136, Pepito Tey, Cienfuegos (**© 43/54-5334**), was begun by U.S. sugar magnate Edwin Atkins in 1904, and taken over by Harvard University in 1919. With more than 2,000 species of plants covering some 90 hectares (222 acres), it is the largest and most extensive botanical garden in Cuba. The grounds are beautiful to walk around, and the birdwatching is usually good. It's worth picking up one of the excellent guides (Hilda Rangel, for example) at the entrance, as there are no markers. The gardens are 17km (11 miles) east of downtown, via the road to Trinidad. The garden is open daily from 8am to 5pm; admission is CUC$2.50.

Opposite the entrance to the gardens is the old sugar mill town of **Pepito Tey**. It's an interesting diversion for history buffs, with a small museum. Contact guide and resident Nancy Robaina (**© 43/54-5168**).

Farther away is **El Nicho ★**, in the Escambray mountains, a series of waterfalls (some up to 50 ft. high), from which you can plunge into a natural pool; the scenery is lovely, and there's a restaurant onsite. Agencies organize trips for CUC$30, although you can arrange private transport through local casas that works out cheaper.

ON & BELOW THE WATER

While Cienfuegos sits on a large and beautiful protected bay, the best (and really the only) beach is 17km (11 miles) away at **Playa Rancho Luna.** The beach here is a long expanse of white sand, although the sand isn't quite as fine and silky as that found at some of Cuba's more famous beaches. You can book scuba-diving trips out of the **Faro Luna Diving Center** (**© 43/54-8040;** buceocom@nautica.cfg.cyt.cu) or with the **Whale Shark Diving Center** at Hotel Rancho Luna (**© 43/54-8020**) or book through Cubanacán in town.

Marina Cienfuegos, Calle 35 between Avenidas 6 and 8, Punta Gorda (www.nauticamarlin.com; **© 43/51-2891**), is your one-stop shop for all nautical needs. Here you can charter a sailboat or sportfishing excursion, book a cruise around the harbor, rent a Hobie Cat or windsurfer, and go fishing and diving. Contact **Blue Sail Alboran** (www.bluesail-caribe.com), **Platten Sail** (www.platten-sailing.de), or **Dream Yacht Charters** (www.dreamyacht charter.com). The elegant 1920s-built **Club Cienfuegos** entertainment

Benny Moré: The Rhythm Barbarian

Maximiliano Bartolomé Moré, better known as Benny Moré and perhaps most descriptively dubbed "El Bárbaro del Ritmo" (The Rhythm Barbarian), is Cienfuegos' pride and joy. Born in the nearby hamlet of Santa Isabel de las Lajas on August 24, 1919, Moré was probably the greatest Cuban singer and bandleader of his time. He sang and composed in a variety of genres, from mambo to *son* to cha-cha-chá. Tall and thin, with a velvet-smooth voice, Moré was the epitome of the debonair Cuban bandleader of the '40s and '50s. Although he never enjoyed the overseas success of Xavier Cugat or Pérez Prado, in Cuba, Benny Moré is considered the king. His life and voice were immortalized in the 2006 movie "El Benny," and his bronze statue stands on Cienfuegos' main thoroughfare, Prado. The Festival Internacional de Benny Moré is held in November.

complex, Calle 37 between Avenidas 8 and 12 (✆ **43/51-2891;** contacto.club@cienf.palmares.cu), has an attractive pool and a barbecue (Tues–Sun CUC$10; consumo mínimo CUC$7), a small park with rides for children, an attractive bar with views, and a small patch of sand with a little swimming area in front of it; some locals and tourists use it as a place to sunbathe and cool off. Several international regattas, fishing tournaments, and speedboat races are held in Cienfuegos each year.

Shopping

The best arts and crafts shop in town is the **Galería Maroya,** on Av. 54 no. 2506 between Calles 25 and 27, located on the southern flank of the Parque José Martí. There's an excellent cigar shop, **Casa del Habano El Embajador,** at Av. 54 between Calles 33 and 35. An **ARTex** shop on the Bulevar (Av. 54 btw. Calles 35 and 37) stocks a selection of typical souvenirs, and it usually has a good selection of CDs, including some by Benny Moré. Much more interesting is the **Galería Trazos Libres,** Av. 62 no. 4523 between Calles 45 and 47 (✆ **43/51-5173;** santiagom@nauta.cu), a private house featuring works by painter and engraver Santiago Hermes. Another studio worth stopping into is **Galeria-Estudio Vladimir Rodríguez**, Av 56 between Calles 25 and 27 (www.vladimirodriguezvisual.blogspot.com; ✆ **43/59-8094**), for his ceramic skull work. Designer Lourdes Trigo has opened up a clothes shop on the boulevard: **Arte Moda**, Av. 54 between Calles 35 and 37 (✆ **43/51-4494;** lourdestrigo@azurina.cult.cu); it's open Monday through Saturday 9am to 5pm, Sunday noon to 1pm. Look for daily handicraft stalls along Avenida 28 leading south of the main park.

Where to Stay

IN CIENFUEGOS

Hotel La Unión ★ The most attractive hotel in Cienfuegos, this pastel-green 1869 colonial mansion lies in the heart of town and boasts a lovely swimming pool in a pretty, secluded patio with an adjacent, convivial bar. The standard rooms are small, so the upgrade to the junior suites is a worthwhile investment with their burnt-orange thread themes, desks, and paintings of Cuba on the walls. Marble bathrooms feature rain showers and bathtubs. The signature suites are not worth the upgrade; the accessories are horribly dated.

Calle 31 (corner of Av. 54), Cienfuegos. www.gran-caribe.cu. ✆ **43/55-1020.** reserva@union.cfg.tur.cu. 49 units. CUC$110–CUC$143 double; CUC$145–CUC$180 junior suite; CUC$155–CUC$190 signature suite. MC, V. **Amenities:** Restaurant; snack bar; 2 bars; small exercise room; Jacuzzi; outdoor pool; sauna; Internet.

Hotel Jagua & Hotel Perla del Mar ★ This enormous 1950s hotel at the end of Punta Gorda is notable for its views and large pool. Rooms, however, are basic and lackluster (although the views are outstanding), and the food is desultory. (The exception to this is the full pork roast in the Los Laureles garden beside the Palacio del Valle.) A better bet: The connected **Perla del Mar**, which sits diagonally opposite on Punta Gorda. This stylish 1950s mansion has just seven standard rooms and two suites furnished in moss green and cream drapes with bright, mosaic-tiled bathrooms. You'll want the two suites with sea views. The back patio is smartly furnished with wicker chairs, white and tangerine cushions, and two Jacuzzis overlooking the bay. Both the taberna, **El Bodegón**, and the **Palacio de Valle** restaurant (daily noon–3pm and 7–10pm) are part of the hotel. We recommend a drink on the Palace's rooftop terrace (until 10pm) only.

Calle 37 no. 1, Punta Gorda. www.gran-caribe.com. ✆ **43/55-1003.** 149 units. CUC$100–CUC$130 double. CUC$145–CUC$180 suite. Perla del Mar CUC$118–CUC$150. MC, V. **Amenities:** 2 restaurants; bar; snack bar; cabaret; children's pool; outdoor pool; Internet.

Hostal E Palacio Azul ★ A mini blue turreted palace built in 1920 by an Italian architect, this sweet hotel offers just seven rooms out on Punta Gorda with an extraordinary collection of beautiful original tiled floors. A grand marble staircase leads up to the first floor, where you'll find my favorite room, Dalia, a corner unit with a view of the Club Cienfuegos, the harbor, and the sunset. All but two rooms come with a private little balcony. The Margarita is a useful triple room with the third bed in its own small adjoining room.

Calle 37 no. 1201, btw. Avs. 12 and 14, Punta Gorda. www.gran-caribe.com. ✆ **43/55-5828.** 7 units. CUC$80–CUC$145 double. **Amenities:** Restaurant; bar; room service.

Inexpensive

Cienfuegos has scores of good *casa particular* options. You'll find the greatest concentration of casas particulares all along and near the Prado (Av. 37), as well as surrounding the Parque José Martí and on Punta Gorda.

Casa Amistad, Av. 56 no. 2927, between Calles 29 and 31 (✆ **43/51-6143;** leonormh41@nauta.cu), is a colonial house with a wonderful front living room, two rooms, and some hearty home-cooked food (it's a stone's throw from Parque José Martí). Of the handful of rooms at **BellaPerlaMarina,** Calle 39 no. 5818 at Av. 60 (✆ **43/51-8991;** wrodriguezdelrey@yahoo.es), the standout is the suite with Jacuzzi bath and capacity for six. The dining terrace also features a billiards table. Owner Waldo is super helpful and will help organize excursions.

Casa Piñeiro, Calle 41 no. 1402 between Avenidas 14 and 16, Punta Gorda (✆ **43/51-3808;** www.casapineiro.com), is an enormous house with friendly owners and a great outdoor oven. **Villa Lagarto,** Calle 35 no. 4B (✆ **43/51-9966;** http://villalagarto.com), run by the very friendly Tony and Mailín, has three breezy, comfortable top-floor rooms, a garden overlooking the sea right at the tip of Punta Gorda, and one of Cienfuegos' top dining spots (see below).

Up a wooden spiral staircase and run by Miriam and Keila, **Las Estancias Villa,** Calle 35 no. 4B Altos between 0 and Litoral (✆ **5274-2659**), is a gorgeous canary-yellow 1890 gingerbread home with one room with a cute pink and yellow bathroom. **Hostal Colonial,** Calle 47 5609 between 56 and 58 (✆ **43/52-4647;** eliasr1988@yahoo.es), run by Dagmara and Elías Ramos, is a 1916 colonial home with three rooms arrayed off an interior patio and portico.

Where to Dine

In addition to the places listed below, you can get acceptable pizza and pastas at **Pizza Dinos,** Calle 31 between Avenidas 54 and 56 (✆ **43/55-2020**).

Villa Lagarto ★ CONTINENTAL/COMIDA CRIOLLA Tony and Mailín run the best restaurant in Cienfuegos. All meals are charged at CUC$18 and come with a spread of bruschetta, bread, fried bananas, salads, black beans, soup, and grilled aubergine to start followed by a host of delicious barbecued dishes including chicken, roast pork leg, outstanding barbecued lamb and rabbit in tomato sauce. All dishes are accompanied by rice and vegetables and followed by a dessert, coffee, and liqueur. You'll want the tables and leather-and-hide chairs under the ranchón right on the water of the Bay of Cienfuegos. The service here is topnotch. You could also just enjoy a sundowner on the painted wooden chairs on the small jetty.

Calle 35 no. 4B between 0 and Litoral, Punta Gorda. http://villalagarto.com. ✆ **43/51-9966.** Reservations recommended in high season. No credit cards. Daily 7pm–midnight.

Finca del Mar ★ CONTINENTAL/SEAFOOD This new paladar is super smart with cream canvas umbrellas in the garden and tangerine cream and black dining-room colors. It has a view of the bay, but it's obscured by the front wall of the paladar. We dined on the Camerones Finca del Mar, a shrimp dish with apricots, figs, dates, currants, and olives. The service here is good, but the dishes are on the expensive side: Charging CUC$12 for a pasta dish is not justifiable. At these prices, we say stick to the meats and seafood. There's also an air-conditioned dining room on-site.

Calle 35 between 18 y 20, Punta Gorda. ✆ **43/52-6598.** Main courses CUC$12–CUC$17. No credit cards. Daily noon–10pm.

Cienfuegos After Dark

The biggest draw in town is the **Club El Benny,** Av. 54 no. 2907 between Calles 29 and 31 (✆ **43/55-1674**). Its nightly cabaret show (admission CUC$3

Fri–Sun; CUC$2 Mon–Thurs) features the classic sounds and songs of the club's namesake. The place also serves as one of the city's most lively dance clubs. Check out the program at **Los Jardines de la UNEAC** on Parque Martí. Next to the city's historic theater is the **Café Teatro Terry,** Av. 56 between Calles 27 and 29 (© **43/51-0770**), where traditional music can be heard from 9am to 1am (admission CUC$2 evenings).

TRINIDAD ★★★

334km (208 miles) SE of Havana; 261km (162 miles) S of Varadero; 649km (403 miles) W of Santiago de Cuba

Tiny Trinidad is, quite simply, one of the finest colonial towns in all the Americas. Wholly disproportionate to its diminutive size, Trinidad ranks as one of Cuba's greatest attractions. A few square blocks of cobblestone streets, pretty pastel-colored 18th- and 19th-century houses, palaces, and plazas, Trinidad's colonial-era core can be toured in just a few hours. Many visitors find its serenity so soothing, however, that they are easily coaxed into much longer stays. Magically frozen in time and tastefully scruffy where it needs to be, the city has streets that are more populated by horse-drawn carts than automobile traffic, and old folks still crouch by windows, behind fancy wrought-iron grilles, to peer out at passersby.

Founded in 1514 on the site of a native Taíno settlement, Villa de la Santísima Trinidad was the fourth of Diego Velázquez's original seven *villas* (towns). Trinidad quickly grew and later prospered in princely fashion from the sugarcane industry concentrated in the outlying Valle de los Ingenios. The sugar boom that took root by the mid-1700s created a coterie of wealthy local sugar barons, who built magnificent estates in the valley and manor houses in town and imported thousands of African slaves to work the fields. Trinidad's golden age, though, proved to be short-lived. Slave uprisings on plantations, intense European competition, and, finally, independence struggles throughout the Caribbean all took their toll on the Cuban sugar industry.

When the bottom dropped out of sugar by the 1860s, Trinidad's economy collapsed and the town drifted into obscurity. Its economic failure in the late-19th century is a true blessing in the 21st: Trinidad escaped further economic development and modernization that surely would have obscured the colonial nucleus that UNESCO honored as a World Heritage Site in 1988. Even in the 1950s, in prerevolutionary, capitalist Cuba, the beauty and historical value of Trinidad prompted the government to declare it off-limits to further development.

Essentials

GETTING THERE

BY PLANE Chartered **AeroCaribbean** light-aircraft flights from Havana, Cienfuegos, and Varadero arrive in Trinidad at the little **Aeropuerto Alberto Delgado,** Carretera Casilda Km 1.5 (© **41/99-6393;** airport code TND), a couple of kilometers beyond the historic center of Trinidad. A taxi from the airport to Trinidad costs around CUC$5.

BY BUS The **Terminal de Omnibuses** (✆ **41/99-4448**), in Trinidad is on Gustavo Izquierdo between Piro Guinart and Simón Bolívar.

Víazul (www.viazul.com; ✆ **41/99-4448** in Trinidad) journeys regularly to Trinidad. From Havana, buses depart daily at 7am, 10:45am, and 2pm, taking almost 6 hrs.; the fare is CUC$25. From Varadero, buses leave at 7:30am, taking 6.5 hrs. (CUC$20). From Santiago de Cuba, buses leave at 7:30pm and arrive at 7am the following day (CUC$33). Return buses leave Trinidad for Havana at 7:30am, 8:15am, and 4pm; for Varadero at 7:30am; and for Santiago at 8am. A new bus to Santa Lucia leaves at 10am (CUC$23). A bus leaves from Viñales at 6:45am and arrives in Trinidad at 4:15pm (CUC$37); there is no return bus journey.

BY CAR From Havana, the fastest route is to drive along the Autopista Nacional to Santa Clara (about 4 hrs.), and then drop down through Jibacoa to Trinidad along the local road south. (See "Autopista Scam," earlier in this chapter.) Another option is to continue on the Autopista Nacional to Sancti Spíritus (perhaps stopping for a look, if you're not planning an overnight visit there), and circle back southwest to Trinidad for a scenic drive through the Valley of the Sugar Mills (see "Side Trips from Trinidad," later in this chapter). If you're driving in from Cienfuegos, there are actually two routes. We prefer the coastal road, which gives you some good sea views as you near Trinidad.

GETTING AROUND

Getting around Trinidad is a simple affair. Almost everything of interest in town is clustered around the Plaza Mayor in the historic center. The streets of old Trinidad were made for exploring on foot, and you can easily get around the whole of the old city, and most of the newer parts just beyond the colonial core, very easily on foot.

BY TAXI Taxis are available for travel back and forth between Playa Ancón and Trinidad, up the hill to Hotel Las Cuevas, or private hire for excursions. Call **Cubataxi** (✆ **41/99-8080**). Taxis charge CUC$8 to Playa Ancón.

BY CAR Although it is far easier to sign on for an organized tour to visit the surrounding area, including Topes de Collantes in the Sierra del Escambray, you might want to rent a car to explore central Cuba or travel to more distant destinations. The drive northeast to Sancti Spíritus through the Valle de los Ingenios is particularly alluring. The major car-rental companies are **Cubacar** (✆ **41/99-6110**) and **Vía Rent a Car** (✆ **41/99-6388**). Rates range from CUC$45 per day for a standard car to CUC$80 and up per day for a 4WD.

BY BICYCLE **Osbel** (✆ **5296-1007**), at Calle Maceo 409, opposite the post office, rents Swiss bikes with gears and helmets for UC$6 per day that you can use to get back and forth to the beach. Be forewarned, however: It's downhill, then flat, on your way to the beach, but the final few kilometers coming home will be uphill.

BY BUS The **Trinidad Bus Tour** departs at 9am, 11am, 2pm, 4pm, and 5pm from the Havanatur office, Calle Lino Perez 368 between Gracia and

Trinidad

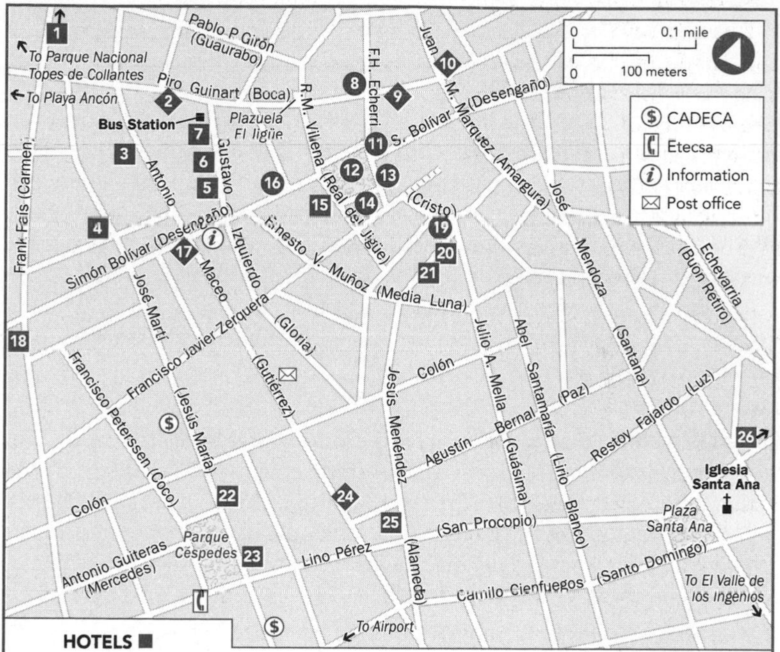

HOTELS ■
Casa Bastida **3**
Casa Elda y Roberto **20**
Casa Font **5**
Casa Mauri **7**
Casa Meyer **6**
Casa Sotolongo **15**
Hostal Alameda **21**
Hostal Casa Muñoz **4**
Hostal Oasis **18**
Hotel E La Ronda **22**
Hotel Las Cuevas **26**
Iberostar Grand Hotel Trinidad **23**
La Casona **1**
Maison Alameda **25**

RESTAURANTS ◆
Café Don Pepe **9**
Café Las Begonias **17**
El Dorado **2**
Taberna La Botija **2**
Restaurant San José **24**

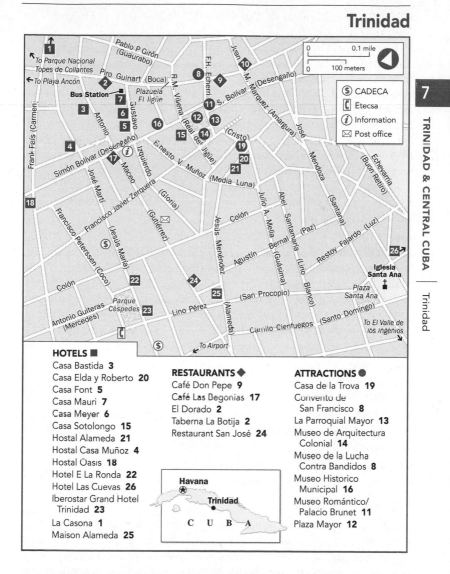

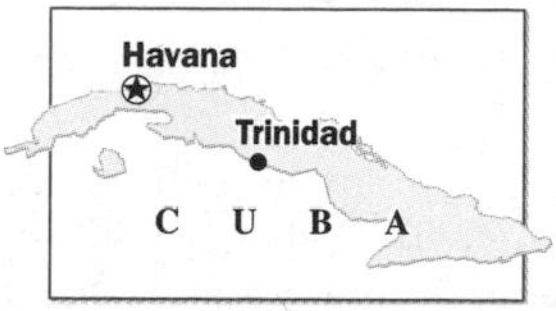

ATTRACTIONS ●
Casa de la Trova **19**
Convento de San Francisco **8**
La Parroquial Mayor **13**
Museo de Arquitectura Colonial **14**
Museo de la Lucha Contra Bandidos **8**
Museo Historico Municipal **16**
Museo Romántico/Palacio Brunet **11**
Plaza Mayor **12**

Antonio Maceo, and picks up at a few stops in town, including the Cubatur office, before heading to Playa La Boca and the hotels on Playa Ancón. It returns from the beach at 10am, 12:30pm, 3:30pm, 5:15pm, and 6pm. The fare is CUC$2 per person.

ORIENTATION

The streets of Trinidad go by both original colonial and newer, post-Revolution names and are haphazardly labeled. Locals usually don't know both; what one person may call Boca another calls Piro Guinart. Many longtime residents use the old names, but most businesses and institutions adopt the newer names, which are used in this section. Be prepared to encounter some confusion if asking for an address, though Trinidad is so small that it's nearly impossible to be lost for long.

VISITOR INFORMATION

For information about Trinidad and nearby excursions, the **state-run travel agencies** have locations in town. **Cubatur** (© **41/99-6314;** www.cubatur.cu) is at Antonio Maceo at the corner of Francisco Javier Zerquera. **Cubanacán** is located on José Martí between Francisco Javier Zerquera and Colón (© **41/99-6142**), and at Cafe Las Begonias. **Infotur** is next to Bar Yesterday, Calle Gustavo Izqueirdo between Simón Bolívar and Piro Guinart (© **41/99-8258**).

For something more personal, tailor-made, and adventurous, contact **Trinidad Travels** (© **5282-3276**; www.trinidadtravels.com) at Maceo 613A between Pablo Pisch Girón and Piro Guinart.

FAST FACTS

BANKS/ATMS **Banco de Crédito y Comercio** is located at José Martí 264 between Colón and Francisco Javier Zerquera (© **41/99-2405**). It's open Monday through Friday 8am to 3pm and Saturday 8am to 11am and has ATMs. A **CADECA** is at José Martí 166 (© **41/99-6263**); its hours are Monday through Saturday 8am to 6pm and Sunday 8am to 1pm. Another CADECA can be found at Calle Maceo between Camilo Cienfuegos y Lino Pérez.

INTERNET **Internet terminals** are at the Etecsa office on Lino Pérez (on the east side of Parque Céspedes, between José Martí and Miguel Calzada). The Iberostar resort's Wi-Fi can also be accessed from the same park using Nauta Internet cards.

MEDICAL For medical attention, go to the 24-hour **Clínica Internacional** located at Lino Pérez 103, at the corner of Reforma (© **41/99-6492**). It also has an in-house pharmacy.

POST OFFICE The main **post office** is situated at Antonio Maceo 418, between Colón and Francisco Javier Zerquera (open Mon–Sat 8am–7pm).

Exploring the Area

Unquestionably, the greatest attraction in Trinidad is the town itself. Trinidad's cobblestone streets contain a treasure trove of small and grand colonial homes, churches, and quiet squares. Walking aimlessly about the curving streets of the old town is unmatched in Cuba for tranquillity and charm. Remarkably, as quaint as it is, Trinidad feels like a real town where Cubans live and work, rather than the film set it first appears to be.

A good way to get your bearings in Trinidad is to trace a path from the **Plaza Mayor,** the heart of the old town, heading west on Echerri and then down Piro Guinart to **Plazuela El Jigüe,** a pretty little square. Then head down Peña to Simón Bolívar and east on Antonio Maceo, the closest thing there is to a main drag in Trinidad.

A couple blocks south of here, along Lino Pérez, is **Parque Céspedes,** the focal point of the "new" town (though newer than the colonial core of Trinidad, it remains anything but shiny and modern).

Northeast of the old town, following Fernando H. Echerri to José Mendoza for several blocks, you'll reach **Plaza Santa Ana** and the ruins of **Iglesia Santa Ana,** which looks ancient, but dates only to 1812. On the square is a former 19th-century prison, **Real Cárcel,** which today houses an unremarkable, touristy restaurant.

Horseback riding tours can be arranged through Casa Munoz (p. 169) and La Casona (p. 254). Julio Munoz also offers immersive **photo tours** and **street photography workshops ★★** (www.photo.trinidadphoto.com).

Dance classes can be taken at the Casa de la Cultura, Calle Rosario between Medio Luna and Real) with Julio Reinosa Espinosa (✆ **41/99-4308/**5810-7104)

AROUND THE PLAZA MAYOR ★★

The neo-baroque, 19th-century Plaza Mayor, elaborately adorned with serene sitting areas, statuary, towering palm trees, and gardens enclosed by white wrought-iron fences, is one of Cuba's most beautiful plazas. It's ringed by magnificent palaces and pastel-colored houses with red-tile roofs and wood shutters. On the northwest corner is the cathedral, Iglesia de la Santísima Trinidad, which most locals refer to as **La Parroquial Mayor.** The cathedral, completed in 1892, replaced the original 17th-century church that was destroyed in 1812 by a hurricane. The new construction, completed at the end of the 19th century, is rather simple on the outside, but the restored interior reveals a Gothic vaulted ceiling and nearly a dozen attractive carved altars. The cathedral can be visited Monday through Saturday from 10:30am to 1pm. Mass is at 4pm on Saturday, 10am on Sunday, and 8pm Tuesday through Friday.

The highlight of the Plaza Mayor, and the most evocative reminder of Trinidad's glory days, is the lovingly restored **Palacio Brunet,** Fernando H. Echerri 52 at the corner of Simón Bolívar. The colonial mansion dates to 1704 (the first floor was built in 1808) and houses the **Museo Romántico ★★** (✆ **41/99-4363**). Its splendid collection of period antiques culled from a number of old Trinitario families convincingly evokes the life of a local sugar baron in the 1800s. Don't miss the enormous kitchen, covered in *azulejo* (glazed ceramic tiles), and its wood-burning stove. The views from upstairs are marvelous. The museum is open Tuesday through Sunday from 9am to 5pm. Admission is CUC$2; camera use CUC$1; allow about 45 minutes for your visit.

On the east side of the Plaza Mayor, in a squat, sky-blue mansion once belonging to the Sánchez Iznaga family, the **Museo de Arquitectura Colonial** (✆ **41/99-3208**) features moderately interesting exhibits that trace the development of Trinidad, including examples of woodwork and ironwork, maps, models, and photographs. What is on display, though, can hardly compare to the real-life exhibits beyond the museum's doors. It's open Monday, Thursday, Saturday, and Sunday from 9am to 5pm. Admission is CUC$1.

The former Palacio Cantero, a palatial 1830 residence built by a noted sugar baron, houses the **Museo Histórico Municipal ★★**, Simón Bolívar 423 between Peña and Gustavo Izquierdo (✆ **41/99-4460**). In addition to antiques and 19th-century furnishings, it holds bits and pieces of slave history, old bank notes, and exhibits of revolutionary Cuba. For many visitors, though, the highlight is the climb up the narrow and rickety wooden stairs, surrounded by stunning frescoes, to the tower, which has terrific bird's-eye views of Trinidad and the surrounding area. The museum is open Saturday through Thursday from 9am to 5pm; admission is CUC$2. Allow about an hour for your visit, a bit longer if you want to linger over the views.

The second of Trinidad's two major towers is the picturesque yellow-and-pastel-green domed bell tower belonging to the former 18th-century **Convento de San Francisco (Convent of Saint Francis of Assisi),** Fernando H. Echerri at Piro Guinart. Today the building hosts the dogmatic, but rather fascinating **Museo de la Lucha Contra Bandidos** (✆ **41/99-4121**), which focuses on revolutionary Cuba and the continuing "struggle against bandits." Exhibits document Fidel's battles against counterrevolutionaries—the *bandidos* in question—who sought to overturn the regime's ideals by winning support among *guajiros* (poor rural farmers) and fighting in the Sierra del Escambray in the 1960s. In addition to newspaper reports, you'll find machine guns, military maps, a CIA radio, and photos of the ragtag principals who finally, and quite extraordinarily, overthrew the Batista government in 1959. As is the case with the Museo Histórico, though, the biggest draw may be the panoramic views from atop the bell tower. The museum is open Tuesday through Sunday from 9am to 5pm; admission is CUC$1. Allow 45 minutes or so, including the visit to the tower.

Where to Stay

Trinidad has hundreds of *casas particulares,* including several in fine colonial homes that rank as excellent bargains and are particularly appropriate accommodations in this beautifully preserved old town.

Visitors who arrive on the Víazul bus will be confronted by a rabble of dozens of card- and placard-waving folks hoping to get you to follow them to their homestays. They are perfectly innocuous and, for the most part, honest folks just trying to make a buck. Not all the *casas* are as close to the colonial center as you might wish to be, so have a map ready so they can show you clearly where their houses are located. If you already have the name of a *casa,* don't mention that you are looking for "José" or "María" (for example); the homeowner you're talking to will morph into that person in no time. Houses in the old center of town generally charge CUC$25 to CUC$35 per double; those a bit farther out (usually no more than a 15-min. walk from the Plaza Mayor) charge CUC$20 to CUC$25 per double. Alternatively, you could stay at one of the large resorts on Playa Ancón, 12km (7½ miles) away.

Know Where You're Going

Be careful: *Jineteros* (hustlers) meet incoming buses and taxis with the names of tourists they've gleaned from friends inside the bus or taxi company. They then proceed to tell the tourists either that their reservation at a specific *casa particular* has been canceled, or that they are taking them to that casa, when in fact they are bringing them to a different casa altogether. Some locals have also resorted to putting up copied house signs and numbers to deceive people. *Jineteros* have also been known to enter a false key into the door of the house that tourists have booked into only to find that the door is "locked" and so the casa owner is not there and they should therefore come to the *jinetero*'s casa or *jinetero*'s friend's casa instead. If you have and trust your confirmed reservation at a *casa particular,* make sure you know the exact address and location of the house, and distrust touts who take you elsewhere. Beware of people who wish to escort you—especially *jineteros* on bicycles. Know that not all folks are suspicious, however; many are *arrendadores* (owners of legal *casas particulares*) who have not had the good fortune to be listed in a guidebook. Don't dismiss them all; just check that they have a genuine license.

IN TRINIDAD

The venerable old **Hotel E La Ronda,** José Martí no. 246 between Lino Pérez and Colón (www.hotelescubanacan.com; ✆ **41/99-8538;** reservas@cuevas.co.cu), is a restored 1868 building with 17 high-ceilinged rooms named after famous boleros. Four rooms have balconies overlooking the street (nos. 215–218), but if you're noise sensitive these may not be the best choices. Guests here can use the pool at Hotel Las Cuevas (CUC$143–CUC$170 double). The **Pansea Trinidad** (www.pansea.com/Pansea_Trinidad_Cuba.html) is currently under construction, incorporating the remains of the Iglesia de la Popa church, as is the central **Hotel E Palacio Iznaga** (www.hotelescubanacan.com).

Expensive

Iberostar Grand Hotel Trinidad ★ This grand, pastel-green hotel offers the most sumptuous hotel accommodations in town in a remodeled old building lining the leafy Parque Céspedes. The large lobby is centered around a fountain with chairs to relax in, while the rooms are reached via a marble staircase, or elevator. Rooms are extremely spacious and come with elegant furnishings decked in gold and claret colors with smart beige marble bathrooms with bathtubs and chrome rain showers. My favorite rooms are the first-floor standard units, nos. 106 through 111, with balconies facing the park. The restaurant buffet offers quite a spread with a notable cheese board. A hotel spa is due to open next door.

Calle José Martí 262 (at Calle Lino Perez), Trinidad. www.iberostar.com. ✆ **41/99-6070.** reservas@iberostar.trinidad.co.cu. 40 units. CUC$95–CUC$210 double; CUC$120–CUC$235 suite. Rates include breakfast. MC, V. A request needs to be made to the management to accommodate children under 15. **Amenities:** Restaurant; bar; butler service; game room; room service; smokers' salon; Wi-Fi.

Moderate

La Casona ★★, Frank País 759 (final; www.lacasona759trinidad.com; ✆ **41/99-8692**), is a sprawling, stylish property with six rooms, stables, and a hilltop swimming pool. Owner Kenia has fashioned all-white rooms decorated with the work of local woodcraft artist Lázaro Niebla, and tadelakt-style Moroccan bathrooms. The grounds are overflowing with mango, avocado, and hibiscus (doubles CUC$100–CUC$120; advance reservations necessary).

Mansion Alameda ★, Calle Alameda 69 between Lino Pérez and Paz (www.mansionalameda.com; ✆ **41/99-8313**), a handsome 300-year-old property, was the birthplace of Dalia Soto de Valle, Fidel Castro's second wife. It has been converted into a 10-room property centered around a tree-shaded patio and fountain. The rooftop views are incredible (CUC$135–CUC$200 including breakfast).

Hotel Las Cuevas Las Cuevas is perched on a hill 1.6km (1 mile) north of (and up above) the old colonial core of Trinidad, a bit of an inconvenient location. It's a 20-minute (downhill) walk to the restaurants and nightlife of Trinidad and a taxi ride home. Nevertheless, the hotel is popular with tour groups. The main appeal of this place, really, is the swimming pool and the surreal underground-cave dance club (a short distance from the property). The basic rooms (with mostly twin beds) are in bungalows scattered around the pool.

Finca Santa Ana, Trinidad. www.hotelescubanacan.com. ✆ **41/99-6133.** reservas@cuevas.co.cu. 114 units. CUC$85–CUC$125 double. Rates include breakfast and dinner buffet. MC, V. **Amenities:** 2 restaurants; 3 bars; dance club; nightly show; outdoor pool; outdoor tennis court; Internet.

Inexpensive

Hostal Alameda, Calle Alameda 156 between Cristo and Media Luna (www.mansionalameda.com; ✆ **41/99-8298;** hostalalameda.trinidadcuba@yahoo.com), is an über-stylish haven created by Canadian Daniela with two rooms with iron beadsteads, cream linens, white drapes, and tadelakt walls. Daniela's cinnamon buns and homemade jam and bread are a treat. Daniela also offers horseback riding for CUC$20 per person. **Hostal Oasis ★** Frank País 389 between Simón Bolívar and Francisco Javier Zerquera (✆ **41/99-4589**; tereleria@gmail.com' www.hostaleloasis.com), with three rooms, is run by the super-friendly and welcoming Teresa; it has a rooftop bar with city views. **Casa Mauri,** Gustavo Izquierdo 119 between Simón Bolívar and Piro Guinart (✆ **5247-4272;** msvm@nauta.cu) is an enormous house built in 1780 that's run by Miguel A Suárez del Villar Mauri. The colorful house offers three rooms—one of which boasts an ancient bathtub.

The welcoming **Casa Bastida ★** Maceo 537, between Simón Bolívar and Piro Guinart (www.hostalbastida.com; ✆ **41/99-6686**), boasts wonderful rooftop views. One room has a cute balcony overlooking the street, and there's an attractive communal dining area under a bamboo roof. **Casa Elda y Roberto,** Jesús Menéndez 166, between Fernando H Echerri and Ernesto V Muñoz (http://eldayroberto.trinidadhostales.com; ✆ **41/99-3283;** mdleon@pol1tdad.

Check in Before You Check In

When you make a reservation with a *casa particular*, it's a very good idea—if not essential—to reconfirm your reservation a couple of days in advance. *Casas* often let out rooms that haven't been reconfirmed.

ssp.sld.cu), is run by a friendly couple; of the two rooms in the house, the choice room ★ is perched in the garden out back with a small patio and views across the rooftops. **Casa Sotolongo,** Real 33 between Francisco Javier Zerquera and Simón Bolívar (✆ **41/99-4169**; galinkapuig@gmail.com), is located right on the main plaza with an interesting radio collection and antiques. **Casa Font**, Gustavo Izquierdo 105 btw. Piro Guinart and Simón Bolívar (www.casafonttrinidad.jimdo.com; ✆ **41/99-3683;** viatri@yahoo.es), is a divided late-18th-century mansion with two rooms; one room has a bed dating from 1800 and richly decorated with mother-of-pearl. The house also has stunning *modernista mampáras* doors (half doors in the Modernista design).

Casa Meyer ★, Gustavo Izquierdo 111 between Piro Guinart and Simón Bolívar (www.hostalcasameyer.com; ✆ **41/99-3444**) is a spectacular, 200-year-old colonial home, with a garden courtyard. The house has very high, wood-beamed ceilings. One bedroom is huge, with antique beds, one decorated with mother-of-pearl, while the second room set back in the garden is just as nice and perhaps even more tranquil, with a huge, bronze four-poster bed. An original pram and 1903 gramaphone grace the main front room. **Hostal Casa Colonial Muñoz ★**, José Martí 401, corner of Santiago Escobar (www.casa.trinidadphoto.com; ✆ **41/99-3673**), is a charming place run by English-speaking Julio and his wife, Rosa. A breezy and centrally located colonial house built in 1800, it has several bedrooms with en-suite bathrooms, one with a mezzanine, and a shady patio, plus a rooftop terrace with fantastic views. Julio is a photographer (p. 165) and horse whisperer (p. 173) and has considerable advice on Trinidad's cultural scene. Guests can also access Wi-Fi using nauta cards at his home.

PLAYA ANCON

Brisas Trinidad del Mar Of the current hotels on Playa Ancón (Iberostar and Meliá are in the process of building properties), the Brisas is the most appealing. This intimate all-inclusive is arrayed around an attractive central pool shaded by sprightly palm trees, with hanging wicker chairs lining a portico. All the buildings imitate the colonial core of Trinidad. Rooms are spacious and functional, but you'll spend most of your time by the pool or on the beach, a short walk away. Sun loungers are easily snatched up early in the day, so you'll want to claim one sooner rather than later. Unfortunately, the food continues to be desultory. There are better holiday resorts in Cuba, but if this fits in with your travel plans, it's the best of the handful of hotels here.

Península Ancón, Trinidad. ✆ **41/99-6500.** www.hotelescubanacan.com. 241 units. CUC$121–CUC$131 double. Rates are all-inclusive. MC, V. **Amenities:** 3 restaurants; 2 bars; snack bar; children's center and programs; gym; outdoor pool; room service; sauna; bike rental; 2 outdoor tennis courts; Internet.

Where to Dine

The dining scene in Trinidad has exploded. Just 5 years ago, there were three licensed paladares, now there are nearly 100.

The best dining establishment in Trinidad, owned by a Cuban American, is the **Restaurante San José ★★**, Calle Maceo 382, between Colón and Smith (www.sanjosetaste.com; ✆ **41/99-4702**; main courses CUC$5–CUC$15), in a supremely elegant dining room (with an air-conditioned dining room at the back) under whirring wooden ceiling fans and pink and cream Spanish tiles, serving up huge grilled seafood platters with sweet potatoes and vegetables, plus pizzas and sandwiches. It's open noon to 10:30pm daily.

Taberna La Botija ★, Calle Amargura 71-B between Boca and San José (✆ **41/99-2670;** main courses CUC$7.50–CUC$16) is a rustic *taberna* with Cuban blue doors and decorated in antiques and items relating to Trinidad's slave trade by collector and owner Douglas Pineda Gregorio. The best dish: shrimp in garlic served up in earthenware dish. It's open 24 hours.

A cute garden hideaway with tree-trunk tables and leather-and-hide chairs, **Café Don Pepe**, Calle Piro Guinart between FH Echerri and Amargura (✆ **41/99-3573**), serves up iced coffees and teas from CUC$1, accompanied by a square of chocolate. It's open 8am to midnight.

El Dorado, Calle Piro Guinart 228 between Gustavo Izquierdo and Maceo (www.restauranteldorado.hostl-cuba.com; ✆ **41/99-3849;** main courses: CUC$7.50–CUC$18), is a breezy colonial home serving up excellent home-cooked food with topnotch service. The Pargo "El Dorado," tender snapper bathed in rosé wine with mushrooms, pumpkins, and rice, is highly recommended. It's open noon to 11pm.

Dulcinea, also known as Café Las Begonias, corner of Simón Bolívar and Maceo, is the perfect refreshment stop for cakes, pastries, sandwiches, and ice creams. It has an Internet café attached.

Shopping

Trinidad is now a shopping emporium. Lining the cobblestoned streets are dozens of stalls or shopfronts selling **lace ★, woodwork,** and **handicrafts.**

ART & CERAMICS

The art gallery on the south side of the Plaza Mayor, **Galería de Arte ARTex,** has two floors of contemporary art, much of it very accessibly priced. Trinitario artist **Yudit Vidal Faife**, Calle Simón Bolívar 294 between José Martí and Frank País (www.yuditvidal.com; ✆ **41/99-4706**; Mon–Sat 9am–8pm), is currently involved in a project that nurtures the artistic value of the embroidery work famous in Trinidad. Woodwork artist **Lázaro Niebla** recycles doors and window pieces, carving characterful portraits of local personalities into the wood at **Galería Lázaro Niebla Castro**, Calle Real No. 11 (✆ **5294-0210**). **Galería TallerDeustua**, Calle Maceo 396 between Colón and Smith (✆ **5338-5219;** aledeustua@gmail.com; Mon–Sat 9am–10pm and Sun 10:30am–10pm), showcases the colorful ceramic work of artist Alejandro López Bastida.

Many of the ceramic wares you see for sale around Trinidad are produced by the Santander family, whose history in this art form goes back generations. You can visit their small factory, **El Alfarero Casa Chichi,** Andrés Berro 51, between Abel Santamaría and Pepito Tey (✆ **41/99-3146**), although it's best to call in advance and tell them you're coming.

CIGARS

The place to go for cigars and tobacco paraphernalia in town, **La Casa del Tabaco,** has two branches and carries all the finest Cuban cigars, carefully stored. The shop at Lino Pérez 296 (at the corner of José Martí) is open daily from 10am to 6pm; the branch on Francisco Javier Zerquera (at the corner of Maceo) is open daily from 10am to 6pm.

Trinidad After Dark

While most of Trinidad's old-town streets are coffin-quiet after dark, several joints bop with live Cuban music nightly. One of the best spots to sit outside, have a *mojito* or beer, and hear good traditional bands is the small plaza midway up the steps leading to the **Casa de la Música ★**. The dance floor is usually a good mix of polished, semiprofessional locals and foreigners whose hips are somewhat less smoothly oiled. The steps are often overflowing with people checking out some free music under the stars from 8:30pm until midnight. Inside the Casa de la Música, a more raucous environment prevails until the wee hours for a cover charge of CUC$1. Just around the corner on Fernando H. Echerri, **Palenque de los Congos Reales ★★** has an open-air stage where you can catch Grupo Folklórico performing Afro-Cuban music and dance. At other times, there may be a standard *trova* or *son* group playing. It's open daily from 10am to 1am, and until 10pm on Saturday. The **Casa de la Trova,** Fernando H. Echerri 29, a block east of the Plaza Mayor, is the traditional spot to listen to Cuban bands and try out a few dance steps; it's open daily from 10am to 1am, and there's a cover charge of CUC$1. The **Ruinas del Teatro Brunet**, Maceo between Zerquera and Simón Bolívar, offers a mixed program.

La Canchánchara, Rubén Martínez Villena at Pablo P. Girón, sometimes has a few musicians assembled, but it's mostly just a little open-air courtyard bar in an atmospheric colonial house, a good place to kick back in old wooden chairs and have a *mojito* or the eponymous house drink, made with *aguardiente* (firewater), lime, and honey. It's open daily from 8:30am to 2am. Another bar set in a delightful open-air courtyard in the ostensible ruins of a colonial home, the **Ruinas de Segarte**, Jesús Menéndez s/n between Callejón Gado and Juan Manuel Marquéz, is an intimate affair and open from 10:30am to 1:30am daily, and also has live music most nights.

One of the most unusual nightspots in Cuba has to be the dance club carved out of a deep two-level cave, **Discoteca Ayala,** also called La Cueva (© **41/99-6133**). Though it can be deadly hot, and the kitsch factor is undeniable, it's still pretty cool to dance to blasting disco-salsa tunes as colored lights bounce off stalactites. The crowd on weekends is largely Cuban. Now if they could only install air-conditioning to go with the lights and sound system, nocturnal spelunking would be even more appetizing. To get here, you can either walk up a path leading directly behind the cathedral, off Juan Manuel Márquez, or take the longer route from Hotel Las Cuevas (it's not actually on the premises of the hotel, though it's under the same management). It's open Tuesday to Sunday 10pm to 2am (later Fri–Sat); admission is CUC$3.

Side Trips from Trinidad

Though the colonial streets of Trinidad are the main draw, the town is perfectly situated for quick trips to the beach (one of the best on the southern coast) and gorgeous surrounding countryside, which includes the Sierra del Escambray mountains and a picturesque valley that was once home to the sugar plantations that made Trinidad wealthy in the 18th and 19th centuries.

PLAYA ANCON

It can't quite compare with Cayo Largo, Varadero, Cayos Coco and Guillermo, Cayo Santa Maria, or Guardalavaca—Cuba's prettiest and most prestigious beaches—but Playa Ancón is still an attractive beach with one distinct advantage over those other, isolated stretches of sand: proximity to Trinidad. At just 13km (8 miles) from town, Ancón, a 3km (2-mile) strip at the end of a peninsula, is a quick and easy ride to and from Trinidad, so beach lovers can stay here and visit the colonial wonder of Trinidad at their will. The beach is made up of white sand, and there's good snorkeling and diving at some 30 offshore dive sites. (It's a shame, then, that the first few meters offshore are littered with beer cans.) The Brisas Trinidad del Mar hotel (p. 169), as well as the major travel agencies in town, offer diving and snorkeling excursions beginning at CUC$35 per person in addition to watersports.

Cayo Blanco is a tiny offshore island with iguanas; local operators offer "seafari" expeditions to Cayo Blanco, with boat trips to the island, lunch, and snorkeling (from CUC$50). Trips depart from the Marina Nautica Marlin (© **41/99-6205**).

Northwest of Playa Ancón, about 8km (5 miles) from Trinidad, is **La Boca,** a small fishing village that's the popular beach spot among locals. Few tourists make it to La Boca, though there are a couple of *casas particulares* that rent rooms, including the **Hostal Vista al Mar,** Calle Real 47 (© **41/99-3716;** hostalvistaalmartri@gmail.com), a cute royal-blue bungalow overlooking the beach. The best room is at the front of the house.

To get to Playa Ancón, take a taxi (CUC$6), or the Trinidad Bus Tour. Alternatively, energetic folks can rent a bike; see "Getting Around," earlier in this section.

VALLE DE LOS INGENIOS ★

Trinidad grew rich off the sugar trade back in the 18th and 19th centuries, and the Valle de los Ingenios (Valley of the Sugar Mills) was one of the most productive sugarcane growing areas in all of Cuba. The gorgeous, verdant valley is no longer king of the sugar trade, which once supported 56 mills, but for visitors, it makes a wonderful day trip. The zone has been declared a UNESCO Cultural Heritage Site. When it's working, a train, especially for tourists, departs daily for the valley, making the journey out to one of the old sugar estates, **Manaca-Iznaga,** in just over 30 minutes from Trinidad (CUC$10), leaving at 9:30am and returning at 2:30pm. The operative word is "working," however: The train breaks down regularly. Best to call or visit the train station, Calle Antonio Guiteras Final (✆ **41/99-6368**), to see if things are operational. The old manor house (Casa Hacienda) remains and is now a pretty good tourist restaurant; however, the main attraction is the fantastic, 45m-high (148-ft.) pointed tower, built in 1845, which visitors can ascend (for a fee of CUC$1) for spectacular views of the surrounding area. A huge bell once hung here and tolled for the toiling slaves in the fields, signaling the beginning and end of their working days. The surprisingly good little restaurant in a hacienda-style manor home serves up a filling lunch for between CUC$4 and CUC$8. **Hacienda Guáimaro** which features the restored frescoes of Italian artist Daniele Dal'Aglio; and the remains of the **San Isidro de los Destiladeros mill** are worth visiting, too.

Julio Muñoz of Casa Muñoz (p. 169) offers **horseback riding** excursions into the Valle de los Ingenios for CUC$26 per person (including entrance to a waterfall; www.trinidadphoto.com/riding.html).

PARQUE NACIONAL TOPES DE COLLANTES (SIERRA DEL ESCAMBRAY) ★★

Northwest of Trinidad, along dangerously curving roads, are the densely pine-covered mountains of the Sierra del Escambray, a beautiful range that cuts across central Cuba. From Trinidad, the Topes de Collantes National Park, which covers 175sq. km (68 sq. miles), is the main draw, a cool refuge from the heat that usually bakes the stone streets of Trinidad. It's a splendid area for hiking, and there's the surreal Art Deco **Kurhotel,** which provides therapeutic treatments.

Of the several well-established trails, the most popular route is **Salto de El Caburní,** a hike that begins near a graffiti-covered house, the Casa de la Gallega (where simple lunches are served), and terminates in a great 75m (246-ft.) waterfall and swimming hole. The clearly marked trail, through forests of palm, pine, and eucalyptus trees, is fairly challenging, with several steep descents, often along a muddy, narrow path. The water in the deep green pool makes for a brisk swim. Another popular hike, which also has a waterfall as its reward at the end, is **Salto Vegas Grandes.** Each of these trails is a 4km (2.5-mile) hike each way.

The Topes de Collantes resort, about 20km (12 miles) from Trinidad, welcomes mostly Cubans, but several of its hotels accept foreign guests. Much more appealing is the B&B ★ **El Manantial** (✆ **42/54-1325;** manantial@nauta.cu), a local haven buried in peach and avocado trees with a natural pool for swimming and its own mirador for views. The delicious food is cooked on firewood. (*Comida criolla* and roast pork lunches can be reserved in advance by nonguests.) The monumental former TB sanitorium **Kurhotel Escambray** (✆ **42/54-0180;** kurhotel@topescom.cu) is most notable as a spa offering a variety of therapies, including hydrotherapy. Still, it's hard to recommend this place, when most visitors have access to vastly better services at home. There is, however, vast potential here (CUC$45–CUC$50 double). Reservations must be made at an office at the resort complex or by phone (✆ **42/54-0219**) or at a tourism desk in town.

The **Museo de Arte Contemporáneo**, featuring the works of Flora Fong, Manuel Mendive, and Tomas Sánchez, is worth a tour (daily 8am–5pm; CUC$2). Stop in at the **Casa del Café** for an iced coffee (7am–7pm daily).

Though it's possible to rent a car and explore the region on your own, paying a CUC$9 entrance fee at the **Complejo Turístico Topes de Collantes** (✆ **42/54-0219;** reserva@topescom.co.cu; run by Gaviota), hikers are advised to sign on for organized bookings, since many trails are not well marked. The Trinidad travel agencies, such as Havanatur and Cubatur, offer Sierra del Escambray jeep excursions from CUC$29 to CUC$55 per person.

SANCTI SPÍRITUS

70km (43 miles) NE of Trinidad; 386km (240 miles) E of Havana

Sancti Spíritus lies smack-dab in the middle of the island and is the capital of the province of the same name. Perched on the banks of the Río Yayabo, the old town is a warren of corkscrew streets, many lined with fine, if weathered, colonial homes. Like Trinidad, the town was one of the original seven *villas* (towns) founded by Velázquez in the early 16th century. Today, Sancti Spíritus is a small and not greatly significant, mostly modern provincial capital with an unassuming, lived-in feel. When it celebrated its 500th anniversary in 2014, it began to renovate some of its more important colonial buildings, including one of the finest house-museums and one of the best-preserved colonial churches in the country, with the hopes of attracting a greater percentage of the travelers stopping off in nearby Trinidad.

Essentials

GETTING THERE

BY BUS **Víazul** (www.viazul.com; ✆ **41/32-4142**) has three daily buses to Sancti Spíritus on the Havana–Santiago de Cuba line. From Havana, the trip takes just over 5 hours. The fare is CUC$23. Víazul also makes the 1-hour trip to Sancti Spíritus directly from Trinidad (CUC$6) twice daily at 8am and 10am. There are also connections from Santiago, Varadero, and Santa Lucía.

Sancti Spíritus

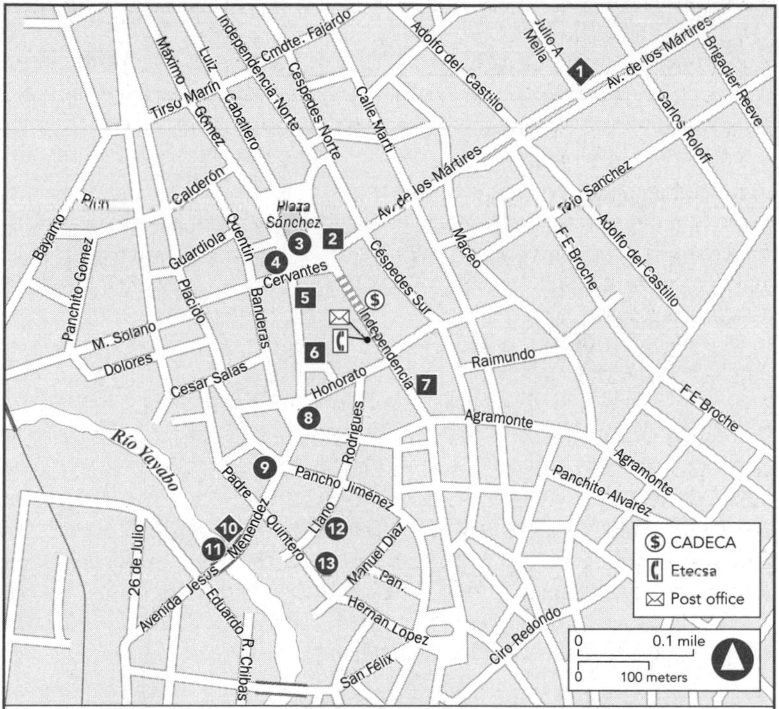

HOTELS ■

Hostal Encanto del Rijo **6**
Hostal Paraíso **5**
Hotel E Don Florencio **7**
Hotel E Plaza **2**

RESTAURANTS ◆

Paladar Las Delicias del Paseo **1**
Taberna Yayabo **10**

ATTRACTIONS ●

Biblioteca Provincial Rubén Martínez **4**
Calle Llano **12**
Casa de Guayabera **13**
Iglesia Parroquial Mayor del Espíritu Santo **8**
Museo de Arte Colonial **9**
Plaza Serafin Sánchez **3**
Puente Yayabo **11**

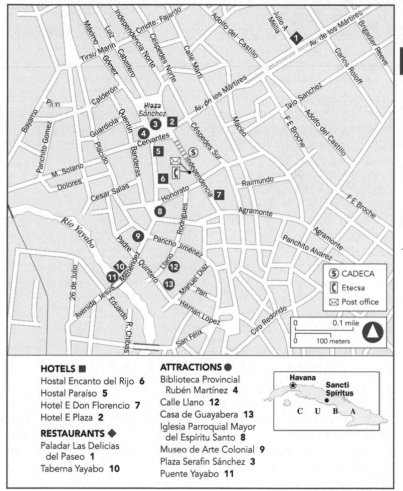

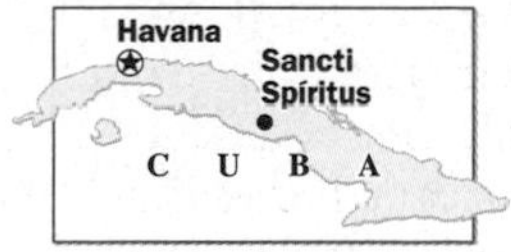

The bus terminal in Sancti Spíritus is located at Carretera Central Km 388, between Circunvalación and the Carretera de Jíbaro. Taxis charge CUC$3 for a ride to the center of town.

BY CAR Driving from Havana, the fastest route is along the Autopista Nacional (A1) to Santa Clara, and then continuing along the Carretera Central to Sancti Spíritus (about 5 hrs.). (See "Autopista Scam," earlier in this chapter.) The short drive from Trinidad, along the Circuito Sur, is one of the prettiest in Cuba, as the road rolls through fields of sugarcane with the Sierra del Escambray looming in the background. From Santiago de Cuba, start out northwest on the unfinished A1 and then take the Carretera Central through Bayamo, Camagüey, and Ciego de Avila (about 6 hrs.).

GETTING AROUND

Call **Cubataxi** (✆ **41/32-2133**) for a taxi, or hop aboard one of the horse-drawn *coches* (carriages), which officially only accept pesos, but most will accept an offer for the fare of CUC$1 to CUC$2. To rent a car, call **Cubacar** (✆ **41/32-8533**); rates are CUC$55 to CUC$95 per day for a four-door car.

ORIENTATION

For a relatively small town, Sancti Spíritus is rather spread out. You're unlikely to spend much time beyond the old town, however, where you can easily walk everywhere. You'll only need a taxi (or horse-drawn *coche*) for getting to the bus terminal.

VISITOR INFORMATION

The closest Sancti Spíritus comes to having a tourist information office is the travel agency **Cubatur** (✆ **41/32-8518**), Máximo Gómez 7, on the west side of Plaza Sánchez.

FAST FACTS

BANKS/ATMS The **Banco Financiero Internacional,** Independencia 2 between Plaza Sánchez and Honorato (✆ **41/32-8479**), is open Monday through Friday 8:30am to 3:30pm. The BPA, just up the street, has ATMs. The **CADECA** branch at Independencia 31 (✆ **41/32-8535**) is open Monday through Saturday 8am to 4:30pm and Sunday 8:30am to 11:30am.

INTERNET You can access the internet and make long-distance or international phone calls at the **Etecsa** office on Independencia 10 Sur between Plaza Sánchez and Honorato opposite the CADECA; it's open daily from 8:30am to 7pm.

MEDICAL The **Hospital Provincial Camilo Cienfuegos** is located on Carretera Central at Bartolomé Masó (✆ **41/32-4017**).

POST OFFICE The **post office** is at Calle Independencia 8 (Mon–Sat 8am–6pm).

Exploring the Area

It won't take much more than a morning or afternoon to check out Sancti Spíritus's principal attractions. The old town is very nontouristy and unassuming, and perfect for an easygoing stroll.

Calle Llano is the most atmospheric street in Sancti Spíritus, a bent-elbow cobblestone alleyway (one of the only remaining stone streets in town) of pastel-colored and tiled-roof houses. It's often very still, except for a few kids playing stickball. **Puente Yayabo,** the bridge over the river at the southern edge of the old town, is a 19th-century take on a European Romanesque stone bridge said to be built of sand, lime mortar, and donkey milk. Locals bound over it at great speed, on bicycles, in horse-drawn wagons, and in 1950s Chevys on their way to and from the Colón residential district.

The main hub of life in Sancti Spíritus is **Plaza Serafín Sánchez,** a large public square with a handful of fine colonial buildings. It certainly doesn't qualify as one of Cuba's most attractive plazas, but it is perennially busy with cars buzzing around and people meeting up. One of the most notable edifices on the square, on the corner of Solano and Máximo Gómez, is the **Biblioteca Provincial Rubén Martínez ★**, an early-20th-century library that looks more like the local opera house. Head inside to see one of the largest crystal chandeliers on the island (Mon–Fri 8am–5pm and Sat 8am–4pm). The main sights in town are a short walk south of here.

Perhaps Sancti Spíritus's most splendid colonial home, **Museo de Arte Colonial ★★**, Plácido 74 at Jesús Menéndez (**© 41/32-5455**), is the city's standout attraction. The opulent 1744 former palatial mansion of one of Cuba's most elite families, the Valle-Iznaga clan, who fled Cuba after the Revolution, it became the property of the state in 1961. Ninety percent of what you see inside, from furniture to paintings, is original. Though the family obviously kept an impressive collection of Limoges porcelain, French gilded mirrors, Italian marble tables, and Baccarat crystal chandeliers here, this wasn't their primary residence; the house was used mostly to host family members in transit, so the furnishings were rather eclectic. The three bedrooms are decorated in grand style, though, with handmade lace, embroidered sheets, and hand-painted glass. Note the gorgeous and very Cuban leather *sillón fumador* (smoking chair) and, in the music room, the 1800 American piano, one of only two of its type in Cuba. In the second bedroom is the family seal, which says a lot about the arrogance of the rich and powerful: *"El que más vale no vale tanto como Valle vale"* ("He who has the greatest worth isn't worth as much as a Valle is worth"—playing off the Spanish word for "worth" with the family surname). The museum is open Tuesday through Saturday from 9:30am to 5pm and Sunday from 8am to noon. Admission is CUC$2 with a guided tour in English, Spanish, or French; there is a fee of CUC$1 to take photos.

Iglesia Parroquial Mayor del Espíritu Santo ★, Jesús Menéndez between Honorato and Agramonte, is one of the best-preserved colonial churches in Cuba and the oldest building in Sancti Spíritus. A small, blue church with a bell tower, the newly painted construction dates to 1680. The church's massive Mudejár ceiling and domed altar ceiling are impressive, as is the blue-and-gold painted nave. Though the church is unlikely to wow most visitors, it is a quietly evocative, authentic colonial sight that recalls a day when Sancti Spíritus may have looked more like Trinidad. It's open daily from 9am to 5pm; admission is free.

Next to the Museo de la Guayabera in the former Restaurant Santa Elena (Padre Quintero btw. Llano and Manolico Díaz) is the **Casa de Guayabera,** where Angel (**© 5809-5812**) will make your own *guayabera* (Cuban traditional shirt) from CUC$40 against the backdrop of the world's largest guayabera (5m x 3m). It's open Tuesday through to Sunday 9:30am to 5pm.

Where to Stay

Sancti Spíritus has two charming boutique hotels, as well as a good collection of *casas particulares* clustered within easy walking distance of the old town's main attractions. **Hostal Paraíso ★**, Máximo Gómez 11 Sur between Honorato (Parque Honorato) and Cervantes (http://paraiso.trinidadhostales.com; ✆ **41/33-4658** or **5271-1257;** hectorluisparaiso64@gmail.com), has four comfortable rooms—one in an old doctor's consulting room where an original glass cabinet is embedded in the wall—and a garden patio for filling breakfasts and delicious dinners.

Hostal Encanto del Rijo ★ This handsomely restored, duck-egg-blue colonial mansion on Plaza Honorato del Castillo is part of a growing trend in elegant boutique hotels. The 1827 house was in complete ruins just several years ago, but it has been completely redone and now exudes colonial character and charm. The rooms are huge, especially nos. 5, 6, 7, and 8, which look out onto the plaza and have balconies with views of the tower of La Parroquial church. The accommodations décor is restrained, with cream and chocolate color threads and old photos of Sancti Spíritus. The two-story structure is built around a lovely patio with a fountain, where you'll find the hotel's little restaurant. There's also a nice cafe and bar that opens onto the plaza. The suite, with three balconies, is the standout room, but if you're noise sensitive, you'll want to opt for an interior room.

Honorato del Castillo 12. www.islazul.cu. ✆ **41/32-8588.** rperurena@islazulssp.tur.co.cu. 16 units. CUC$80–CUC$100 double; CUC$100–CUC$120 suite. **Amenities:** Restaurant; bar; room service; Internet.

Hotel Encanto Don Florencio★ This handsomely restored 1918 doctor's house with royal blue columns and lots of planters is really the pick of the town thanks to a location set away from the traffic on a pedestrian boulevard. Opt for one of the upstairs rooms, with their high ceilings, smart chairs, and plush textiles in orange, honey, maroon, and gold. Only two rooms feature balconies; of these you'll want the largest (no. 8). You can while away the afternoon in the two Jacuzzis in the courtyard (a little overlooked by the attractive bar area) or play the piano upstairs on the landing surrounded by original Louis XV furniture. This hotel has another unique attribute: A masonic lodge operates on the premises.

Independencia Sur 632. www.islazul.cu. ✆ **41/32-8306.** 12 units. CUC$80–CUC$120. **Amenities:** Restaurant; bar; 2 Jacuzzis; room service; Internet.

Hotel E Plaza This small blue hotel right off Plaza Sánchez is on a busy corner of the city, so you'll want to choose your rooms wisely and perhaps not be tempted by rooms with balconies. My favorite is the very spacious room 212, with a king-size bed and threads in bronze, taupe, and chocolate. Although the interior courtyard provides a cool retreat from the heat of the sun, this property lacks the charm of the other two city center hotels.

Independencia 2 (Plaza Sánchez), Sancti Spíritus. www.islazul.cu. © **41/32-7102.** 27 units. CUC$60–CUC$75 double. Rates include breakfast. MC, V. **Amenities:** Restaurant, bar; room service; Internet.

Where to Dine

Taberna Yayabo (Calle Jesús Menéndez between Padre Quintero y Puente Yayabo 106; 5383-7552), is a new state enterprise with flair in a great position overlooking the River Yayabo. Settle into one of the cute balconies overlooking the river, at the bar tables inside or on the tambores-turned-bar seats at the bar. Tapas, wines, and fixed-price menus are on offer. We recommend the grilled shrimps in garlic—not least because you're guaranteed large shrimps, now rare in Cuba as they are being exported. Slip down into the basement *cava* for champagne and slices of jamón serrano imported from Spain. It's open 9am to 11pm daily.

Just 5 minutes' walk from the main plaza, **Paladar Las Delicias del Paseo,** Avenida de los Mártires 255, corner of Julio A Mella (www.lasdelicias delpaseo.com; © **41/32-1325**), is worth the diversion for the tender fillet of fish cooked in parsley and lemon. This is a no-frills paladar—with pasta and other *comida criolla* options—but it's the best in town. It's open noon to 10pm daily.

CAMAGÜEY & THE NORTHEASTERN COAST

8

The extraordinary, powdery, dazzling white beaches of Cayo Coco and Cayo Guillermo, the cays that lie off the Cuban mainland and jut into the deep aquamarine blue of the Atlantic Ocean, are the primary attractions of the Ciego de Avila province. It is a remote area, but one with the infrastructure and natural gifts that make it perfect for idyllic sun, sand, and sea holidays.

The namesake provincial capital **Ciego de Avila** and other towns and cities in this province hold few attractions for visitors. A little farther east, the predominantly flat, low-lying **Camagüey province,** southeast of Ciego de Avila, is the largest in the country, though it is also the least densely populated. It occupies the widest swath on the island, 120km (75 miles) from the Atlantic coast to the Caribbean coast. **Camagüey,** the provincial capital, is Cuba's third-largest city, after Havana and Santiago de Cuba, and is a fine colonial city that is worth exploring. Its architectural wealth was recognized by UNESCO in 2008, when its historic core was named a World Heritage Site.

CAYO COCO & CAYO GUILLERMO ★★

98km (61 miles) N of Ciego de Avila; 550km (342 miles) E of Havana; 270km (168 miles) NE of Trinidad; 202km (126 miles) NW of Camagüey

One of Cuba's premier beach destinations, distinguished by some of the most pristine sand and seas on the island, Cayo Coco and Cayo Guillermo are cousin cays *(cayos)* reached by crossing a 27km (17-mile) *pedraplén,* or man-made causeway, that extends from the mainland over the shimmering, shallow waters of the Atlantic. The cays share some of the same attributes as Varadero, but with a more isolated and natural feel, and without the interminable string of hotels—although rapacious hotel development is now changing all that.

Cayo Coco & Cayo Guillermo

ATLANTIC
OCEAN

Cayo Media Luna
Playa del Medio
Guillermo Diving Center
Playa Pilar
Playa El Paso
CAYO GUILLERMO
Dolphinarium
Marina

Playa los Perros
Playa Los Flamencos
Playa Prohibida
Playa Concha
Playa Las Coloradas
Gasolina

Cayo Botella

CAYO COCO

Aeropuerto Internacional

Cayo las Cayamas

B a h i a d e P e r r o s

Cayo Romano

0 5 mi
0 5 km

$ Bank
Beach

HOTELS ■
Gran Caribe Club
 Cayo Guillermo **2**
Meliá Cayo Coco **6**
Meliá Cayo Guillermo **1**
Sol Cayo Coco **5**

ATTRACTIONS ●
Acuavida Spa-Talaso **4**
La Cueva de Jabalí **3**

Isla de Turiguanó
San Rafael
To Morón
Manatí

Havana The Cayos Cayo Alto
C U B A
Cayo Judas

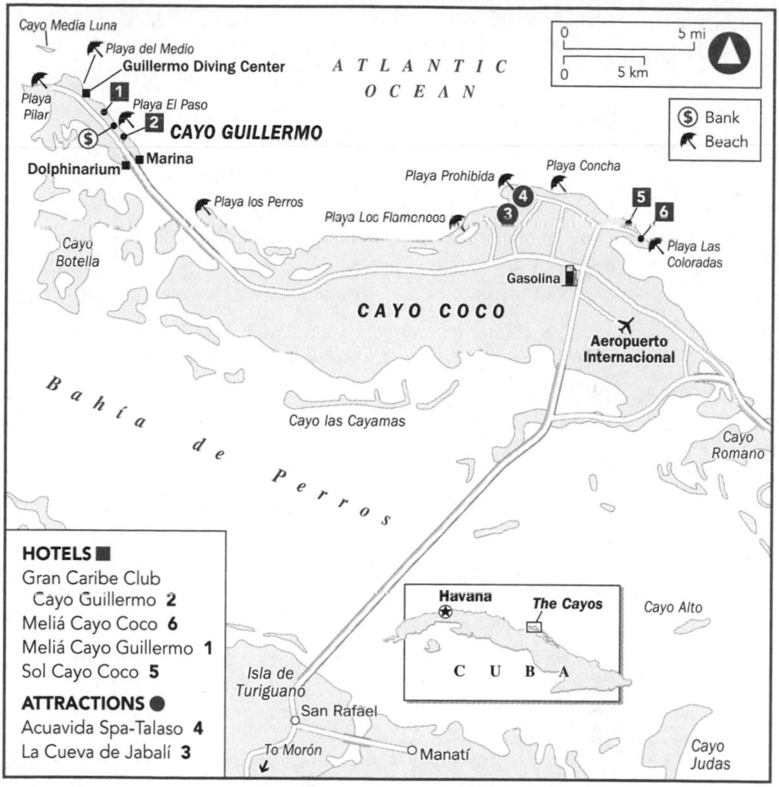

Though these cays were explored way back in 1514, when Diego Velázquez named the stretch of islands and cays along the north coast **Jardines del Rey (the King's Gardens),** Cayo Coco was only developed for tourism in the early 1990s. Until construction of the causeway in 1988, the Cayos remained completely isolated, exclusively known to local fishermen, adventurous sailors like Ernest Hemingway, and pirates who would stow their treasures.

The cays are part of the Archipélago de Sabana-Camagüey, which extends 300km (186 miles) along the north coast and consists of some 400 large islands and small cays. Cayos Coco and Guillermo, the most developed of the entire stretch, are populated by an increasing number of resort hotels. The unspoiled beaches have spectacular white and powdery sand and the waters are a classic Caribbean-style crystalline turquoise. A third cay—east of Cayo Coco, Cayo Romano, and the beaches out on Cayo Paredón Grande—is the next bull's-eye targeted for Cuban hotel development in the archipelago. The area's natural gifts are some of the best in Cuba: nearly 400km (250 miles) of coral reefs, plus an ecotourist's bundle of lagoons, marshes, and one of Cuba's most abundant populations of birds, with more than 200 species. The latter includes one of the Americas' largest native colony of pink flamingos, estimated at upwards of 10,000 birds, which often appear as a gauzy pink haze shimmering on the horizon, as well as herons, pelicans, black and white egrets, white ibis, and other tropical species. (The white ibis, known as "coco" in Cuba, gave the cay its name.) The waters off the cays are flush with grouper, snapper, and mackerel, while deeper off the coast, fishermen find marlin and swordfish.

The focus for most guests is trained squarely on the beaches, swimming pools, watersports, dining and drinking, in-house activities, and nightly entertainment; rare is the traveler who comes seeking something else. If you have other activities in mind, your sense of isolation could be significant, although for those who get antsy, all the hotels offer local excursions as well as day trips and overnights to Trinidad, Santa Clara, Cienfuegos, Camagüey, and Havana. Private taxis also abound; you will be approached about classic car tours in all the hotels.

Essentials

GETTING THERE

BY PLANE The **Aeropuerto Internacional Jardines del Rey,** Cayo Coco (© **33/30-9165;** airport code CCC), accepts international flights from Canada, Argentina, and the U.K. There are three daily domestic flights on **AeroGaviota** (© **33/30-2260**) from Havana for CUC$101.

The hotels offer airport pickup services for clients. If you have not prearranged transportation to your hotel, there are usually a couple of taxis hanging about. The fare from Aeropuerto Internacional Jardines del Rey is CUC$10 to CUC$15 to Cayo Coco and CUC$15 to CUC$25 to Cayo Guillermo.

BY BUS/TAXI If you're traveling independently to the cays from within Cuba, getting there on your own without a rental car or authorized taxi is complicated. The only bus services that travel across the checkpoint are those belonging to official tour operators. All of these operators offer package deals and transportation options to the cays from all of their major operational points, including Havana, Santiago, Varadero, Trinidad, Santa Clara, Cienfuegos, and Camagüey.

A more complicated way to the cays is to take a **Víazul** bus (www.viazul.com; © **33/20-3086**) to Ciego de Avila, and then hire a taxi all the way to the cays for between CUC$80 to CUC$120. Bargain very hard. All Víazul buses on the Havana-Santiago route stop in Ciego de Avila. The fare is CUC$27 from Havana and CUC$24 from Santiago. Make sure you hire a driver who is authorized to transport foreigners to the cays. The nearest town to the cays with legal *casas particulares* is Morón (p. 186).

BY CAR/TAXI To drive to the cays, head north out of Ciego de Avila toward the city of Morón, and follow the signs out to the cays. Call **Cubataxi** (© **33/26-6666** in Ciego de Avila). A taxi from Trinidad costs CUC$140. A taxi from Morón to Cayo Coco is CUC$45 and to Cayo Guillermo CUC$55 to CUC$65. From Ciego to Avila to Morón it's CUC$15 to CUC$25. You have to pass a guarded checkpoint with a toll each way of CUC$2 to access the *pedraplén* that bridges the distance between the mainland and the cays. Remember that if you travel from Morón to the cays for the day you will need to show your passport at the checkpoint. There are rental offices in Morón and Ciego de Avila.

GETTING AROUND

You won't get very far on foot. The cays are deceptively large, and there's no place to go on foot anyway, unless you want to visit an adjacent hotel. The best way to get around the cays—and off the beaten track—is by **moped.** Most of the hotels have mountain bikes (free for guests) and mopeds that rent for CUC$25 a day.

A tourist bus, **Jardines del Rey Bus Tour,** makes the entire circuit from one end of Playa Coco to Playa Pilar at the far end of Cayo Guillermo. The bus runs six times a day in each direction, and costs CUC$5 (for the day), taking in all the hotels, the dolphinarium, spa, and market. A **tourist train** also circulates around the eastern Cayo Coco hotels from the Melia Cayo Coco to the market and back (CUC$3 return).

All of the hotels can call you a cab, or you can try **Cubataxi** (✆ **33/30-1414**) on Cayo Coco. If you prefer to drive yourself, car-rental companies are located on both Cayo Coco and Cayo Guillermo, and most hotels have agencies on the premises. **Cubacar** has an office at Calle Libertad between Honrato del Castillo and Maceo, Ciego de Avila (✆ **33/21-2570**) and at Av. Tarafa, Morón (✆ **33/50-2115**); **Cubacar** also has an office at the bus terminal in Ciego de Avila (✆ **33/22-5105**) and in the Hotel Morón in Morón (✆ **33/50-2028**). All have operational centers on Jardines del Rey. Thanks to high demand and isolation, rates are relatively expensive on the cays, about CUC$80 to CUC$100 per day for a standard four-door vehicle. You're sometimes better off renting a car in Ciego de Avila or Morón before traveling to the cays.

All the hotels offer a variety of **organized excursions** that transport guests by bus or minibus from one cay to the other or to other destinations, such as Playa Pilar on Cayo Guillermo.

FAST FACTS

BANKS/ATMS **Banco Financiero Internacional** is in the Servicupet at the Rotonda at the entrance to Cayo Coco (✆ **33/30-1252**) and at the **Iberostar Daiquirí** in Cayo Guillermo (✆ **33/30-1607**).

INTERNET Hotels operate Nauta Internet with cards selling at CUC$4.50/hr. Wi-Fi is often limited to the lobbies of hotels. International and domestic mail can be handled at any of the hotels.

MEDICAL For medical attention, go to **Clínica Internacional Cayo Coco** (✆ **33/30-2158**). The Hospital General Docente de Morón has a designated foreigners' ward.

PAPA & THE cayos

Ernest Hemingway's love of sailing and deep-sea fishing is well documented, a great source of his love affair with Cuba. The novelist was one of the first to explore Cayo Guillermo; in the '30s and '40s, Hemingway used to set sail off the coasts of the northern cays in dogged pursuit of marlin and swordfish in the Atlantic. The celebrated beach on Cayo Guillermo, Playa Pilar, is even named for the author's beloved fishing boat, *Pilar.* In an episode befitting his he-man, roguish character, Hemingway enlisted his crew and boat to hunt for Nazi submarines off Cuba's northern cays at the height of World War II (according to some, the island was awash with Nazi sympathizers and agents). Papa's companion was, as ever, Gregorio Fuentes, the model for the aged fisherman in *The Old Man and the Sea.*

In Hemingway's novel *Islands in the Stream*, the main character looks longingly across the bay at Cayo Guillermo, asking rhetorically, "See how green she is and full of promise?" Evidently the Cuban authorities, intent on developing the cays a half century after Hemingway first explored them, feel the same way.

What to See & Do

The best-known **Cayo Coco beaches ★★** are **Playa Larga** and **Playa Las Coloradas. Playa Los Flamencos** is a few kilometers west, and beyond this is **Playa Prohibida.** They're among the most stellar beaches to be found in all of Cuba. In the interior of the cay are lagoons and marshlands, havens for the local bird and animal populations.

Cayo Guillermo is connected to Cayo Coco by a 15km (9-mile) *pedraplén.* **Cayo Guillermo beaches ★★** (**Playa El Paso and Playa del Medio**) are every bit as spectacular as those on Cayo Coco; in fact, at low tide, the crystal-clear waters are so shallow that you can comfortably wade out several hundred meters. The landscape is very similar to Cayo Coco, but Guillermo boasts the most spectacular beach of either cay: **Playa Pilar ★★**, long ago explored by Ernest Hemingway and today a popular day trip for hotel guests on both cays. Playa Pilar features high sand dunes, an attractive blue-and-white walkway and a restaurant on the beach serving up seafood (CUC$6.50–CUC$15) and other dishes from CUC$3. Sun loungers are charged at CUC$2 a day; Balinese sunbeds at CUC$10. Just one kilometer away is **Cayo Media Luna,** a popular spot for snorkelers. Unfortunately, Playa Pilar's virgin status is about to be wrecked by the opening of several large hotels.

El Parque de Escalada (Torre de Cristal Rocarena) is a large circular structure with a circuit of ropes on three levels; it will feature 90 attractions of different grades of difficulty for adventure lovers when it opens.

DIVING & OTHER WATERSPORTS

With long, pristine stretches of coral reef and warm, crystal-clear waters, the cays are a popular diving spot. There are 28 dive sites, including five superior sites easily accessible from the cays, which range in depth from 4 to 30m (13–98 ft.). All the hotels on Cayo Coco and Cayo Guillermo can organize diving excursions, but you may want to consult one of the main outfits directly, like **Blue Diving** (© **33/30-8179**), at the Meliá Cayo Coco; **Coco Diving** (© **33/30-1020**; cocodiving.cav@tur.cu), at Tryp Cayo Coco; and **Green Moray** at Meliá Cayo Guillermo (© **33/30-1627**), which offers certified programs, several dive packages, and diving excursions to Playa Santa Lucía and Trinidad. A two-tank dive runs around CUC$83, including equipment.

Most of the hotels have their own catamarans, sailboards, and other vehicles and facilities for watersports; **kitesurfing** is also popular from October through April. **Marlin Jardines del Rey** on Cayo Guillermo (© **33/30-1515** or 33/30-1581) has a wide range of watersports programs, including "seafari" catamaran trips to Paredón Grande, east of Cayo Coco and a complement of kayaks and windsurfing boards. The **International Marina** on Cayo Guillermo (© **33/30-1737/1323**) has a pier and facilities, including diving and sportfishing trips. Full-day catamaran trips run about CUC$79 per person; half-day trips are CUC$43. **Boat Adventure ★** (© **33/30-1516**) offers 2-hour small-speedboat trips (self-driven, with a guide) through a maze of mangrove canals, marshes, and wetlands in Cayo Guillermo, a scenic trip with stops for snorkeling; CUC$46 per person. Glass-bottom-boat excursions with snorkeling run CUC$25. Private boat charters are also possible but expensive, costing from CUC$480. Fishing is available from CUC$240 for a half-day. Call © **33/30-2139** for information or contact **Ecotur** at © **33/30-8163.**

ORGANIZED TOURS

All the hotels offer day trips to remote beaches, including the finest in the cays, **Playa Pilar** (CUC$59), as well as **city tours** by minibus to Morón, Ciego de Avila, Santa Clara, Trinidad, and Camagüey, or to Havana (CUC$189–CUC$289) by plane. Other options include **sugarcane tours** that take visitors to a decommissioned sugar factory that now produces sweets, tours of the **Criadero de Crocodrilos** (crocodile breeding center), a boat trip on Redonda lagoon (see below; CUC$65), and visits to **Sitio La Güira** (a purpose-built dude ranch; CUC$75 with lunch). Horseback treks and jeep safaris (CUC$79) through the interior of the cays and to Morón are also available. A popular trip is to **Laguna de la Leche ★**, a massive lake on the outskirts of Morón with plenty of pelicans and other native birds. The lake's name comes from the water's murky, milky appearance (caused by limestone deposits). Another, much smaller lake that's worth a visit is **Laguna La Redonda,** where you'll find thick mangroves, swamps, and funky woodlands growing out of the still waters. It's best seen by *lancha* (motorboat) tour leaving from the entrance of the little restaurant (CUC$4 for a 45-minute trip). On a cruise, you'll see huge spider webs, massive mounds of termites in trees, and thick Spanish moss. Both lakes are most often visited in combination with a city tour of Morón (CUC$40).

TIME FOR SOME PAMPERING

The **Acuavida Spa-Talaso** (www.servimedcuba.com; © **33/30-2158;** yusnaisydida@gmail.com) offers a wide range of massage and spa treatments. Options range from mud baths and seaweed scrubs to full-body massages and a host of water-based treatments. The large facility has five pools in a range of sizes and temperatures. Some are freshwater pools, while others take advantage of the neighboring seawater. It's open Monday to Saturday 9:30am to 7pm.

Where to Stay & Dine on Cayo Coco

Almost all visitors to Jardines del Rey come as part of an all-inclusive package and take all their meals at their hotels. If you want to take a break from your hotel fare, check out the simple state-run Ranchón shacks selling seafood on a couple of the beaches. The number of hotels on both cayes now runs to nearly 20. We have distilled the best. On Cayo Coco we also recommend the more reasonably priced **Sol Cayo Coco** (www.meliacuba.com; ✆ **33/30-1280;** 270 units; CUC$173–CUC$360 double).

EXPENSIVE

Meliá Cayo Coco ★★★ An elegant hotel on a beautiful swath of beach, this is the Meliá flagship hotel in the Jardines del Rey (Gardens of the King). Rooms splashed in candy pink are divided between blocks scattered in a circular route around the gardens; rooms that are more modern and bright are located in casitas overlooking the lagoon. You'll want the attractive first-floor rooms, done in sea-blue colors with modern artworks in blues and pinks on the walls. The stylish **Arena Beach Bar** is well positioned right on the beach; just behind is a pool area surrounded by gazebos and thatched umbrellas. The only down side? The pool bar is not as close as it could be to the pool. The hotel's popular main restaurant, **Las Caletas,** on the lagoon, serves an international dinner menu and also doubles as a private breakfast arena for some guests.

A STOPOVER IN morón

Located 37km (23 miles) north of Ciego de Avila, Morón (Moh-*rohn*) is the small gateway city to the cays, and home to most of the Cubans who work at the resort hotels. With just a few dusty streets traveled by bicycles, horse-drawn carriages, and antique American autos, low-key Morón is most notable for its splendid, if dilapidated, collection of colonial buildings that lines the main street, **Calle Martí.** Most visitors arrive by bus or taxi from Ciego de Avila or Camagüey or on an organized tour from one of the hotels on the Cayos. Though Morón possesses an evocative **1920s railway station** and a **Municipal Museum,** Calle Martí 374 (✆ **33/50-4501;** admission CUC$1), with pre-Columbian artifacts and idols, most travelers are content to stroll up and down Martí, absorbing the relaxed local flavor. The town mascot is the cock of Morón, a bronze statue placed at the foot of a clock tower near the Hotel Morón.

Some visitors decamp to Morón as a less-expensive alternative to the all-inclusive luxury hotels on the cays. The best lodging options are the *casa particulares.* **Casa Xiomara,** Calle 8 no. 2-C, between Calle Sordo y Calle C (✆ **33/50-4236;** lisbet74@nauta.cu), is a modest, modern family home that offers one excellent air-conditioned guest room in an independent *casita.* Dine on Xiomara's wonderful food—try the *flan de leche*—while relaxing under hibiscus flowers and mango trees.

Note: Casita S21 is quite exposed, so guests staying there might not get the privacy they are seeking. The daily program of activities is extensive and the staff committed. As a Meliá guest, you can dine at other Meliá properties on the cayes between 9am and 5pm.

www.meliacuba.com. ✆ **33/30-1180.** 250 units. CUC$202–CUC$342 double. Rates are all-inclusive. MC, V. Children under 18 not allowed. **Amenities:** 4 restaurants; snack bar; 5 bars; bikes; dive center; gym; outdoor pool; room service; sauna; scooter rental; smoke-free rooms; 2 lit outdoor tennis courts; watersports equipment; Internet.

Where to Stay on Cayo Guillermo

EXPENSIVE

Meliá Cayo Guillermo ★★ This large luxury hotel is less intimate than the flagship Meliá Cayo Coco but sits on a stunning stretch of beach that in my mind is more beautiful than that of Cayo Coco. The Meliá here also boasts a jetty that stretches out into the shallow turquoise sea. Pull up a sun lounger under one of the four thatched ranchóns on the pier for one of Cuba's most exquisite views. Set in luxuriant grounds, the large property is centered around a swimming pool crisscrossed by white bridges and featuring an in-pool bar cascading with water and the well-positioned beach grill. The best rooms in the property that are close to the beach are the low-slung standard rooms 3101 and 3102 in cream, taupe, and caramel colors.

www.meliacuba.com. ✆ **33/30-1680.** 301 units. CUC$181–CUC$370 double; suite CUC$231–CUC$400. Rates are all-inclusive. Children's rates available. MC, V. **Amenities:** 4 restaurants; snack bar; 4 bars; dance club; children's center and programs; dive center; fitness center; outdoor pool; sauna; scooter rentals; smoke-free rooms; 2 lit outdoor tennis courts; watersports equipment; Internet.

MODERATE

Gran Caribe Club Cayo Guillermo ★ Formerly Villa Cojímar, this budget option is a great place to stay and has even had a makeover in recent years. Divided between older-style bungalows that sit right on a fantastic stretch of beach and newer wooden cabañas set back in gardens, this represents the best value in the Gardens of the King. The two pools have new sun loungers, umbrellas, and two inflatable poolside slides. Although the food is nothing like that available at the smarter all-inclusives, it has improved and is adequate. The small hotel beach has a lovely pier, and coconut palms abound. This is also a favorite spot for kitesurfers. The shallow sea and the kid's club make this perfect for families—although the 7pm buffet dinner start is not necessarily family friendly. Two new a la carte restaurants have been built in the grounds.

www.gran-caribe.cu. ✆ **33/30-1712.** 324 units. CUC$180–CUC$220 double. Rates are all-inclusive. Children's rates available. MC, V. **Amenities:** 3 restaurants; snack bar; 3 bars; dance club; children's club; 2 outdoor pools (1 for children); sauna; scooter rental; nightly show; 2 outdoor tennis courts; watersports equipment.

Jardines del Rey After Dark

Most folks simply take advantage of the bars and nightly shows at their all-inclusive resorts. The disco at **La Cueva de Jabalí ★** (✆ **33/30-1206;** open

Tues and Thurs 10:30pm–2am; CUC$25, including open bar), 5 kilometers (3 miles) from the Cayo Coco hotel strip, is set in the belly of a small underground cave. Bring insect repellent to fight off the mosquitoes inside the cave. Another alternative is **La Bolera** (© **33/30-1697**), a four-lane bowling alley that also serves as a bar and cabaret, located near the Meliá Cayo Guillermo.

Farther South: Jardines de la Reina ★★★

South of Ciego de Avila is the protected pristine chain of islands known as the **Archipíelago de los Jardines de la Reina (Gardens of the Queen)**, with hundreds of uninhabited virgin cays. But the real attraction lies underwater, where some of the best diving and fishing in the Caribbean is found. Some 80 dive sites offer the possibility of seeing whale sharks, hammerhead sharks, bull sharks, reef sharks, silky sharks, nurse sharks, and hawksbill turtles, among others. (High season for whale sharks runs Aug–Jan, with the peak months being Oct–Dec.) Anglers can hope to catch an abundance of bonefish, tarpon, permit fish, horse-eye jacks, mutton snapper, and silky sharks.

There is only one authorized diving and fishing operation based out of Júcaro, south of Ciego de Avila: **Avalon** (www.cubandivingcenters.com or www.cubanfishingcenters.com), which runs 6-night diving and fishing packages on five live-aboard boats (the best is the new, luxury *Avalon II,* although the top rooms on this boat are oddly configured) or the floating hotel La Tortuga. Prices run from 2,089€ to 3,622€ for diving (including accommodations, meals, drinks, transfers, and dives, but excluding 324€ inscription fee and $CUC50 park fee).

CAMAGÜEY ★★

553km (344 miles) E of Havana; 110km (68 miles) E of Ciego de Avila; 328km (204 miles) W of Santiago de Cuba

One of Cuba's most historic and important cities, Camagüey is an excellent place to get a feel for Cuba's colonial-era grandeur. Founded as the sixth of Cuba's original seven *villas* in 1514—as a port town originally named Santa María del Puerto del Príncipe—the city was later moved to a different spot by Diego Velázquez himself in 1516 and transplanted again to its present, inland location in 1528. The town didn't receive its final name, which means "Son of the Tree" in the Taíno language, until after the conclusion of the Spanish-American War in 1898.

Camagüey retains a strong colonial imprint, with a highly irregular layout and warren of narrow, bending streets and alleyways, handsome colonial houses, two of the most dignified colonial plazas in Cuba, and an unequaled collection of impressive, if evocatively dilapidated, 16th-, 17th-, and 18th-century churches. In fact, Camagüey is often called *la ciudad del Barroco* (city of baroque) or *la ciudad de las iglesias* (city of churches). Another symbol of the city is the *tinajón,* a massive terra-cotta water jug used in the 18th and 19th centuries to collect rainwater. These now largely decorative items can still be seen in the serene gardens and courtyards of the city's colonial houses. Its

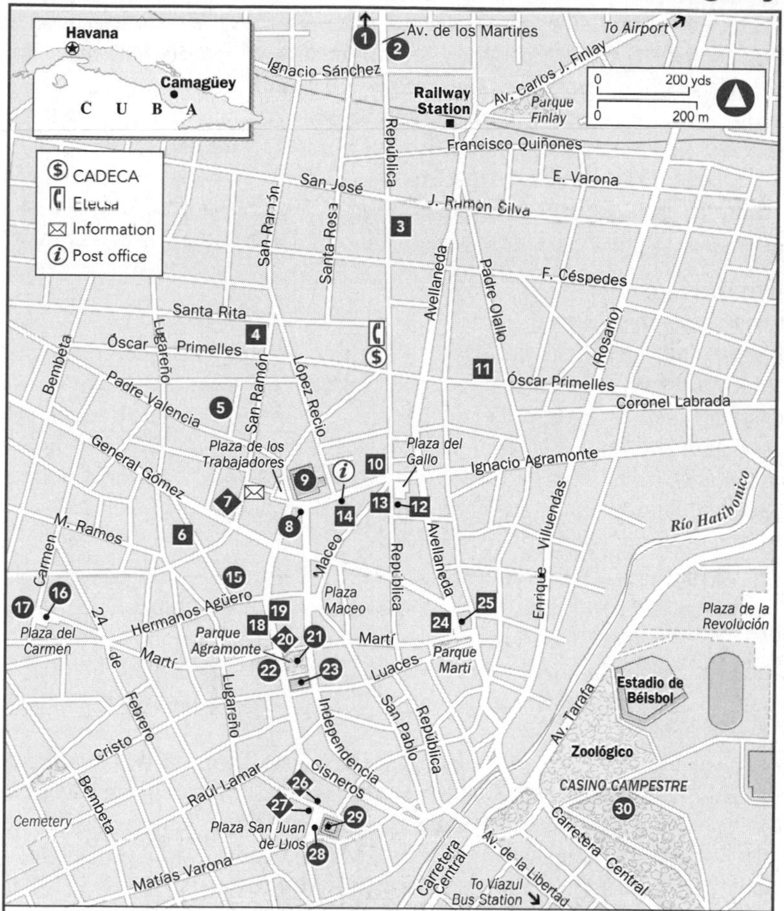

ATTRACTIONS ●

Casa de la Trova **22**
Casa Natal del Mayor (Ignacio Agramonte) **8**
Casa Natal Nicolás Guillén **15**
Casino Campestre **30**
Hospital de San Juan de Díos **29**
Iglesia de Nuestra Señora de la Merced **9**
Iglesia de Nuestra Señora del Carmen **17**
Iglesia San Juan de Díos **29**
La Catedral **23**
Museo Provincial General Ignacio Agramonte **2**
Parque Agramonte **21**
Plaza del Carmen **16**
Plaza San Juan de Díos **28**
Teatro Principal **5**
Tifereht Israel Synagogue **1**

RESTAURANTS ◆

Café de la Ciudad **20**
Casa Italia **7**
La Campana de Toledo **26**
Restaurante 1800 **27**

HOTELS ■

Casa Caridad **11**
Casa Eduardo y Geraldine **6**
Casa Los Vitrales **24**
Casa Xiomara & Rodolfo **4**
Gran Hotel **14**
Hotel Camino de Hierro **13**
Hotel El Marqués **19**
Hotel Islazul Colón **3**
Hotel La Avellaneda **12**
Hotel La Sevillana **18**
Hotel Santa María **10**
Natural Caribe **25**

historical and architectural wealth was recognized by UNESCO in 2008 and the historic core is now a World Heritage Site.

Travelers intent on experiencing the cultural offerings of urban, interior Cuba should not skip Camagüey. The birthplace of Cuba's national poet, Nicolás Guillén, Camagüey claims some of the strongest artistic and literary traditions in Cuba and one of the country's most vital cultural scenes, with an active community of artists (worth the stop alone) and the internationally renowned Camagüey Ballet. Travelers could conceivably blow through and see the principal attractions in a day, but Camagüey requires at least 2 or 3 days or more to unfurl its significant charms and take in visits to the artists' studios.

Essentials

GETTING THERE

BY PLANE You can fly from Havana to Camagüey on **Aerocaribbean** (© **32/29-1338**) four times a week for CUC$89; there are also international charter flights from Canada. Flights arrive at **Aeropuerto Internacional Ignacio Agramonte,** Carretera Central Nuevitas Km 8 (© **32/26-1010;** airport code CMW), 9km (6 miles) west of the city. A local bus runs from the airport to Parque Casino and back, but a taxi is probably your best bet. A taxi from the airport to the city is CUC$10.

BY BUS **Víazul** (www.viazul.com; © **32/27-0396** in Camagüey) travels four times daily to Camagüey on the Santiago de Cuba-Trinidad line; from Santiago, 7½ hours (CUC$18); from Trinidad, one departure daily (CUC$15); and Havana–Santiago de Cuba lines. From Havana, the bus departs four times daily, and the ride takes about 9 hours (CUC$33). From Varadero, the bus travels overnight (CUC$25).

The main bus terminal for long-distance buses, the **Terminal de Omnibuses** (© **32/27-1668**) is located 2km (1¼ miles) southeast of the city, at Carretera Central 180 at the corner of Calle Perú. Taxis/bicitaxis charge CUC$5 to CUC$6 from the terminal to the city center. For buses to locations within Camagüey province, a separate **Terminal Municipal** (© **32/28-1525**) is located several blocks north of the old center, near the intersection of Padre Olallo and Avenida Carlos J. Finlay (just north of the railway station).

GETTING AROUND

The labyrinthine layout of Camagüey's old town is extremely complicated, though it is pretty compact. The best way to get to know the historic center is on foot. In fact, in and around Camagüey, you will mostly depend on leg power, though bicitaxis may be necessary to get back and forth between a couple of places.

BY TAXI There are a few taxis around town. Call **Cubataxi** (© **32/28-1247**) for local and long-distance hire. Bicycle-powered rickshaws also function as taxis around the historic center. A taxi to Playa Santa Lucía is CUC$60.

BY CAR A car isn't necessary if you are planning to stay put in Camagüey, but if you're looking to go beyond the city, the major car-rental company is

Cubacar (© **32/28-7067**). There are also company offices in the airport. Rates are about CUC$45 to CUC$85 per day for a standard four-door car.

VISITOR INFORMATION

An **Infotur** office is located on Ignacio Agramonte in the Callejón de los Milagros between República and López Recío (© **32-25/6794**); there's also an Infotur office at the airport.

Most of the major Cuban tour agencies operate several tour desks around Camagüey, and at all the major hotels. **Cubatur** operates at Ignacio Agramonte 421 (© **32/25-4785**); **Ecotur** (© **32/24-3693**), Calle San Esteban 453 (Hotel Isla de Cuba); **Cubanacan** (© **32/29-4905**), in the Gran Hotel; **Gaviota Tours** (© **32/25-3570**), Plaza Maceo. Cultural promoter **Paradiso,** Ignacio Agramonte 413 (© **32/28-6059;** paradscm@artex.cu), can arrange trips to see ballet rehearsals and a ballet shoe factory for CUC$5; you can also tour local artists' studios (CUC$5). It also offers city tours and courses in dance, singing, and ceramics (office open Mon–Fri only).

FAST FACTS

BANKS/ATMS You'll find a **Banco Financiero Internacional** (© **32/29-4846**) at Independencia 221, at Plaza de Maceo. It's open Monday through Friday 8:30am to 3pm. There is a **CADECA** (© **32/29-5220**) at República 353, open Monday to Saturday 8am to 6pm and Sunday 8am to 1pm. There are several other banks and money-exchange houses around the city.

MEDICAL If you need medical attention, **Servicios Médicos Internacionales** is located at Ignacio Agramonte 449, opposite the church of La Merced (© **32/33-6370**).

INTERNET An **Etecsa** Telepunto telephone and Internet center is on Calle República 453; it's open daily from 8:30am to 6:30pm. The main branch of **Correos** is at Ignacio Agramonte 461; it's open Monday through Saturday from 7:30am to 8pm.

What to See & Do

Camagüey's *casco histórico* (old quarter) is the primary draw, and most sights of interest are within easy walking distance of its epicenter, just north and west of the Hatibonico River. The historic zone represents one of the largest colonial sectors in Cuba, spread over 300 hectares (741 acres), and Camagüey boasts more than a dozen colonial churches. As in Havana, the office of the city historian is actively engaged in restoring as many of the city's historic buildings as it can manage, and by law, all businesses in the district contribute 2 percent of their revenues toward the restoration cause. Calle Maceo and Calle República are now pedestrian boulevards.

Parque Agramonte, which occupies the spot where the old Plaza de Armas existed in 1528, shortly after the transfer of the city to its present location, is the best place to get your bearings. In its center is a bronze and pink granite equestrian statue of the most famous citizen of Camagüey, Ignacio Agramonte. Each corner of the park is marked by a tall royal palm, planted to pay tribute to four local martyrs of the struggle for independence, who were executed in the square by Spanish forces for treason. The park is an agreeable spot, with elegant street lamps and marble benches popular with locals. It is flanked by attractive colonial houses, including the **Casa de la Trova** (where live traditional Cuban music can be heard daily), and the early-18th-century **Catedral** on the south side. The church is a good example of the city's ongoing efforts to resurrect neglected historic buildings. Dedicated to Nuestra Señora de la Candelaria, patron saint of Camagüey, the cathedral has been transformed from a dull and uninspiring church to an attractively austere house of worship, showing off beautiful *vigas* (wood ceiling beams). It is open Monday to Friday from 8 to 11:45am and 2 to 5pm, Saturday 3 to 4pm and Sunday 8 to 11:30am. Climb the tower (CUC$5) for wonderful photo opportunities.

Calle Maceo, just north of Parque Agramonte, is the city's principal shopping avenue, a busy pedestrian artery stuffed with shops and bars. The other principal reference point of downtown Camagüey is the much-trafficked but disappointingly pedestrian **Plaza de los Trabajadores (Workers' Square).** On it are two of the city's more important sights: the **birth house of Ignacio Agramonte** and the church of **La Merced.**

Southeast of the historic core, across the unspectacular Hatibonico River, lies **Casino Campestre,** Cuba's largest natural city park. Inaugurated in 1860, it was transformed into a public park at the beginning of the 20th century. Its tall, shady royal palms, public monuments, and kids' attractions make it a favorite with Camagüeyanos. Nearby, on the other side of the Cándido González baseball stadium, the massive but cold square **Plaza de la Revolución** honors Cuba's revolutionary legends past and present: Agramonte, Che, and Fidel.

THE TOP ATTRACTIONS

Casa Natal del Mayor (Ignacio Agramonte) Ignacio Agramonte y Loynaz, Camagüey's favorite son and the national hero of the independence struggle—known to all as "El Mayor"—was born December 23, 1841, in this pale yellow 18th-century house. Agramonte's birthplace displays classical colonial elements, both baroque and Hispanic-*mudéjar* (Hispanic-Moorish). The house, now a national monument, may interest those with a thirst for Cuban history; others may simply be interested in viewing the lovely carved wooden ceilings upstairs and period furnishings (only some are original to the house) of an authentic colonial house. A number of artifacts aim to reveal Agramonte's boyhood life here and his later achievements, with documents including love letters to Amalia Simoni (who would later become his bride), photographs, newspaper accounts of battles, and Agramonte's pistol.

Ignacio Agramonte 459, Plaza de los Trabajadores. ✆ **32/29-7116.** Admission CUC$2; camera use CUC$5. Tues–Sat 9am–4:30pm; Sun 9am–noon.

Casa Natal Nicolás Guillén Camagüey's most important literary figure, considered Cuba's national poet, was born in this house, which stands as a simple tribute to his life and enduring work. Guillén, born here in 1902, only lived in the house for 2 years, though he returned to Camagüey after studying law in Havana and worked as a journalist for a local paper. The house now functions primarily as a research and cultural center, with occasional poetry readings and concerts. A smattering of photographs, personal memorabilia, and copies of a handful of poems connect the house to the life and work of Guillén.

Calle Hermanos Agüero 58 (btw. Cisneros and Príncipe). ✆ **32/29-3706.** Free admission. Mon–Fri 8am–5pm.

Iglesia de Nuestra Señora de La Merced ★ The most significant structure on the rather plain Plaza de los Trabajadores is this massive, 18th-century brick church, Camagüey's most distinguished and, in its day, the largest in Cuba. A chapel existed on this spot in 1601; the present structure dates to 1748 (it was reconstructed in 1848 and again in 1909 after a fire). The old convent still houses a rapidly decreasing number of nuns. The church is an eclectic architectural mix. Adorning the ceiling are surprising Art Nouveau murals, added in the 20th century. Also of note: the painted wood, neo-Gothic altar and the **Santo Sepulcro,** a 1762 casket elaborately fashioned from 25,000 silver coins and carried high by eight men during Easter processionals. Down narrow stairs behind the principal altar is a mysterious crypt, the remains of an extensive underground cemetery. Most of it was closed off after fire damage, but six macabre tombs with skeletons remain and are on creepy view alongside a small museum of 18th- and 19th-century objects uncovered at the church.

Av. Agramonte 4 (Plaza de los Trabajadores). ✆ **32/29-2783.** You'll have to tip to gain access to the padlocked catacombs; free admission to the church. Mon–Sat 8am–noon and 4pm–5.30pm; Sun 8am–10am and 5:30–7pm. Access to the catacombs Mon–Sat 9am–1pm.

Museo Provincial General Ignacio Agramonte This large museum, housed in a 19th-century former barracks several blocks north of the pedestrianized Calle República, holds a large collection of Cuban art featuring the works of Wifredo Lam, Victor Manuel, and Amelia Peléaz, among others. It also has a selection of decorative arts, including furnishings and porcelain from the colonial and Republican periods. The natural-history rooms display native Cuban species, such as sharks, fish, and exotic fauna. The grand patio is known for its collection of *tinajones* (large ceramic pots).

Av. de los Mártires 2 (btw. Ignacio Sánchez and Rotario). ✆ **32/28-2425.** Admission CUC$1 adults, free children under 12. Tues–Sat 9am–4pm; Sun 9am–noon.

Camagüey's Synagogue

Camagüey has one of the more active, if still tiny, Jewish communities in Cuba, and many Jewish visitors from overseas visit the city's small synagogue, **Tifereht Israel,** Calle Andrés Sánchez 365, between Capdevila and J. de Agüero, La Vigía (✆ **32/28-4639**). Inaugurated in 1998, the synagogue serves just a handful of families, and the community is in the process of restoring the city's small Jewish cemetery, which had suffered from neglect. Visits are preferred after 5pm, so it's essential to call beforehand, although the synagogue is open all day.

Plaza del Carmen ★★ A narrow, pedestrian-only street of pastel-colored colonial row houses opens onto an irregularly shaped square. Renovations have revamped the 18th-century square with street lamps, huge *tinajones*, and slightly larger-than-life sculptures of locals in various poses of daily work and pleasure by ceramicist Martha Jiménez. This restored spot has done much to uncover a classic Camagüey colonial plaza.

Not long ago, the church and convent at the end of the open square stood roofless, in utter ruins. The baroque-style **Iglesia de Nuestra Señora del Carmen,** which dates to 1825, is now immaculately restored. It is the only church in Camagüey, and indeed in the whole eastern half of Cuba, topped by two towers. The church is open Tuesday to Saturday 8am to noon and 3 to 5pm. The early-19th-century **Monasterio de las Ursalinas (Ursuline Convent)** next door is now an architectural showpiece distinguished by handsome arches framing the expansive patio. Built in 1829, the convent later became a refuge for hurricane victims and a school for the poor. In the years following the Revolution, it served several purposes; most recently, it was a nondescript warehouse. The building was taken over in 1999 by the city historian's office, and today the convent is a beauty, with thick mustard-yellow columns, *tinajones*, and *mediopunto* (semi-circular stained-glass windows above wooden doors). You may visit the courtyard if the door is open.

Plaza del Carmen. Daily 24 hr.

Plaza San Juan de Dios ★★★ A national monument and one of the most remarkable colonial relics in Cuba, this elegant and serene square looks like a meticulously designed movie set. Its charms are subtle but undeniable. The colonial arches, cobblestones, and houses with red-tile roofs and window grilles speak volumes about Camagüey's colonial past. The square, whose present design dates to 1732, holds great significance for Cubans: The body of the national independence war hero Ignacio Agramonte was brought here, after being burned by the Spaniards, for identification in 1873.

On one side of the square are the 17th-century church and hospital of the order of San Juan de Dios. **La Iglesia San Juan de Dios** features a baroque colonial interior with dark-toned woods and the original brick floor. The church adjoins the handsome **Hospital de San Juan de Dios,** established to serve the poor. Padre José Olallo Valdés (1815–89), who furthered that mission, was beatified in 2008. Off one side of the cloisters are the remains of Agramonte, making the buildings even more of a sacred place for Camagüeyanos. The city now puts on art exhibits, concerts, and historical displays, such as old pharmaceutical objects, in one corner of the hospital. The understated but noble colonial structure contains a notable courtyard, thick doors, and an elegant wood staircase. Climb the stairs to the tower, from which there is a splendid view of all the church belfries spread across the skyline of the *centro histórico*.

Plaza San Juan de Dios. ✆ **32/29-1318.** Admission CUC$1. Mon–Sat 9am–4pm.

Shopping

You'll find *artesanía* (handicrafts) stands set up on **Plaza San Juan de Dios** Friday through Sunday.

If you want to visit **artists' studios,** we highly recommend the work of amiable husband-wife team Joel Jover and Ileana Sánchez. Their home studio is Calle Martí 154, on the north side of Parque Agramonte (✆ **32/29-2305;** jover@pprincipe.cult.cu). Jover also has a **gallery** on Plaza San Juan de Dios (open Mon–Sat 8am–noon and 2–6pm). Ileana's studio, **El Gato Azul**, is just off the plaza on Calle San Juan de Dios 30.

At Calle San Juan de Dios 26B, in a restored 1740 home, are the fascinating wooden sculptures of **Magdiel Garcia Almanza** (www.magdielescultor.com; ✆ **32/28-6842;** open daily 9am–7pm). Another well-known and very welcoming artist is Oscar Rodríguez Lasseria, a talented **ceramicist** whose studio "Iris" is on Calle Ignacio Agramonte 438, corner of López Recio (✆ **32/28-1400**; lasseri@pprincipe.cult.cu). His work "Senor Presidente usted ha sido re-electo" ("Mr. President you have been re-elected")—a series of donkey dictator busts in uniform—is worth a visit alone.

Ceramic artist and painter Martha Jiménez, creator of the statue ensembles in Plaza del Carmen, has her workshop on the square (www.martha-jimenez.es; ✆ **32/25-7550;** daily 8am–8pm). Drop in at **Galería Osmar Yero**, Plaza del Cármen 253A (daily 9am–12:30pm and 3-7:30pm) to buy gorgeous cloth and leather bags imprinted with colored leaves, the work of Sandra Arset and Yanaya Acosta. ***Note:*** If you purchase any artworks in Camagüey, you'll need to take them to the **Registro de Bienes Culturales,** Avenida de la Libertad 112 (✆ **32/29-2877** or 32/28-5382), to get official permission and documentation to export them from Cuba; fees vary.

Those interested in Cuban memorabilia, stamps, and coins should drop in at Ignacio Agramonte 433 between Lopez Recio and Independencia.

Where to Stay

Camagüey has an appealing supply of attractive and affordable hotels. For visitors interested in homestays, Camagüey also has a host of excellent private accommodations.

MODERATE

The tour agency **Cubanacán** (www.hotelescubanacan.com; ventas@ehoteles.cmg.tur.cu) has opened a raft of small hotels in the center of Camaguey that offer groups and families solid, historic-core accommodations at moderate rates (CUC$91–CUC$140 double). Of these, the most attractive include the **Hotel El Marqués** (in an old 1926 doctor's home), with just six rooms (room no. 4 is supremely elegant with a king-size bed in natty navy-blue and cream) and a Jacuzzi in the interior patio (Calle Cisneros 222 btw. Hermanos Agüero and Martí, ✆ **32/24-4937**). The **Hotel La Avellaneda**, also an erstwhile doctor's colonial home, boasts a sumptuous suite in dark chocolate and orange hues and another eight rooms (Calle República 226 btw. Ignacio Agramonte and Callejón del Castellano; ✆ **32/24-4958**); the drawback, here, is that breakfast must be taken across the road at the lovely, pivotal **Hotel Camino de Hierro** (Plaza de la Solidaridad 76 btw. Maceo and República; ✆ **32/28-4264**). Of the 10 rooms, the standout is room no. 5 with three balconies and antique dressers with gray marble tops, faded mirrors, a marble sink, and handsome mahogany bed. The bar here is open 24 hours and spills out onto the street, with pretty umbrellas for shade. The **Hotel Santa María** (Calle República, corner of Ignacio Agramonte; ✆ **32/24-4944**), with 31 rooms, is the least attractive but it's the only one with Wi-Fi in the lobby. The new **Hotel La Sevillana** was due to open opposite El Marqués.

Gran Hotel ★ Camagüey's old-world 1939 hotel is still a classic place to stay despite the competition from nearby new "boutique" accommodations. It's also the only hotel in town with a pool. It's all dark precious woods, old elevator, and cubbyholes for drinking—very Graham Greene. The top-floor restaurant **Salon Caribe** and roof terrace are popular spots for dining and drinking (with a good-value buffet dinner for CUC$12; daily noon–3pm and 7–10pm). Of the rooms, you'll want the corner rooms (rooms no. 1 and 7 on each floor)—the largest in the hotel. Clients who are not staying at the hotel can use the pool for CUC$10 (consumo mínimo CUC$8). Don't miss the 9pm water ballet every Monday, Tuesday, Thursday, and Saturday.

Maceo 64 (btw. General Gómez and Ignacio Agramonte), Camagüey. www.islazul.cu. ✆ **32/29-2093.** 72 units. CUC$76–CUC$86 double. Rates include buffet breakfast. MC, V. **Amenities:** Restaurant; cafeteria; 2 bars; nightly show; small outdoor pool.

INEXPENSIVE

The **Hotel Islazul Colón,** Calle República 472, between San José and San Martín (www.islazul.cu; ✆ **32/25-1520;** CUC$64–CUC$74), opened in 1927 by Catalan owners and featuring a standout precious-wood lobby bar, has rather lost its mojo and position with the new Cubanacan property openings.

Camagüey has many excellent *casas particulares*. **Casa Los Vitrales,** Calle Avellaneda 3, between General Gómez and Martí (✆ **32/29-5866;** requejobarreto@gmail.com), is a centrally located colonial casa in a former seminary run by a very helpful family. The four rooms are spacious and quiet, the breakfasts are filling, and there is a lovely courtyard. **Casa Caridad**, Calle Oscar Primelles 310A between Bartolomé Masó and Padre Olallo (✆ **32/29-1554;** caridadgarciavalera@gmail.com), has three quiet ensuite rooms with super-comfy orthopedic beds. The real draw of this house is the huge courtyard garden with attractive white wrought-iron furniture and beautiful hanging white flowers. **Eduardo y Geraldine**, Calle Gollo Benítez (Príncipe) 61 between San Rámon and Gral Gómez (✆ **32/29-0995;** edudelav@gmail.com), has a great upstairs apartment with two spacious ensuite rooms, a roof terrace, and a shaded plunge pool. **Casa Xiomara & Rodolfo,** Oscar Primelles 615, between Lugareño and San Ramón (✆ **32/28-1948;** cubarentur@gmail.com), has an amazingly large and well-equipped apartment that's a very nice option for two couples or a family traveling together. **Natural Caribe**, Avellaneda 8 between Keiser and Martí (© **32-29/5866;** requejoarias@nauta.cu), a colonial home reworked into a minimalist tropical fantasy by a young architect, offers two rooms and spacious living areas.

Where to Dine

In addition to the places listed below, **Café Callejón de la Soledad** (© **32/29-1961**) is an atmospheric outdoor cafe on a cobblestone alley, just beside the 18th-century Iglesia de Nuestra Señora de la Soledad. **Café Ciudad,** Parque Agramonte, Calle Martí at Cisneros (© **32/28-8412;** daily 9am–11pm), features striking antique prints of old Camagüey under a glorious mudejár ceiling with iron candelabras. Unfortunately, half the coffee menu is unavailable, but there's still plenty of choice from CUC$0.50. Coffees come with a chocolate bonbon. Grab a window seat and a cup of coffee, and watch children playing in the park.

Casa Italia, Calle San Rámon 11 between Astileros and Gral Gómez (© **32-25/7614**), is an attractive haven with mint-green Doric columns running alongside two loggias just behind Plaza de los Trabajadores. Run by a Sardinian, it has an authentic pizza oven, jamón serrano, a whole host of pasta dishes, and tasty, filling lasagnas (daily noon–11pm; no credit cards). The elegant **Restaurante 1800** (www.restaurante1800.com; © **32/28-3619**), in a restored colonial building—all sparkling glassware and silver service—dominates an enviable corner of Plaza San Juan de Dios. The menu lists beef, *langosta* (shrimp), fish, and substantial *criolla* dishes, but much of it was unavailable on our visit. The restaurant gets rave reviews, but we found the service a little on the cold side. Diagonally opposite Restaurante 1800 is **La Camapana de Toledo,** a rustic, state-run affair in an 18th-century house that looks out onto the restored Plaza San Juan de Dios. The house specialty is *boliche mechado*, beef stuffed with fatty bacon and accompanied by French fries (San Juan de Dios 18, btw. Ramón Pinto and Padre Olallo, Plaza San Juan de Dios; © **32/28-6812;** daily 10am–10pm).

Camagüey After Dark

A **Cartelera Cultural board** (www.pprincipe.cult.cu) posts weekly events listings in a building at 432 Ignacio Agramonte.

Built in 1850, the neoclassical **Teatro Principal,** Padre Valencia 64, between Tatán Mendéz and Lugareño (© **32/29-3048**), is an elegant showpiece with a grand marble staircase and chandeliers. The theater often showcases the distinguished **Ballet de Camagüey ★★**, which celebrates the Festival de Ballet in February. Camagüey's **Casa de la Trova ★★**, Salvador Cisneros 171 (© **32/29-1357**), is one of the liveliest in Cuba, with good bands and great local crowds. It's open Tuesday through Thursday from noon to 6pm and 9pm to midnight; Friday and Saturday from noon to 6pm and 9pm to 1am; and Sunday from 11am to 4pm and 9pm to 1am. Admission is CUC$3 and includes CUC$2 worth of drinks. **El Cambio,** Calle Martí and Independencia, is a small, atmospheric bar on the main park, whose walls are plastered with graffiti.

Excursions From Camagüey

Some 110km (68 miles) north of Camagüey are the white sands and aquamarine seas of **Santa Lucía.** There are a handful of hotels and a dive school along the 21-km (13-mile) stretch of fine white sand. At the western end is **Playa Los Cocos,** which is known for its **bull sharks,** which feed in the area from July to September and February to March. Along this north coast are **Cayo Sabinal, Cayo Cruz,** and **Cayo Romano.**

For tours to Bonita Beach (CUC$72) or snorkeling tours (CUC$25), contact **Cubanacán** (✆ **32/33-6449**) or **Ecotur** (✆ **32/33-6109**) at Playa Santa Lucía. The bull sharks tend to appear around the turning of the tide, so dives are timed to give visitors the best chance of seeing the sharks; many dives include a visit to the "Mortera" wreck, a Spanish galleon that sunk in 1905. For details, contact **Shark's Friends Diving Center** (✆ **32/36-5182**) between Hotel Brisas Santa Lucía and Gran Club Santa Lucía. There are some 34 dive sites, and dives run from CUC$40; the shark dive costs CUC$69.

At Playa Los Cocos, **Restaurante Bar Bucanero** (✆ **32/36-5226**) serves seafood and slices of smoked beef under a thatched roof. Los Cocos is very popular with locals and has a more authentic feel than the hotel strip.

Santa Lucia has a gas station, a bank, shops, an Etecsa office, a car-rental office, and an international clinic. The one daily bus to Santa Lucía from Camaguey leaves at 2:45pm and returns at 11am (2 hr.; CUC$8).

WHERE TO STAY

Day passes are available for many Santa Lucía hotels, but considering its distance from Camagüey, most visitors opt to spend the night in the area. The most comfortable of the hotels is the **Hotel Brisas Santa Lucía** (www.hotelescubanacan.com; ✆ **32/33 6317;** from CUC$40 double).

EL ORIENTE

The region known as El Oriente is less known and visited than the western half of Cuba but is every bit as rewarding for travelers—perhaps more so. The farther east you go, the more emphatically Caribbean it feels. This region's remarkable landscapes include the north coast's exuberant banana and coconut groves, the aquamarine seas off Guardalavaca, the densely wooded peaks of the Sierra Maestra, and the east coast's tropical rainforest.

9

Prior to the 1959 Revolution, the eastern half of Cuba was a single province, straightforwardly called El Oriente, or the East. Most Cubans still refer to everything east of Camagüey—a region much more scenically and historically interesting than most of central Cuba—as El Oriente, even though it is now composed of the distinct provinces of Holguín, Granma, Santiago de Cuba, and Guantánamo.

The wars of independence began in El Oriente in the 1860s, and nearly a century later, Castro concentrated his power base in the inaccessible **Sierra Maestra.** Quiet but dignified **Bayamo,** which played a pivotal role in Cuba's revolutionary struggles, is the capital of Granma province. The gorgeous beaches and warm seas of **Guardalavaca,** part of Holguín province, make it a favorite resort area in Cuba, while tiny, remote **Baracoa,** where Columbus first dropped anchor at the extreme northeastern edge of Guantánamo, is one of the most beautiful, rugged spots on the island. The former capital city of the Spanish colony, **Santiago de Cuba,** is not only known as a vibrant musical center, but also as the cradle of the Revolution; see chapter 10 for full coverage of Cuba's "Second City."

The eastern end of Cuba was especially hard hit from Hurricanes Gustav and Ike in September 2008, and Hurricane Sandy walloped the city of Santiago in 2012. In Holguín, the main areas affected in 2008 were Banes and Gibara, and repairs to those damaged towns remain ongoing.

GUARDALAVACA ★★

56km (35 miles) N of Holguín; 190km (118 miles) NW of Santiago de Cuba; 258km (160 miles) NE of Camagüey

Guardalavaca's white sands, hidden coves, stunning aquamarine seas, and underwater life make it a top beach destination. And though a lineup of all-inclusive resort hotels gazes out over some of the finest beaches in Cuba, Guardalavaca remains charmingly low-key. Its location, close to historic towns and cities, also makes it a good base for inland exploration. As a result, Guardalavaca is one of the most popular beach destinations on the island.

Guardalavaca is the finest, and really the only resort cluster in the eastern half of the island. Guardalavaca's appeal is its three-stripe canvas of intensely green tropical vegetation, stone-white sand, and pristine turquoise seas well protected by coral reefs.

Christopher Columbus first sailed around the coast at Guardalavaca, landing just to the west at the Bay of Bariay in late 1492 (the Baracoans, however, think he landed there first). He declared the island "the most beautiful land that human eyes have ever seen." Columbus may have been given to hyperbole, repeatedly touting the unrivaled virtues of the places where he dropped anchor, but his assessment of Guardalavaca remains pretty accurate. The area was originally home to several indigenous groups, and today the region is recognized as Cuba's archaeological capital, primarily for the discovery of the 15th-century Arawakan Indian village and burial site near Guardalavaca, one of the most important pre-Columbian sites in the Caribbean. The *bohíos* (thatched-roof huts) that dot the thickly wooded hills still evoke a sense of Caribbean discovery more than 500 years later.

The foundations of Guardalavaca's resort development were laid in the late 1970s: Fidel Castro himself inaugurated the first hotel here, swimming laps in its large, square pool. "Guardalavaca" now denotes not only the eponymous town and beach, but is also used to refer to the entire resort, strung along several nearby beaches and continuing to expand to the west, including Playa Esmeralda and Playa Pesquero.

The backdrop to the beaches is a bucolic region thick with sugarcane fields, grazing cattle, and luxuriant, rolling hills sprinkled with royal palms. In addition to scuba diving at a dozen dive sites, hiking, biking, and horseback-riding trips are available. A dozen nature preserves, including one declared a UNESCO World Biosphere Reserve, dot the region. Side trips from Guardalavaca are easy to arrange.

Essentials

GETTING THERE

By Plane

Aeropuerto Internacional Frank País, Carretera Central Vía Bayamo Km 11.5 (✆ **24/47-4525;** airport code HOG), is about 70km (43 miles) south of Guardalavaca, and 14km (8¾ miles) south of Holguín, the provincial capital. The airport is about an hour from hotels in and around Guardalavaca. Both national and direct international flights (including various package charters) arrive at the airport here. The main domestic carrier is **AeroCaribbean** (www.fly-aerocaribbean.com; ✆ **24/46-8556** in Holguín), which offers daily flights from Havana for CUC$97 each way.

El Oriente

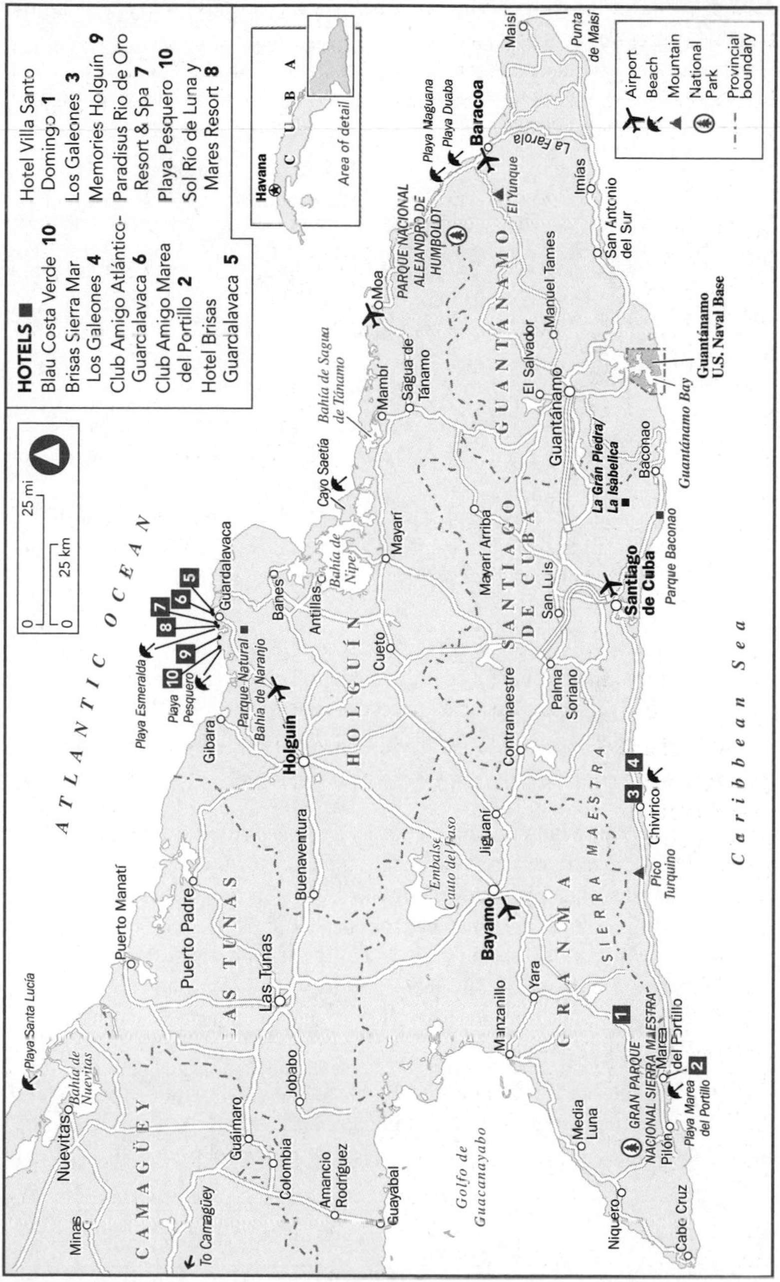
HOTELS ■
Blau Costa Verde 10
Brisas Sierra Mar Los Galeones 4
Club Amigo Atlántico-Guardalavaca 6
Club Amigo Marea del Portillo 2
Hotel Brisas Guardalavaca 5
Hotel Villa Santo Domingo 1
Los Galeones 3
Memories Holguín 9
Paradisus Rio de Oro Resort & Spa 7
Playa Pesquero 10
Sol Río de Luna y Mares Resort 8
25 mi
25 km
Havana
C U B A
Area of detail
Airport
Beach
Mountain
National Park
Provincial boundary
A T L A N T I C   O C E A N
C a r i b b e a n   S e a
Golfo de Guacanayabo
CAMAGÜEY
LAS TUNAS
HOLGUÍN
GRANMA
SANTIAGO DE CUBA
GUANTÁNAMO
SIERRA MAESTRA
Playa Santa Lucía
Bahía de Nuevitas
Nuevitas
Minas
To Camagüey
Guáimaro
Colombia
Amancio Rodríguez
Guayabal
Jobabo
Puerto Manatí
Puerto Padre
Las Tunas
Buenaventura
Gibara
Holguín
Parque Natural Bahía de Naranjo
Playa Esmeralda
Playa Pesquero
Guardalavaca
Banes
Antillas
Bahía de Nipe
Cayo Saetía
Bahía de Sagua de Tánamo
Mambí
Moa
Sagua de Tánamo
Cueto
Mayarí
Mayarí Arriba
Embalse Cauto del Paso
Bayamo
Jiguaní
Contramaestre
Palma Soriano
San Luis
Santiago de Cuba
Parque Baconao
La Gran Piedra/ La Isabelica
Baconao
Guantánamo
Guantánamo Bay
Guantánamo U.S. Naval Base
El Salvador
Manuel Tames
San Antonio del Sur
Imías
PARQUE NACIONAL ALEJANDRO DE HUMBOLDT
El Yunque
Playa Maguana
Playa Duaba
Baracoa
La Farola
Maisí
Punta de Maisí
Manzanillo
Yara
Media Luna
Niquero
Cabo Cruz
Pilón
Playa Marea del Portillo
Marea del Portillo
GRAN PARQUE NACIONAL SIERRA MAESTRA
Pico Turquino
Chivirico

When *Not* to Come to Guardalavaca

The month of May in Guardalavaca is heavy with tropical rains, as is the early part of June. August is sweltering and too humid for all but the most committed sun worshipers.

The hotels all have airport pickup services for clients. If you have not prearranged transportation, there are usually some taxis hanging about. Rates run between CUC$35 to CUC$45 to Guardalavaca, CUC$15 to Holguin, CUC$30 to Gibara, and CUC$40 to Bayamo.

By Bus

Víazul (www.viazul.com; ✆ **24/42-2111** in Holguín) travels to Holguín on its Havana-Santiago and Trinidad-Santiago lines. The ride takes 12½ hours from Havana (CUC$44). From Varadero, the daily bus takes 12 hours (CUC$38). From Trinidad, the daily service takes 8 hours, 40 minutes (CUC$26). From Santiago (six daily departures) it's 3½ hours (CUC$11).

The main bus station in Holguín is located on Carretera Central between 20 de Mayo and Independencia (✆ **24/42-2111**), just west of downtown. A fare to downtown costs CUC$3.

During summer months, **Transtur** (✆ **24/43-0273**) may run Saturday and Sunday return buses from La Begonia restaurant on Parque Calixto García between 8:30am and 5pm for CUC$5.

By Car/Taxi

The easiest way to get to Guardalavaca, if you don't have a prearranged bus service to take you from the airport, is by rental car or taxi; contact **Cubataxi** (✆ **24/47-3535**). Getting from the airport, through the city of Holguín, and out onto the highway to Guardalavaca is quite confusing. One of the best ways to navigate it is to hire a local tout for a few CUCs to ride with you until you're on your way.

If you arrive by Víazul, there are plenty of touts with cars to take you up to Guardalavaca. The fare is approximately CUC$30 to CUC$35; bargain hard.

Guardalavaca's beauty and proximity to areas of interest, including Baracoa, make it one of the better areas in Cuba to rent a car for some regional sightseeing. Car-rental agencies in Holguín include **Cubacar** (www.transtur.cu; ✆ **24/46-8414**), **Transgaviota** (✆ **24/43-0047**), and **Rex** (✆ **24/46-4644**). Almost all of these have desks at the airport, as well as at one or more beach resorts.

GETTING AROUND

Playa Guardalavaca is small enough that you can easily walk from any of the hotels here to the market area. Playa Esmeralda is about 3km (1¾ miles) from Guardalavaca, a manageable walk. The rest of the beaches and attractions are quite far.

The best way to get around the beaches of Guardalavaca is by **bicycle** (if you're feeling fit) or **moped** *(moto)*. Most of the hotels have mountain bikes (free for guests) and mopeds that rent for CUC$25 a day. There are also *coches* (carriages), but this isn't a cheap way to travel.

Day Trips to Guardalavaca

The relatively expensive all-inclusive hotels pretty much have a lock on the splendid beaches around Guardalavaca. If you want to visit the beaches and spend the day there without paying for the privilege of sleeping at one of the hotels, you can design a day trip from Holguín if you have a rental car. (***Note:*** If you don't have your own wheels and have to take a taxi, the cost could equal the cost of staying in one of the less-expensive all-inclusives or a *casa particular,* and you'd have to travel 1½ hr. back to your hotel in Holguín, making it hardly worth the effort.) The major hotels sell day passes (*pasadías*), generally from CUC$20 to CUC$133, that allow you to use the facilities, including pool and beaches, and eat and drink all you wish.

Any of the hotels can arrange a taxi for side trips in the area. You can also call **Cubataxi** (✆ **24/43-0139**) directly on Playa Guardalavaca; taxis to Esmeralda cost CUC$7; Pesquero CUC$15; Gibara CUC$35; and Banes CUC$25. All the hotels also offer excursions either directly or through tour operator representatives.

Each of the major hotels has representatives of one or more car-rental agencies on the premises. You could also contact **Cubacar** (✆ **24/43-0389)** on Playa Guardalavaca.

One interesting alternative for touring the area is the **Guardalavaca Bus Tour,** which runs a hop-on/hop-off service in the area that now includes Chorro de Maita. The fare is CUC$5 for the day. The **HolguínBusTour** (✆ **24/43-0273**) leaves daily from all the hotels (first departure from Brisas at 8:45am) and returns from Parque Calixto García at 1pm (CUC$15 return).

VISITOR INFORMATION

The best sources of **visitor information** are the Guardalavaca hotels themselves and the representatives of the major tour operators (Havanatur, Cubatur, and Cubanacán) that operate out of the hotels. In Holguín, **Infotur,** Edificio Pico Cristal, C/Libertad, corner of Martí (✆ **24/42-5013**), has limited information.

Currency exchange and **postal services** are available at any of Guardalavaca's hotels. There are a couple of grocery stores, a photo processing store, and a branch of the cigar store La Casa del Habano.

The Club Amigo has a pharmacy on the premises; several other hotels also have pharmacies.

Exploring the Area

Most folks come here on all-inclusive packages, and many are content to spend their entire time in a chaise lounge on the beach or beside the pool. However, a wide range of tours and activities are available for the more active.

BEACHES, DIVING & OTHER WATERSPORTS

The spectacular beaches around Guardalavaca are this resort area's main attraction. Tracing the coast are more than 1,200km (746 miles) of pure white beaches lined by royal palm trees, framed by exuberant vegetation, and fronting some of the clearest, most inviting waters of Cuba. The best beaches are **Esmeralda, Pesquero, Yuraguanal,** and **Guardalavaca**—all of which have major hotels lining them—and small **Don Lino.** Many of the beaches are long and wide expanses of sand, but the jagged coastline is also peppered with tiny coves that are nearly private. Guardalavaca has a dozen excellent dive sites, including Corona, Laberinto, Cuevas 1–2, Sierena, and Punta Inglés, and is well-known for its abundant and vibrant sponges. **Eagle Ray** (✆ **24/43-0316**) is on Playa Guardalavaca, and **Marina Gaviota Oriente** (formerly Sea Lovers Scuba Diving Center; ✆ **24/43-0132**) is on Playa Esmeralda. Each offers dive packages and diving gear rental. Certification programs are also provided with several dive packages; a single dive costs CUC$45. Note that hotel reps take a large commission cut, so we recommend you book directly at the dive centers. Transfers from the hotels are included in the price.

The most popular watersports are sailing, kayaking, windsurfing, canoeing, and pedal boating. Most of the hotels have their own catamarans and other facilities for watersports. **Marina Internacional Puerto de Vita** (✆ **24/43-0465**) operates catamaran cruises around the coral reef beyond the cays for either a half- or full day. **Marlin** (✆ **24/43-0491**) has a wide range of watersports programs, including seafaris with snorkeling to Playa Pesquero and yacht rentals for sportfishing. Other excursions include a seafari to Cayo Saetía (CUC$79), a snorkeling trip on a catamaran (CUC$69), a speedboat adventure (CUC$29), a trip to Gibara (CUC$79), horseback riding (CUC$16), and a trip to Santiago (CUC$86).

Note: While masks are new and tend to fit well, the snorkels these companies use tend to be cheap and ill-fitting; bring your own if you plan to do a lot of snorkeling.

PARQUE NATURAL BAHIA DE NARANJO

The **Bahía de Naranjo,** about 5km (3 miles) west of Guardalavaca, is a 1,000-hectare (2,471-acre) nature park of mangrove swamps and thickly wooded wilderness. Within the park, visitors can take boat rides. There are plenty of man-made attractions to round out the more ecologically oriented offerings. The **aquarium** (✆ **24/43-0439**) at Cayo Naranjo, a sliver of an island reached by boat, isn't really a large-scale aquarium in the traditional sense; it's part of a tourist complex, but it does feature tropical fish as well as a daily marine show at noon (CUC$50) and an opportunity to swim with dolphins for CUC$108, both of which includes transport and guide from the hotels. While we are normally fairly appalled by the conditions of most dolphin attractions, including others around Cuba, this place has some of the largest natural ocean pens you'll find anywhere. You'll also find watersports and a seafood restaurant with an Afro-Cuban show.

ON DRY LAND

One of the most popular activities on dry land here is **horseback riding.** There's plenty of wide-open terrain and wonderful sea views to be enjoyed. Most hotels can arrange a riding excursion for you. There are stables in front of Hotel Club Amigo Guardalavaca. ***Note:*** Be sure to bring plenty of sunscreen as protection from the often-brutal sun here.

BANES

A slow-moving, dusty little town about 30km (19 miles) southeast of Guardalavaca, with a significant collection of Art Deco buildings, Banes is best known for its unlikely association with the towering figures of 20th-century Cuba. Fulgencio Batista, whose government the rebels deposed in 1959, was born here in 1901. Fidel Castro and his brother, Raúl, were born nearby in Birán.

Fidel married the daughter of the conservative mayor of Banes in 1948 at the small **Iglesia de Nuestra Señora de la Caridad,** on a plaza at the edge of the park. (They divorced 6 years later.) Of perhaps greater significance in town is the **Museo Indocubano ★**, Av. General Marreo 305 (✆ **24/80-2487**), specializing exclusively in Cuba's pre-Columbian history. Its collection is among the best in Cuba; among the 22,000 or so items, exhibits include fragments of ceramics, jewelry, tools, and a valuable replica 13th-century gold "idol of Banesa," just 4cm (1½ in.) high. The museum is open Tuesday through Saturday from 9am to 5pm, and Sunday from 8am to noon; admission is CUC$1; camera use CUC$5.

Tucked into the hills of the Banes zone are 96 archaeological sites from the Native American groups that once populated the area. **Museo El Chorro de Maíta (Maíta's Stream Museum) ★**, Cerro de Yaguajay (✆ **24/43-0201**), represents the largest and most important discovery of a Native American cemetery in Cuba. The community dates from 1490 to 1540. The burial ground contains the remarkably well-preserved remains of 108 Taíno men, women, and children, including a single Spaniard, most likely a friar, whose body is marked by a cross. A *cacique* (tribal chief), lying in a fetal position, is distinguished by a copper medal placed on his shin. Several skulls are deformed, the result of a beautification practice that involved applying two pieces of wood to the head with ropes. Found among the remains were Spanish ceramics and jewelry and objects crafted from gold, copper, coral, and quartz; many are displayed in cases. The museum is open Monday to Saturday 9am to 5pm, Sun 9am to 1pm. Admission is CUC$1; camera use CUC$5.

Where to Stay

The entire area is developed around the **all-inclusive-resort** concept. Playa Guardalavaca was the original resort beach (developed in the late 1970s), but today, resort hotels are distributed on several beaches along the coast, principal among them Playa Esmeralda, Playa Turquesa, and Playa Pesquero, where the hotels are more upscale than in Guardalavaca, and the beaches even finer. The non-resort area of Guardalavaca features a few shops, a taxi stand, market, and a large park; a second park has been bulldozed to make way for a new five-star hotel complex: the Albatross. At Playa Pesquero, behind the resorts, is the new Pueblo **Plaza Pasquero,** a small shopping complex offering bowling, artisan stalls, a beer garden, and an ice cream parlor.

The area also has a small handful of ***casas particulares*,** including the comfortable **Villa Bely** (www.villabely.orgfree.com; ✆ **5261-4192**), which offers three rooms and a bar and grill just 5 minutes' walk from the beach.

PLAYA GUARDALAVACA

Club Amigo Atlántico Guardalavaca The Club Amigo is a sprawling amalgam of several resorts. The oldest hotel at this resort, the Atlántico, was built in 1976, and its age shows in its basic structure. The best rooms are in the much more modern villa section, with marble bathrooms and small terraces; some have good sea views. Keep in mind, however, that these are much farther from the restaurant and public beach than the older rooms but are close to slivers of coves and a slightly larger cove beach with a statue of Christopher Columbus; you have to walk west along a boardwalk to get to the real expanse of public beach. The food is desultory, but it's a decent hotel and the cheapest on the beach.

Calle 2, No 1, Guardalavaca. http://hotelescubanacan.com. ✆ **24/43-0180.** 747 units. CUC$56–CUC$122 double; CUC$82–CUC$CUC$158 villa. Children 12 and under stay free in their parents' room; children 3–12 pay 50 percent of full price to stay in a separate room. Rates are all-inclusive. MC, V. **Amenities:** 9 restaurants; 2 snack bars; 10 bars; bike rental; children's programs; concierge; dance club; gym; 4 outdoor pools for adults; 4 outdoor pools for children; sauna; nightly show; 2 outdoor tennis courts; minigolf; watersports equipment; Internet (with charge).

Hotel Brisas Guardalavaca ★ Brisas incorporates an older building with newer, more attractive accommodation in villa complexes. The two sections are connected and considered one property, but guests would be wise to draw a firm distinction; the one-star rating we have given applies only to the villas, which are more attractive, intimate, and in much better condition. Mediterranean in style and set amid pleasant gardens, the pastel-colored, red-tile-roof villas are large and luxurious, with balconies. The atmosphere is one of tranquility, with easy access to an attractive stretch of beach. The standard hotel next door doesn't fare well in comparison; rooms are ill-maintained and not good value. Of the a la carte restaurant options, the international restaurant offers delicious choices.

Calle 2, No 1, Guardalavaca. www.brisasguardalavaca.com or www.hotelescubanacan.com. ✆ **24/43-0218.** 437 units. CUC$116–$238 double. Villa CUC$116–CUC$238. Suite CUC$156–CUC$218. Children under 12 stay for free in room; children 6–12 pay half price in a separate room. Rates are all-inclusive. MC, V. **Amenities:** 8 restaurants; snack bar; 11 bars; babysitting; bikes; children's programs; concierge; dance club; Jacuzzis; nightly show; 2 outdoor pools for adults; 2 outdoor pools for children; 2 lit outdoor tennis courts; watersports equipment; Internet.

PLAYA ESMERALDA

Paradisus Río de Oro Resort & Spa ★★★ One of Cuba's most luxurious all-inclusive resorts, this adults-only Meliá flagship is embedded in beautifully landscaped gardens and perched above a low, rocky cliff overlooking the fine Playa Esmeralda. Handsome two-story blocks of rooms and slightly more exclusive casitas, consisting of two apartments with separate terraces and outdoor showers, are dotted about the grounds. The rooms are very large and well-appointed, with separate sitting areas and balconies. The plush Royal Service rooms are close to the small Caleticas beach coves, but the choicest rooms—and easily the top accommodations in Guardalavaca—are the two massive Royal Service Garden Villas, each with private swimming pool. All the specialized restaurants are in high demand, especially the excellent Japanese Tsuru, so it's a good idea to make reservations for the duration of your stay upon arrival. The superb main beach is a short walk down some stairs built into the cliff; the tiny cove beaches accessed through the gardens are only for those staying in Royal Service rooms or using the YHI spa.

www.meliacuba.com. Playa Esmeralda. ✆ **24/43-0090.** 354 units. CUC$380–CUC$650 junior suite; CUC$540–CUC$810 master junior suite Royal Service; CUC$1,565 villa. Rates are all-inclusive. MC, V. Children not allowed. **Amenities:** 8 restaurants; 6 bars; bikes; gym; Jacuzzi; 3 pools; room service; sauna; nightly show; spa; 3 lit outdoor tennis courts; watersports equipment; Internet (no charge in Royal Service).

Sol Río de Luna y Mares Resort ★★ This bright and breezy unified double hotel complex is popular with families thanks to a raft of children's programs and its setting on a glorious, ample stretch of Playa Esmeralda. Rooms are clustered around an open-air lobby and medium-size pool, while family suites are scattered closer to the beach. The bright, colorful rooms on the third and fourth floors here have excellent views, and the junior suites are immense, with massive terraces.

www.meliacuba.com. ✆ **24/43-0060**. 464 units. CUC$133–CUC$210 double; CUC$133–CUC$190 suites. Rates are all-inclusive. Children under 2 stay free in parent's room; children 3–12 stay for half-price in parent's room. MC, V. **Amenities:** 8 restaurants; 8 bars; babysitting; bikes; children's and teenage center and programs; dance club; gym; Jacuzzi; 2 outdoor pools; sauna; nightly show; spa; 2 lit outdoor tennis courts; watersports equipment; Internet.

PLAYA YURAGUANAL

Memories Holguín ★★ A medium-size resort characterized by a huge hacienda-style lobby and known for its seven pools, five of which are connected by cascading waterfalls on several levels that descend to the hotel's essentially private beach. The restaurants are located at the reception level while the hotel accommodations are closer to the sea. It has a lot of steps, but the hotel's golf buggies swing by the beach to take sun worshippers up and down the hill on a regular basis. Rooms, set in grounds of mango, banana, and malanga plants, are huge and boldly colored with large, cool ceramic tile floors in a checkerboard pattern, and stylish wrought-iron headboards over the beds. All have private balconies featuring attractive slouchy fabric chairs. You'll find several good a la carte dining options, as well as the ubiquitous large buffets. The pizza and ice-cream stand on the beach is a big hit here, and the little *guarapo* (sugarcane juice) stand is a thoughtful touch.

www.bluediamondresorts.com. ✆ **24/43-3540.** 531 units. CUC$125–CUC$200 double; CUC$200–CUC$250 suite. Rates are all-inclusive. First child stays free in parent's room; 2nd child 2–12 pays half price. MC, V. **Amenities:** 4 restaurants; 1 snack bar; 6 bars; babysitting; children's center and programs; concierge; dance club; gym; sauna; 7 outdoor pools; nightly show; 8 lit outdoor tennis courts; watersports equipment; Internet and Wi-Fi (Wi-Fi access cheaper).

PLAYA PESQUERO

Blau Costa Verde ★★ This resort has a decidedly tropical feel, daubed in orange and sapphire-blue hues. It has expanded considerably with the addition of 440 rooms in a new section known as BlauCostaVerde Plus. The original section is clustered around a large figure-eight pool with ocean-themed rooms. Despite new bedspreads and TVs, these rooms still have a dated look. The sands are a 50m (164-ft.) walk away, but the beach is lovely, and the water has amazing crystal-clear turquoise tones. Unfortunately, the extra capacity of the new Plus section means the beach is now quite crowded. The Plus area—set farther away from the beach—is quiet, with its own inviting pools and no blaring music or shows. The Plus suites are smart, with Jacuzzi baths. The resort's kids' club, kiddie pool, playground, shallow "children's beach," and childcare will appeal to families. The food is good for a large-scale all-inclusive.

www.blau-hotels.com. ✆ **24/43-3510.** 749 units. CUC$108–CUC$184 double. Plus CUC$128–CUC$204 double. Rates are all-inclusive. Children under 6 stay free in parent's room; children 7–12 stay for half price in same room; children under 12 stay for half price in a separate room. All rooms with ocean view cost CUC$10 more. MC, V. **Amenities:** 6 restaurants; snack bar; 5 bars; babysitting (daytime only) children's center and programs; concierge; dance club; gym; Jacuzzi; 2 outdoor pool for adults; outdoor pool for children; sauna; nightly show; 3 lit outdoor tennis courts; watersports equipment; Internet & Wi-Fi.

Playa Pesquero ★★ This massive hotel has a new addition in the form of the adults-only Premium Playa Pesquero, with super-smart rooms featuring Jacuzzi baths, butler service, immense minibars, and its own restaurant and reception set next to the Río Bariay and just a short stroll to a stunning curve of beach. This section also hosts the swanky new spa open to all guests. The open-air lobby of the original section is decorated with lily pools and large sculptures, and a funky train carriage serves coffee. Standard rooms are all in two-story blocks spread around the massive grounds ringing the large free-form pool, gym, and entertainment area. This resort has a whole host of organized activities and entertainment options, as well as a broad selection of restaurants and bars. Of the a la carte restaurants here, **La Gondola** is appealing. Be sure to reserve one of these in advance if you're looking for a romantic dinner.

Next door is the Gaviota-run **Playa Costa Verde** (www.gaviotia-grupo.com).

✆ **24/43-3530.** www.gaviota-grupo.com. 1000 units. CUC$200–CUC$280 double; CUC$260–CUC$360 suite. Premium CUC$350–CUC$450. Rates are all-inclusive. Children under 2 stay free in parent's room; children 2–11 stay for half price in same room. MC, V. **Amenities:** 7 restaurants; 2 snack bars; 6 bars; babysitting; children's center and programs; dance club; gym; 4 Jacuzzis; sauna; massive outdoor pool; nightly show; 3 lit outdoor tennis courts; watersports equipment; Internet & Wi-Fi (no charge in Premium).

Where to Dine

Few visitors eat anywhere besides their all-inclusive hotels. But if you're day-tripping in Guardalavaca, you have some options to choose from. **El Ancla,** Playa de Guardalavaca (✆ **24/43-0381**), serves seafood in a rather charmless building set on a bluff. Other tourist restaurants in the zone include **Mongo Viña,** on the road to Playa Esmeralda with a pastoral view (✆ **24/43-3463**), as well as **Restaurante Cayo Naranjo** (✆ **24/43-0132**), within the tourist complex of Parque Natural Bahía de Naranjo, and **Yaguajay Restaurant** (✆ **24/43-0422**) in the Aldea Taína opposite the Museo del Chorro.

Side Trips from Guardalavaca

The following are the most common and easily accessible side trips from Guardalavaca. Though it may seem unfair to characterize the largest city and provincial capital, Holguín, as a day trip from the beach, the fact of the matter is that the overwhelming majority of visitors to this section of northeastern Cuba have sun and surf on their minds.

HOLGUÍN ★

56km (35 miles) SW of Guardalavaca; 734km (456 miles) E of Havana; 134km (83 miles) NW of Santiago de Cuba

The provincial capital, officially called San Isidoro de Holguín, may be known across Cuba as the "city of parks," but it doesn't get a whole lot of tourist traffic, which also makes it appealing. Holguín is a pleasant but unremarkable city with only a modicum of attractions. Still, it makes a good day trip for resort visitors who would otherwise see nothing of Cuba save Guardalavaca's all-inclusive hotels and brilliant beaches.

Holguín, the fourth-largest city in Cuba, has a compact center that's easy enough to get around; visitors can manage the highlights in an unhurried day. The city's few elegant plazas, colonial buildings, and small dose of museums do not rival the highlights of Trinidad or Santiago, and much of the city's historical character has been subsumed by industrial expansion. The great majority of the city's buildings date from the 19th and 20th centuries.

Pleasant **Parque Calixto García** (also called Parque Central), named for a 19th-century patriot, represents the heart of the city. The hero of the wars of independence is paid tribute with a large marble statue in the park's center. Benches are usually occupied by locals watching the town and time pass by. Two nearby churches of note are the domed **Iglesia de San José** (on Plaza Carlos Manuel de Céspedes), which has an unusual baroque interior to go with its remade neoclassical facade, and the modest 18th-century **La Catedral de**

San Isidro de Holguín (Calle Mandulay, on Parque de las Flores), which features *mudéjar* (Moorish-style) carved wooden ceilings.

Of special note in Holguín is the lime-green and mustard **Museo de Historia Natural Carlos de la Torre y Huerta** (Calle Maceo 129) building with its striking original tiles and wrought-iron work; its contents are lackluster.

La Loma de Cruz (Hill of the Cross), 3km (1¾ miles) north of the city, can be climbed by ascending the nearly 500 steps to the top, where there's a wooden cross that was placed there in 1790. Though the often-windy hill has excellent views of Holguín in the flat valley and the surrounding countryside, the hilltop is a little forlorn. The **Mirador de Mayabe** is the other acclaimed viewpoint, about 10km (6 miles) from the city center. On the hill, **Cerro de Mayabe,** is a hotel (✆ **24/42-2160**) and restaurant.

Holguín's **Cabaret Nocturno**, Carretera Central Vía Las Tunas, km 2 (✆ **24/42-9345**), is an open-air cabaret show running Tuesdays, Fridays, and Saturdays from 10pm. Admission is CUC$2.

The **Villa Liba,** C/ Maceo 46, corner of 18 (✆ **24/42-3823;** marielayoga@cristalhlg.sld.cu), is a 1950s mansion, decorated with original furniture, that has been converted into a wonderful *casa particular.* Relax on the interior patio fragranced by mariposa flowers. The owner, Jorge Mezerene, who is of Lebanese descent, cooks with organic ingredients and is known for his vegetarian food. His wife Mariela is a yoga and reiki practitioner who can offer massages to guests.

Restaurante San José (C/ Agramonte 188; ✆ **24/42-4877**) is a quiet spot for some tasty barbecued food. Alternatively, try the filling house specialty, roast leg of lamb in tomato sauce; Holguín's first fancy place, **nueva havana** (C/ Maceo 256; ✆ **24/42-2464**) is a friendly spot for tapas and piña coladas.

GIBARA ★

35km (22 miles) N of Holguín

A sleepy, charming early-19th-century provincial port, **Gibara**—sometimes referred to as *La Villa Blanca,* or the White Village, thanks to its one-time whitewashed appearance—is home to a number of fine colonial buildings. Unfortunately, Hurricane Ike pummeled Gibara in 2008, and many historic attractions are still waiting to be restored. This modest fishing town offers great scenery and overlooks a wide natural bay, with a very tranquil atmosphere. Two pretty little beaches and a *malecón* (promenade) line the picturesque bay, and inland is the **Silla de Gibara,** a flat-topped mountain that locals claim is the hill described by Columbus when he first happened upon Cuba (it is much more probable that he landed in Baracoa, much farther east of here, and that the mountain described in his journal is El Yunque).

On the top of Los Caneyes hill are the ruins of an old fortress, which protected merchants involved in trade with Europe and the U.S. (a 30-min. walk up the hill rewards hikers with excellent views of the town and bay). Trade soon diminished with the introduction of the railroad, and the fortunes of Gibara suffered, leading to an exodus of a significant portion of its population.

Gibara's moment in the sun is still reflected in the handful of grand mansions and public buildings.

The main plaza, Calixto García, is marked by an attractive yellow church, **San Fulgencio,** which dates back to 1850 and has red-tiled cupolas and African oak trees. Of greatest interest is the **Museo de Artes Decorativas,** Independencia 19 (✆ **24/43-4687**), housed in an impressive neoclassical house constructed in 1872. The sumptuous mansion, which once belonged to an elite merchant, was severely damaged by the 2008 hurricane. Its saved features include huge mediopunto stained-glass windows, yellow and blue tiles, and quality period furnishings. Museum staff may be happy to show you the unique-in-Cuba 1910 *alfiletero*, an egg-shaped needle store with a tiny panorama of a Jordanian scene viewed through a tiny pin-sized viewer in its "shell." Also of note is the well-known mixed-media picture, *La Copa del Amor* (1872), which features human hair. Lovers Adolfo Ferrin and Ygnacia Nates were separated as he traveled for work. On his return he found his betrothed gravely ill. After 17-year-old Ignacia died (of typhus), local businessman Adolfo asked her father if he could cut some of her hair to incorporate into a picture. *La Copa del Amor* depicts the tomb of Ygnacia in the Gibara cemetery, shaded by the branches of the sauce llorón tree. The tree, with its branches—made of hair and tree—is seen as a tree of tears.

Explorers should head to the town's **Cavernas de Panaderos** to see bats and pictographs (site of the town's quirky annual mid-March cave cinema festival) with local expert and guide José Corella (✆ **24/84-5107;** gibara@baibrama.cult.cu). Cave divers can explore caves and cenotes with Cuba Cave Society expert Arturo Rojas Cruz (✆ **5291-5251;** acave@nauta.cu).

Gibara holds the biennial **Festival Internacional del Cine Pobre** (www.cubacine.cu/cinepobre or www.festivalcinepobre.cult.cu/) in April; the **Cine Jibe** on the main plaza is the star screen in town.

The handsome **Hotel Ordoño** (C/J Peralta 9; www.hotelescubanacan.com; ✆ **24/84-4448**) is comfortable and central; the standout Felipe and Isabel suite, named after the owner of the 1927 building, Spanish merchant Felipe Ordoño and his wife, Isabel Camps, with the frescoed bathroom is a steal (CUC$74; suite CUC$104). **Villa Caney** (C/Sartorio 36; ✆ **24/84-4552;** tleticia@nauta.cu) offers two comfortable rooms in a huge colonial home with patios and a restaurant. **Bar La Loja** on Parque Colón is a cute taberna in a historic property with occasional live music.

For all intents and purposes, there's no public transportation available to tourists connecting either Holguín or Guardalavaca to Gibara. It is quick and convenient to take a taxi there and back for around CUC$25. Gibara is also featured as a day trip by most of the tour operators in Guardalavaca.

CAYO SAETIA ★

130km (81 miles) SE of Guardalavaca

This pristine cay, on the eastern side of the Bahía de Nipe, isn't terribly easy to get to, but if isolated and totally unpopulated sugar-white cove beaches, turquoise seas, and wild game are of interest to you, it is worth the effort. This erstwhile exclusive game resort was once the private stomping and hunting grounds of Cuba's military and political brass. The cay has an exceptional roster of flora and fauna, which includes not only imported deer and wild boar, but also a wild collection of exotics such as antelopes, ostrich, water buffalo, and zebras. Most excursions include snorkeling, boat rides, jeep safaris, horseback riding, and lunch on the beach. There's only one hotel on the cay, **Villa Cayo Saetía** (✆ **24/51-6900;** www.gaviota-grupo.com), with just a dozen simple but tasteful rooms and cabanas. Cayo Saetía is about 90 minutes from Guardalavaca by car. Contact **Gaviota Tours** (✆ **24/43-0434**), which runs the place, or any of the hotels or travel agencies in Guardalavaca. A great option is to take the catamaran cruise around the coast to the cayo, and enjoy lunch and a jeep safari among the wild animals (CUC$79). Note that the gorgeous beach is 8km (5 miles) from the cabanas, so you'll need a rental car.

BAYAMO & THE SIERRA MAESTRA ★

757km (470 miles) E of Havana; 201km (125 miles) E of Camagüey; 127km (79 miles) W of Santiago de Cuba; 73km (45 miles) S of Holguín

Granma province is unusually easygoing and lethargic, even by the standards of stifling hot and dry eastern Cuba, but its retiring pace belies a turbulent, indelible role in modern Cuban history. Bayamo, the capital of the province, and the densely forested, impenetrable mountains of the Sierra Maestra at the extreme southwest corner of the Oriente region have long been at the forefront of political turmoil and rebellion. The otherwise unassuming region may just be the place where Cuba's independent streak runs deepest.

Bayamo, one of Cuba's original seven *villas* and today a midsize city and the capital of Granma province, is considered the birthplace of Cuban independence. The *himno nacional,* or national anthem, was first sung here after the city was seized by the Liberating Army and became the capital of the Republic at Arms in 1869. South of Bayamo, the Sierra Maestra, a national park comprising a spectacularly verdant and rugged range that reaches right down to the Caribbean coast, is where Fidel Castro and his band of rebels sneaked back into Cuba in 1956 after a period of exile in Mexico. The rebels hid in the mountains, depending upon the assistance of sympathetic *guajiros* (peasants), and based their long-shot revolution there, covertly raising the antenna of Radio Rebelde and scoring decisive victories on the road to eventual triumph. How influential was the province as a turning point in 20th-century Cuban politics and society? Important enough that, after the Revolution, it received the name of the yacht in which Fidel and his brothers in arms sailed from Mexico, and the government-owned and operated national daily newspaper is also named after the boat: Read all about it in *Granma.*

Today, Bayamo and the Sierra Maestra are considerably better known for their historical associations than they are as travel destinations. Bayamo is pleasant and peaceful, but its citizens and well-maintained colonial structures don't really try too hard to impress visitors, making it a tranquil stopover. Meanwhile, much of the Sierra Maestra remains difficult to penetrate due to controlled access. However, it is relatively simple (and rewarding) to trace the revolutionary steps of Fidel and Che Guevara, visiting the fascinating installations of the rebel group—preserved as they were in the tense days of the late 1950s—tucked high in the mountains. The dramatic coastline that bends around the southeastern base of the Oriente, where the mountains scrape the edge of the sparkling Caribbean, makes an excellent, if time-consuming, ground approach to Santiago de Cuba, and is worth the trip for the scenic value alone. Hurricane damage has blasted the roads in part, but it is passable if a little hair-raising at times. A handful of package tourism hotels are perched on the rocky coast, where the sands aren't much to speak of, but the incomparable sea and mountain views, not to mention diving and hiking opportunities, more than compensate for that.

Essentials

GETTING THERE

By Plane

You can fly from Havana to Bayamo on **Aerocaribbean** (✆ **23/42-3916** in Bayamo) on Tuesday and Friday; the fare is CUC$104 one-way. Flights arrive at **Aeropuerto Carlos Manuel de Céspedes,** Carretera a Holguín (✆ **23/42-7514;** airport code BYM), 10km (6 miles) north of the city. By registered taxi, the trip to town is about CUC$5.

By Bus

Víazul (www.viazul.com; ✆ **23/42-4036** in Bayamo) is the most convenient mode of transportation for traveling to Bayamo. On the Trinidad–Santiago de Cuba line, there is one daily departure; 10 hr. 15 min. (CUC$26). Six daily departures from Santiago bound for Bayamo take 2½ hr. (CUC$7). On the Havana-Santiago line, there are three daily departures; 14 hr. (CUC$44). On the Varadero-Santiago line the daily evening departure takes 13½ hr. (CUC$42).

The main bus terminal for long-distance buses, the **Terminal de Omnibuses,** is located on the outskirts of downtown, on Carretera Central near Avenida Jesús Rabi, on the road to Holguín. Horse-drawn carriages and private taxis await passengers to ferry them downtown for CUC$3.

GETTING AROUND

The compact old town of Bayamo is very simple to get around on foot. You're only likely to need a taxi to get back and forth to the airport or bus station to move on. Contact **Cubataxi** (✆ **23/42-4313**) for local and long-distance taxis. Alternatively, you can take a horse-drawn or bicycle taxi anywhere in town for CUC$1 to CUC$2.

Getting to the Sierra Maestra mountains is rather more complicated, necessitating a rental car, hired *carro particular,* or organized excursion. If you wish to explore the Sierra with any degree of independence, or make the coastal drive to Santiago de Cuba, your own wheels are virtually indispensable. There are **Transtur** offices within the Sierra Maestra Hotel (✆ **23/48-2990**). To get to the Sierra Maestra for a day's hike, it's often cheaper to organize the excursion with a *casa particular* than it is to go with a state travel agency.

Anley Rosales Benitez of **Bayamo Travels Agency**, Carretera Central 478, opposite the bus station (www.bayamotravelagent.com; ✆ **5292-220;** anley82@yahoo.es), can help with most journeys. **Ecotur**, which is the only agency selling tickets for the Sierra Maestra trails, can be found in the Hotel Sierra Maestra (✆ **23/48-7006;** agencia@grm.ecotur.tur.cu) or directly in Santo Domingo (✆ **23/56-5613**).

ORIENTATION/VISITOR INFORMATION

Bayamo's historic center sits on a high bluff overlooking the Bayamo River. For information about excursions in the province, visit one of the major tour operators. **Cubanacán** has an office inside the Hotel Royalton (✆ **23/42-2290**).

FAST FACTS

BANKS/ATMS A **Banco Popular de Ahorro** branch (with ATMs) is on General García corner of Saco. It's open Monday through Saturday 8am to 7pm. There is a **CADECA** on Saco No. 5 between Donato Mármol and General García; it's open Monday through Saturday 8:30am to 4pm.

INTERNET An **Etecsa** center with Internet access is at General García 109; it's open daily 8:30am to 7pm.

MEDICAL For medical attention, go to **Hospital General Carlos Manuel de Céspedes,** Carretera Central, on the way to Santiago de Cuba (✆ **23/42-2144**).

PHARMACY The **Farmacia International** is on Calle García between Lores and Figueredo (✆ **23/42-9566**; closed Sun).

POST OFFICE The main **post office** is on the west side of Parque Céspedes. It's open Monday through Saturday 8am to 8pm.

Bayamo

The second Spanish city founded in Cuba in 1513, as Villa de San Salvador de Bayamo, is small and quiet for a provincial capital. The laid-back town welcomes relatively few visitors, except for day-trippers, and locals refrain from hassling foreign visitors—unless it involves singing the Cuban national anthem for you, the city's pride and joy.

Bayamo grew wealthy in the 17th and 18th centuries from contraband and later sugar and cattle. Many of the local elite were privileged enough to send young men off to Spain and France to study, and a number of them returned with enlightened ideals about colonialism and a strong desire for Cuban independence. Carlos Manuel de Céspedes (1819–74) was a wealthy businessman who, in 1868, freed his slaves and formed a small army that set about achieving that goal. The movement was known as the *Grito de Yara,* a call for independence or death. His forces succeeded in capturing Bayamo and giving life to the War of Independence against Spain. The rebels held Bayamo for 3 months until it was evident that the superior numbers of Spanish troops would

Bayamo

HOTELS ■
Casa Arturo &
 Esmeralda **8**
Casa Olga Celeiro
 Rizo **9**
Hotel Royalton **3**

RESTAURANTS ◆
Bar La Esquina **5**
Casa de La Trova **7**
La Bodega **1**
Los Beatles **13**
Paladar Bar Beran's **10**
Paladar San Salvador
 de Bayamo **6**
Tropicrema **12**

CADECA ⑤
Etecsa 🄲
Post office ✉

ATTRACTIONS ●
Casa Natal de Céspedes **4**
La Catedral de Bayamo/
 Capilla de La Dolorosa **2**
Museo de Cera **14**
Parque Céspedes **11**

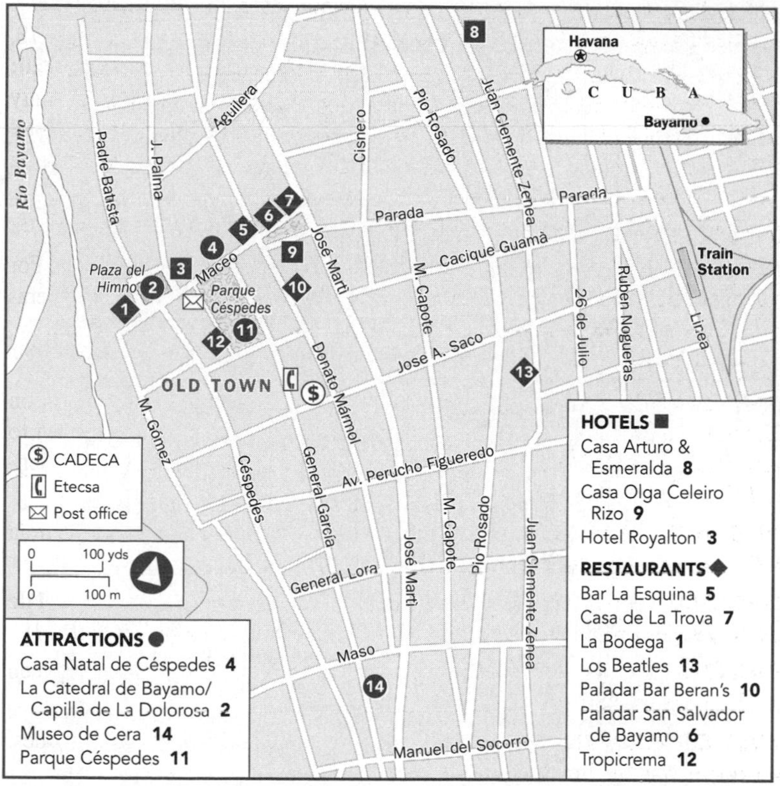

soon defeat them. Rather than surrender, the rebel army audaciously chose to burn the city, in the ultimate act of sedition. Most of the city was wiped out by this act of self-immolation in 1869.

EXPLORING THE AREA

Parque Céspedes ★ is the focal point of downtown Bayamo. It's an exquisite, peaceful square flanked by tall royal palm trees. The light-cream and claret building at one end of the square, which housed a pharmacy, is where the great blaze began. At one end of the plaza is a marble bust of the independence fighter Perucho Figueredo, which carries the words and music to "La Bayamesa" (later the national anthem), imploring followers not to fear "a glorious death" and encourages Cubans that to "die for the homeland is to live." At the other end of the plaza is a stately granite and bronze statue of Carlos Manuel de Céspedes. Ringing the square are handsome, pastel-colored, arcaded colonial-style (post-1869) buildings. Had the city not been consumed by fire, in all likelihood it would resemble the remarkable colonial core of Trinidad.

Next to the Hotel Royalton on the north side of the square, the **Casa Natal de Céspedes ★**, Calle Francisco Maceo Osorio 57 (© **23/42-3864**), the birthplace of the "father of the Cuban nation," is the only house on the square that escaped destruction from the fire. The significance of it alone being saved is not lost on Cubans. Today it is a museum, open Tuesday through Friday from 9am to 5pm, Saturday from 9am to noon and 8 to 10pm, and Sunday from 10am to 1:30pm; admission is CUC$1. The house has been lovingly restored; the two-story building holds a chronological exhibit about the Céspedes family, elegant 19th-century colonial furnishings, objects belonging to Céspedes (such as his ceremonial saber), and a few odds and ends that help piece together the story of Bayamo's independent streak (including the original printing press that produced the first newspaper of free Cuba, *El Cubano Libre,* in 1868). The standout item, however, is the extraordinary, huge four-poster bronze bed complete with two oval shields depicting towns in mother-of-pearl decoration; the imagery changes as you glance at the depictions from left to right. Céspedes is remembered for refusing to trade his surrender for the life of his son, who was captured by the Spanish army; the Cuban patriot replied in writing that all Cubans were his sons and he could not be expected to trade their independence for the life of one man. The Spaniards promptly shot his son Oscar.

Just west of the museum and Parque Céspedes, dominating a small open square called **Plaza del Himno,** is **La Catedral de Bayamo** (or La Catedral del Santísimo Salvador), an immense, 16th-century church that succumbed to the 1869 fire. Rebuilt several times over the course of its life, the church has been magnificently restored. It features a high-peaked wood-beam ceiling, two beautiful stained-glass windows of the coat of arms of Cuba, and of Bayamo by artist Juan Carlos Fernández, and, above the altar, an attention-getting battle mural commemorating a pivotal local episode when the parish priest blessed the rebel army flag. This blurring of the lines between church and state was not the only overtly political statement to take place in the cathedral; the first singing of the revolutionary anthem was staged here in 1869. The cathedral is open to visitors Monday to Friday from 9am to noon and 2:30 to 4:30pm and on Saturday from 9am to noon. To one side of the cathedral, the small chapel **Capilla de La Dolorosa (Chapel of the Lady of Sorrows),** which dates to 1740, is distinguished by a lovely Moorish-style, carved wooden ceiling and fine baroque altarpiece; it was only one of three important buildings to survive the 1869 blaze (the others were the Casa de la Trova and Céspedes' home).

Heading south from Parque Céspedes, Calle General García has been turned into a pleasant pedestrian mall, with several shops, simple restaurants, and tour agency offices.

The only wax museum in Cuba, the **Museo de Cera,** is worth visiting to see the work of self-taught local Rafael Barrios and family. Some 16 expertly fashioned giants of Cuban history and culture—José Martí, Compay Segundo, Bola de Nieve, and Juan Formell among them—along with two esteemed foreigners (Gabriel García Marquez and Ernest Hemingway) form part of the tiny museum. Wildlife enthusiasts will be tickled by the Cuban birds and animal section. It's open Tuesday to Sunday 9am to 5pm; admission is CUC$1; guided CUC$5; camera CUC$5 (Calle García between Bartolomo Masó and Marmol de Socorro).

WHERE TO STAY

Quite a few *casas particulares* can be found in the old center of Bayamo. **Casa Arturo & Esmeralda,** Calle Zenea 56A between William Soler and Capote (www.casa-bayamo.com; ✆ **23/42-4051**) offers two air-conditioned rooms with TVs and minibars in a modern, welcoming house. **Casa Olga Celeiro Rizo,** Calle Parada 16 (Altos) between Martí and Mármol (✆ **23/42-3859;** maillo@nauta.cu), is a friendly home with two comfortable, air-conditioned rooms and a great terrace overlooking the pleasant Francisco Maceo Osorio plaza.

Hotel Royalton ★ With its zesty yellow façade, the Royalton, refurbished under Cuba's boutique Hoteles Encanto brand, sits in a prime position facing Parque Céspedes. The cavernous, uninviting lobby of the 1940s building leads up to the compact rooms decorated in chocolate, beige, and gold threads with smart bathrooms with rain showers. All rooms except three feature twin beds. Four of the rooms have balconies overlooking the main square, but you'll want rooms 208 or 308 for their park-view balconies as well as side-window views of the church. The **Restaurante Plaza**'s sidewalk terrace is a great place for a cooling beer.

Calle Maceo 53, Bayamo. ✆ **23/42-2246**. 33 units. CUC$56–CUC$76 double. Rates include breakfast. MC, V. **Amenities:** Wi-Fi (with charge).

WHERE TO DINE & DRINK

Bayamo's private dining scene is very small, and standards are not up to the level found in other provincial capitals. **Paladar San Salvador de Bayamo,** at Calle Maceo 107, between Martí and Mármol (✆ **23/42-6942**), is a popular tour group stop so is best avoided at the lunch hour. Although the place is striking, with two dusty pink Moorish horseshoe arches and original tiling, it's understaffed, which can mean a lengthy wait at dinnertime. The menu, with prices in *moneda nacional*, is full, but some dishes are, not uncommonly, unavailable. We recommend the surf-and-turf kebabs and the fulsome lasagna made with *picadillo de res*. **Paladar Bar Beran's** at Donato Mármol 175, between Canducha Figueredo and Parada (✆ **23/42-1992**), is a little down-at-heel, but the chicken a la Barbacoa is particularly tasty amid the principally *criollo* food, with main courses ranging around CUC$5 toCUC$8. There's also a **Dino's Pizza** at General García 111, as well as a host of restaurants along pedestrian Calle General García that are open from noon to 10pm. For dessert, stand in line with the locals at the ice-cream parlor **Tropicrema,** located just off the southwest corner of Parque Céspedes.

The loveliest place to kick back with a *cerveza* is **La Bodega** at 34 Plaza del Himno (✆ **23/42-1011**). This sweet bar and café has a fetching view of the river and is the perfect spot for a sunset drink. There is occasionally live music.

DEAR granma

In early December 1956, Fidel Castro, his brother Raúl, Ernesto (Che) Guevara, and a group of idealist revolutionaries, including some who had previously stormed the barracks in Santiago de Cuba and Bayamo, sailed back to Cuba from exile in Mexico with weapons and an audacious plan: to overthrow, once and for all, the Batista government. They set sail aboard a yacht christened the *Granma,* purchased from a couple of Americans in Veracruz. The stealth journey was beset by all manner of hitches, including bad weather and scarce provisions. Just 82 men disembarked at Las Coloradas beach 2 days later than planned, with few weapons and virtually no supplies.

Batista forces had been tipped off to the operation, and prompt aerial bombing killed about half the rebels; the others fled for the mountains in small groups. After suffering an ambush, only 16 men remained, and when the survivors eventually met up at Cinco Palmas in the Sierra Maestra, only a dozen men remained. They had but eight rifles to their names. Against monumental odds, they nonetheless began to plan their offensive. Batista, no doubt convinced that the attempted sedition had been effectively quashed, announced to the world that Castro and the other leaders had been killed and withdrew government forces from the area—a fatal mistake.

Crafty Castro slowly but surely began to gain adherents and advance the rebel cause of the 26th of July movement. Astonishingly, a band of just over a dozen fighters at the campaign's inception—propped up by a growing network of *guajiros* (poor rural farmers) and vast, inaccessible terrain—somehow ended up toppling the Batista regime just 2 years later.

Today, the spot where the rebels landed ashore, at the southwestern tip of Cuba near Cabo Cruz, is a national park, **Parque Nacional del Desembarco del Granma** (admission CUC$5; museum CUC$5; open daily 7am–6pm). A monument features a replica of the *Granma;* the real vessel is in the Museo de la Revolución in Havana.

The small, air-conditioned **Bar La Esquina,** on the corner of the small, shaded Francisco Maceo Osorio plaza, is a cool spot for a drink. At the other end of the plaza on Calle Maceo is the **Casa de La Trova,** which has regular live performances. **Los Beatles,** Calle Zenea between Saco and Figueredo (closed Mondays), is an outdoor venue that hosts cover bands.

Sierra Maestra ★★

Cuba's highest and longest mountain range stretches about 140km (87 miles) west to east, across three provinces: Granma, Santiago de Cuba, and Guantánamo. Its highest peaks are only several kilometers from the coastline, making for some exciting views, whether you're perched up in the mountains or cruising along the coast. The entire range forms part of the **Gran Parque Nacional Sierra Maestra,** and its thickly forested, rugged terrain, with steep, deep green mountains swathed in wispy clouds, is impenetrable for most traffic, though the area is splendid for hikers. While there are many trails just begging to be explored, until recently most remained closed to the public; hardcore hikers should perhaps anticipate encountering some closed trailheads. The heart of the Gran Parque is a park-within-a-park, the **Parque Nacional de Turquino ★**, which includes Turquino, the nation's highest summit at just under 2,000m (6,562 ft.).

Deep folds and craggy ravines make these mountains very inaccessible, and they are, not surprisingly, sparsely populated, with only small numbers of *guajiros* (poor rural farmers)—many of whose families once gave shelter and support to the rebels in their midst—living very simply in *bohíos* (thatched-roof huts) with no electricity or running water. Also tucked away in the mountain range are dozens of endemic species of birds and plants.

Unless you're a physically prepared hiker with all your own equipment and several days or more for hikes, your best bet is to head to Turquino Park, where there is, at least, minimal infrastructure; there's also the lasting legacy of Fidel Castro and his committed band of rebels, which formed the **Comandancia de La Plata,** a base command for their guerrilla war in 1956 after returning from exile in Mexico (see "Dear *Granma,*" above). The two main trails into the mountains are the **Pico Turquino Trail** and the **La Plata Trail;** the latter visits the rebels' base camp.

The road south from Bayamo is a long, lush, tropical adventure; it cuts through beautiful sugarcane fields where pigs, peacocks, and machete-wielding farmers roam, with the rounded, green peaks of the Sierra Maestra looming in the background. **Santo Domingo,** 65km (40 miles) south of Bayamo by a good road, is where you'll find the entrance to the national park, as well as a rustic hotel and restaurant that serve as a perfect base camp for those who want to trace the trail of Fidel and Che, ascend Pico Turquino, or just explore the rugged beauty of the national park. The **Hotel Villa Santo Domingo** (www.islazul.cu/es/hotel/villa-santo-domingo; ✆ **23/56-5568**), where Fidel and his brother Raúl have been frequent guests in the past (Fidel favored cabin no. 6), sits down a bit on the left side of the road, on the banks of the Yara River. The 20 little cabins have twin beds, private bathrooms, air-conditioning, TVs, solar-powered hot water, and fridges. The cabins cost CUC$50 to CUC$65 double, including breakfast. They have been joined by some smart rustic cabanas that are more comfortable but set farther away from the river (CUC$84–CUC$90 with breakfast). Also on the grounds are a good restaurant and outdoor grill, as well as a bar, and video/game room. The rustic, open-air **Restaurant La Yamagua** offers standard *comida criolla* (Cuban creole food), several different preparations of chicken, and pork steak. Better food can be found at the great *casa particular* across the river (reached by a new bridge or stepping stones): The four rooms of the **Casa Sierra Maestra** (✆ **53/23564491**; casasierramaestra@gmail.com) are an appealing option. The ensuite rooms, and a great restaurant, are run by the friendly Ulises and family. The area has two other *casa particulares.*

HIKING IN THE SIERRA

Hiking deep into the Sierra Maestra is a superbly rewarding experience for any hiker, but, given the mountains' historic role in the success of the

Revolution and the fact that much of the Sierra remains a military zone, the Cuban government zealously protects access to it. By law, you need permission and a guide to explore the national park. Remember, Fidel's cronies hid from Batista's forces and the CIA for more than 2 years in the dense forest of the Sierra, so finding your way around is a complicated task. Park authorities don't look kindly upon foreigners seeking to explore the park on their own.

Guides can be contracted at the official entrance to the national park, the **Centro de Visitantes,** about 200m (656 ft.) along the road beyond the Hotel Villa Santo Domingo. It is open daily from 7:30 to 9am. (Take your passport). Visitors now pay a minimum CUC$27 fee to enter the park, which includes a guide for hikes into the Sierra. An additional CUC$5 is payable to take pictures of La Comandancia. This also is the spot to arrange for treks and bird-watching. You will need to arrive with all necessary gear, as no one in the area rents equipment. The center offers a number of different hikes and prices. All prices are per person and include a guide:

- **Comandancia La Plata del Ejército Rebelde** (see below): CUC$27, including return transport from the park entrance to the trails' access, guide, box lunch, and one small bottle of water
- **Santo Domingo to Pico Turquino:** Includes 1 night in the Aguada de Joaquin refuge, which has 20 beds and mattresses, sheets and blankets, all food, and three bottles of water: CUC$68
- **Santo Domingo–Aguada de Joaquin–Pico Turquino–Las Cuevas:** Includes one night of camping: CUC$68

To gain access to the Pico Turquino or La Plata trail, hikers must either climb or take a 15-minute 4WD ride one way up a treacherously steep paved road, with thrilling hairpin turns, to **Alto de Naranjo,** 5km (3 miles) from the visitor center. This trip is now included in the entrance fee.

For more information about trekking in the Sierra Maestra, go to **Ecotur** (p. 114), **Bayamo Travel Agent** (p. 214), or your *casa particular*. Taxi costs start from CUC$35 for a one-way trip to Santo Domingo from Bayamo.

Pico Turquino ★★

The hike to Pico Turquino, the highest summit in Cuba, requires a minimum of 2 nights in the area (one night camping). The trek from Alto de Naranjo is about 15km (9 miles). Experienced, fast hikers can do the ascent and descent in a day, but most people choose to camp overnight at the *refugio* (refuge), several kilometers below the summit. The trek through an amazing array of tropical ferns, vines, and dense cloud forest, punctuated by the sharp calls of unseen birds, is terrific, with stunning panoramic views all around, and only really difficult at the steep end. It gets quite cold at night, so make sure you're prepared with proper clothing and equipment. Although food and some water is included in the hike price, you would be wise to bring a sleeping bag, plenty of snacks, and a water sterilizer such as a Steripen.

Comandancia de la Plata ★★

Though not nearly as challenging a hike—you can do the 6km (4 miles) up and back in about 3 hours—the trail to La Plata perched on a mountain ridge reverberates with thrilling history, no matter on which side of the political fence you fall. Visiting the rudimentary installations of Fidel Castro's rebel base camp is a remarkable experience. When you learn the story of the rebellion and visit the crude installations from which Fidel directed his offensive, it's hard not to have at least some appreciation for why this man clung so tenaciously to power and the ideals of the Revolution: Look what he did to get there.

After about 20 minutes on the trail, about 800m (2,625 ft.) above sea level, hikers come to the **Alto de Medina,** a small wooden house. Situated at the entrance to the base camp, it was the checkpoint building. Farther up along the trail, you come to a **small museum,** which tells the story of the guerrilla warfare waged in these mountains. You'll see what, at one time, was a small hospital, and eventually, you'll arrive at the huts where Fidel lived with his *compañera* (partner) Celia Sánchez. Fidel never allowed anyone but Celia inside the shack; the bench outside the door where he conducted interviews is still there. Ingeniously constructed under the cover of thick forest, the installations make it quite apparent how the rebels eluded capture and assassination. The hilltop rising above the camp is where the guerrillas covertly erected the antenna to broadcast their rebel message on the nascent Radio Rebelde.

As with the Pico Turquino trek, carry plenty of snacks and additional water. If you stay the night at the hotel before the trek, be advised that the breakfast at the hotel is insufficient to power you through.

The Coastal Road to Santiago de Cuba

The Sierra Maestra stretching down to the rocky beaches and black sands of the south coast, against the sparkling blue waters of the Caribbean, is one of the most dramatic sights in Cuba. To trace the coastline to Santiago de Cuba is to take the scenic route; it's a roundabout way to get to your destination, for sure, but well worth it if you're a fan of rugged, bravura landscapes. The road and bridges have suffered damage from hurricanes but are still passable—ask about the status of the road in Niquero, Pilón, or Santiago before setting out on your trip, and take it slow. It takes around 8 hours from Pilón to Santiago and is the most scenic drive in the country. If you're pressed for time and headed to Santiago, the inland route from Bayamo is much more direct. The road east from Chivirico to Santiago is now fully paved.

The coastline is remarkably absent of any sort of villages or installations for long stretches at a time: It's just you, the open road (watch for rockslides), and the sea to your right and Sierra Maestra to your left. While you can usually make the trip in any normal sedan, a four-wheel-drive vehicle is recommended for the added clearance, if nothing else. The beaches, such as they are, range from passable soft gray stone to forbidding big black rock.

You'll find a smattering of large resort hotels at certain points along the coast, and while it's a stretch to describe them as beach resorts, they do offer splendid sea views, a host of watersports, and plenty of trekking opportunities. Most are package-tourism confines, aimed largely at seniors. Canadian charter planes fly direct to Manzanillo, then the hotels bus in groups of 100 vacationers or more for an inexpensive, weeklong, coastal Cuban vacation. Whether those guests arrive expecting fine, white, powdery Caribbean sand we don't know (and certainly hope not). Although we were initially turned off by the notion of an all-inclusive hotel hovering illogically on "beaches" that suffer so in comparison with those along the north coast, we do admit that a couple of the hotels wouldn't be awful places to vacation, as long as your expectations are simple, such as the **Club Amigo Marea del Portillo,** Carretera Granma Km 12.5, Pilón (www.hotelescubanacan.com; © **23/59-7081**).

From Marea del Portillo, the road continues another 40km (25 miles) or so to Santiago de Cuba province. The views take in desertlike landscapes, the massive dry mountains of the Sierra Maestra, black rocky beaches, and large waves crashing ashore; it's a highly scenic drive. The only village of any real size is **Chivirico,** a small fishing settlement about 75km (47 miles) outside of Santiago de Cuba. The best hotel en route to Santiago de Cuba is the all-inclusive **Brisas Sierra Mar Los Galeones** (www.hotelescubanacan.com; © **22/32-9110**), a massive, multitiered hotel overlooking a sandy brown beach. Though the overall facilities are fairly impressive—restaurants, bars, tennis courts, a large swimming pool, watersports center—the rooms are standard, undermaintained, and uninspiring. There are plenty of better all-inclusive hotels in other parts of Cuba, but this place is quiet, the views are extraordinary, and mountain exploration close to Santiago is its appeal. You can also dive the warship *Cristóbal Colón*. Rates are CUC$144 to CUC$150 double, all-inclusive. Just outside the resort is the **Océano Restaurant** (© **5226-4717**), serving up seafood daily between 11am and 3pm and 6 and 9pm. **Los Galeones** ★ (© **22/32-6160**) is a small, pretty, adults-only hotel (CUC$130) located atop a peak, and offers outstanding views, which is part of the Brisas complex and connected to it by a bus three times a week (or taxi service: CUC$10). From here, it's another hour or so to Santiago; see chapter 10 for full coverage.

The Road to Baracoa

Guantánamo province, by virtue of a Cuban song seemingly known the world over ("Guantanamera") and an attention-getting, anachronistic U.S. military base, gets more ink and initial interest than it probably deserves. The easternmost province on the island only has one true draw, but it's one of the highlights of Cuba: the tiny tropical town of Baracoa. The only real reason to stop over in the sweltering and unappealing city of Guantánamo is to visit the distant lookout trained at the contentious **American naval base** isolated on Cuban soil. That's as close as you'll get—and honestly, outside of the novelty factor, there's not too much to see. The new **Mirador los Gobernadores**

GOIN' (OR NOT) TO gitmo

On the radio in Guantánamo city and along the road to Baracoa, the unmistakable sounds of English-speaking DJs and American pop music can be heard, seemingly out of nowhere. The programming is courtesy of the U.S. government, emerging from behind barbed-wire fences at the base at Guantánamo Bay, known to American military personnel as "Gitmo." The base is an eyebrow-raising anomaly in revolutionary Cuba, as it's probably the least likely spot in the world for the U.S. to have a naval base. Washington continues to hold an indefinite lease on the base, which was established in 1903 as a reward for the U.S. role in the Spanish-American War—making it the oldest overseas American naval base.

Pursuant to the original agreement, signed by President Theodore Roosevelt, which called for an annual payment of 2,000 gold coins (worth US$4,085 in 1903), the U.S. government continues to send rent checks for that original amount, even though Fidel Castro has never cashed a single one since 1959. Castro understandably would rather forgo the paltry sum than lend legitimacy to the American presence in Cuba. A 1934 treaty that reaffirmed the lease of the base stipulated that both the U.S. and Cuba must mutually agree to terminate the lease

Though it has official missions (refueling and reconnaissance), in peace times the Guantánamo base has existed primarily to continue to poke thorns in Castro's side. That is, until 2001, when the U.S. military decided to send Al Qaeda prisoners captured in the conflicts in Afghanistan and Iraq to Guantánamo. Since then, the base has been a source of international news and controversy. Most of the detainees continue to be held and interrogated without access to lawyers or the filing of any formal charges.

Cubans have grudgingly learned to live with the base. They no longer expect a U.S. invasion at any moment, and the U.S. now returns those Cubans who, rather than attempting to cross the Atlantic, try to escape Cuba by crossing over to the American base. The last handful of Cuban workers who crossed military checkpoints every day to get to their jobs on the base retired in 2012.

Gitmo has about 3,000 full-time residents, who, though surrounded on three sides by Cuba, live as if they were in American "suburbotopia," with typical suburban homes, U.S. products, American cars, cable TV, a golf course, and, of course, a McDonald's. However, on the Cuban side this gated community has a sign that reads REPUBLICA DE CUBA, TERRITORIO LIBRE DE AMERICA (Republic of Cuba, Free Territory of America).

(signposted) is open 7am to 9pm with the viewing platform open until 4pm (CUC$1, including loaned binoculars). Especially curious visitors can arrange to stay at **Hotel Caimanera** (www.islazul.cu; CUC$32 including breakfast), the only hotel on Guantánamo Bay itself, with a pool and small museum on the premises. The stay must be arranged through Islazul at Hotel Guantánamo with 72 hours' notice (✆ **21/38-64-66;** adrian.rivas@hotelgtmo.co.cu); guests must be accompanied by a guide on the way in (CUC$5 per person).

The parched landscape of the southern coast begins to change gradually in color along the spectacular 40km (25-mile) road **La Farola ★★★**, which courses southeast of Santiago and wends its way through the mountains along the route to Baracoa. Things get more and more lush, with thick tropical vegetation and beautiful views at every turn. ***Be forewarned:*** In addition to its beauty, this is a tight and winding road with a seemingly endless series of white-knuckle hairpin turns. Baracoa, isolated from the rest of Cuba before the building of the road, is a beguiling little town, known for its chocolate and coconut and connections to Columbus. It's been known to bewitch more than a few travelers into staying much longer than they'd planned.

BARACOA ★★★

236km (147 miles) NE of Santiago de Cuba; 150km (93 miles) NE of Guantánamo; 332km (206 miles) E of Holguín

Swathed in generous tropical vegetation—royal palms, coconut palms, coffee bushes, and cacao plants—and refreshed by 10 rivers, Baracoa is perhaps the most picturesque spot in all of Cuba. It's also my favorite place in Cuba, after Havana. The historic town sits on a lovely oyster-shaped bay, **Bahía de Miel (Honey Bay) ★★★**, and the landmark flat-topped mountain known as **El Yunque (the Anvil)** looms in the background.

Not only is Baracoa, for my pesos, the most beautiful place on the island, it's also the oldest. That Baracoa was the first settlement established by Diego Velázquez in 1511—making it the second oldest colonial city in the Americas—is not in doubt. Christopher Columbus is thought to have first landed at this spot in late November 1492, and locals claim that he planted a wooden cross here to mark his arrival.

After its founding, Nuestra Señora de la Asunción de Baracoa remained the capital of the new Spanish colony for just 4 years; when Velázquez moved the capital west to Santiago, on a bigger and deeper bay, Baracoa's isolation had already begun. The small fishing and farming village remained virtually cut off from the rest of Cuba, with no true road in until the 1960s, when a scenic roller coaster of a highway was cut through the mountains.

For such a small, isolated settlement, Baracoa is loaded with things to do and see. It swims with possibilities for hiking, rafting, swimming, and boating. Baracoa really shines the first week of April, when heady street parties (part of a *semana de cultura,* or cultural week) commemorate the date General Antonio Maceo disembarked at nearby Playa Duaba in 1895, marking the beginning of Cuba's War of Independence. The greatest pleasure Baracoa offers, though, is just being here. Most people make the trek just to take in its extraordinary beauty, tranquility, and abundant charms. A UNESCO Biosphere Reserve, the tropical seaside town is tucked into green hillsides covered with cocoa and coconut groves, and surrounded by beaches lined by royal palms. As the abundant greenery attests, Baracoa is huddled in the midst of the wettest region in Cuba.

Baracoa

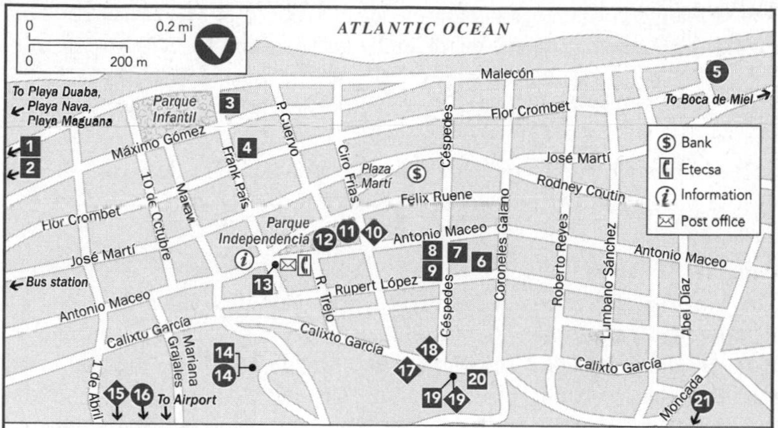

ATTRACTIONS ●
El Castillo de Santa Bárbara **14**
El Yunque **16**
Fuerte Matachín/Museo Matachín **5**
Nuestra Señora de la Asunción **11**
Museo Arqueológico **21**
Parque de la Independencia **12**

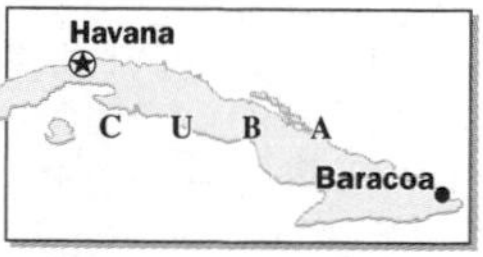

HOTELS ■
Casa Barbara Almeida Cesar **9**
Casa Brisas del Atlántico **3**
Casa Colonial Lucy **7**
Casa Colonial Yalina & Gustavo **4**
Casa Daniel Salomón Paján **8**
Casa de Hidiolvis Real Domínguez **2**
Casa la Colina **19**
Casa Walter **6**
Casa Ysabel Garrido **20**
Hostal La Habanera **13**
Hotel El Castillo **14**
Villa Maguana **1**

RESTAURANTS ◆
Calalú **18**
El Buen Sabor **17**
El Poeta **10**
La Colina **19**
La Rosa Nautica **15**

Essentials

GETTING THERE

By Plane

There are flights four times a week on **Aerocaribbean** or **Aerogaviota** from Havana to Baracoa; however, flights are often booked weeks ahead. Fares are CUC$126 one-way with Aerogaviota and CUC$164 with Aerocaribbean. The Aerocaribbean office is at Calle José Martí 185 (✆ **21/64-5374**). Flights arrive at the small **Aeropuerto Gustavo Rizo** (✆ **21/64-5376;** airport code BCA), west of the bay near the Hotel Porto Santo and about 4km (2½ miles) west of downtown. By taxi, the trip to town costs CUC$5. Should the Baracoa flights be full, Moa, 38km (24 miles) down the road, has flights on Monday and Thursday from Havana, for CUC$150 one-way.

By Bus

Most visitors arrive overland; the ride from Santiago de Cuba is especially spectacular, if lengthy. A **Víazul** bus (www.viazul.com; ✆ **22/62-8484** in

Santiago, or 21/64-1550 in Baracoa) departs Santiago daily at 1:30am and 8am and arrives in Baracoa at 6am and 2pm respectively; the fare is CUC$15. The bus stops in Guantánamo. Buses depart Baracoa at 8:15am and 2:15pm for Santiago and Havana arriving in Santiago at 2:15pm; the 2:15pm departure arrives in Santiago as its final stop at 7:05pm. The route is very popular, especially in high season; make reservations for the trip at least several days in advance—these buses sell out frequently and fast.

The Baracoa **Terminal de Omnibuses** (✆ **21/64-1564**) is located at the end of José Martí near Avenida de los Mártires, diagonally opposite the La Punta restaurant.

By Car

You can drive to Baracoa from either Santiago de Cuba, along the scenic La Farola highway (see "The Road to Baracoa," above), or from Guardalavaca/ Holguín along the northern coastal road through Moa (although the latter road is hideously bad in places, but still passable). Allow 4 to 5 hours for either route. Gaviota organizes a Saturday daily departure to Holguín via Moa at 8am (minimum 7 people; CUC$30; 6 hr.).

GETTING AROUND

You can easily get around most of Baracoa on foot or *bicitaxi* (bicycle carriage). To reach the beaches, rivers, and mountains around Baracoa, you'll either need to contract a taxi, rent a car, or sign on for an organized excursion. **Cubataxi** (✆ **21/64-3737**) makes local and long-distance runs.

A car is a good idea if you really want to do some independent exploration of the surrounding area, or travel to, say, Santiago de Cuba or Guardalavaca. A **Cubacar** desk is located in the Havanatur office (www.transtur.cu; ✆ **21/64-5225**), and **Vía Rent a Car** (✆ **21/64-5137**) has offices in Cafetería El Parque (✆ **21/64-1671**) and at the airport (✆ **21/64-1665**). *Motos* can be rented from this company too from CUC$20. Rates are CUC$60 to CUC$80 per day for a standard four-door compact car.

VISITOR INFORMATION

The **Infotur** office at Maceo 129A (✆ **21/64-1781**) offers information and Internet access only. More useful are agencies selling tours, including **Cubatur,** Maceo 149, corner of Pelayo Cuervo (✆ **21/64-5306**) next to the church; **Gaviota Tour** in Cafetería El Parque (✆ **21/64-5164;** buro.gtours@gavbcoa.co.cu), and **EcoTur,** Calle Ciro Frías, at the corner of Rubert López (✆ **21/64-2478;** ecoturbc@enet.cu), which specializes in outdoor trips in the area.

FAST FACTS

BANKS/ATMS A **Banco de Crédito y Comercio** branch is on Calle Antonio Maceo 99. Traveler's checks can be cashed at the Hotel El Castillo.

MEDICAL For medical attention and a pharmacy, go to the **Clinica Internacional Baracoa,** Calle Martí, between Roberto Rey and Linvano Sánchez (www.servimedcuba.com; ✆ **21/64-1037/38**).

POST OFFICE The main **post office** is on Calle Antonio Maceo 136, near Plaza Independencia; it's open Monday through Saturday 8am to 10pm and Sunday 8am to 8pm.

INTERNET/PHONE You can make local, long-distance, and international phone calls or use one of the computer terminals for Internet at the **Etecsa** office on Calle Antonio Maceo, opposite Plaza Independencia; it's open daily from 8:30am to 7:30pm. Wi-Fi is available in Baracoa's hotels.

Exploring the Area

Baracoa is its own greatest attraction. Its bustling streets are lined with gaily painted clapboard houses, and the rivers, beaches, and mountains beyond the city are perfect for outdoor exploration.

In the 18th and 19th centuries, Baracoan settlers built three fortresses to protect the town from pirate attacks. **El Castillo de Santa Bárbara,** the oldest of the bunch, sits high above town, with splendid views of the bay and surrounding countryside; it has now been converted into a hotel. **Fuerte de la Punta,** facing the seaside promenade, is now a restaurant. The third, **Fuerte Matachín,** near the entrance to town, houses the municipal museum, **Museo Matachín,** Calle Martí s/n at the Malecón (✆ **21/64-2122**). It holds a number of interesting historical exhibits related to the history of Baracoa and its legends and myths. The museum also has a collection of extraordinary, vividly colored and striped *polimitas* (snail shells), which locals used to make into necklaces sold to tourists before the supply dried up. (It is now illegal to sell them.) The museum is open Monday to Saturday from 8am to noon and from 2 to 6pm and Sunday from 8am to noon; admission is CUC$1 with a guide, and photo privileges cost an extra CUC$1. Ask here about a city tour for CUC$5.

Nuestra Señora de la Asunción, Maceo 152 (✆ **21/64-3352**), the rather austere cathedral, was constructed in 1511, though it was burned by the French in 1652. The current structure was rebuilt at the beginning of the 19th century. It underwent a significant restoration for the 500th anniversary of the city's foundation in August 2011. It is most notable for the **Cruz de la Parra,** a small wooden cross on display in its own niche to the left of the main entrance. Locals insist that Columbus himself planted the cross on the banks of the bay in 1492, shortly after disembarking on Cuban soil for the first time. Whether or not there's any truth to that claim, carbon dating has in fact established that the cross is more than 500 years old (making it one of the oldest Christian relics in the Americas, if not the oldest). The hardwood is native to Cuba, though, so if Columbus did leave it, the cross must have been fashioned in situ rather than having been brought with him, as was originally believed. The cross has greatly dwindled in size, thanks to devout visitors who over the years thought nothing of slicing off a memento for themselves. The church's opening hours are Monday through Saturday from 8am to 11am and 4pm to 8pm and Sundays from 7am 11am.

Next to the church is the **Parque de la Independencia** (also called Parque Central), a popular gathering spot for locals and tourists enjoying a few lazy days in Baracoa. A bust of the rebel Taíno Indian leader Hatuey (whose countenance today appears on beer bottles) adorns the square. Hatuey took up arms against the early conquistadores until he was caught by the Spanish and burned at the stake.

The area around Baracoa has as many as 50 **pre-Columbian archaeological sites** related to the major Native American groups that inhabited the area (Siboney, Taíno, and Guanturabey). The only native group to survive is the Yateras, a small community that has succeeded in preserving its traditions, marrying only among each other and living along the Río Toa.

Above the town is the **Museo Arqueológico** in Reparto Paraíso, open Monday to Friday from 9am to 5pm and weekends from 9am to noon; admission is CUC$3 (entrance costs CUC$2 if you buy through Ecotur). The remains of Taínos can be seen in a cave, as well as in a random collection of ceramics and artifacts supposedly belonging to this pre-Columbian tribe. The museum is only really worth the entrance fee to climb to the ***mirador*** ★★★, where you can admire and survey the entire bay; on a clear day, the vista is stunning.

Those with young children will find the enclosed restored **Parque Infantil** (Calle Máximo Gómez between 10 de Octubre and Frank País) a dream attraction with its playgrounds and onsite café (open daily 8am–6pm; CUP$20; CUP$40 adults).

Outdoor Excursions Around Baracoa

The spectacular area around Baracoa affords excellent opportunities for treks and whitewater rafting. The region features patches of secondary rainforest and abounds in banana, yucca, mango, coconut, and tall royal palm trees, and at least 10 flowing rivers. The earth here is rich in iron, which gives it a red hue.

Distinctive **El Yunque** ★★, described in Spanish chronicles as an anvil-shaped, high (575m/1,886 ft.), and square mountain, dominates the landscape; Columbus wrote of seeing it on his approach to the bay, an the slopes have been declared a UNESCO Biosphere Reserve. Frequently bathed in mist, the flat-topped limestone mountain is about 10km (6¼ miles) west of Baracoa, and its slopes can be climbed in 4 hours round-trip. El Yunque is part of the Parque Natural Duaba and is home to scores of bird species and unique plants. In fact, 16 of Cuba's 24 endemic bird species can be found in this area. You can also spot the endemic *coco thrinas* palms, which look like tall dandelions. The trek through tropical forest, with views of rare ferns and orchids, is beautiful, but it can be intensely humid and is a challenging slog with a 2-hour ascent. Those who aren't up for the hike can always drive, though it's rough going along the unpaved road. Tours are offered in town for CUC$16, including transport. Adventurers in search of rafting possibilities should check out **Río Toa,** the widest river in Cuba and part of a national park. Tours to Río Toa are CUC$18 to 22. Tours to the **Río Yumurí** ★, a beautiful, luscious deep-river canyon 30km/19 miles east of Baracoa that can be accessed by boat and by walking on river islands, cost CUC$20 (CUC$26 with lunch). If you have your own transport boat, trips on these rivers cost CUC$3 per person.

The UNESCO Natural World Heritage Site of **Parque Nacional Alejandro de Humboldt,** a mountainous rainforest area with karst scenery that extends for 32,560 hectares (80,458 acres) north of Baracoa, is rich in biodiversity. It is home to the ivory-billed woodpecker, Cuban parrot and parakeet, colorful *polimita* snails, Caribbean manatee, and rare Cuban *solenodon* (an insectivorous mammal). It also provides habitat for the world's smallest bat, smallest frog, smallest bird, and smallest male scorpion. Tours are offered from town for CUC$23 and include a boat adventure into paradise—a slow tour around the **Bahía Taco ★★★**, where you can take in the mangroves and the stunning vista of royal and coconut palms, and search for manatee. If you have your own transport you can drive the 56km (35 miles) in 1¼ hours along the bad road. The park opens at 8am, and guided walks can be bought from there too (trails cost CUC$8 per person). Baracoa is blessed with a few superb beaches, which, due to the town's isolation, haven't yet been built up with huge all-inclusive hotels. **Playa Maguana ★** is about 22km (14 miles) from town on the road to Moa. It's a peaceful place with picture-perfect golden sands and is popular with local families and fishermen. There's a small hotel here (see "Where to Stay," below) and some new B&Bs. Cubatur runs day excursions here from 10am to 4:30pm (CUC$5 per person) that can be organized on the morning you wish to go.

Playa Duaba is a black-sand beach surrounded by wild vegetation and close to the mouth of the Río Duaba. A small monument in the community here marks the exact spot where Antonio Maceo and the independence fighters landed on April 1, 1895. This 1924 monument has been replaced by a larger 1929 obelisk close to the Hotel Porto Santo, and this is the monument to which the townsfolk process every year. The **Parque Espeleo-Arqueológico Majayara** is a new protected area beyond the delightful fishing community of **Boca de Miel ★★★**. Walk out of town past the hurricane-damaged stadium along the black-sand beach of Playa Baracoa, which curves around the Bahía de Miel, until you reach the long wooden bridge that crosses the mouth of the River Honey. Here you can see locals fishing with nets against a scene of bucolic charm: mountains studded with thousands of coconut palms and, in the distance, the flat-topped El Yunque. After crossing the bridge, turn left before reaching the park kiosk. A 10-minute walk beyond is **Playa Blanca** (entrance CUC$2). The white sand is not silky, but the water is beautiful and there are rock pools and a shallow entrance for children. Farther into the park is a stunning **Balcón Arqueológico ★★**, a 500-meter-long (1,640-ft.) limestone balcony with panoramic views of the entire coastline. Admission, which comes with a guide who can point out flora, fauna, and petroglyphs in the park, ranges from CUC$10 to CUC$15 and should be bought from Ecotur (lunch and access to Playa Blanca is included in the price); the park is open daily from 8:30am to 5:30pm. Visitors should be fit and prepared to climb up a ladder and almost sheer rock face to the balcony. Before hiking, look for locals who make bars of chocolate and coconut (much rarer than you would imagine), as well as banana and almond *dulces*.

A new, great-value trip that encompasses the best of Baracoa's bounty—**Mountain and Sea**—takes in El Yunque, a waterfall, Finca Duaba (a cacao-processing ranch), Rancho Toa, a boat trip on the River Toa, and a visit to Playa Maguana. It costs CUC$40, including lunch, and is sold by Cubatur.

Where to Stay

There's nothing fancy or especially luxurious in easygoing Baracoa—except the spectacular views of the bay and surrounding mountains—but one of the main hotels, in the oldest fortress in town, is a charmer. The little town is populated by more than 150 *casas particulares*, most right within the old town; several are excellent and among the best deals of their kind in Cuba.

MODERATE

Hotel El Castillo ★★ Perched on a small hill with the most outstanding views of Baracoa and the mountains, this is the top place to stay in town. The original rooms of the hotel occupy the area of the old fort and collect around the attractive pool. A newer block was built away from the older property in 2009; rooms here are larger but lack ambience. The real appeal of this hotel is not in the rooms but in the outstanding location, the superb views, and the inviting pool. Nonguests may use the pool for CUC$10 (and consume CUC$8 worth of food and drink). The elevated Mirador bar (daily 3–11pm) is worth the climb up the stairs for the five-star views.

Calle Calixto García, Loma el Paraíso, Baracoa. www.gaviota-grupo.com. ✆ **21/64-5194.** 62 units. CUC$58–CUC$65 double. Rates include breakfast. MC, V. **Amenities:** Restaurant; snack bar; 2 bars; outdoor pool; Wi-Fi.

Villa Maguana ★★ These rustic cabanas, tucked into a private cove in eastern Cuba 21km (13 miles) from Baracoa, are the closest Cuba has to boho living right on a beach. On a small, manicured plot of land, three tall cabanas with 12 spacious rooms and balconies overlook a tiny cove sandwiched between the larger fine curve of Playa Maguana and several unnamed beautiful coves lapped by stunning sapphire seas. Four other ground-floor rooms are older in style but closer to the beach; of those, just two rooms (201 and 204) come with matrimonial beds; the rest of the property's rooms have large twin beds.

Carretera de Moa a Baracoa, Km 20. www.gaviota-grupo.com. ✆ **21/64-1204.** 16 units. CUC$73–CUC$83 double. Rates include breakfast. MC, V. **Amenities:** Restaurant; bar; Wi-Fi (with charge).

INEXPENSIVE

Baracoa has more than 150 *casas particulares*. Recommended *casas* include **Casa Daniel Salomón Paján ★**, Calle Céspedes 28, between Rubert López and Maceo (✆ **21/64-1443**; daniels@nauta.cu), which is one of the friendliest *casas* in Cuba. Daniel works at the local museum and knows a lot about Baracoa's history. He has two comfortable rooms and a central covered patio. Mountain bikes are also available for rent. **Casa Ysabel Garrido ★**, Calle

Calixto García 164A (✆ **21/64-3515;** ysabel.gtm@infomed.sld.cu), has a large terrace and a small balcony overlooking the street; there's also a separate entrance to three upstairs bedrooms that share a sitting room and small kitchen.

Casa Walter, Calle Rubert López 47, between Céspedes and Coroneles Galanos (www.casa-walter.com; ✆ **21/64-2346**), is a central option with a third-floor terrace that has a high-pitched red-tile roof with dining tables and a bar. The two rooms share a sitting room and have independent entrances. **Casa Brisas del Atlántico ★**, Calle Frank País 3, between Malecón and Máximo Gómez (✆ **21/64-5798;** orlandoin@nauta.cu), has three rooms with a separate entrance, a large inviting communal area, and a rooftop terrace with sea views. You'll want to take the large room fronting the terrace at **Casa La Colina ★**, Calle Calixto García 158 altos, between Céspedes and Coroneles Gulano (✆ **21/64-2658**; choco.al@yahoo.es), which has a superb terrace.

Spacious **Casa Colonial Lucy**, Calle Céspedes 29, between Rubert López and Maceo (✆ **21/64-1061;** astralsol36@gmail.com), offers five rooms and a top terrace with sun loungers. **Casa Colonial Yalina & Gustavo**, Calle Flor Crombet 125, between Frank País and Pelayo Cuervo (✆ **21/64-5809;** gustavoyyalina2013baracoa@gmail.com), is a wonderful 1898 house with five rooms and a terrace—perfect for groups of friends. **Casa Barbara Almeida Cesar**, Calle Céspedes 30 between Maceo and Rubert López (✆ **21/64-3027;** pacoya@correodecuba.cu), is run by the kind Victor and Kany. It has one huge ensuite room with its own independent entrance.

Hostal La Habanera ★ Right in the heart of the action is this small, handsome porched colonial hotel. Just four of the 10 rooms, which all feature necessary blackout curtains, offer balconies that look out onto a veranda overlooking the main street—these are the top rooms. Consult the cute coffee menu during your stay.

Calle Maceo 68, corner of Calle Frank País. www.gaviota-grupo.com. ✆ **21/64-5273.** 10 units. CUC$40–CUC$45 double. Rates include breakfast. MC, V. **Amenities:** Restaurant; snack bar/bar; Wi-Fi (with charge).

Playa Maguana

Casa de Hidiolvis Real Dominguez ★, Playa Maguana (✆ **5310-4875**), is one of just two *casas particulares* at Maguana. Set back around 70 meters from the beach, this gorgeous little painted wooden house features two charming rooms. There are hammocks and a small dining table set up on a wooden walkway shaded by the boughs of a vast mango tree—heavenly.

Where to Dine

Diners resigned to the plain, unimaginative food in the rest of Cuba are in for a treat in Baracoa. The town and region revel in a unique cuisine found nowhere else in Cuba, one that makes ample use of local coconut and chocolate. The region produces about three-quarters of Cuba's coconuts, so logically it plays a strong part in the local diet. Try *cucurucho,* a coconut snack with fruit or almonds and honey wrapped in a palm-leaf cone; fresh fish embellished with coconut sauce; and the drinks *sacoco,* rum and coconut milk drunk from green coconuts, and *chorote,* chocolate with cornstarch. **Casa de Chocolate,** Maceo 121, is the place to get thick hot chocolate and locally made candies. In addition to the *paladares* listed below, the prices are good value for a full spread of Baracoan food at **Restaurante Calalú** (Calle Calixto García 151, corner of Céspedes; ✆ **5310-4810;** call for hours); and **La Colina** (Calle Calixto García 158; ✆ **21/64-2658;** daily 5–11pm) offers barbecued dishes on its top terrace.

BARACOA

El Poeta ★ BARACOAN/CRIOLLAN The rose-pink clapboard El Poeta is part restaurant and part theater. Owner Pablo approaches your table and composes poetry on the spot (no mean feat), and after dinner there's another treat (which we won't spoil by writing about it). The "show" is not designed to deflect from the cuisine, however. The tasty, well-curated Baracoan spread includes *ajiaco* (a traditional meat and vegetable stew) served in a guiro; *bacán* (mashed crab and banana in coconut milk and lemon boiled in banana leaf); *tetí* (the tiny local fish harvested during the waning moon); and coconut ice cream served in a coconut husk.

Calle Maceo 159, corner of Ciro Frias. ✆ **21/64-3017.** Complete dishes CUC$12–CUC$15. Daily 10am–10pm.

El Buen Sabor BARACOAN/CRIOLLAN Run by Alcides and Maba, this is one of Baracoa's most professionally run *paladares,* and is popular with couples, groups, and families. Opt for a spot on the terrace, garlanded in fairy lights, choosing a fish filet in coconut sauce or the lamb fricassee. The duck meatballs, compliments of the house, were a welcome treat.

Calle Calixto García 134 (altos). ✆ **21/64-1400.** Main courses CUC$8–CUC$18. Daily noon–10pm.

La Rosa Nautica SEAFOOD/BARACOAN/CRIOLLAN Baracoa's only fine-dining restaurant is wrapped in a nautical theme and offers great, tasty cuisine in elegant, elevated surrounds. Start first with the refreshing house cocktail La Rosa Nautica (rum, lemon, cacao liquor, and coconut) before tucking into abundant seafood, skewered meats, or marinated rabbit. The *pescado a Santa Barbara* (dorado in an exquisite coconut sauce) is delicious. The downsides are that the staff is a little pushy on the starters, the music swings from reggaeston to Amy Winehouse, and you need to review your bill. A 10-percent service charge is automatically added.

Calle 1 de Abril 185 (altos). ✆ **21/674-5764.** Main courses CUC$5.50–CUC$25. Daily noon–midnight. You'll need a *bicitaxi* to get here (CUC$2) or you can walk (15 min.).

PLAYA MAGUANA

Run by Piero from Turin and his Cuban wife, **Restaurant Maguana Beach**, Playa Maguana (✆ **5442-0724**), offers Italian dishes and *mariscos* eaten under a thatched roof overlooking the beach, all complemented by vegetables and herbs grown in the on-site garden. It's open daily noon to 9pm. Tucked into the crook of the cove to the east of Playa Maguana is **Restaurant Inolvi** (✆ **5278-0678**), known as the "casa amarilla" for its yellow clapboard exterior. Up in the garden, feast on beer, meat dishes, and river shrimp. On the main beach is the 24-hour **El Pulpo** (✆ **5227-8598**), serving fish in coconut sauce as well as octopus (*pulpo*).

Baracoa After Dark

Baracoa has an amazingly lively, after-dark scene for a town so small. In fact, its nightlife ranks among the best in Cuba. Virtually all the clubs and live-music venues are conveniently located on a single street, **Calle Antonio Maceo,** making Baracoa throb most nights like a tiny, tropical New Orleans, with traditional Cuban and contemporary dance music and revelers spilling out into the street until the wee hours. Unique to Baracoa are the enthusiastic *animadores,* or emcees, that introduce songs and bands and entertain audiences with florid language, poetry, and humor. Club cover charges are generally CUC$1 to CUC$3.

The first place to stop is the local **Casa de la Trova ★★**, Maceo 149, a comfortable, well-lit place loaded with locals and featuring good bands and a gregarious emcee. If you're lucky, you'll get to hear **Maravilla Yuqueña,** a wonderful group with a venerable old lead singer who should be far more famous than he is. Across the street, **La Terraza** is a huge, open-air terrace on top of a building. It has a Friday, Saturday, and Sunday show (10pm–midnight) and full-throttle, decibel-busting music under the stars, with dancers and occasional dance contests as well as top comedians—if your Spanish is up to it. Tuesday to Thursday nights feature a live band such as Orquesta Baracoa. A more sedate spot, within shouting distance of the sound system of La Terraza, is **El Patio,** a cute, brightly colored cafe with red lamps and a corrugated tin roof. The live music is pure Cuban *son* (Cuban salsa). Next door is the **Casa de la Cultura** (Maceo 124), which hosts traditional music on Saturdays from 9pm and folkloric music on Sundays. Dance classes are available here with teacher Eider López Milian (✆ **21/64 2772;** eiderim@correodecuba.cu).

Indigenous Baracoan music is called *Kiribá* and *Nengón.* It predates *son.* You can hear this music and see a dance performance by arranging a **fiesta ★**. It's a great day out in the countryside and you'll sample a fantastic spread of local food. Contact ***Grupo Kiribá* y *Nengón*** (Teresa Roché; ✆ **21/64-3447**). Three days' notice is required; cost is CUC$10 per person.

Baracoa is also well known for its annual **Culture Week** (at the end of March) and its yearly **carnival,** which runs the first 2 weeks of April.

SANTIAGO DE CUBA

10

The country's second-largest city, Santiago de Cuba ★★★ swings to the sound of *son* and *salsa*. Vibrant, tropical, and often sweltering, Santiago is the country's liveliest cultural showpiece, outside of Havana. With a population just under a half-million people, Santiago is a world apart, with a unique history and rhythms all its own. The city has produced some of Cuba's greatest contemporary musicians as well as several of its most stalwart revolutionaries, and has served as the stage for some of the most storied events in Cuba's modern history. As the capital of the old Oriente province, it has the largest Afro-Cuban population in Cuba and a resolutely Afro-Caribbean feel that distinguishes it from the rest of Cuba.

Founded in 1515, Santiago was one of the first of seven towns in Cuba and the Spanish colony's capital until 1553. Diego Velázquez, the founder of the original seven *villas,* built his mansion here, and the house still stands in the heart of the historic quarter. The Spanish character of the city would soon be supplemented by other influences. After the 1791 revolution in Haiti, a large number of French coffee plantation owners fled with their African slaves and made their way to Santiago. Black Haitian workers followed, as did large contingencies of West African slaves, sold to work on the plantations.

While downtown Santiago has the requisite noise, traffic, and urban chaos of a large city, it retains the intimate, friendly feel of a provincial capital, with peaceful neighborhoods where men play dominoes outdoors on hilly streets.

Santiago continues to earn its reputation as one of the liveliest and most individualistic cities in Cuba. The city's annual Carnival celebrations in July are famous throughout Cuba, predated by the boisterous and entertaining Festival del Caribe and Fiesta del Fuego at the beginning of the month. Afro-Cuban religious traditions, including Santería and other forms of worship, have their strongest hold here. And Santiagueros are also recognized for their take on Cuban Spanish, with a unique vocabulary and singsong rhythm.

Santiago fans out from a large, deep natural bay—guarded by the 16th-century El Morro fortress—and sits at the base of low mountains. Interesting excursions await visitors with time to explore outside the city: **El Cobre ★★** is a sacred shrine set in the beautiful foothills of the Sierra Maestra, while **Gran Piedra** is a rocky area just outside the city that invites hiking in its cool environs.

Hurricane Sandy in 2012 did much damage to Santiago's buildings and trees, but the city has undergone renovations and refurbishments as part of the 500th-anniversary celebrations in 2015.

ORIENTATION

Arriving & Departing

BY PLANE Direct international scheduled and charter flights arrive at the **Aeropuerto Internacional Antonio Maceo** (✆ **22/69-8614;** airport code SCU). Airlines regularly servicing Santiago include **Aerocaribbean** from Santo Domingo and Puerto Principe, **Aerogaviota** to Kingston, and **Cubana.** Charter flights run between Miami and Santiago several times each week.

Twice-daily flights connect Santiago with Havana via **Cubana** (www.cubana.cu; ✆ **22/65-1578** in Santiago) for CUC$135. **AeroCaribbean** (✆ **22/68-7255** in Santiago) flies twice a week for CUC$135. **AeroGaviota** (✆ **22/69-8625**) flies twice a week to Havana. Flights are about 2 hours.

The airport is 8km (5 miles) south of the city. There are several car-rental agencies at the airport. The quickest and safest way to the city is by taxi; the trip into town costs CUC$10.

BY BUS **Víazul**'s (www.viazul.com; ✆ **22/62-8484** in Santiago) Havana–Santiago de Cuba line is the best way to get to Santiago by bus, especially if you're planning to see any points of interest between Cuba's two main cities. For the trip from and to Havana, buses depart four times a day (16 hr.); the fare is CUC$51 one-way. From Trinidad (✆ **41/99-4448**), a bus leaves daily (11½ hr.); the fare is CUC$33 one-way. From Varadero, there is an overnight departure (14½ hr.); the fare is CUC$49 one-way.

Víazul also has twice-daily service between Santiago and Baracoa. Duration is 4 hours and 50 minutes; the fare is CUC$15 one-way. Note that no Cuban agencies sells Víazul tickets, which means a schlep out to the bus station. The ticket office is open from 8am to 12:45pm, 2 to 3pm, and 4 to 6:45pm. The **Terminal de Omnibuses** (✆ **22/62-8484**) for Víazul is located on Avenida de los Libertadores at the corner of Avenida Yarayó, about 2km (1¼ miles) from Parque Céspedes. A taxi to downtown costs about CUC$3, but the *taxistas* at the exit will demand up to CUC$5.

BY TRAIN The Cuban *ferrocarril* (railway) is not dependable, and delays, midrun breakdowns, and other problems are quite common. Taking the train is a potentially adventurous experience for those who wish to see the "real Cuba," but may be frustrating for those who need to adhere to a schedule.

In Santiago, the large, modern **Terminal Central de Ferrocarriles** is located on Avenida Jesús Menéndez at Paseo de Martí (✆ **22/62-2836**), across from the Caney rum factory.

Santiago de Cuba

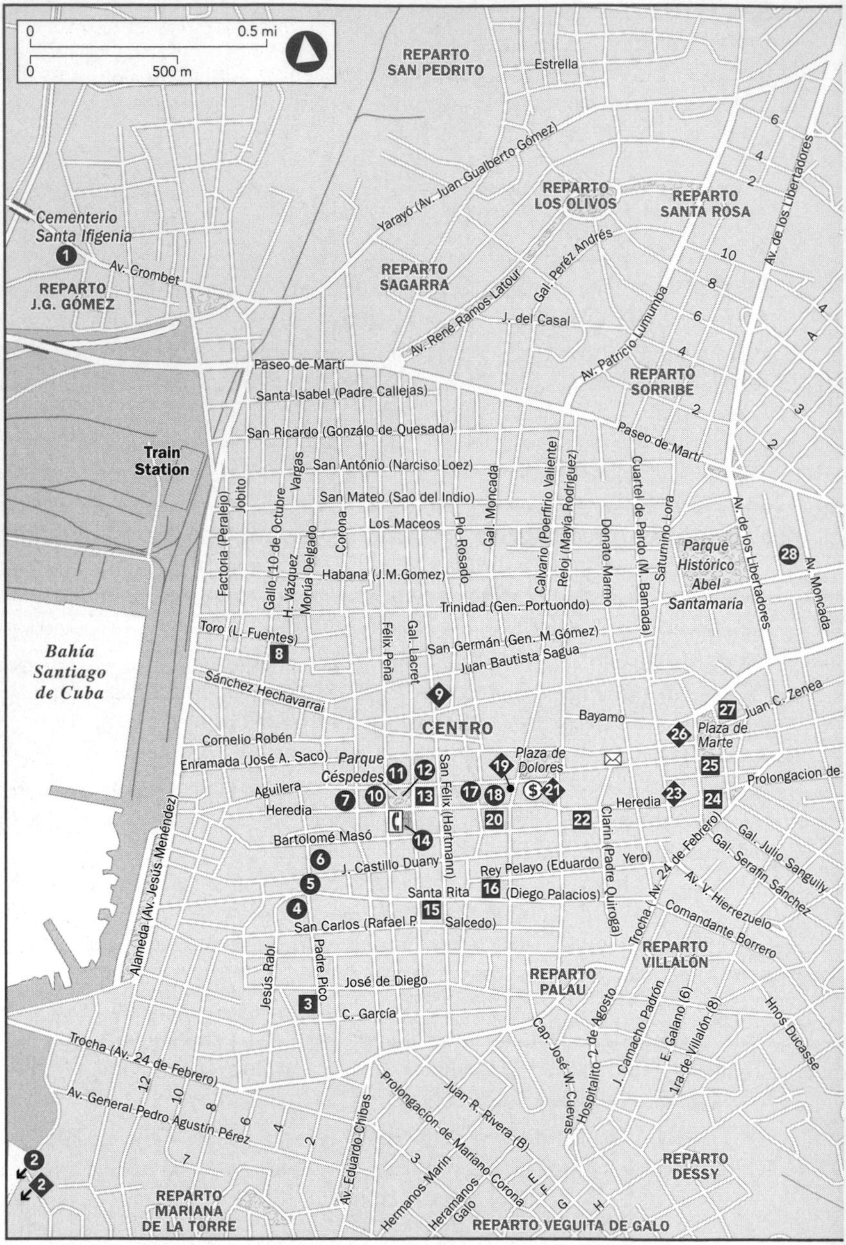
0
0.5 mi
0
500 m
REPARTO SAN PEDRITO
Estrella
Yarayó (Av. Juan Gualberto Gómez)
REPARTO LOS OLIVOS
REPARTO SANTA ROSA
Av. de los Libertadores
Cementerio Santa Ifigenia
1
Av. Crombet
REPARTO J.G. GÓMEZ
REPARTO SAGARRA
Av. René Ramos Latour
Gal. Peréz Andrés
J. del Casal
Av. Patricio Lumumba
REPARTO SORRIBE
Paseo de Martí
Santa Isabel (Padre Callejas)
San Ricardo (Gonzálo de Quesada)
Train Station
San António (Narciso Loez)
San Mateo (Sao del Indio)
Los Maceos
Habana (J.M.Gomez)
Trinidad (Gen. Portuondo)
Factoria (Peralejo)
Jobito
Gallo (10 de Octubre)
Vargas
H. Vázquez
Morúa Delgado
Corona
Pio Rosado
Gal. Moncada
Calvario (Poerfirio Valiente)
Reloj (Mayía Rodriguez)
Donato Marmo
Cuartel de Pardo (M. Bamada)
Saturnino Lora
Parque Histórico Abel Santamaría
28
Av. Moncada
Toro (L. Fuentes)
8
Bahía Santiago de Cuba
Félix Peña
Gal. Lacret
San Germán (Gen. M Gómez)
Juan Bautista Sagua
Sánchez Hechavarrai
9
CENTRO
Bayamo
27
Juan C. Zenea
26
Plaza de Marte
Cornelio Robén
Enramada (José A. Saco)
Parque Céspedes
11
12
San Félix (Hartmann)
19
Plaza de Dolores
25
Prolongacion de
Aguilera
7
10
13
17
18
21
Heredia
23
24
20
22
Clarín (Padre Quiroga)
Bartolomé Masó
14
6
J. Castillo Duany
Rey Pelayo (Eduardo Yero)
5
Santa Rita
16
(Diego Palacios)
4
15
San Carlos (Rafael P. Salcedo)
Gal. Julio Sanguily
Gal. Serafín Sánchez
Av. V. Hierrezuelo
Comandante Borrero
Trocha (Av. 24 de Febrero)
REPARTO VILLALÓN
Alameda (Av. Jesús Menéndez)
Jesús Rabí
Padre Pico
José de Diego
3
C. García
REPARTO PALAU
Cap. José W. Cuevas
Hospitalito 2 de Agosto
J. Camacho Padrón
E. Galano (6)
1ra de Villalón (8)
Hnos Ducasse
Trocha (Av. 24 de Febrero)
Av. General Pedro Agustín Pérez
Prolongación de Mariano Corona
Juan R. Rivera (B)
Av. Eduardo Chibas
Hermanos Marin
Heramanos Galo
REPARTO DESSY
2
REPARTO MARIANA DE LA TORRE
REPARTO VEGUITA DE GALO

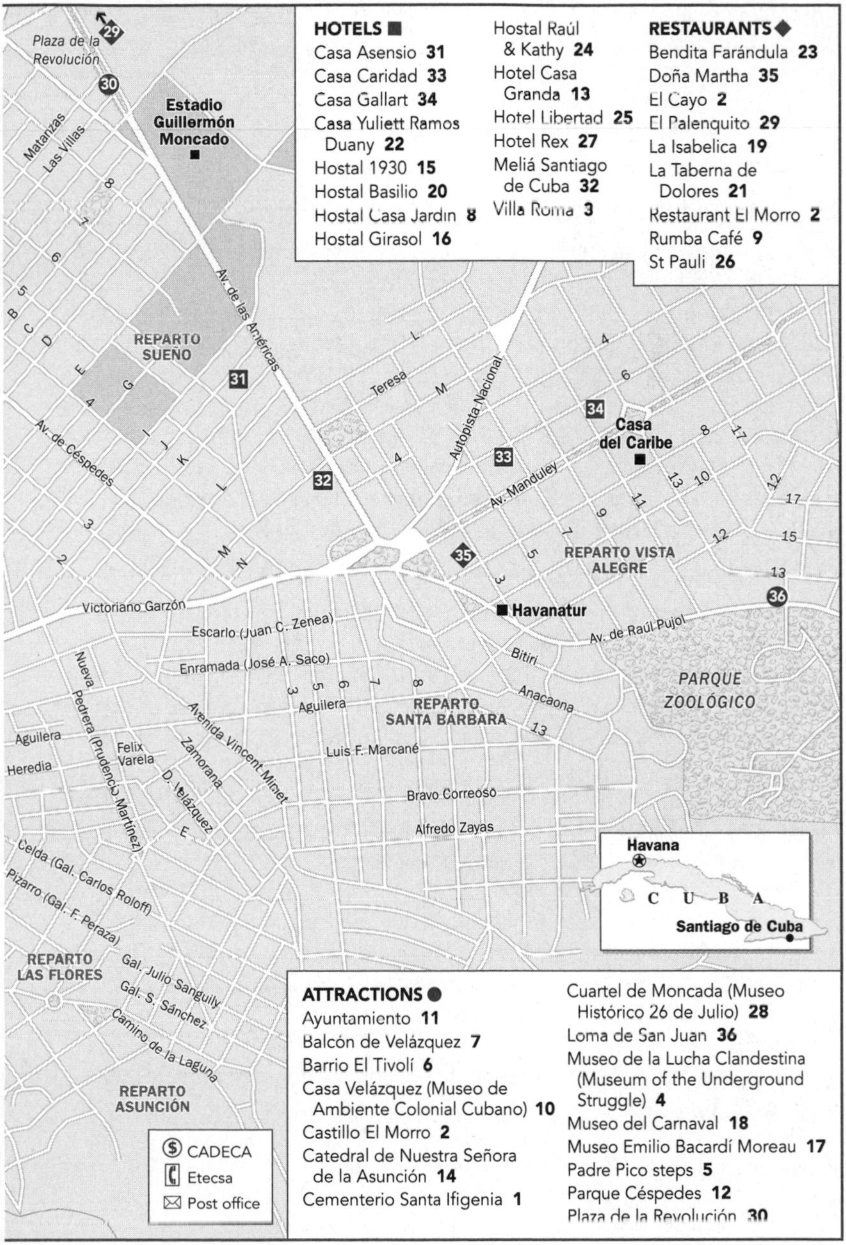
HOTELS ■
Casa Asensio 31
Casa Caridad 33
Casa Gallart 34
Casa Yuliett Ramos Duany 22
Hostal 1930 15
Hostal Basilio 20
Hostal Casa Jardín 8
Hostal Girasol 16
Hostal Raúl & Kathy 24
Hotel Casa Granda 13
Hotel Libertad 25
Hotel Rex 27
Meliá Santiago de Cuba 32
Villa Roma 3
RESTAURANTS ◆
Bendita Farándula 23
Doña Martha 35
El Cayo 2
El Palenquito 29
La Isabelica 19
La Taberna de Dolores 21
Restaurant El Morro 2
Rumba Café 9
St Pauli 26
ATTRACTIONS ●
Ayuntamiento 11
Balcón de Velázquez 7
Barrio El Tivolí 6
Casa Velázquez (Museo de Ambiente Colonial Cubano) 10
Castillo El Morro 2
Catedral de Nuestra Señora de la Asunción 14
Cementerio Santa Ifigenia 1
Cuartel de Moncada (Museo Histórico 26 de Julio) 28
Loma de San Juan 36
Museo de la Lucha Clandestina (Museum of the Underground Struggle) 4
Museo del Carnaval 18
Museo Emilio Bacardí Moreau 17
Padre Pico steps 5
Parque Céspedes 12
Plaza de la Revolución 30
CADECA
Etecsa
Post office
Plaza de la Revolución
Estadio Guillermón Moncado
Reparto Sueño
Av. de las Américas
Autopista Nacional
Teresa
Casa del Caribe
Av. Manduley
Reparto Vista Alegre
Av. de Céspedes
Victoriano Garzón
Escarlo (Juan C. Zenea)
Enramada (José A. Saco)
Havanatur
Av. de Raúl Pujol
Bitiri
Anacaona
Parque Zoológico
Reparto Santa Bárbara
Aguilera
Heredia
Nueva Pedrera (Prudencio Martínez)
Felix Varela
Avenida Vincent Minet
Zamorana
D. Velázquez
Luis F. Marcané
Bravo Correoso
Alfredo Zayas
Celda (Gal. Carlos Roloff)
Pizarro (Gal. F. Peraza)
Reparto Las Flores
Gal. Julio Sanguily
Gal. S. Sánchez
Camino de la Laguna
Reparto Asunción
Matanzas
Las Villas
Havana
CUBA
Santiago de Cuba

BY CAR Driving to Santiago is a good way to see the breadth of the country. The six-lane, toll-free Autopista Nacional (A1) and the Carretera Central run the length of Cuba, straight down the spine of the country from Pinar del Río to Santiago. However, east from Sancti Spíritus, it is just two lanes almost the entire way to Santiago, and the going can be slow at times, since equal numbers of cars, trucks, horse-drawn carriages, bicycles, and pedestrians make use of the Carretera Central. Santiago is 860km (534 miles) east of Havana, 127km (79 miles) east of Bayamo, and 134km (83 miles) southeast of Holguín.

Visitor Information

Infotur, inside the Cubatur office, Calle Lacret 701, corner of Heredia (✆ **22/66-9401**; open daily 8am to 5pm); another Infotur office at the airport (✆ **22/69-2143**); **Cubanacán,** Calle M, corner of Avenida Las Américas (✆ **22/64-2202**); and **Cubatur,** Calle Lacret 701, corner of Heredia (✆ **22/68-7096**) all offer guided city and area tours. Excursions to El Cobre cost CUC$15, to La Gran Piedra CUC$46, and to Baconao CUC$66. The best value tour takes you around the city, out to Cayo Granma, El Morro, and El Cobre for CUC$54, including lunch. Contact the recommended **Paradiso**, Calle Heredia 304 e/ Calvario y Carnecería (✆ **22/62-7037;** paradisoscu@scsc.artex.cu), if you want to learn more about music, culture, and religion in Santiago.

City Layout

The historic center of the city rolls across low hills to the east of the **Bahía de Santiago,** where work is underway to build an attractive Malecón. The focal point of colonial Santiago is **Parque Céspedes.** This historic square boasts perhaps the oldest house in the Americas. **Calle Heredia,** which leads east from the square, is a popular street with plenty of foot traffic and is lined with live music venues, colonial houses, and museums. South of Parque Céspedes is the charming, hilly **El Tivolí** district and its emblematic Padre Pico steps. Heading east of Parque Céspedes is **Plaza de Dolores,** an attractive and shady little square that's a popular and easygoing hangout ringed by a handful of restaurants, bars, and cafes. **Plaza de Marte** marks the divide between old Santiago and the newer section, leading along the long and wide avenue Victoriano Garzón out toward the nicest suburbs in Santiago and districts where you'll find several hotels and *casas particulares:* **Reparto Sueño,** the elegant **Reparto Vista Alegre,** and **Reparto Santa Bárbara.**

Note that old and new street names (pre- and post-Revolution) are used interchangeably in Santiago. The most common pre-Revolution street names used in the old colonial center are: Enramada (for José Antonio Saco); San Basilio (Bartolomé Masó); San Pedro (General Lacret); Santo Tomás (Félix Pena); Marina (Aguilera); and Carnicería (Pío Rosado).

Getting Around

BY TAXI **Cubataxi** (✆ **22/64-1965**) and private taxis congregate near the cathedral on Parque Céspedes and at the major tourist hotels. Be sure to ask about fares before hiring one, as tourist gouging is a favorite local pastime

santiago, CITY OF STRUGGLE & REBELLION

Santiago has long demonstrated a fiercely independent streak. Among Cubans, the city is known affectionately as the *cuna de la Revolución,* or the cradle of the Revolution. The first slave uprisings in Cuba occurred in Santiago, and the city had prominent roles in the wars of independence against the Spanish in 1868 and 1895. Antonio Maceo rejected a pact with the colonial power, laying the foundation for continued resistance, and became one of the leaders of the rebel army. Each of the 29 generals during the 30-year war against the Spanish came from the city, and the Bay of Santiago was the site of the 1898 naval battles between the U.S. and Spain. Teddy Roosevelt and his Rough Riders stormed the Loma de San Juan, a low hill just east of the city, in battles against the Spanish, which led to Spain's imminent defeat and withdrawal from Cuba (though Cuba's independence was effectively usurped by the Americans in the years after the Spanish-American War).

In 1953, the young Fidel Castro and a band of insurgents attacked the Moncada military barracks in Santiago (the failed, but famous 26th of July episode). After many of his rebels were tortured and killed by the army, Castro was captured and issued his famous declaration, "History will absolve me," in defense of his seditious actions. A local Santiago schoolteacher, Frank País, sparked an uprising of university students in 1957, attacking police headquarters. Assassinated by the Batista army in the streets of Santiago, he became a martyr of the Revolution. Castro returned from exile in Mexico in 1956 to wage war from the cover of the Sierra Maestra, west of Santiago, and 2 years later the rebel leader ultimately announced victory, on January 1, 1959, from the balcony of the governor's mansion (today Town Hall) in Parque Céspedes. Castro rewarded the city that supported him with the title "Heroic City of the Revolution."

(from the Meliá Santiago to Parque Céspedes, the fare should be CUC$2–CUC$3; from downtown to El Morro CUC$12–CUC$15). Gran Car charges CUC$0.90 a kilometer. Cheaper private taxis can be found parked around Plaza Marte. With the latter, negotiate a price, but understand that the driver may be uncomfortable taking you directly to the door of your hotel if he's not officially licensed to carry foreigners.

There are also *bicitaxis* (bicycle taxis), which are convenient and inexpensive (usually CUC$1–CUC$3) but occasionally hair-raising for many passengers.

BY CAR **Cubacar** (www.transtur.cu; ✆ **22/68-6107**) has offices at the airport, opposite the Cupet gas station on Carretera Central; Hotel Casa Granda; Hotel Las Américas; Meliá Santiago; and Hotel Villa San Juan. **Vía Rent a Car** (✆ **22/62-4646**) is inside the Cubatur office, Lacret 701, corner of Heredia. Rates are from CUC$60 per day for a standard four-door compact car.

BY FOOT The area of greatest activity and cultural interest to many visitors in the historic center—the few streets around Parque Céspedes is easy to get around on foot, though some areas, such as the Tivolí district, are extremely hilly. However, many hotels are at least a couple of kilometers from the city center, and a good number of the city's foremost attractions, such as El Morro, are beyond the city and require transportation.

[FastFACTS] SANTIAGO DE CUBA

Airport See "Arriving & Departing," above.

Banks/ATMS/Currency Exchange A **CADECA** (✆ **22/65-1383**) branch is on Calle Aguilera 508. The local branch of **Banco de Crédito y Comercio** (✆ **22/62-3316**), where you can exchange traveler's checks and get cash advances, is on Félix Pena 614. **Bandec** (✆ **22/62-7581**), with similar services, is on Félix Peña between Aguilera and Heredia with an ATM. Both are open Monday through Friday 8am to 1pm and Saturday 8 to 11am. ATMs can be found at most banks. An ATM is at the **Banco Popular de Ahoro** (✆ **22/64-2454**) on Plaza Dolores; it's open Monday through Saturday 8am to 7pm. You can also change money at the Meliá Santiago and most other hotels in the city.

Car Rentals See "Getting Around," above.

Emergency Dial ✆ **106** for police or ✆ **185** for an ambulance.

Hospitals & Medical Assistance **Clínica Internacional,** Avenida Raúl Pujol at Calle 10 in Reparto Vista Alegre (✆ **22/64-2589**), has 24-hour emergency services, a dentist, and English-speaking doctors. There are **pharmacies** at the clinic and along Calle José Antonio Saco.

Internet Access The **Etecsa Multiservicios Céspedes on Heredia,** corner of Sto Tomás (✆ **22/62-4784**) provides telephone and Internet service daily from 8:30am to 7:30pm. You can also find Internet at the Meliá Santiago and Casa Granda.

Police The police station is located at Corona and San Gerónimo (✆ **106**). However, the probability of finding an English speaker is remote. In case of an emergency, one of the better hotels (such as the Casa Granda or Meliá Santiago) should be able to help or at least interpret for the police.

Post Office The main post office is on Calle Aguilera 517 between Reloj y Clarín (✆ **22/65-2397**); it's open Monday through Saturday 8am to 8pm. All the major hotels have basic postal facilities. A **DHL** office can be found at Calle Aguilera 310 at the corner of San Félix (✆ **22/68-6323**).

Safety Santiago is a safe city, but the local *jineteros/as* are relentless in accosting foreigners. They are, for the most part, innocuous. Still, if you're attending a street festival, concert, or Carnival, put your money in a money belt and leave your watch, jewelry, and knapsack behind (these items will be safer in your hotel or *casa particular*). Also, be careful and keep an eye on your bags at the Santiago bus and train stations.

Taxis See "Getting Around," earlier in this chapter.

Telephone You can make local, long-distance, and international phone calls with a phone card from **Etecsa** (see "Internet Access," above).

EXPLORING THE AREA

Many visitors in search of what makes Cuba unique actually prefer the country's second city to the capital. Santiago is unpolished. To get to know its city, music, and colonial architecture, an immersion of more than a few days is recommended.

The Top Attractions

A major gathering spot day and night for Santiagueros, aggressive *jineteros,* and travelers alike, **Parque Céspedes ★** is a menagerie of eclectic architecture, to put it mildly. Its benches, growing post-Sandy trees, and gas lamps are ringed by colonial, 19th-century, and modern structures, including the ancient mansion of Diego Velázquez (see "Casa Velázquez," below), as well as the handsome colonial governor's mansion (Town Hall), the baroque cathedral, the Club San Carlos, and the city's oldest hotel, Casa Granda.

The **Ayuntamiento,** or Town Hall, a huge white building on the north side of the square with blue wooden grilles, was originally built in 1515. It was greatly renovated in the 1950s after an earthquake, but has retained its elegant colonial lines, balcony, and patio. Fidel Castro addressed the adoring masses here on January 1, 1959, after the rebel army had taken the city and announced the triumph of *La Revolución.*

Across the park, the early-19th-century **Catedral de Nuestra Señora de la Asunción** is a massive, ornate, newly painted silvery-gray basilica with twin towers—the fourth church to occupy the site since 1522. The frescoes on the arches and dome of the interior have been restored. Inside is a massive pipe organ, as well as the remains of the Spanish conquistador Diego Velázquez, although, since a 1678 earthquake, the whereabouts of those remains in the building are unknown. The graves of the first (Spanish) archbishop of Cuba and the first Cuban archbishop are clearly visible. The cathedral is open Tuesday through Saturday 8am to 12:30pm and 5 to 7:30pm, and Sunday 8 to 11am and 5 to 6:30pm.

Casa Velázquez (Museo de Ambiente Colonial Cubano) ★★ The mansion (ca. 1516) that once belonged to Diego Velázquez, founder of the original seven *villas* in Cuba, still stands despite the unrepentant fumes of tour buses and fires that have threatened it. The house has a notable Moorish influence, with a wonderful carved cedar ceiling (most of which had to be reconstructed after a fire). The top floor was the living quarters; the ground floor was the commercial part of the house, where Velázquez maintained offices and horse carriages were kept. The majority of the house's elaborate frescoes have been supplemented by very amateurish reproductions, a real sin against the authenticity that is so apparent elsewhere. The museum aims to depict the varied styles and epochs of colonial life, seen through period furnishings from the 16th to the 19th century. You'll find some splendid pieces of French, British, Spanish, and Cuban furniture; Spanish ceramics; carved chests; and French porcelain. Several dressers have extraordinary inlaid designs, proof of the wealth of the bourgeoisie in colonial Cuba. A second 19th-century house in back, blue and white, with an attractive courtyard, is not part of the original Velázquez house. Peñas are held in the courtyard on a weekly basis.

Félix Pena 612, Parque Céspedes. ✆ **22/65-2652.** Admission CUC$2; CUC$1 to take photos, CUC$5 to take video. Guided tours in Spanish or English available. Sat–Thurs 9am–5pm; Fri 1–5pm.

Cuartel de Moncada (Museo Histórico 26 de Julio) ★ The yellow barracks of the Spanish army, east of downtown, represent a pivotal episode in modern Cuban history. The ocher-colored exterior is still pockmarked with bullet holes, a reminder of the day in July 1953 when Fidel

Castro and a band of ragtag but idealistic rebels launched an assault on the barracks, with the intention of stealing arms and jump-starting a revolution. First built by the Spanish in 1859, the barracks were burned down and then rebuilt in the late 1930s. Today, the Art Deco–style barracks house a museum focused on that day and the revolutionary struggle. For anyone interested in Cuban history, regardless of ideology, a visit to the museum is a must.

Fidel and his poorly funded troops, including his brother Raúl and Abel Santamaría, arrived in the early hours of July 26 dressed like army soldiers (though the street shoes they wore, rather than military boots, would give them away). Some 120 men attacked the barracks, but the plan failed miserably and 61 were killed. The others escaped, but were soon captured; many were tortured to death by Batista's army. Batista announced to the press that 500 well-funded militiamen had attacked the barracks and been killed in a gun battle. A young journalist succeeded in getting photographs of the tortured and murdered young revolutionaries out of Santiago and to Havana, where the pictures were published, galvanizing many Cubans against the Batista regime.

The museum exhibits the rebels' small rifles and pistols, bloodstained uniforms, photographs, letters, and other documents that tell the amazing story of the subsequent exile of the surviving rebels and guerrilla warfare in the Sierra Maestra. Exhibits are labeled in Spanish only, so a guide might be a good idea.

Calle Trinidad (corner of Moncada). ✆ **22/62-1157.** Admission CUC$2; CUC$1 to take photos; CUC$5 to take video. Free guided tours are available in English, French, and Italian. Tues–Sat 9am–4:30pm; Mon & Sun 9am–12:30pm.

Museo Emilio Bacardí Moreau ★ Begun by Emilio Bacardí, the founder of the political and rum dynasty in 1899, this highly personal collection constituted one of the first museums in Cuba. Now a provincial museum, it remains an eclectic art and historical assembly. The grand, gleaming white neoclassical building was erected in 1928 to house the idiosyncratic collection. On the first floor is a wide variety of artifacts documenting indigenous peoples, slavery, and the wars of independence, including an extensive array of armaments and a peculiar coffin-shaped torpedo used by the Mambíses. Bacardí also collected personal items belonging to Cuban national heroes, including those of Antonio Maceo and Carlos Manuel Céspedes. Don't miss the tiny stage set of a colonial Santiago street (through a door on the south side of the first floor). In an annex, which must be entered from a side door on Calle Aguilera, is an archaeology room holding an Egyptian mummy (smuggled out of Egypt in 1913), a pair of Peruvian mummies belonging to the Paracas (pre-Inca) culture, various ceremonial objects, pre-Columbian ceramics, and an extraordinary decorated shrunken head from the Amazon. The second floor is an art museum exhibiting national and international paintings. There are several contemporary pieces, including a larger-than-life sculpture of Che Guevara in heroic pose. Allow an hour to see it all. All of the display information here is in Spanish, but English-speaking guides are available.

Calle Pío Rosado (at Aguilera). ✆ **22/62-8402.** Admission CUC$2. Free guided tours are available in English. Mon noon–4:15pm; Tues–Sat 9–4:15pm; Sun 9am–noon.

Other Attractions

Barrio El Tivolí A charming, hilly neighborhood just south of Parque Céspedes (loosely bordered by Av. Trocha and Calle Padre Pico), El Tivolí was once the most fashionable place to live in Santiago. Today, it's a relaxed place of steep streets, weathered and decrepit wooden houses, and a couple of attractions, but mostly it's a good place to wander.

The famous **Padre Pico steps** are named for a Santiaguero priest who aided the city's poor. Castro once roared fire and brimstone down on the Batista government here, but today you'll find more pacifistic chess and dominoes players who've set up all-hours tables on the steps. Take the steps up to the **Museo de la Lucha Clandestina (Museum of the Underground Struggle),** General Rabí 1 between Santa Rita and San Carlos (✆ **22/62-4689**), which is housed in a handsome 18th-century-replica mansion on a hill, Loma del Intendente. Inside are disorganized exhibits related to the November 1956 attack on this former police headquarters, led by rebel leader and schoolteacher Frank País and his brother Josué, both executed by the army. Frank País's funeral was massively attended by Santiagueros, a signal that the Revolution would have significant local support. Other photos and documents attest to the phenomenal years of tension, rumors, and conflict that led to the rebels' triumph (labels are in Spanish only).

Barrio El Tivoli, just south and west of Parque Céspedes. Admission CUC$1; photography permit CUC$5. Tues–Sun 9am–4:45pm.

Cementerio Santa Ifigenia ★★ Northwest of the city center, this sprawling cemetery, dating to 1868, is a small city of the dead, populated by elaborate marble tombs and sarcophagi, including several spectacular mausoleums (many of which are pre-1868, having been moved here from other cemeteries). By far the most famous is that of José Martí, a massive stone and marble circular structure built in 1951 (Martí died in 1895). Don't miss the solemn changing-of-the-guard ceremony. The Lincolnesque mausoleum is near the entrance to the cemetery, at the end of a private path. Martí once wrote that he wished to die, "without a homeland, but without a master" and to be buried with "a bouquet of flowers and a flag." In addition to Martí, the remains of Emilio Bacardí, Carlos Manuel de Céspedes, Pedro (Perucho)

Terrace with a View

The **Balcón de Velázquez,** at the corner of Heredia and Corona at the edge of El Tivolí district, is a marvelous lookout over the red-tile rooftops of the city as it slopes down to the Bay of Santiago. Named for the Spanish conquistador who founded the city, the terrace was reconstructed in the 1950s; it has been said that the original terrace in this very spot was used by Velázquez himself to observe incoming ships in the bay. An escape tunnel once ran from the spot, protected by cannons, all the way to the bay. Admission is free, but you'll have to pay CUC$1 if you want to take photographs.

Figueredo (author of the Cuban national anthem), and heroes of the Moncada 26th of July rebel attack are interred here. The newest addition to the celebrated figures buried here is the great musician and native son Compay Segundo. The cemetery's palm-lined paths abound with a wealth of other fascinating tombs for families both famous and unknown.

Calle Raúl Perozo s/n. ✆ **22/63-2723.** Admission CUC$1, CUC$5 to take photos. Daily 7am–5pm.

Loma de San Juan This low-rise hill in the center of Reparto Vista Alegre, a leafy, upscale neighborhood, is where the decisive last battle of the Spanish-Cuban-American War was fought. Teddy Roosevelt and his army of an estimated 6,000 Rough Riders stormed the hill and defeated the Spanish troops. At the entrance to the park is the **Arbol de la Rendención (Tree of Surrender)**, where the Spanish forces capitulated to the Americans. Something that still irks Cubans today, besides the commonly used name of the war that leaves them out, is that the Cubans were not even signatories to the surrender. While there are several plaques and monuments in the neatly manicured park that pay tribute to the North Americans who participated and died in the war, there are few dedicated to the Cuban fighters (though the **Tomb of the Unknown Mambi,** or independence fighter, can be found there).

Reparto Santa Bárbara, at the intersection of Av. de Raúl Pujol and Carretera de Siboney Km 1.5 (next to the Hotel San Juan).

Museo del Carnaval Santiago's Carnival is the most famous in Cuba, and this small museum, in one of the oldest houses on Calle Heredia, aims to give visitors some historical perspective. Unfortunately, exhibits are ragtag and many of the displays are unlabeled. It would be wise to hire a guide to navigate the collection of black-and-white photos, instruments, and capes. Of note is the beautiful 1945 cape belonging to a participant of the Conga de los Hoyos group and a 2011 cape dazzling with sequins and featuring the Five Cuban Heroes (p. 27). **Folklore and music and dance events** are held at the museum (except in inclement weather) Monday through Saturday at 4pm, Saturday at 7pm, and Sunday at 10am. Plan to spend about 20 minutes viewing the displays.

Calle Heredia 303 (corner of Pío Rosado). ✆ **22/62-6955.** Admission CUC$1; CUC$5 for a guide; CUC$5 to take photos. Sun–Mon noon–5:15pm, Tues–Fri 9am–5:15pm, and Sat 9am–10pm.

Plaza de la Revolución This massive, raised platform monument to Antonio Maceo is an emphatic statement, to be sure, featuring a startling equestrian statue of the great patriot surrounded by 23 enormous iron machetes slicing toward the sky, like daggers in the sides of colonial power. Maceo, a Cuban of mixed blood, was called the "Bronze Titan" of the Cuban independence wars. Beneath the work is an eternal flame. An underground room houses a small and rather uninspiring museum dedicated to the man.

Av. de las Américas (at Los Desfiles and Carretera Central). ✆ **22/64-3768.** Admission to museum CUC$1; CUC$5 to take photos. Tues–Sat 9am–4pm; Sun 9am–1pm.

Bay of Santiago

Santiago's deep natural bay is one of the city's defining characteristics. In 2015 work was begun by a Chinese consortium to deepen the bay for commerce and prettify the Malecón for locals. The narrow entrance to the Bahía de Santiago, past the Castillo El Morro, stretches 8km (5 miles). During the Spanish-American War, the contingency of Spanish ships was huddled within the bay, and the Americans were perched on the coast waiting to ambush them.

Today, Santiago's marina is popular with European and U.S. yachts and sees twice-weekly visits from cruise ships. Visitors can book a 40-minute trip around the entire bay (daily 9am–4pm; CUC$12). If you just want to cross over to the fishing village on the tiny island of Cayo Granma for lunch, the ferry is CUC$3 round-trip. For more information, contact the **Santiago Marina,** Calle 1 no. 4, Punta Gorda (✆ **22/69-1446;** mercado@marlin.acu.tur.cu).

WHERE TO STAY

Santiago may not be blessed with the range of hotels that Havana has—in fact, it has less than a half-dozen hotels within easy reach of downtown—but it has enough variety among its few hotels that most guests shouldn't have trouble finding a decent place to stay at any price level. Only one of Santiago's major hotels is within the historic district, which is lively and fun, but may be too noisy and chaotic for many visitors.

Especially popular in Santiago are *casas particulares*. The city has hundreds of these state-sanctioned private homestays, several in historic homes in the heart of the old district and others in tranquil, leafy suburbs.

For those who prefer to stay outside the city as an overnight excursion or even with plans to make a day trip out of Santiago, there are a couple of hotels along the coast and near some of the outlying attractions. Those hotels are listed in "Side Trips from Santiago de Cuba," later in this chapter.

Centro Historico

MODERATE

Hostal Basilio ★ A small, sweet hotel tucked back off the street and garlanded by a twin staircase entrance. The forest-green Basilio operates under Cubanacán's Hotel Encanto brand and features eight high-ceilinged rooms stylishly arranged with colonial furniture and done in maroon and mustard threads. Most rooms come with twin beds except rooms no. 3 and 5, which feature king-size beds. Room no. 5 is also the largest on the property. Amid the interior patterns of green decor is a small garden patio with seats, a quiet spot for tea and reading. The hotel has a small in-house restaurant serving reasonable local and international fare.

Calle Basilio 403 (btw. Calvario and Carnicería). www.hotelescubanacan.com. ✆ **22/65-1702.** 8 units. CUC$84–CUC$90 double. Rate includes breakfast. MC, V. **Amenities:** Restaurant; bar.

Hotel Casa Granda A large, elegant building right on Parque Céspedes, this hotel is a landmark in the city. Graham Greene's character Wormold, from *Our Man in Havana,* stayed in the 1914 hotel. Best known perhaps for its terrace bar with live music and its roof garden with great views over the cathedral and Santiago, the Casa Granda is one of the best places to stay in the city for its location only. The hotel features large rooms with high ceilings and restrained décor, but many rooms are looking tired and dated. As with most state-run hotels in Cuba, double beds are at a premium here; in fact, just 18 rooms come with a queen-size bed, and the rest have two twins. Rooms either have views of the park, Calle Heredia, or the interior—guests should opt for the latter as street and park noise may not allow for a good night's sleep. Unfortunately, you'll need to review the bar prices, check your bill, and double-check your change at the popular people-watching terrace bar.

Heredia 201 (btw. San Félix and General Lacret). www.hotelescubanacan.com. ✆ **22/65-3021.** 58 units. CUC$96–CUC$112 double; CUC$115–CUC$140 junior suite. Rates include breakfast. MC, V. **Amenities:** 1 restaurants; 2 bars; room service.

Hotel Rex ★ The restored 1950s Rex hotel is a good choice for those on a budget. Just off Plaza Marte, and with a rooftop terrace and bar (open Thurs–Tues 6:30pm–1:30am) for relaxation, it offers renovated rooms with flatscreen TVs, luggage racks, bedside lamps (still uncommon in Cuba), and brand-new bathrooms. Most rooms come with twin beds; rooms with views of the city and mountains are the top choices here (no. 41 and 35). Room no. 36 is preserved as a museum dedicated to the stay of Abel Santamaría, who took part in the Moncada assault on July 26, 1953.

Avenida Garzón no. 10 (btw. Pérez Carbó and Pizarro). ✆ **22/68-7032.** 24 units. CUC$54–CUC$64. Rates include breakfast. MC, V. **Amenities:** Restaurant; bar.

INEXPENSIVE

Downtown Santiago offers scores of *casas particulares*. Prices run between CUC$25 and CUC$30 for a double.

Hostal 1930, Calle Santa Rita 302 between San Pedro and San Félix (✆ **22/65-8589;** juanmarti13@yahoo.es), is a stunning house with three rooms and a wealth of beautiful antiques and highly unusual *mamparas* (half-door screens inlaid with plain or decorative glass), which have engraved French scenes compressed between the glass. The choice room is off the back patio (complete with fountain and rocking chairs) with a huge mahogany bed, pink and green original tiles, and a prominent chandelier. **Hostal Casa Jardin**, Calle Máximo Gómez 165 between Rastro and Gallo (✆ **22/65-3720;** mariaelsaas@gmail.com), is a wonderful house, run by the helpful Mari, with three rooms and a delightful patio garden. The top terrace, too, is overflowing with flowering plants and a swing chair.

Casa Yuliett Ramos Duany, San Basilio 513 between Clarin and Reloj (✆ **22/62-0546;** isabelycarlos686@gmail.com), is a friendly household with young children. The three rooms are smartly furnished and are comfortable with plently of storage space. The second room has its own separate kitchen. There's a front terrace and a roof terrace. **Villa Roma,** Calle Padre Pico 614 between Princesa and San Fernando (✆ **22/62-2801;** niurkis.www2013@yahoo.es) is a lovely house with a plant-filled terrace and a magnificent view up to the cathedral. Niurkis and her Italian husband, Gianni, offer a warm welcome and tasty Italian food. You'll need to be nimble for the second of the two bedrooms—its bathroom is on a cute mezzanine reached by a spiral staircase.

Hostal Girasol, Calle Diego Palacios (Santa Rita) 409 between Pío Rosado (Carnicería) and Calvario (✆ **22/62-0513**; hostalgirasol1983@gmail.com), is run by super-friendly Jeannette and Julio. Girasol has five rooms scattered across the house, which is decorated with sunflower artwork. One room boasts a cute independent terrace, and another room has its own interior terrace. Breakfast is served up on the roof terrace with views across Santiago's rooftops.

Hotel Libertad, Calle Aguilera 658 (Plaza de Marte; www.islazul.cu; ✆ **22/65-1589**), fronts the busy Plaza de Marte and is a reliable budget option in the heart of the city. Many of the 17 rooms, plainly furnished with compact bathrooms, do not have windows. No. 214 is the hotel's largest and best room. The real draw here, apart from the central location, is the popular rooftop bar (Wed–Mon 6pm–2am). **Hostal Raúl & Kathy**, Calle Heredia 610.5 between Paraiso and Marte (www.facebook.com/HostalRaulSantiagocuba; ✆ **22/62-4472** or 5271-7833; morel.barca@gmail.com), is a lovely, welcoming home with rooms scattered around two properties. If you're a light sleeper, you'll want the interior rooms away from the street noise. Breakfasts and dinners are served up on the communal tables on the top terrace, which has outstanding views of the city and surrounding mountains.

The Outskirts

EXPENSIVE

Meliá Santiago de Cuba ★★ This prominent bold-red postmodern high-rise is the largest hotel in Santiago and the most luxurious. It's about 2km (1¼ miles) from the historic core, perfect for guests who want to get away from the busy pace of downtown and like to end their day with a dip in a pool. The Melia's pool is the best in the city, with gazebos and a poolside grill. It's also got a multitude of restaurants and bars. The rooms are spacious and enjoy fantastic views of the city and mountains. Royal Service rooms—all tangerine, beige, and gold threads—come with a host of associated amenities such as late checkout and breakfast in bed. Royal Service Junior suites boast Jacuzzi baths. The hotel has a show on Saturday and Wednesdays in its atmospheric **Santiago Café,** which is an indoor reconstruction of a miniature colonial city. Nonguests can use the pool facilities for a fee of CUC$14, which includes pizza and two drinks.

Av. de las Américas (at Calle M), Reparto Sueño, Santiago de Cuba. www.meliacuba.com. ✆ **22/68-7070.** 302 units. CUC$120–CUC$143 double; CUC$183–CUC$248 junior suite. Royal Service rooms (standard, junior suite, master suite, and presidential suite) CUC$183–CUC$350. Free for children under 2; free for one child 3–12 sharing an adult's bedroom. Breakfast CUC$10 per person. MC, V. **Amenities:** 4 restaurants; 4 bars; gym; sauna; Saturday show; 3 outdoor pools; volleyball court; Wi-Fi (with charge; free for Royal Service rooms).

INEXPENSIVE

In the elegant Vista Alegre district, you'll find **Casa Gallart**, Calle 6 no. 302, corner of 11 (✆ **22/64-3307;** maydepedro@yahoo.es), run by Pedro Gallart and Mayde Tauler, with two rooms and a cozy back patio; and **Casa Caridad Cisneros Ferrer,** in a 1950s modernist home located at Calle 6, no. 158, between Calles 5 and 7 (✆ **22/64-2871**).

Casa Asensio ★ This fine house with an upstairs apartment is run by the friendly Isabel. The huge apartment has a large, private rooftop terrace. There's an independent entrance and a separate kitchen, a large, comfortable bed, and a good-size bathroom plus a second shower room and sofabed in the living room for friends or family. Abstract art is painted on the walls, and you have access to the home's little garden.

Calle J, no. 306 (btw. Calle 6 and Av. de las Américas), Reparto Sueño, Santiago de Cuba. ✆ **22/62-4600.** manuel@medired.scu.sld.cu. 1 unit. CUC$25 double. No credit cards.

WHERE TO DINE

Santiago's dining scene has not taken off in the same way as that of Havana. There are, however, a few choice places to eat in the city and we have included those here.

For coffee, beer, and refreshments we recommend **Café Ajedrez,** Calle Enramada at Felix Peña (no phone), located in a tiered 1966 Art Deco building by architect Walter A. Betancourt. The cafe features stylized metal tresses, Deco lamps, and stone tables with chess boards (*ajedrez*). It's open Tuesday to Sunday 10am to 3pm. Another great spot is the atmospheric **Café La Isabelica** on Plaza Dolores, corner of Calle Aguilera and Calvario, which has been serving patrons since 1868. The two signature coffees are *rocio con gallo* (coffee with rum) and the Café Isabelica (coffee, *aguardiente*, and honey) which costs CUP$7 but 10 times as much in convertible currency CUC$3. The cafe is reminiscent of an old inn with leather-and-hide-covered chairs, local characters, and gossiping old men. It is open daily from 6:40am to 10:45pm. On the same square, **La Taberna de Dolores** serves drinkers in local pesos from midday to 8am the following morning. For your ice cream hit, wend your way down to **Jardines las Enramadas,** which serves up flavors in *moneda nacional* in Art Nouveau–ish glasses on leafy grounds (open Tues–Fri 9:45am–10:45pm, Sat and Sun 9:45am–11:45pm). Santiagueros' refreshment of choice is Pru, a tea-colored drink of fermented sugar, spices, pepper leaf, and roots. It's sold for CUP$1 a bottle at the **Casa del Pru,** Calle Reloj e/Enramadas and Aguilera (Tues–Sat 9am–9pm, Sun 9am–noon).

Centro Historico

INEXPENSIVE

Rumba Café ITALIAN/INTERNATIONAL Run by an Italian Fabio, this new cafe-bar is a godsend in Santiago. It's in a great spot and is a perfect place to kick back with a pasta dish, a milkshake, a bite-size bun (*pulguitas*) or an ice-cold daiquiri. The front living room is all bright red cushions, tiled floor, chandeliers, and red wooden cabinets, while the leafy patio out back is more reminiscent of a Marrakech bolthole with cushioned seats, wrought-iron tables, and planters backed by colors of tangerine and Majorelle blue.

Calle San Felix 455A (btw. San Francisco and San Gerónimo). ✆ **5802-2153.** Main courses CUC$3.90–CUC$6. No credit cards. Mon–Sat 9:30am–10:30pm.

St Pauli ★★ SEAFOOD/CRIOLLA Hidden away down a decorated alley behind an unassuming black entrance door, St Pauli is a find. Although St Pauli was named after Hamburg's red-light district, the ambience is anything but. Beer-hall tables and chairs fill a backyard area where a menu starring seasonal ingredients is fashioned in the kitchen by enthusiastic staff under the tutelage of renowned Cuban chef Jorge Bringas Sotera. Portions are huge, presentation is exquisite, and value is excellent. The deliciously fresh *concasse* of vegetables in yogurt sauce is as generous as it is delicious; we also recommend the pork meatballs in Dijon sauce. Main courses are chalked up daily on the blackboard. A fulsome platter of octopus *al ajo arriero* was tasty and filling.

Enramada 605 (btw. Barnada and Plaza de Marte). ✆ **22/65-2292.** Main courses CUC$4.50–CUC$15. No credit cards. Mon–Thurs noon–11pm, Fri–Sun noon–midnight.

Bendita Farándula ★ SEAFOOD/CRIOLLA This small tavern with graffitied tangerine walls and leather-and-hide-backed chairs is run by the warm and friendly Sussana Carrasquero Reece, whose grandfather was English. The hole-in-the-wall affair serves up delicious grilled snapper and shrimp in garlic, as well as traditional regional staples such as *ropa vieja* and pork chops.

Calle Barnada 513 (btw. Aguilera and Heredia). ✆ **22/65-3739.** Main courses CUP$90–CUP$300. No credit cards. Daily noon–11pm.

The Outskirts

MODERATE

El Palenquito ★★★ BBQ/CRIOLLA One of Santiago's top restaurants, El Palenquito serves up tantalizingly delicious barbecued food to those in the know. Huge platters of seafood are served up at garden tables surrounded by mango trees and hibiscus flowers with views towards the Sierra Maestra. Owner Avelino Vasquéz Crespo used to work at the Melia Santiago and brought all his expertise to play at El Palenquito, which he opened in 2012. The only downside? You need transport to get here. Oh, and don't arrive late for lunch or you might find some of the platters already sold out.

Av del Río 28 (btw. Calle 6 and Carretera del Caney), Reparto Pastorita. ✆ **22/64-5220.** Main courses CUC$3.75–CUC$12. No credit cards. Daily noon–midnight.

Doña Martha ★ CRIOLLA In a rustic setting just off Vista Alegre's smart main avenue, beneath a thatched roof surrounded by potted plants, the unassuming Doña Martha serves up fantastic and good-value food to Cubans and foreigners in the know. A favorite is the stellar grilled fish accompanied by rice, potatoes, and mixed salad—all for under CUC$3.

Calle 3ra no.152 (btw. Calle 8 and Ave Manduley), Reparto Vista Alegre. © **22/64-1177.** No credit cards. Daily noon–midnight.

Bahia de Santiago

MODERATE

El Cayo CRIOLLAN This relaxing spot for lunch is a boating excursion and dining outing rolled into one. In a pretty blue-and-white clapboard waterfront house on a tiny island in the middle of the Bay of Santiago—you have to take a CUC$3 round-trip ferryboat from the **Santiago Marina** (© **22/69-1446**) to get there—this breezy, tranquil restaurant is popular with organized groups but is perfect for independent travelers, too. Sit on the covered wraparound balcony overlooking the water and try any of the seafood specialties: Spanish mackerel, lobster, red snapper, marlin, or fish soup.

Cayo Granma, Bahía de Santiago. © **22/69-0109.** Reservations recommended for lunch. Main courses CUC$6–CUC$18. MC, V. Daily 11am–6pm.

Restaurant El Morro ★ CRIOLLAN A hugely popular and pleasant open-air place, perched on the coast near the fortress of the same name and boasting spectacular views of the sparkling blue Caribbean Sea. It also serves a good-value lunch (with choices) for groups. Try the lobster if you're in a mood to splurge; otherwise, sample fish filet stuffed with cheese accompanied by shrimp in a tomato sauce, roast chicken, or lobster. A wood-beamed canopy shades the long tables, a most welcome refuge from the scorching sun that makes midday at El Morro fortress a daunting proposition.

Carretera del Morro, Km 8.5, Bahía de Santiago. © **22/69-1576.** Reservations recommended for lunch. Main courses CUC$5–CUC$20. Offers CUC$8 and CUC$10. V. Daily noon–4:30pm.

SHOPPING

Art, Books & Handicrafts

Vendors and craftspeople can be found at **Proyecto Espiral**, Calle Enramadas corner of Gallo, featuring a range of handicrafts and souvenirs, including sculptures of shapely (as well as rail-thin) women carved from ebony and other precious woods, paintings, masks, papier-mâché dolls, musical instruments, and jewelry. **Luis Hodelin Puente**, "el Rey del Disco de Vinil," Calle Aguilera 609 (© **22/62-9189**), sells books and records Monday through Saturday from 9am to 4pm.

At the **Casa del Abanico**, Calle Heredia corner of Carnicería, Maruchi Sánchez fashions fans from cedar and hibiscus woods. **La Escalara**, Calle Heredia 265, offers books, records, stamps, posters and memorabilia. At **Casa Quitrín**, Calle Enramadas 458 between Calvario and Reloj, purchase pretty white cotton clothes and *guayaberas* (pleated men's shirts).

Locally produced abstract and figurative art is available at a handful of galleries, including the **Galería de Arte Oriente** on Calle General Lacret 653, between Aguilera and Heredia.

> **Bring on the *Béisbol***
>
> Santiago is yet another baseball-mad Cuban city, and the local professional team is usually among the best in the national league. The *pelota* (as it's popularly known) season begins in late winter and continues through the spring. Games are held at the **Estadio Guillermo Moncada** on Avenida de las Américas (✆ **22/64-5640**). Ask at your hotel about getting tickets (it's usually possible to purchase them right before game time at the stadium ticket booth).

Cigars & Rum

The **Barrita de Ron Caney,** in the rum factory that was the original Bacardí plant before the Revolution (when the owners fled to the Bahamas and the U.S.), has a gift shop selling an array of types and vintages of Cuban-produced rum, as well as cigars, nice silver jewelry, and other souvenirs. You can taste before you buy. The factory and shop are on Av. Jesús Menéndez 703 between San Antonio and San Ricardo (✆ **22/62-5576**), across from the train station. The shop is open daily from 9am to 5:30pm. Alternately, you can check out the **Museo de Ron** (✆ **22/62-8884**), at San Basilio 358 esq a Carcineria, which offers a brief illustrated guide to the history and process of rum production. It's worth the entry to view the 1889 home of Colonel Mariano Gómez Villasana with its marble floors and chandeliers—with delicately carved bronze flowers and cascading crystals. The museum is open Monday through Saturday 9am to 4:30pm; the CUC$2 entrance fee includes a *trago de ron* (shot of rum).

Cigars can be purchased at hotel shops or **Casa del Habano,** next door to the Caney rum factory (✆ **22/62-2366**), which has a smokers' lounge and bar.

Music

Santiago is the capital of *son* and other indigenous forms of Cuban music, and there are a few good spots to pick up CDs and tapes of Santiaguero musicians (though overall, Havana has a much better selection of music stores). Of the artists you may have an opportunity to see perform live, most sell CDs at their performances. The **Casa de la Trova** (p. 254) has an **ARTex** store. Musical intstruments, including the bongó, maracas, the tres guitar, and the lute can be bought at the new **Tienda de Sindo Garay,** Calle Garzón 5, Plaza de Marte (✆ **22/66-9186;** Tues–Fri 9am–5pm, Sat 9am–9pm, Sun 5–9pm).

SANTIAGO DE CUBA AFTER DARK

The Performing Arts

Besides the locally grown Cuban music scene, another nighttime draw is slick music and audio visual night Locomoción at **Cabaret Tropicana Santiago,** Autopista Nacional Km 1.5, north of Santiago (✆ **22/64-2579**) on Saturday evenings at 11pm; there's also a dance club on the premises, open Tuesday to Sunday from 11pm until 6am. (CUC$5). The cabaret show—different from the one in Havana—with excellent singers and dancers and extraordinarily elaborate costumes, is only available on sufficient demand on Mondays for CUC$25n.

You'll find a much more scaled-down and less-expensive Wednesday-night show at the **Santiago Café** ★ (✆ **22/68-7070**), in the Meliá Santiago. The cover here is just CUC$5 per person, which includes one drink.

The top spots for cultural events such as dance and theater are the sleek **Teatro Heredia,** Avenida de los Desfiles, across from the Plaza de la Revolución (✆ **22/64-3178**). Keep an eye out for performances by **Ballet Folklórico Cutumba** ★★★, an extraordinary Afro-Cuban troupe that has toured in North America and Europe. Cutumba has returned to Santiago and has its base at the old Cine Galaxia, Calle Trocha corner of Santa Ursula (Av V. Hierrezuelo; www.cubanfolkloricdance.com/cutumba.php; ✆ **22/62-3201**). Cutumba stages performances on Saturdays and Sundays at 7pm (CUC$3) and can be seen at the Noche Santiaguera on Saturday nights in Calle Trocha. Also keep an eye out for **Conjunto Folklórico de Oriente,** which performs at Teatro Martí. You may not catch all the spiritual and cultural elements embedded in their show, but the music and dance are infectious nonetheless. Teatro Heredia is the headquarters for the **Festival del Caribe** ★★ in July, but the entertainment also takes place in the streets and the Casa del Caribe. Some events require reservations; contact **Agencia Paradiso** (p. 87) or the **Casa del Caribe** (see below).

Finding out what's going on in Santiago can be difficult. Visit the **Centro de Información Cultural** (Calle Enramadas btw. San Félix and Carnicería; ✆ **22/65-5708;** Mon–Fri 8am–4:30pm, Sat 8am–noon and 5–9pm).

Live Music

Santiago is all about the music. Some of the biggest personalities on the Cuban music scene, such as **Compay Segundo, Eliades Ochoa,** and **La Vieja Trova Santiaguera,** hail from Santiago. Although Compay died at 95 in 2003, Ochoa is still active, touring both in Cuba and internationally. Calle Heredia, just off Parque Céspedes, is Cuba's version of Bourbon Street, but much less commercialized. Four or five places burst with addictive live, traditional Cuban music on any given night, and several have bands during the day, too. Personal local favorites include **Los Jubilados,** a band of gregarious septuagenarians who often play at the Casa de la Trova; **Kokoyé,** a folkloric band playing traditional Afro-Cuban and Afro-Haitian music; and the **Vocal Divas,** a talented women's a cappella group.

Several of the spots below are not only great for hearing live music, but also for watching local patrons who make dancing to Cuban music a sultry art form all their own. Give it a try and don't worry about looking foolish; unless you've had professional training, you simply can't compete with Cubans on the dance floor, so don't even try. If you're without a partner, there's usually

carnival & OTHER SANTIAGO FESTIVALS

Santiago is well known among Cuban cities for its sparkling music festivals, which thrust Afro-Caribbean culture and the local musical genius to the forefront of urban life. If you can stand the stultifying heat in late July, Carnival is the most exciting time to visit the city.

In Santiago, *Carnaval* is not a pre-Lenten celebration as it is in other Latin American countries. In the 17th century, slaves reshaped the traditional (and much more solemn) Catholic veneration of the city's patron saint, Santiago Apóstolo, and the attendant religious processions, into a festive celebration. The slaves' revelry was much more raucous than that of the white Christians, who began to refer to the slaves' participation as the *Fiesta de Los Mamarrachos* (Party of the Crazies). Gradually, the rest of Santiaguero society began to appreciate and even participate in Carnival. French and Haitian elements were incorporated after the 18th-century influx of those populations. By the 20th century, Santiago's Carnival had gone the way of samba and *Carnaval* in Brazil, which was appropriated from marginal black communities and transformed into a mainstream cultural affair.

Today, unsurprisingly, even Carnival is linked to politics. The 5-day celebration also serves to commemorate the 26th of July Movement, which was the foundation for the Revolution. Each year, at 5am on July 26, a reconstruction of the Moncada attack is made, complete with a cavalcade of old cars and gunshots. It's a surreal event. Yet politics seems light-years away from the popular explosion that erupts on Santiago's sweltering streets. Garish floats, with parade queens atop, glide through the streets, frenetic drum-beating conga parades rock the neighborhoods (the biggest are the barrio congas of day 1), and masked *diablitos* (devils) dart daringly through the throngs. African elements, including representations of *orishás* (Yoruba gods), are omnipresent. *Comparsas,* the Carnival band processions, have marchers who don papier-mâché masks and brightly colored costumes.

Today, Carnival still manages to be exuberant, even though funds for fancy costumes are tough to come by and homemade instruments predominate (during the years of the so-called Special Period in the mid-1990s, economic conditions were so tough that Carnival had to be canceled for a couple of years). Some conga ensembles, such as Los Hoyos, trace their origins back to 1902. Be on the lookout for the following excellent dance troupes: Cabildos, La Placita, and Izuama y Olugo. The focal points of Carnival activities are along Avenida Jesús Menéndez and Victoriano Garzón, where the parade and float judging takes place. Congas sally forth on the 24th (dia de San Juan) and 29th of June, and July 18. Tickets for the grandstand seating can be bought in wooden kiosks along Victoriano Garzón from 1 hour before the children's parades at 5pm and the adults' parades at 10pm ($2MN). If you can't bear the crush and need some space, pay for optimum viewing in the foreigners' stand—and be charged CUC$5 for the privilege.

Preceding Carnival is the **Fiesta del Fuego,** or **Festival del Caribe,** in the first week of July, which brings a cornucopia of cultural workshops, theater, and artistic performances to Santiago. On the last day of this festival, an effigy of the devil is burned *(Quema del Diablo),* and a conga line shimmies all the way from Parque Céspedes down to the water at 5pm—buy a bottle of rum, dance the conga (*arroyar*), and join the end of the line.

no shortage of Cuban men and women (most of whom will invariably be *jineteros* or *jineteras*—hustlers) willing to give you a whirl. At places like the Casa de la Trova and other spots around town, you're likely to find music throughout the day, beginning around noon and going well into the night. At most clubs, the music starts around 9pm and really heats up from around 10pm until 2am.

Casa de las Tradiciones ★★★ More cramped and heaps more intimate than the more touristy Casa de la Trova (see below), this old house (called "La Casona" by locals) in the Tívoli section of town is loaded with character and decorated with dozens of paintings and photos on the walls. It gets perfectly steamy when the tight band is playing and more than two couples are working the dance floor. Calle Rabí 154. ✆ **22/65-3892.** Cover CUC$2. Daily 9pm–midnight.

Casa de la Trova ★★★ Decades of raw and infectious Cuban music seep from the walls of this legendary live-music venue, the greatest of the country's Casas de la Trova. Old-timers may complain that it doesn't have the character it once did, thanks to makeovers, but its front room and back patio and the grand upstairs salon still outclass almost any other Cuban music joint. All the greats have played here; you may catch an up-and-coming star or a band of octogenarians who rightly should be every bit as famous as the guys in Buena Vista. They aren't, but you'll enjoy their music all the more for their relative obscurity and the chance to see them in such a welcoming environment. Heredia 206 (btw. San Felíx and San Pedro). ✆ **22/65-2689.** Cover CUC$1 daytime, CUC$5 at night. Programming varies daily.

Casa del Caribe ★ This cultural center has a full schedule of music events and other goings-on starting after 6pm Thursday to Sunday. The program is eclectic, ranging from poetry to folkloric dancing to rumba and steel bands. It's best to call beforehand before making the trek out here. Concerts are held on two leafy outdoor patios. There are also cultural conferences and workshops. Contact the *casa* for the Fiesta del Caribe program. Calle 13, no. 154 (corner of Calle 8), Vista Alegre. ✆ **22/64-3609.** Cover CUC$3 for la Peña de la Rumba on Sun.

Patio de ARTex Stop by this happening venue for live Cuban music every afternoon and night of the week; there's a gorgeous courtyard out back. Heredia 304 (btw. Pío Rosado and Porfirio Valiente). ✆ **22/65-4814.** Cover CUC$2 evenings only. Live traditional music 5–7pm (CUCC$1) and 9pm–midnight (CUC$2).

Patio de los Dos Abuelos This place on the Plaza de Marte is a good spot to listen to *boleros* and *filin* (feelin', a musical genre). The scene is a little older and more sedate than most of the places listed above, but folks still get up and dance. Moreover, the patrons and players show real love for the romantic ballads and tragic love songs that are the staples here. Calle Pérez Carbó 5 (across from the Plaza de Marte). ✆ **22/62-3302.** Live music 9:30pm–midnight. Cover CUC$2.

Iris Jazz Club A new jazz club offers up local and international players in new surrounds including Giselle Lage, Angel Toirac, Camilo Vestrio, and Roberto Fonseca. Diners can eat before the show with food provided by the folk behind the Compay Gallo *paladar;* during the show, tapas is offered to those seated at the tables. Calle Paraíso (btw. Aguilera and Enramadas; Plaza del Marte). ✆ **22/62-6201.** Cover CUC$5. Wed–Mon; bar open from noon; show runs 1:30pm–2am.

Bars & Clubs

In general, bars open around noon and stay open as long as there are patrons, usually between midnight and 2am. Dance clubs and music joints tend to get going around 10pm and stay open until at least 2am.

La Claqueta The choice place for salsa dancing with a patio opposite the cathedral, an elevated stage for the regular live bands, and covered bar. Programming varies; stop by to read the board to see what's on. It gets going around 10pm with a healthy mix of locals, *jineteros,* and foreigners. Calle Felix Pena (btw. Heredia and San Basilio). Daily 10pm till closing.

Bello Bar This bar occupies the entire 15th floor of the Meliá Santiago hotel and has stunning 360-degree views of Santiago. Live jazz is heard on Thursdays and Cuban tunes can be heard daily. In Meliá Santiago hotel. (Av. de las Américas at Calle M, Reparto Sueño). ✆ **22/68-7070.** Cover CUC$5. Daily 6pm–2am.

Hotel Casa Granda Terrace Bar & Rooftop Garden A great spot for people-watching over the Parque Céspedes, this convivial terrace/balcony bar is always busy, even though the service is eternally subpar and shortchanging is rife. The hotel also has a **Rooftop Garden bar** on the top floor with excellent views of the cathedral and Santiago Bay; it's open from 9am to 2am with a dance show starting at 10pm. On Fridays, Septeto Santiaguera play at 10pm. Hotel Casa Granda, Calle Heredia 201 (btw. General Lacret and San Félix). ✆ **22/65-3021.** Entrance to the Rooftop Garden is CUC$3 with consumo mínimo CUC$2 from 9am–7pm; after 7pm entrance fee is CUC$5 with consumo mínimo CUC$4. Rooftop Garden bar and Terrace Bar open 9am–2am.

La Taberna de Dolores This local hangout—my favorite low-rent watering hole in Santiago—is in the pretty, leafy patio of an old colonial house that was formerly the home of Don Sebastian Kindelan, governor of Oriente province between 1800 and 1813. This joint always has cheap draft beer in plastic mugs. The crowd is mostly Cuban, with a few backpacker sorts. With a minimal bit of Spanish (like *cerveza,* meaning beer), you should be able to pay in Cuban pesos—be sure to ask about paying in *moneda nacional,* although be sure you have some *moneda nacional* in your pocket when they hand you the bill. Calle Aguilera 468 (at Reloj), Plaza Dolores. ✆ **22/62-3913.** Daily noon–8am.

SIDE TRIPS FROM SANTIAGO DE CUBA

Excursions to all the places listed below, as well as to Guantánamo and Baracoa (see chapter 9), can be arranged at the tour desks found in most hotels, or with tour agencies (see Santiago de Cuba Visitor Information, p. 238).

Castillo El Morro ★★

15km (9 miles) S of Santiago de Cuba

Guarding the entrance to the Bahía de Santiago, this seemingly impregnable fortress is built atop a rocky promontory and entered across a formidable drawbridge. The medieval and Renaissance-style structure, a UNESCO World Heritage Site, is a warren of platforms, passageways, and cells spread across five levels and protected by 1.5m-thick (5-ft.) walls. It was engineered in 1638 by the Italian architect who built similar fortresses in Havana, as well as Cartagena, Colombia, and San Juan, Puerto Rico, to protect against pirate attacks (which it didn't do so well—pirates including Henry Morgan succeeded in ransacking the place).

The site, where the sun beats down unrelentingly, has magnificent views of the bay and the Caribbean coastline stretching all the way to the Sierra Maestra. Inside the fortress, built above a dry moat, is a sparse museum (with display explanations in Spanish only) detailing the history of piracy, El Morro, and Santiago de Cuba. One room contains artifacts related to the 1898 Spanish-American War—its principal naval battles were fought right in the Bay of Santiago. The 19 modern American ships sank all seven Spanish ships; ironically, the Spanish ship *Cristóbal Colón* was the last to sink, thus closing the door on the history of Spanish colonialism in the Americas.

A daily ceremony, called the Puesta del Sol, takes place at sunset (if it rains, it's canceled), recalling the importance of the fortress in the 19th century. Youngsters dressed as *mambises,* or members of the Cuban rebel army, lower the flag and shoot off an ancient Spanish cannon to cries of "¡Viva Cuba Libre!" Visiting El Morro for the day-ending ceremony, when it has cooled off some, is an excellent idea. You'll need about an hour to tour the complex. Avoid the midday hours of 11am to 4pm at all costs.

To get there, an organized excursion or a car or taxi is required. The Castillo El Morro is open daily from 8am to 5:20pm; admission is CUC$4, and it's an additional CUC$1 to take photos and CUC$5 to take video. Free guided tours are available in English, French, and Italian. For details, call ✆ **22/69-1569.**

Basílica del Cobre

18km (11 miles) W of Santiago de Cuba

The most important shrine for Cubans and the most famous church in the country is lodged in the foothills of the Sierra Maestra near the old copper mines that give it its name. The triple-domed church with the name of **El Sanctuario de Nuestra Señora de la Caridad del Cobre,** built in 1927, rises on Maboa hill and is photogenically framed by green forest. The faithful come from across Cuba on pilgrimages to pay their respects to (and ask for protection from) a black Madonna, the *Virgen de la Caridad* (Virgin of Charity). She is nothing less than the protectress of Cuba, and her image, cloaked in a glittering gold robe, can be seen throughout the country. Her parallel figure in Afro-Cuban worship is Ochún, goddess of love and femininity, who is also dark-skinned and dressed in bright yellow garments. In 1998, the pope visited and blessed the shrine, calling the Virgin "La Reina de los Cubanos" (Queen of Cubans), and donated a rosary and crown.

According to legend, the statue of Cuba's patron saint was discovered bobbing in the Bay of Nipe in 1612 by three young fishermen (or miners, depending on who's telling the story) about to capsize in a storm. The Madonna wore a sign that read YO SOY LA VIRGEN DE LA CARIDAD (I am the Virgin of Charity). With the wooden statue in their grasp, the fishermen miraculously made it to shore. Pilgrims, who often make the last section of the trek on their knees, pray to her image and place *votos* (mementos) and offerings of thanks for her miracles; among them are small boats and prayers for those who have tried to make it to Florida on rafts. Ernest Hemingway—whose fisherman in *The Old Man and the Sea* made a promise to visit the shrine if he could only land his marlin—donated his Nobel Prize in Literature to the shrine, but it was stolen (and later recovered, but never again to be exhibited here). The Virgin sits on the second floor, up the back stairs, encased in glass. The annual pilgrimage is September 8, and the patron saint's feast day is July 25. The Basílica is open daily from 6:30am to 6pm; admission is free.

You can take a taxi to El Cobre for CUC$25 round-trip, but an agency tour is cheaper. Buses run between Santiago and El Cobre, leaving from the Calle 4 bus station in Santiago every half-hour. To enhance the spiritual experience, or merely to have a serene and incredibly cheap overnight stay, an inn behind the church, **Hospedería de la Caridad El Cobre,** welcomes foreigners who abide by the strict rules (10pm curfew and repeated requests for quiet); a stay costs a mere 20 national pesos (CUC$1) a night. The inn has 25 austere, but well-kept rooms, and it's so popular you must reserve by phone (© **22/34-6246**) at least 15 days in advance. It has a large, breezy dining room too.

La Gran Piedra & La Isabelica

27km (17 miles) E of Santiago de Cuba

A tortuous coastal road east of Santiago ascends the mountains to **La Gran Piedra (The Big Rock) ★★★**, an enormous 25m-high (82-ft.) rock perched 1,200m (3,937 ft.) above sea level. You can climb a half-hour on foot to the top of the rock for a panoramic view of thickly wooded eastern Cuba and the majestic Sierra Maestra that extends to the Caribbean and as far as the eye can see. The air is much sweeter and cooler than in Santiago. Admission is CUC$2, which includes a drink. Near the foot of the trail is the modest **Gran Piedra** (www.islazul.cu; © **22/68-6147;** CUC$24 double), a rustic little hotel with a restaurant, as well as the **Jardín Ave de Paraíso,** a small botanical garden with birds of paradise and temperate flowers, straddling the old coffee plantation ruins of La Siberia. The garden is open daily 8am to 5pm, and admission is CUC$2; camera use is CUC$5.

About 2km (1¼ miles) beyond Gran Piedra, a passable dirt track leads to **Museo La Isabelica,** Carretera de la Gran Piedra Km 14, an early-19th-century coffee plantation *finca* (country house) that once was the property of newly arrived French immigrants who fled Haiti after the slave revolt there in 1791. The owner named La Isabelica for his mistress (and later wife), a beautiful slave. The house was a stone mansion built in the style of rural French manor houses in Haiti. It was one of about 60 coffee plantations in the area, which proved very hospitable for planting coffee beans. The 200 Arabica coffee plantations in the region helped Cuba become the number-one coffee producer in the world until 1850, when it was surpassed by Brazil. These Franco-Haitian plantations are UNESCO World Heritage sites. On the premises of La Isabelica is a workshop, along with the original furniture and slave instruments. It's open daily 8am to 5pm; admission is CUC$2; camera use is CUC$5.

Gran Parque Natural Baconao

25km (16 miles) SE of Santiago de Cuba

A UNESCO Biosphere Reserve, **Parque Baconao** is spread over some 40km (25 miles) but was heavily damaged during Hurricane Sandy in late 2012. The local dark-sand beaches are scruffy and the hotels are isolated.

The road leading southeast out of Santiago is lined with 26 monuments to revolutionary heroes who died in the attack on the Moncada barracks. The **Museo Nacional del Transporte (Automobile Museum),** Carretera Baconao Km 8.5 (✆ **22/39-9197**), has a decent number of old cars, some more valuable and in better shape than others. One vehicle, a 1951 Chevrolet, was driven by Fidel's brother Raúl to the Moncada attack (he got lost); a Cadillac on view belonged to the legendary singer Beny Moré. The museum's collection of vintage American cars has been built by the novel practice of offering Cubans new Russian-built Ladas for their old Cadillacs and Chevys. Next door is a collection of several thousand model and Matchbox cars. The museum is open daily from 8am to 5pm; admission is CUC$1; an extra CUC$5 is charged to take photos.

On the coast, at Km 27.5, the **Acuario Baconao** (✆ **22/35-6156**) is a rather sad little aquarium that was badly damaged by Sandy. Today it runs daily dolphin and sea lion shows. Admission is CUC$7. You can also swim with the dolphins for around 15 minutes for CUC$40.

PLANNING YOUR TRIP TO CUBA

11

Planning a trip to Cuba is both an exciting challenge and a bit of a headache. There are complexities and nonsensical issues that will drive you nuts, and obstacles you cannot surmount. If you go with an open mind, a flexible plan, and a good sense of humor, however, you will find that the best travel experiences in Cuba don't come as you planned them, and most likely will be the moments you cherish the most. As Cuban author Pedro Juan Gutiérrez wrote in *Our GG in Havana*: "In Cuba, nothing is exact. That is the appeal of the place."

STRATEGIES FOR SEEING CUBA

This chapter gives you the nitty-gritty on plotting your trip to Cuba. (For more resources in Cuba, please turn to "Fast Facts," on p. 289.) First, some key issues to keep in mind when planning your trip:

- Despite the nascent thawing of U.S./Cuba relations, **American citizens are not allowed to travel directly to Cuba without traveling in accordance with one of 12 categories** permitted under a U.S. Treasury Department general license. Travel is sometimes arranged through a third country instead (see "Entry Requirements," below). Once in Cuba, U.S. citizens will encounter no restrictions.
- All travelers must be aware that **hurricanes may strike from June until November**. Cuba has a very effective hurricane response operation.
- Be aware that if you have **dietary restrictions,** travel may prove problematic: There is little variety in food in Cuba.
- If you take regular medicines, bring them all with you. In fact, **if you need anything in particular while you travel, bring it with you.** There is very little to buy in Cuba.

In addition, here are some general strategies to help you enrich your time and travels in Cuba.

Rule # 1: Weigh the pros and cons of renting a car.

Cuba is served by an efficient tourist bus service, Víazul, that provides daily services linking key towns across the island (see p. 273). It is reasonably priced and comfortable, but a sweater is required for night journeys because of the aggressive use of air-conditioning. To get to places beyond these key points, travelers will need a car or to hire a taxi. Renting a car allows greater freedom and flexibility. Gas stations have increased in number and official parking lots are available for nighttime parking. Travelers will need the *Guía de Carreteras* (road map), available in Havana. See also p. 270 for driving details and the lowdown on Cuban hitchhikers.

Rule # 2: If you do rent a car, get a good road map and a phrasebook to ask for directions.

Cuba is a large island, and although there's little traffic on the roads, some journeys take longer than anticipated thanks to the serious lack of decent road signs. Even with a good road map (and you'll need one; see p. 294), it is inevitable that you will need to stop and ask directions. A good phrasebook, pen and paper may be useful if you don't speak Spanish.

Rule # 3: Allow for down time.

Don't cram your days full of activities. Cuba is a tropical country, and the heat can be intense, especially in the midday hours between 1 to 3pm. Coupled with the fact that you may have unexpected bureaucracy to tackle, always have a plan B. If you are on the road and thinking about a lunch break, it is usually a smart idea to pull over at the first roadside restaurant/gas station you see. It is quite likely this may be the only one for miles. In general, these will not be places to linger; they are purely (limited) refreshment stops.

Rule # 4: Time your visit right.

Cuba's cultural calendar is fit to bursting. If you plan to visit during an important carnival, make arrangements for your accommodations and rental car in advance; the supply of rental cars sometimes runs out.

If you are a party animal, you must brave the suffocating heat of Santiago in July. If you are a movie fan, it is December. For cigar aficionados, a festival takes place in February, and during this time the tobacco fields are in bloom. If you want the coolest months possible, come between December and March. If you want to enjoy a non-commercialized Christmas, come for a winter break; Christmas is low-key in Cuba.

Rule # 5: Decide whether to hotel-hop or stay in one place.

Cuba is a sprawling country, but many of the region's most popular stops are relatively near one another. By choosing a base for several days and exploring the surrounding area on day trips, you'll save time checking in and out of rooms. However, should you wish to explore from some of the beach resorts (Cayo Santa María, Cayo Coco, and Guardalavaca), you'll need to travel the surrounding area with a car. In these cases, it may simply be more relaxing to book tours with the hotel's tour desk.

Rule # 6: Take children into account.

Unfortunately, many of Cuba's museums make little attempt to engage young visitors with what's on display. This is not helped by the lack of English-language signage. Cuba's greatest appeal for children is its vibrant street life, range of natural assets, and glorious white-sand beaches. Remember to stock up on bottled water wherever you go; children dehydrate faster than adults. Also know that many *casa particular* owners are very accommodating to travelers with children.

WHEN TO GO

The tourist high season runs from November through April, coinciding with the winter months in most northern countries. It also coincides with Cuba's dry season. Throughout this season, and especially around the Christmas and Easter holidays, the beaches and resorts are full, rates are higher, and it may be harder to find an available rental car or room. Cuba also has a mini high season in July and August. Overbooking—a widespread problem in the Cuban tourism industry—is much more of a problem during the high season. Interestingly, Cuba's low-season months have shrunk since the U.S. announced a political thaw in December 2014. Discounts are still available during the low season, of course, and resorts and attractions are less crowded, but rates are less favorable than they used to be. The low season is also the time when temperatures are higher, humidity can be high, and periods of extended rainfall are not uncommon.

Climate

Cuba has two distinct seasons: rainy (May–Oct) and dry (Nov–Apr). The dry season is characterized by consistently sunny and temperate weather, with daytime temperatures averaging between 75° and 80°F (24°–27°C).

WHAT TO pack

Pack everything you think you might need while traveling in Cuba. Most consumer products in Cuba are either non-existent or scarce. Bring all medicines, special toiletries, contact lenses, special foods, reading materials, clothes, and sun protection. Opticians do exist, but pack a prescription just in case. Sunscreen is available at resorts, but you'll pay exorbitant prices for it. Baseball caps can be found in some stores but proper sun hats cannot. Bring sturdy luggage and locks; luggage is now sold in a few places but locks cannot be replaced. Also, bring electricity adaptors and any unusual batteries. Women's tampons are not common; sanitary napkins are fairly easily found.

Temperature swings are greater during this period, however, and it can actually get somewhat chilly when cold fronts—or "northers"—creep down the eastern seaboard of the United States, particularly in the months of January and February. In contrast, the rainy season is overall a slightly warmer period in Cuba, with less dramatic same-day temperature swings. There's a small dry spell most years during August, which is also the hottest and most humid month to visit Cuba. The entire Caribbean basin is affected by an annual hurricane season (June–Nov), with September and October having the highest occurrences of storms.

Public Holidays

Cuba has a very limited number of official holidays, and aside from Christmas Day, and Good Friday, no religious holidays are recognized by the state. The official holidays are **January 1** (Liberation Day), **Good Friday**, **May 1** (May Day, or Labor Day), **July 26** (Revolution Day), **October 10** (anniversary of the beginning of the 1868 War of Independence), and **December 25** (Christmas Day). However, the state has such total control that it's not uncommon for mass rallies or entire national mobilizations to be called as it sees fit. Other important dates that sometimes bring Cuba to a de facto state of national holiday include: **January 28** (Birth of José Martí), **February 24** (anniversary of the beginning of the 1895 War of Independence), **March 8** (International Women's Day), **April 19** (anniversary of Bay of Pigs victory), **July 30** (Day of the Martyrs of the Revolution), **October 8** (anniversary of the death of Che Guevara), **October 28** (anniversary of the death of Camilo Cienfuegos), and **December 7** (anniversary of the death of Antonio Maceo).

Calendar of Events

Cuba has a packed schedule of festivals, congresses, and carnivals. If no specific information for a particular event is offered below, you can contact **Paradiso** (www.paradiso.cu; ✆ **7832-6928**), the tour-agency arm of the national arts and cultural organization ARTex. Paradiso organizes theme tours and escorted trips based around most of the major festivals and cultural events occurring throughout the year. You can also find information at www.cubatravel.cu, www.cubaabsolutely.com, and **www.congressesincuba.com**.

FEBRUARY

International Book Fair, Havana. This large gathering of authors, publishers, and distributors is really only of interest to those who can read in Spanish. But if you can, this is an excellent Latin American book fair. For details, go to www.cubaliteraria.cu or http://feriadellibro.cubaliteraria.cu.

Habanos Festival, Havana. Cigar smokers won't want to miss this annual celebration of the Cuban stogie. It's run by the official state cigar company, Habanos, S.A., and events include lectures, factory visits, tastings, and a gala dinner with an auction of rare cigars. For more information, visit www.habanos.com.

MARCH

International Festival of "La Trova" Pepe Sánchez, Santiago de Cuba. If you like the sounds of traditional Cuban folk music, you'll want to hit this festival. Local Santiagueros are the heart of the festival, but singers and groups come from the entire island and throughout Latin America.

MAY

May Day parades, nationwide. If you're in Cuba on May Day, the traditional socialist celebration of Labor Day, you'll want to join (or at least watch) one of the many parades and public gatherings. The big daddy of them all takes place at the Plaza de la Revolución in Havana, where more than 100,000 people gather to listen to the president's annual May Day speech. May 1.

Havana Biennial, Havana. One of the premier Latin American art shows brings together and exhibits a variety of contemporary Latin American artists who work in a broad range of mediums and styles. Havana's celebrated month-long arts' fair, forum, and festival takes place across a variety of venues in the capital. Each Biennial has a different theme. Occurring every 3 years, the most recent Biennial was held in 2015. Go to www.bienalhabana.cult.cu.

International Blue Marlin Tournament, Havana. The Marina Hemingway is the fitting site for this annual big-game fishing tournament. Call ✆ **7/208-9920,** ext. 223, or visit www.cubanacan.cu. Late May.

JUNE

Ernest Hemingway International Billfishing Tournament, Havana. Marina Hemingway/Marina Tarará is the host to this annual big-game fishing tournament, now in its 65th year. Call ✆ **7204-5088** or go to www.internationalhemingwaytournament.com.

International Festival "Boleros de Oro," Havana, Santiago, and other locations. You'll be crying in your *mojito* (Cuban highball cocktail)—and loving it. Theaters, clubs, and concert halls across Havana fill with the sweet and melancholy sounds of bolero. Mid-June.

JULY

Fiesta del Caribe/Fiesta del Fuego, Santiago de Cuba. This event features lectures, concerts, parades, and street fairs celebrating Afro-Caribbean culture. Speakers, guests, and musical groups from around the Caribbean are invited, and each year the festival is dedicated to a Caribbean area or country. For details, visit www.casadelcaribe.cult.cu; for reservations, contact **Paradiso** (✆ **22/62-7037;** paradisoscu@scsc.artex.cu). July 3–9.

Rally de Regularidad Copa Castrol, Havana. Organized by the A Lo Cubano car club, this 2-day event sees classic cars and motorbikes parade through Havana. Go to www.facebook.com/clubalocubano. July or August.

Carnival, Santiago de Cuba. Santiago throws an excellent annual carnival, the best in Cuba. Street parties and concerts are everywhere, and the colonial city is flooded with masked revelers and long conga lines. Second half of July.

AUGUST

Carnival, Havana. Although not nearly as colorful or charismatic as Santiago's Carnival, it still provides a good dose of public merriment, street parties, open-air music concerts, and the occasional parade for 10 days.

Carnival, Matanzas. Although not as massive or elaborate as Carnival celebrations in Havana or Santiago, Matanzas still puts on a good party. The town has strong Afro-Cuban roots, and you'll experience this in body, flesh, food, and song throughout the week. Third week of August.

Jornada Nacional de Hip Hop, Havana. As Havana sizzles, hot Cuban hip-hop music is performed and celebrated at various venues around Havana. The festival is based at La Madriguera (Calle Infanta y Jesús Peregrino final). For details, contact the Cubana el Rap agency (✆ **7832-3503**).

SEPTEMBER

Fiesta de la Virgen del Cobre, El Cobre, Santiago de Cuba. Cuba's national saint, the Virgin of Cobre, is revered by Roman Catholics and Santería followers alike. There are pilgrimages to her altar in the small town of El Cobre and celebrations in her honor nationwide. September 8.

OCTOBER

Days of Cuban Culture, nationwide. In yet another show of Cuba's omnipresent anticolonial spirit, the period traditionally marking Christopher Columbus's stumbling upon the New World is given over to celebrations of Cuban and Afro-Cuban culture. October 10–20.

International Festival "Matamoros Son," Santiago de Cuba. The silky sounds of Cuban *son* fill the streets and theaters of Santiago. This is a great chance to hear a solid week of some wonderful music. Got to www.cultstgo.cult.cu. Third week of October.

Havana International Ballet Festival, Havana. Alicia Alonso, amazingly, is still going strong as the director of the Cuban National Ballet, one of the most highly regarded troupes on the planet. Alicia uses this cachet to stage a wonderful biennial international festival in the Gran Teatro de La Habana. Call ✆ **7835-2945** or visit www.balletcuba.cult.cu. Occurs in even-numbered years. Late October.

International Fishing Tournament Jardines del Rey. This event was inaugurated in 2010 on Cayo Guillermo. Captured fish—blue marlin, sailfish, dolphin fish, and wahoo—accrue points exchanged for silver prizes. It takes place at the Cayo Guillermo International Marina in Jardines del Rey. For details, contact Naútica Marlin, Jardines del Rey (✆ **33/301-323**). Mid-October.

DECEMBER

International Festival of New Latin American Cinema, Havana. One of the premier film festivals in Latin America. A packed schedule of films is shown in theaters throughout Havana over 10 days. Go to www.habanafilmfestival.com. Early December.

International Jazz Plaza Festival (aka Havana International Jazz Festival), Havana. Since 1996, this 10-day festival has been organized by none other than Chucho Valdés. The event draws a handful of top international bands and soloists to share the stage and billing with a strong stable of Cuba's top jazz talents. Visit www.decubajazz.cult.cu. Mid-December.

Las Parrandas, Remedios. This extravagant public carnival features late-night parades with ornate floats, costumed revelers, and a serious amount of fireworks. The big event occurs on December 24, but between the preparations, practice runs, and smaller iterations in neighboring towns, you'll be able to catch some of the excitement throughout most of late December.

ENTRY REQUIREMENTS

Passports

All travelers to Cuba must possess a valid passport, a return ticket, travel insurance policy with medical coverage, and a visa or tourist visa. Unlicensed U.S. citizens may be allowed a stay of up to 90 days upon entry. British citizens are granted 30 days upon entry. This can be extended for another 30 days, and then a further 30 days at immigration offices in Cuba. Canadian citizens are granted a visa for 90 days. This can be extended for 90 days only.

Visas

Tourist visas are generally issued by the ticketing airline or travel agent. (If you book a flight with Air Canada, the visa is included in the price.) Visas are sold at Cancún airport by Havanatur and at London Gatwick by Virgin Holidays. You will not be permitted to board a flight without a visa.

For U.S. and Canadian citizens, tourist visas cost around US$25, depending upon the issuing agent, and are good for up to 90 days, although immigration agents will sometimes issue them for just 30 days or until the date of your return flight, unless you request otherwise. They can be extended for another 30 days (90 days for Canadians) once you arrive in Cuba for an additional minimum CUC$25 fee. In order to extend your tourist visa, you must personally go to any immigration office in the country. An additional 90-day extension for Canadians can be granted once at any immigration office for a cost of approximately CUC$25.

In the U.K., if you buy a ticket for an independent flight, you will need to purchase a separate tourist visa. While the visa is also available from the **Cuban Embassy** in London for £15 plus postage (http://embacuba.co.uk), the most efficient and reliable place to get a visa is directly from www.visacuba.com. U.K. citizens are granted entry for 30 days. This can be extended for an additional 30 days, and then a further 30 days at any immigration office for CUC$25 per extension.

When seeking a **tourist visa extension** (***la prórroga de estancia*),** before going to the immigration office you need to purchase bank stamps (*sellos para la visa*) for the value of CUC$25 at a branch of the **Banco de Crédito y Comercio**, the only bank authorized to sell the stamps.

In the event that you need a specific work visa, or if your travel agent or airline will not provide you with the tourist visa, you should contact the Cuban consulate or embassy in your home country.

FOR RESIDENTS OF THE UNITED STATES

While it is not illegal for U.S. citizens to travel to Cuba, most are prohibited from spending any money in Cuba. This, in effect, is the "travel ban." The complicated prohibition, which allows for various exceptions, is governed by the U.S. Treasury Department and the Office of Foreign Assets Control (OFAC). For more information, visit www.treasury.gov/resource-center/sanctions/Programs/pages/cuba.aspx.

Rules regarding travel to Cuba were relaxed and updated in January 2015. The Treasury Department now grants a general license for **travel in 12 categories**: "family visits; official business of the U.S. government, foreign governments, and certain intergovernmental organizations; journalistic activity; professional research and professional meetings; educational activities; religious activities; public performances, clinics, workshops, athletic and other competitions, and exhibitions; support for the Cuban people; humanitarian projects; activities of private foundations or research or educational institutes; exportation, importation, or transmission of information or information materials; and certain authorized export transactions."

Travel arrangements for visitors traveling in accordance with the 12 authorized categories can be made by travel providers operating under a general OFAC license offering charter flights. As the law stands at press time, there are no scheduled flights from the USA to Cuba. Those travel-service providers

Pick Your Poison

Some operators and guidebooks recommend lying if asked whether or not you were in Cuba. If you lie, you then place yourself at risk for perjury charges, which in the end are easier for the United States government to prosecute and are potentially more serious. I recommend you say little or nothing about your travel to Cuba, but I don't recommend that you lie. Remember, under U.S. law you have the right to refuse to incriminate yourself.

with the strongest presence in the market are those that were authorized under the previous rules. These include **Marazul** (www.marazul.com; ✆ **800-223-5334**) and **ABC Charters** (www.abc-charters.com; ✆ **305/263-6829**).

Be careful about signing on for a "fully hosted" trip. According to the regulations, a U.S. citizen can travel to Cuba without violating the Treasury ban provided he or she does not pay for any goods or services, including food and lodging, or provide any services to Cuba or a Cuban national while in the country. This provision had been widely used by U.S. citizens to buy packages from Canadian, Mexican, or Bahamian tour agencies. However, the Treasury Department has caught on to this tactic and declared that any "fully hosted" trip that is clearly for pleasure or tourism is in violation of the regulations. Go to www.treasury.gov/resource-center/sanctions/Programs/Documents/cubatrav.pdf for clarification.

Failure to comply with Department of Treasury regulations may result in civil penalties and criminal prosecution upon return to the United States. For more information, contact the **Office of Foreign Assets Control,** U.S. Department of the Treasury, 1500 Pennsylvania Ave. NW, Treasury Annex, Washington, DC 20220 (✆ **202/622-2000;** www.treasury.gov/resource-center/sanctions/Programs/Pages/cuba.aspx).

As far as Cuba is concerned, U.S. travelers are welcomed with open arms. In general, Cuban immigration does not actually stamp U.S. passports, but you should ask the officer to be sure, as occasionally they have—instead, officers stamp the tourist visa. For current information on Cuban entry and Customs requirements, you can contact the **Cuban Embassy** (✆ **202/797-8518;** www.cubadiplomatica.cu/sicw/EN/ConsularServices.aspx).

UNLICENSED TRAVEL Thousands of U.S. citizens travel to Cuba each year without a Treasury Department license. The vast majority of travelers use third-country gateway cities like Toronto, Montreal, Cancún, Mexico City, Nassau, George Town on Grand Cayman, or Kingston in Jamaica.

WHAT TO DO IF YOU GET BUSTED Officially, U.S. citizens who violate the travel ban face up to 10 years in prison, $250,000 in criminal fines, and $55,000 in civil fines. If you are stopped upon returning from an unlicensed trip to Cuba and directly asked by the Customs and Immigration agents, you should give as little information as possible. United States citizens cannot be compelled to provide self-incriminating information. Furthermore, you cannot be denied reentry into the U.S. for traveling to Cuba. You will likely face a long and uncomfortable search and questioning session, and then be sent on your way. This will probably be followed by the receipt of a pre-penalty notice from the OFAC. The letter will request specific information to prove or disprove your alleged travel to Cuba, and may threaten the imposition of various fines and penalties. The **Center for Constitutional Rights** (www.ccrjustice.org; ✆ **212/614-6464**) no longer represents U.S. citizens who have traveled to Cuba without a license, but it provides helpful information for those who encounter problems. Go to www.ccrjustice.org/ccrs-cuba-travel-project.

FOR CUBAN NATIONALS

The Cuban government doesn't recognize dual nationality of travelers from other countries who are Cuban-born or are the children of Cuban parents, particularly those who chose exile in the United States. The Cuban government requires some individuals it considers to be Cuban to enter and depart Cuba using a Cuban passport. Using a Cuban passport for this purpose does not jeopardize one's foreign citizenship; however, you will probably have to use your home country's passport to exit and enter that country. Other Cuban nationals and exiles just need a visa, but acquiring this visa is more complicated than acquiring the simple tourist visa used by most other travelers.

If you are Cuban-born or the child of Cuban-born parents, you should check with the Cuban embassy or consulate in your country of residence, as well as your local immigration authorities. In Canada, contact the **Cuban Embassy** in Ottawa (www.cubadiplomatica.cu/canada; ✆ **613/563-0141**); there are also consulates in Montreal and Toronto. In the U.K., contact the **Cuban Embassy,** 167 High Holborn, London, WC1 6PA (http://embacuba.co.uk; ✆ **020/7240-2488**). In the U.S., contact the **Cuban Embassy,** 2630 16th St. NW, Washington, DC 20009 (✆ **202/797-8518**).

Customs

WHAT YOU CAN BRING INTO CUBA

You may bring in all manner of personal effects, including video and still cameras, personal electronic devices, jewelry, personal laptops, flash sticks, MP3 players, DVD players, binoculars, and sports equipment (fishing equipment, non-motorized bicycle, kayak, tennis racquets, and the like). In addition, visitors may bring in up to two bottles of liquor, 400 cigarettes, and up to 10 kilograms of medications, provided they are in the original packaging. By law you may only import up to CUC$1,000 worth of any merchandise, and there is a 100 percent duty on all but the first CUC$51 worth. In practice, most visitors can freely bring in reasonable quantities of basic goods, like dried foods, vitamins, pharmaceuticals, and household supplies, without them being taxed or confiscated. If you want to import satellite communications and/or walkie-talkies, you must declare them on arrival.

For current and more detailed information, check out www.aduana.co.cu.

WHAT YOU CAN TAKE HOME FROM CUBA

U.S. travelers, under license, may now import US$400 worth of merchandise, of which US$100 may be alcohol and tobacco. There is no restriction on the import of artworks and informational materials (like films and music).

Foreign travelers (excluding residents of the U.S.) may export up to 20 cigars with no questions asked, and up to 50 unopened in sealed boxes with no receipts. For more than 50, a sales invoice must be provided by an official Habanos S.A. outlet. There are restrictions on certain works of art, books, publications, and coins. Consult www.aduana.co.cu for further information.

To export serious works of art, you will need a permit from the **Registro Nacional de Bienes Culturales (National Register of Cultural Heritage),** Calle 17 no. 1009 between Calles 10 and 12, Vedado (✆ **7833-9658**). Theoretically, any reputable gallery or shop will provide you with this permit along with your purchase. Those buying artwork at the Almacanes San José market in Havana can purchase the permit for CUC$2 at a kiosk in the building. There's also a *patrimonio* desk at the airport terminals where artworks are checked and permits can be paid.

Note: The CUC$25 departure tax was abolished on May 1, 2015.

Medical Requirements

Since May 2010, all visitors to Cuba must carry proof of medical insurance in order to enter the country. You must have all the vaccines recommended for international travel (tetanus, polio, diptheria, hepatitis A, and cholera). Vaccinations for yellow fever and cholera are not required unless you are arriving from a country where they are prevalent.

GETTING THERE & GETTING AROUND

Getting to Cuba

BY PLANE

Cuba has 10 international airports. Havana is by far the principal gateway, although there are numerous regularly scheduled and charter flights to Varadero (VRA) and Santiago de Cuba (SCU) as well. International charter flights from Canada and Europe also service Cayo Largo del Sur (CYO), Cienfuegos (CFG), Santa Clara (SNU), Camagüey (CMW), Ciego de Avila (AVI), Holguín (HOG), and Cayo Coco (CCC).

It's roughly a 50-minute flight from Miami to Havana; 3 hours and 30 minutes from New York to Havana; 4 hours and 30 minutes from Toronto or Montreal to Havana; and 9 to 10 hours from London to Havana. Most of the principal Caribbean basin gateway cities—Cancún, George Town (Grand Cayman), Kingston, Nassau, and Santo Domingo—are between 40 and 90 minutes to Havana by air.

Airfares vary widely, depending on the season, demand, and certain ticketing restrictions. Since the announcement of the political thaw between Cuba and the U.S. in December 2014, airfares have skyrocketed, in particular from Europe and Central America. It really pays to shop around. If you wish to visit Cuba in July and August, a popular tourist season, book in advance because charter flights often sell out at this time.

Cubana (www.cubana.cu; ✆ **7838-1039** and 7834-4446) is Cuba's national airline and the principal carrier to the island, with regularly scheduled flights to a score of cities throughout the Americas, Europe, and Canada. (Cubana is code-shared with Aerocaribbean.)

Major airlines that fly to Cuba are **Aeroflot** (www.aeroflot.ru); **Air Canada** (www.aircanada.com); **Air France** (www.airfrance.com); Air Transat (www.airtransat.com); **Avianca** (www.avianca.com); **Bahamasair** (www.bahamasair.com); **Cayman Airways** (www.caymanairways.com); **Air China** (www.airchina.com/index.shtml); **Cubana** (www.cubana.cu); **Iberia Airlines** (www.iberia.com); **Lan Airlines** (www.lan.com); **Virgin Atlantic Airways** (www.virgin-atlantic.com).

Budget airlines that fly to Cuba are **Aerogaviota** (www.aerogaviota.com); **Air Europa** (www.aireuropa.com); **Blue Panorama** (www.blue-panorama.it); Condor (www.condor.com); **Edelweiss** (flyedelweiss.com).

As of summer 2015, there were no scheduled services between the United States and Cuba, although there are numerous charter flights from Miami and other key destinations. Licensed U.S. travelers are eligible to use these flights. For more information, see "Escorted General-Interest Tours" and "Special-Interest Trips," later in this chapter.

Getting into Havana from the Airport

Yellow taxis line up outside the arrivals hall, and you will be shepherded to the first in the queue. Yellow Cubataxis have a monopoly on the run from the airport. The official price is a flat fee of CUC$20 to Vedado and CUC$25 to La Habana Vieja. If you arrive at Varadero or Holguin airports, there will be taxis waiting as well as car rental options.

BY BOAT

When arriving by sea, contact the port authorities before entering Cuban waters 19km (12 miles) offshore on VHF channels 16 or 72, or HF channels 2790 or 2760. Skippers do not need to give advance notice or have a prior visa. A visa can be granted on arrival. All crew members must have current passports, and U.S. Treasury Department restrictions (see "Entry Requirements" and "Customs," earlier in this chapter) apply to all U.S. citizens. Skippers will also need to register their vessel upon arrival. A special permit, or *permiso especial de navegación,* is issued. This permit costs around CUC$55 depending on the length of the vessel.

Cuba has a network of state-run, full-service marinas, many run by **Náutica Marli** (www.nauticamarlin.com) and **Gaviota** (www.gaviota-grupo.com). Marinas that function as official points of entry and exit include those in Jardines del Rey, María la Gorda, Cayo Largo del Sur, Cienfuegos, and Santiago de Cuba, as well as the Marina Hemingway in Havana and Marina Gaviota in Varadero.

Getting Around

BY PLANE

Cubana (www.cubana.cu; © **7838-1039** and **7834 4446**) is the principal national and international carrier for Cuba. It is code-shared with **Aerocaribbean** (www.fly-aerocaribbean.com). A full schedule of domestic flights connect Havana and Varadero with Baracoa, Bayamo, Camagüey, Ciego de Avila,

Manzanillo, Nueva Gerona (Isla de la Juventud), Guantánamo, Holguín, Moa, Santiago de Cuba, Las Tunas, Cayo Largo, and Cayo Coco. If you know you'll need an internal flight on your trip, try to have your travel agent or tour operator book it in advance, thanks to high demand (especially on the Nueva Gerona route). If not, book flights with any local tour operator.

BY CAR

Driving a rental car is an excellent way to travel around Cuba. (The legal age requirement is 21.) It gives you great flexibility and allows you to access beautiful off-the-beaten-track places. Many roads are in acceptable condition, while many others are severely substandard. And while there's very little traffic, you'll have to keep a sharp eye out for small and large chasms in the road, horse-drawn carriages, slow-moving tractors, bicyclists, wandering dogs and fowl, and pedestrians taking over major roadways.

It is completely inadvisable to drive at night. There is no lighting on highways, making it very unsafe. Animal-drawn transport, some lorries, bicycles, and pedestrians are also not illuminated, giving rise to highly dangerous driving situations.

The speed limit for cars is 50kmph (31 mph) in the cities, 90kmph (56 mph) on the *carretera,* and 100kmph (62 mph) on the Autopista.

In all cities, there are *parqueos* where you can leave your vehicle attended for 24 hours. This costs from CUC$1 to CUC$2 a night. All *casas particulares* also use *guardias* (night watchmen), and the fee is the same. It may be unwise to leave the vehicle unattended in cities at night, as theft of wheels and wipers, and anything removable, is not unknown.

A handful of state-run car-rental companies offer a large, modern fleet of rental cars to choose from. Prices and selection are rather standard, although improving, with an abundance of small economy Japanese, Chinese, and Korean cars. A standard rental car should cost you between CUC$45 and CUC$85 per day, excluding the daily CUC$10 to CUC$30 insurance and unlimited mileage, depending on the model and the season. Low-season (*temporada baja*) prices are, obviously, cheaper. Some agencies start you off with a full tank of gas for which they charge you—in addition to the rental fee—then give no credit for any gas left in the tank upon the return of the car. Discounts are available for multiday rentals. It's always a good idea to have a reservation in advance, especially during peak periods, when cars can get scarce. There's a Catch-22, however, in that many of the state-run agencies don't have a trustworthy international reservations system. As is the case with rampant overbooking of hotel rooms, when demand outstrips supply the car-rental agencies may not honor your supposedly confirmed reservation, you may not get your choice of automatic car (more expensive than manual), and you may end up paying more for a better model because the economy models have been assigned.

Cubans may now drive rental cars and can be included on your insurance for an additional cost, as can a second foreign driver. Insurance is voided if an accident is shown to be caused by a driver under the influence of alcohol.

Some of the major car-rental agencies in Cuba are **Cubacar** (© **7272-5986**), **Havanautos** (© **7273-2277**), **Rex** (www.rex.cu; © **7835-6832**), **Transtur** (www.transtur.cu; © **7838-3995**), and **Vía Rent a Car** (www.gaviota-grupo.com; © **7207-9502**). All car-rental agencies have desks at the Havana airport and at most hotels around the country. If you book your car online, the best deals are usually found at the rental-car company websites, although all the major online travel agencies also offer rental-car reservation services. It is often cheaper to book your rental car before you arrive in Cuba.

All car-rental agencies in Cuba, except Transtur, offer insurance coverage for between CUC$10 and CUC$30 per day which must be paid in cash separately. Transtur, which runs Cubacar and Rex, charges a minimum of CUC$15. Most agencies carry a deductible of CUC$150 to CUC$1,000. All companies charge CUC$20 extra for picking a car up at an airport. Additional drivers will be charged between CUC$3 and CUC$10 per day. If you drop the car off in a different province than you picked it up from, you will be charged a fee based on mileage between the two points. Some companies do not cover theft, but this is a very minor problem in Cuba. If you hold a private auto insurance policy, you may be covered abroad for loss or damage to the car, and liability in case a passenger is injured. The credit card you use to rent the car also may provide some coverage; be sure to check whether or not your insurance company or credit card coverage *excludes* rental cars in Cuba. (This type of coverage probably does not cover liability if you caused an accident, however). Check your own auto insurance policy, the rental company policy, and your credit card coverage for the extent of coverage. ***Note:*** The daily insurance charge is only payable in cash and never appears to be documented on official literature.

Be very thorough when checking out your car, and make sure that all accouterments (like the spare tire, jack, and radio) are present and accounted for. Moreover, be sure to have the agent note every little nick and scratch, or you run a great risk of being charged for them upon your car's return. You will also be charged for small nicks caused by flying stones on some of Cuba's poorer roads. Gasoline costs about CUC$1.30 especial per liter *(por litro)*, or CUC$1.10 regular per liter. Diesel is CUC$1.10 per liter. Gone are the gas shortages of several years ago. Service stations are plentiful and conveniently located on the major highways and on the outskirts of all major centers, as well as in major towns and cities. Tourist cars should use *gasolina especial.* Service stations are digitized.

Every car-rental agency will provide you with a basic road map. The best road map is the **Guia de Carreteras,** but it is not always widely available (see p. 294).

While driving is generally easy and stress free, there are a couple of concerns for most foreign drivers here. First (and most annoying) is the fact that roads have very, **very few road signs** and directional aids. This means that getting lost will happen. If you don't speak Spanish, you will need a dictionary, phrases, paper and pen, and patience. Second, there's the issue of **hitchhikers.**

Cuba's public transportation network is grossly overburdened, and hitchhiking is a way of life. The highways sometimes seem like one long line, with periodic swellings, of people asking for a lift, or *botella.* While this is not dangerous, you should still be careful about who you pick up—theft of belongings has been reported. It is not advisable to pick up hitchhikers after dark. The biggest hassle of offering rides, however, is twofold: When you stop, you are likely to be swarmed by supplicants, who will want to stuff your car over the brink of its carrying capacity; and most hitchhikers are looking for relatively short hops, so once you pick up a load, you might find yourself suddenly making constant stops to let your passengers off—at which point there will almost certainly be a new rider immediately vying to snag the just-emptied seat. (You can, however, stop at an official *botella* point, identified by the mustard-yellow-uniformed official with a clipboard.) On the positive side, you will be providing the public-transport-starved Cubans with a much-needed ride.

Instead of driving your own rental car, an alternative option is to hire a Cuban driver. While journeying about Cuba in a classic car may sound dreamy, these cars are not particularly comfortable for long journeys thanks to the lack of air-conditioning and headrests. (***Note:*** It is not legal for foreigners to self-drive classic cars.)

One key rule to keep in mind when driving your own rental car: **Stop at all railroad crossings!** It's the law, and it's also an essential safety measure. Cuba's railroad network crisscrosses its highway system at numerous points, and trains rarely slow down. Rarer still are protective crossbars or warning lights.

One final note: If you have a minor accident, you must go to a police station and get a signed report saying what happened and stating that you are not responsible for the damage (if that's the case). If the report does not state you are not responsible, you will be liable. If you are involved in a serious accident, whether or not you are to blame, you may be detained. If someone is killed, call your embassy for assistance and get a translator immediately.

BY TRAIN

The state-run train agency, **Ferrocuba** (✆ **7861-4259**), has offices in each train station. Havana is connected to Pinar del Río in the west, and Santiago de Cuba in the east by rail traffic. One or two trains a day head west, and a half dozen or so head east. Intermediate cities with regular service include Matanzas, Santa Clara, Ciego de Avila, Camagüey, Las Tunas, and Holguín. The principal train station, or **Estación Central,** is located in Havana at Calle Egido and Calle Arsenal, La Habana Vieja (✆ **7861-4259**).

Most trains are in rather bad shape, with uncomfortable seats and limited amenities. Be sure to bring along some food and something to drink. Even if there's a cafeteria car onboard, which isn't always the case, you might not find any of the offerings particularly appealing, and they might just run out of food somewhere along the line anyway. Moreover, train travel in Cuba is notoriously erratic, with frequent schedule changes and delays lasting up to 3 days.

It is always best to check current schedules and conditions before buying a ticket and undertaking a train journey. If you are short on time and not looking for this kind of adventure, it's wise to avoid all trains.

BY BUS

For all intents and purposes, the only buses tourists will ride in Cuba are those run by **Víazul** (www.viazul.com; ✆ **7881-1413**). (*Note:* This website is not always updated; prices are correct, but sometimes the timings are off. It's best to call in at the stations or ask your *casa particular* owner for exact times. If you plan a trip using the displayed timetable, however, your trip won't be completely thrown off-kilter.) Víazul buses are modern and fairly comfortable, with lavatories on board. Now that many Cubans are using the service, it's more important to reserve at least several days in advance in high season. It is possible to reserve and pay online for bookings 7 days in advance, but there is a disconnect between online sales and the information available at each station. This means that those passengers *without* an online reservation or a pre-bought ticket must wait until the last 5 minutes to see if seating is available but will need to queue between 30 minutes to 1 hour before departure to snag those last seats. Those that have tickets in advance (whether bought online or at stations) must still arrive up to half an hour before the bus departure to swap their pre-booked ticket slip for a boarding ticket. Bureaucracy lives on!

Víazul travels to most major tourist destinations in Cuba. The main Víazul station is located in Nuevo Vedado, Havana, across from the metropolitan zoo. Its ticket office is open daily from 7am to 6pm, and from 7pm to midnight. All stations keep different hours. Children ages 5 to 12 pay half price; children 4 and under who do not occupy a seat travel for free. The weight limit is 20kg (10kg for children), and at some stations, including Havana but not with any consistency, you may be charged 1 percent of the value of your ticket per extra kilo of weight. Baby strollers travel free of charge; bicycle charges vary according to the distance traveled.

Note: In high season in some places, such as Baracoa, tickets are booked well in advance and travelers are known to have been stuck for a few days; if you have a tight schedule, buy your return ticket for this route in Santiago de Cuba.

SPECIAL-INTEREST TRIPS & ESCORTED TOURS

Special-Interest Trips

You'll have plenty of options for a special-interest or theme vacation to Cuba. Popular themes include cigars, Ernest Hemingway, classic cars, bird-watching, diving, fishing, and Latin dance.

- **GAP Adventures** (www.gapadventures.com; ✆ **888/800-4100** in the U.S. and Canada, or 0344-272-2060 in the U.K.) is a major international adventure and educational tour operator with a full plate of theme tours to Cuba.

- **Global Exchange** (www.globalexchange.org; ✆ **415/255-7296**) is a non-profit organization working to increase international understanding by conducting small-scale tours that emphasize educational or social aid themes.
- **Paradiso** ★ (www.paradiso.cu; ✆ **7831-7444**) is the tour-agency arm of the Cuban arts and cultural organization ARTex. Paradiso organizes theme tours and escorted trips, including tours based around most of the major festivals and cultural events, as well as participatory learning trips with instruction in a variety of arts.

ADVENTURE TRIPS

Active tourism is a growing interest in Cuba, and opportunities have opened up in the last few years. The island offers myriad ways to add a bit of adrenaline and adventure to your vacation. Watersports are the main draw here, and Cuba abounds with outstanding opportunities to fish, sail, snorkel, and scuba dive. For those looking for some dry-land adventure activities, there are great options for biking and rock climbing, and you might even be able to play some baseball.

BASEBALL Baseball is the national sport and, after dancing and sex, Cuba's greatest national passion. Cuba's amateur players are considered some of the best in the world, and the premier players are aggressively scouted and courted by the major leagues. The regular season runs November through March, and playoffs and the final championship often carry the season on into May. Most major towns and cities have a local team. It's usually easy to buy tickets at the box office for less than 5 Cuban pesos; your hotel or *casa particular* may also be able to get you tickets in advance.

If you want to actually get out and play, you should be able to find a pickup game to join. Check with **Baseball Adventures** (www.baseballadventures.com; ✆ **949/476-2197**), which offers fully hosted trips geared toward serious players looking to play and train with local Cuban pros.

Tip: If you're planning on playing, bring some extra equipment—balls, bats, and gloves—to leave behind. It'll be greatly appreciated and is a great means of getting into a game.

BIKING With a local reliance on bicycles for everyday transportation and a relatively well-maintained road network serving a small motor-vehicular fleet, Cuba is a great country to tour by bicycle. Few local operations rent decent bikes in Cuba, so it's best to bring your own. I also recommend organized trips, since the logistics of traveling through Cuba still make it a bit difficult for independent bike touring. One dependable operation with regular bike tours and quality bike rentals is **Wow Cuba** (www.wowcuba.com; ✆ **902/368-2453**). Anyone thinking of bicycling in Cuba should pick up a copy of Wally and Barbara Smith's *Bicycling Cuba: Fifty Days of Detailed Rides from Havana to Pinar Del Río and the Oriente* (Backcountry Guides, 2002).

BIRD-WATCHING Over 350 resident and migratory species of birds can be spotted in Cuba, including some 25 endemic species. Cuba is also home to the smallest hummingbird in the world, the endemic bee hummingbird. A couple of organized tour options are offered by the British company **www.cubabirdingtours.com** and the Canadian operation **Quest Nature Tours** (www.worldwidequest.com; ✆ **1-800-387-1483**). Some of the best places to go bird-watching in Cuba include **La Güira National Park,** the **Zapata Peninsula, Cayo Coco** and **Cayo Guillermo, La Belen** reserve near Camagüey, the **Sierra Maestra** region, and **Baracoa.** Bird-watchers will want to bring a copy of *Field Guide to the Birds of Cuba* (Comstock, 2000), by Orlando Garrido et al.

CLIMBING Climbing is due to be officially sanctioned by the state down in Vinales. Until then consult: www.cubaclimbing.com

CRUISING **StarClippers** (www.starclippers.co.uk; ✆ **845/200-6145**); **CubaCruise** (www.yourcubacruise.com; ✆ **855/364-4999**), **Thomson** (www.thomson.co.uk/cruise.html; **0871/231-4691**), **Noble Caledonia** (www.noble-caledonia.co.uk; ✆ **020/7752-0000**), and **Fred Olsen** (www.fredolsencruises.com; ✆ **+44 (0) 1473-742424**) cruise to Cuba. In mid-2015, it was announced that 7-day volunteering trips on **Carnival Cruises**' new Fathom brand (www.carnival.com; ✆ **800/764-7419**) and **MSC cruises** (www.msccruisesusa.com; ✆ **877/665-4655**), among others, had been licensed by the U.S. government to sail to Cuba and were awaiting approval from the Cuban government.

FISHING There's fabulous deep-sea sportfishing for marlin, sailfish, tuna, dorado, and more off most of Cuba's extensive coastline, while the Zapata Peninsula and Cayo Largo del Sur may just be some of the best and least-exploited bonefishing spots left in the hemisphere. The mountain lake and resort of Hanabanilla is getting good grades as a freshwater ground for wide-mouth and black bass. Cuba has a broad network of state-run marinas, the greatest number run by **Grupo Empresarial de Náutica y Marinas Marlin** (www.nauticamarlin.com) and **Gaviota** (✆ www.gaviota-grupo.com). All offer sportfishing charters. For information, see individual destination chapters. **Avalon** (www.cubanfishingcenters.com) runs a reputable operation; it operates out of **Jardines de la Reina, Isla de la Juventud, Cayo Cruz,** and **Cayo Largo.**

GOLF The country's only regulation 18-hole golf course is the **Varadero Golf Club** (www.varaderogolfclub.com; ✆ **45/66-8482**). The course is a relatively flat resort course, with lots of water, plenty of sand, great views, and almost no rough. In Havana, the **Club de Golf Habana,** Carretera Vento Km 8, Capdevila, Rancho Boyeros (✆ **7649-8918**), has a decent little 9-hole course.

HORSEBACK RIDING Riding horses is possible in Viñales, around Trinidad and Guardalavaca, and on some beaches such as Cayo Guillermo. **Wild Frontiers** (www.wildfrontierstravel.com) organizes a trip focused on horseback riding.

KITE-SURFING Great kite-surfing can be found on Cayo Guillermo and on Varadero through **Cubakiters** (www.cubakiters.com; ✆ **45/66-8612)** and through the **Havana Kite & Surf Club** (www.hkckite.com) at Tarará and Santa María del Mar.

MOUNTAIN & ROCK CLIMBING These sports are in their infancy in Cuba, but excellent opportunities abound, especially around the Viñales Valley. **Cuba Climbing** (www.cubaclimbing.com) can point you to the right rocks and answer any questions you might have. The state was scheduled to form a climbing company in Viñales in mid-2015.

SAILING Whether you take a day sail, or decide to cruise the coastline for a week or so, opportunities to sail the clear waters off Cuba abound. The state-run marinas in Varadero, Jardines del Rey, Camagüey, Santiago, Cienfuegos, and Cayo Largo del Sur all offer charter sailboats, as well as a variety of day-sailing options. Three private companies offer sailing opportunities out of Cienfuegos (p. 153). See also "Cruising," above. See the individual destination chapters for more information.

SCUBA DIVING & SNORKELING The coral reefs, ocean walls, and ancient wrecks that lie just off Cuba's coasts offer fabulous scuba-diving and snorkeling opportunities. **Los Jardines de la Reina, Isla de la Juventud, Playa Girón Santa Lucía,** and **María la Gorda** are widely considered the absolute top scuba-diving destinations, but in each case, the majority of the accommodations options are either rustic or decidedly geared toward hard-core dive enthusiasts and almost no one else. The only liveaboard operation is at Jardines de la Reina. You will also find acceptable to average dive opportunities in **Varadero, Cayo Coco, Cayo Guillermo, Guardalavaca,** and **Cayo Largo del Sur,** as well as far more comfortable and varied accommodations. For more information, see specific destination chapters.

SURFING Cuba is not considered a world-class surfing destination, and Cuban surfers or surf tourists are few and far between. This, however, is part of the charm of surfing in Cuba, and there are waves and breaks all along the island's long coastline, including right off the Malecón in Havana. For good information and a primer, check out www.havanasurf-cuba.com and **www.royal70.net.** You will definitely have to bring your own board, and I would recommend bringing a board (or two) that you wouldn't mind leaving behind for some very appreciative Cuban surfer.

TENNIS Many of the large-scale beach resorts have tennis courts. Almost all are outdoor courts, and very few are lit. If you're set on playing tennis on your trip, be sure to check in advance whether your hotel or resort has courts. Your options are much more limited in Havana, unless you're staying at one of the few city hotels with a court. Your best bet in Havana is to try to book a court at the **Memories Miramar,** Avenida 5, between Calles 72 and 76, Miramar, Playa (www.memoriesresorts.com/en/resort/havana.aspx; ✆ **7204-3584**), which has six courts (CUC$10/day); or head to the **Club Habana,** Avenida 5, between Calles 188 and 192, Reparto Flores, Playa (✆ **7275-0300**).

TREKKING Most tour operators can arrange trekking tours. **Caledonia** (www.caledoniaworldwide.com; ✆ **0131/621-7721**) organizes trekking trips in the Sierra Maestra.

LANGUAGE, MUSIC, AND PHOTOGRAPHY CLASSES

The **University of Havana** (www.uh.cu) offers language classes from CUC$100 a week starting on the first Monday of almost every month. The **University of the Oriente** (www.uo.edu.cu/tarifas) in Santiago de Cuba also offers Spanish classes from US$250.

Caledonia (www.caledoniaworldwide.com; ✆ **0131/621-7721**) offers Spanish courses in Havana and Santiago from £145 per week. **Caledonia** also offers fantastic music and dance trips to Cuba. (It is also possible to combine these activities with language classes.)

The **International Cuban Music School** (www.jazzsummerschool.com/cuba) is held annually in Havana.

If you're interested in photography, check **www.trinidadphoto.com/workshops** for workshops with Cuban photographer Julio Muñoz based in Trinidad.

The **Escuela de Fotografía Creativa de la Habana** photo school (www.efchabana.com; ✆ **7832-6592**) offers various photographic courses, also open to foreigners.

VOLUNTEER & WORKING TRIPS

The **Cuban Solidarity Campaign** (www.cuba-solidarity.org.uk; ✆ **020/7490-5715**) runs international work brigades twice a year from £650 per person, excluding international flights, and sponsorship-raising cycle trips. See also **Global Exchange,** p. 274.

Escorted General-Interest Tours

There are dozens of travel service providers in the United States; almost all offer charter flights and packages. Some of these operators arrange well-organized escorted general-interest tours. A couple of the best and most reputable are:

- **ABC Charters ★** (www.abc-charters.com; ✆ **305/263-6829**) is an excellent travel service provider and charter company based in Miami.
- **Marazul ★** (www.marazul.com; ✆ **223-5334**) is a dependable company with a long history of operations in Cuba.

FROM CANADA

In addition to the agencies listed below, Canadian travelers and others using Canada as a gateway can check directly with **Transat Holidays** (www.transatholidays.com; ✆ **866/322-6649** in the U.S. and Canada), the tour agency arm of one of the principal charter flight companies to Cuba.

- **Signature Travel ★** (www.signaturevacations.com; ✆ **800/830 1111**) is the largest tour and package operator in Canada.

FROM THE U.K.

- **Cuba Direct ★** (www.cubadirect.co.uk; ✆ **020/3811-1642**) is a good Cuban-owned operator running a variety of tours and selling flights.

Tour Name	Americans? Y/N	Price	Time	Destinations	Type of Trip	Number of Trip Participants
Abercrombie & Kent	Y	$5,700	10–13 days	Las Terrazas, Havana, Cienfuegos, Cayo Santa Maria, Remedios, Caibarièn, Santa Clara	People to people	24
Adventure Women	Y	$6,600	10 days	Havana, Cienfuegos, Island of Cayo Encenachos	Women, cultural, people to people	18
Baseball Adventures	Y	$3,200	1 week	Cienfuegos, Santa Clara, and Havana	Baseball trip	17
Classic Journeys	Y	$5,100	8 days	Havana, Viñales Valley	People to people	12–14
Coda International Tours	Y	$4,500	8 days	Havana, Varadero, Pinar del Rio	People to people, cultural immersion	15–18
Cuba Cruise	Y	$1,400–$4,000	1–2 weeks	Havana, Cienfuegos, Santiago de Cuba	Cruise combined with people to people	1,200 passengers
Discovery Tours by Gate 1	Y	$3,900	9 days	Cienfuegos, Havana	People to people	22
Distant Horizons	Y	$3,500	6 days	Havana	Educational	20
Fred Olsen	N	$1,800	2 weeks	Havana	Cruise	929 passengers
Friendly Planet	Y	$4,000	9 days	Cienfuegos, Trinidad, Sancti Spiritus, Santa Clara, Varadero, Cardenas, Matanzas, Cojimar & Havana	History and culture	24
G Adventures	N	$999	8 days	Havana, Vińales, Maria la Gorda, Soroa	Leisure	12–16
Global Exchange	Y	$3,500	11 days	Matanzas, Yumuri Valley, Cienfuegos, Trinidad, Zapata Penisula, Pinar del Rio, Havana	Volunteerism, cultural education, people to people	1–21

Globus	Y	$2,699	9 days	Santiago De Cuba, Baracoa, Biran, Guardalavaca, Holguin	People to people	8
Go Ahead Tours	Y	$3,500	9 days	Havana, Sancti Spiritus, Cayo Santa Maria	Cultural and historical	27
Grand Circle Foundation	Y	$4,000	12 days	Havana, Trinidad, Cienfuegos	People to people	12–20
Insight Cuba	Y	$4,500	1 week	Havana, Viñales Valley, Pinar del Rìo, Las Terrazas	People to people	16–24
Intrepid Travel	Y	$3,175	9 days	Havana, Viñales, Cienfuegos, Trinidad	People to people	4–6
MSC Cruises	Y	$547	1 week	Havana	Cruise	4,345 passengers
National Geographic Expeditions	Y	$6,000	9 days	Havana, Trinidad, Cienfuegos	Nature, cultural education	25
New York Times Journeys' Cuba	Y	$6,700	9 days	Havana, Las Terrazas, Viñales	People to people	25
Noble Caledonia	N	$7,300	2 weeks	Havana, Cienfuegos, Santiago de Cuba, Isla de Juventud, Maria la Gorda, Casilda	Cruise	100 passengers
Quest Nature Tours	Y	$3,300	2 weeks	Western or Eastern Cuba, depending on tour	Nature	12–16
Road Scholar	Y	$3,700	9 days	Havana, Cienfuegos	Educational, people to people	10–24
Smithsonian Journeys	Y	$6,000	9 days	Havana, Cienfuegos	People to people	30
Star Clippers	N	$895–$2,025	5–10 days	Cienfuegos, Casilda, Cayo Largo, Archipelago de los Canarreos	Cruise	227 passengers
Wild Frontiers	Y	$4,700	12 days	Havana, Cienfuegos, Trinidad, Viñales	Cultural and historical	8–12
Wow Cuba	N	$2,150	1 week	All of Cuba covered depending on trip chosen	Bike tour	5–30

- **W&O Travel** ★ (www.westernoriental.com; ✆ **020/3131-6989**) took over Cuba specialists Regent Travel and offers great tours to Cuba.
- **Journey Latin America** ★★ (www.journeylatinamerica.co.uk; ✆ **020/3432-8461**) is a large U.K.–based operator for trips throughout the hemisphere, with often very good deals on airfare.
- **Thomas Cook** ★ (www.thomascook.com; ✆ 0800/**107-5620**) is a major U.K.–based operator for trips around the world, with excellent operations in Cuba.
- **The Holiday Place** ★★ (✆ **020/7644-1770;** communications@cuba-solidarity.org.uk) offers good package deals to Cuba; it also runs an office in the U.S. (http://holidayplace.co.uk).
- **Esencia Experiences** ★ (www.esenciaexperiences.com; ✆ **01481-714-898**) organizes bespoke luxury tours of Cuba.

FROM AUSTRALIA & NEW ZEALAND

- **Caribbean Destinations** (www.caribbeanislands.com.au; ✆ **1800/354-104**) is an Australian-based specialist in travel throughout the Caribbean.

FROM THE U.S.

- **The New York Times Journeys' Cuba: The Time is Now: A People to People Experience** ★★ (www.nytimes.com/times-journeys/travel/cuba-times-now/; ✆ **855/698-7979**) is an insightful, thoughtful trip to Havana and western Cuba.
- **Smithsonian Journeys** ★★ (www.smithsonianjourneys.org/tours/cuba; ✆ **855/330-1542**) offers excellent trips to Cuba, taking in Havana, Cienfuegos, and Trinidad.
- **Distant Horizons** ★★ (www.distant-horizons.com; ✆ **800/333-1240**) offers insightful, well-organized trips to Cuba.

BANKS, MONEY & ATMS

The Value of the Cuban Convertible Peso vs. Other Popular Currencies

CUC$	US$	CAN$	UK£	EURO (€)	AUS$	NZ$
1	$1.08	C$1.12	£0.70	€0.85	A$1.18	NZ$1.50

Frommer's lists exact prices in the local convertible peso currency. The currency conversions quoted above were correct at press time. However, rates fluctuate, so before departing consult a currency exchange website such as **www.oanda.com/convert/classic** to check up-to-the-minute rates.

Cuba is not a particularly cheap island to travel around for tourists and not cheap at all compared with neighboring Central American countries. You can reduce costs by traveling on the Víazul bus system and staying in *casas particulares* (private homes with rooms for rent), but note that single travelers rarely get a discount on a double room in a private house. You can easily pay out CUC$25 in a 2-week trip just on tipping the ubiquitous music bands that play in restaurants.

Although the U.S. dollar was replaced with the **Cuban convertible peso** (or **CUC**) in 1994, Cuba has always operated under a defacto dollarized economy. The CUC is an internationally unsupported currency and is, for all intents and purposes, pegged to the U.S. dollar. All of the CADECA branches and major banks will change U.S. dollars, euros, British pounds, and Canadian dollars.

There are, in fact, two distinct kinds of currency circulating in Cuba: the *moneda libremente convertible* ("convertible peso," or CUC), and the *moneda nacional* (Cuban peso, or MN, or CUP). Both are distinguished by the dollar $ symbol, leading to some confusion. Both the CUC and *moneda nacional* are divided up into units of 100 *centavos*. To complicate matters, the euro is also legal tender in many of the hotels, restaurants, and shops in several of the larger, isolated beach resort destinations. ***Note:*** In this book, we list prices in the Cuban convertible peso (CUC$), but when an establishment only accepts the Cuban peso (MN) we also list prices in MN.

The convertible peso functions on a near one-to-one parity with the dollar—at press time, the official exchange rate was US$1=CUC$0.93 and £1=CUC1.43. However, U.S. dollars are penalized by a 10 percent surcharge on all money-exchange operations into convertible pesos. For this reason, it is best to carry any hard currency you plan on spending in Cuba as euros, British pounds, or Canadian dollars. All of these are freely exchanged at all CADECA branches and most banks around Cuba. Be sure to bring relatively fresh and new bills. Cuban banks will sometimes refuse to accept bills with even slight tears or markings. Convertible pesos come in 1, 3, 5, 10, 20, 50, and 100 peso bills. Convertible peso coins also come in denominations of 0.1, 0.5, 0.25, 0.50 centavos and 1, and CUC coins. Although the government has long abandoned its official posture of a one-to-one parity between the Cuban peso (MN) and the U.S. dollar, the habit of converting *moneda nacional* prices directly into dollars is still common in many situations. Currently, Cuban pesos can be exchanged legally for CUC (and vice versa) at any CADECA money-exchange office (see below), some banks, and many hotels. The official exchange rate at press time was around 24 Cuban pesos to the CUC. While opportunities for travelers to pay in Cuban pesos are few and far between, it's not a bad idea to exchange around CUC$1 to CUC$2 for pesos soon after arrival. It's possible to pay for some meals, movie tickets, collective taxis, and other goods or services in Cuban pesos—the savings are substantial. If "MN" is displayed on the prices, you should theoretically be paying Cuban pesos. You can exchange any remaining convertible pesos at unfavorable rates for U.S. dollars, sterling, or euros at the airport before leaving. Do so, as the convertible pesos will be useless outside of Cuba.

Note: Cubans still often use the terms *peso* and *dollar* interchangeably. If you are quoted a price in pesos, it may not be the bargain you think it to be. To be clear, "*moneda nacional*" or "MN" always refers to Cuban pesos. Other terms for a CUC include *divisa, chavito, verde,* cooks (CUCS), and *fula.* Cash is known as *efectivo.*

The Cuban government announced in 2013 that it would unify the two currencies, but an official timeline has not been announced.

Cuba's state banking system is trying to keep u p with the rise in international tourism and joint business ventures. Both the **Banco de Crédito y Comercio** and **Banco Financiero Internacional** have opened up branches in most major business and tourist areas; most are open Monday through Friday 8am to 4pm and a handful are open on Saturday mornings. These banks are the place to go for cash withdrawals using your non-U.S.-issued credit cards. They'll also work for cashing traveler's checks or changing currency, but your best bet for money-exchange transactions is the national chain of *casas de cambio* (money-exchange houses), **CADECA, S.A.** You'll find CADECA branches in major cities, major hotels and tourist destinations, as well as at all the international airports. Do note, however, that many Cadecas in hotels in Havana will only change money for guests. The Cadeca in the Melia Cohiba is an exception to this rule. This is also the place to change your CUCs into national pesos *(moneda nacional)*. Most hotels also offer currency exchange to guests at the front reception.

Warning: Do not change money in the street. It is inevitable that you will be given a wad of useless national pesos instead of CUCs. Also, if you are offered the silver three-peso Che Guevara coin as a souvenir, note that it is worth three national pesos and not CUC$3; it can be obtained in a CADECA for $3MN.

WHAT THINGS COST IN CUBA	CUC$
Taxi from Havana airport to downtown	20.00–25.00
Taxi ride from bus station to downtown	5.00-8.00
Double room in an all-inclusive beach resort, moderate	150.00-250
Double room in a provincial city, moderate	80.00–150.00
Room in a *casa particular in Havana*	25.00–50.00
Room in a *casa particular elsewhere*	15.00–40.00
Three-course dinner for one without a drink, moderate	20
Bottle of beer	1.50-2.00
Bottle of water (500ml)	1-2.50
Mojito	2.50–4.00
Cup of coffee	050–3.00
1 liter of premium gas	1.30
1-hour Internet card (terminal and Wi-Fi)	2
Admission to most museums	1.00–5.00

MasterCard and **Visa** are widely accepted at hotels, car-rental agencies, and official restaurants and shops. Those cards issued by a United States bank or financial institution are still not usable in Cuba despite the fact that MasterCard and American Express has said its users can now use their cards in Cuba since early 2015. Credit card users must wait until their banks authorize the use of the card and must wait until Cuban infrastructure is ready to accept them. **Diners Club** is also accepted, although to a much lesser extent. It is always best to check with your home bank before traveling to see if your card will work in Cuba. If you have ignored all advice, contact **Asistur** (p. 292), which can advise you on a company in Santo Domingo that can arrange a transaction between your U.S. bank and Asistur.

You are fabulously ripped off when taking money out on your debit or credit card in Cuba. No matter what the country of origin of your card, your transaction will first be converted into dollars, and then there are exchange fees, bank fees, and goodness-knows-what other fees, thereby incurring a charge of up to a staggering 12.5 percent, before you are given the CUC. On a CUC$800 withdrawal, for example, you'll pay a whopping CUC$100 fee. This also happens at ATMs where your request for CUC is converted to U.S. dollars at that day's exchange rate. You are then charged 3 percent of the transaction in dollars at the point of withdrawal. (If you are in Cuba for any length of time, it is best to bring plenty of cash in sterling, euros, or Canadian dollars.)

Most *paladares* (private-home restaurants), *casas particulares* (private-home accommodations), and small businesses do not accept credit cards. In the more remote destinations, you should count on using cash for all transactions.

If your credit card is lost or stolen while you're in Cuba, call your bank directly. Banks will usually accept collect calls from anywhere in the world. You can also contact Asistur (p. 292).

Cuba has an expanding network of ATMs (automated teller machines) associated with a string of banks, like the **Banco de Crédito y Comercio** and **Banco Financiero Internacional.** No credit or debit cards issued by U.S.–based companies will work yet at any of these machines, although U.S. law now permits them to do so. However, travelers from other countries can easily extract convertible pesos from ATMs at the international airport and major tourist destinations. As with credit cards, it is always best to check with your home bank before traveling to see if your ATM card will work in Cuba.

Note: Remember that many banks impose a fee every time you use a card at another bank's ATM, and that fee can be higher for international transactions (up to $5 or more) than for domestic ones (where they're rarely more than $2 in the U.S.).

TIPS ON ACCOMMODATIONS

Cuba's tourist accommodations range from top-class historic **hotels** to basic budget uniform blocks in urban areas. These are complemented by ***casas particulares,*** a system of excellent-value Cuban guesthouses where Cubans rent out their rooms (or a whole house or an apartment) to guests. At **beach resorts,** hotels range from top-class luxury to above-basic facilities at slightly inflated prices, with a few very good exceptions at the more reasonable/lower end of the market. You won't find many *casas particulares* on Cuba's beaches, but there are now some in Varadero and Guardalavaca. In rural areas, you'll find a mix of high-end to attractive, moderately priced accommodations as well as some unattractive government hotels.

Hotels are either owned or run by the Cuban state or are run as joint ventures with foreign companies. Cuba has no 100 percent foreign-owned hotels.

Most hotel options in Cuba have been divvied up among a few large state-run chains: **Islazul** (www.islazul.cu), **Gaviota** (www.gaviota-grupo.com), **Cubanacán** (www.hotelescubanacan.com), **Gran Caribe** (www.gran-caribe.cu), and **Habaguanex** (www.habaguanex.ohc.cu/hotels/). These chains generally stake out distinct territories. Habaguanex has a monopoly control over the hotel scene in La Habana Vieja in Havana, the exception being the Hotel Saratoga. Their properties tend to be midrange to upper end, and most are in beautifully restored colonial buildings. Gaviota, Cubanacán, and Gran Caribe divvy up the remainder of the midrange to upper-end hotels around the country. Islazul runs the most economical hotels, although it has begun refurbishing some real gems in the colonial heart of some of Cuba's more interesting cities. Cubanacán is also upgrading properties with the Hoteles Encanto brand.

These large, state-run companies sign management contracts with international hotel chains, usually resulting in improved service and hospitality. While the international **Barceló** (www.barcelo.com), **NH Hoteles** (www.nh-hotels.com), **Iberostar** (www.iberostar.com), **Accor** (www.accor.com), and **Blue Diamond Resorts** (www.bluediamondresorts.com) chains run a few hotels each, the major player is the Spanish **Meliá** chain (www.meliacuba.com), which manages 248 midrange to high-end properties in Cuba.

Be prepared for some pitfalls when booking directly through hotel websites in Cuba. Many of the state-run chains—**Gaviota, Habaguanex,** and **Cubanacán**—have primitive or poorly maintained websites, and their online booking mechanisms can be cumbersome and inconsistent. You'll definitely do better with the larger international chains like Meliá.

You'll find consistently competitive live availability deals offered on **www.cubahotelreservation.com ★★**, and hotels honor these reservations with good rooms.

Note: High season (*temporada alta*) runs from December 15 to March 31, July 1 to August 31. Low season (*temporada baja*) runs from April 1 to June 30, Sept 1 to December 14. In 2015, however, the low season in Cuba was very short. Most hotels charge a supplement on Dec 24, 25, and 31.

We have listed rack rates for every hotel listing; any agency booking will be much cheaper than what we have listed. Overbooking is a common issue, and being able to check in on time in Havana hotels is somewhat of a miracle. As of mid-2015, no U.S.–issued credit cards could yet be used in Cuba.

Note: Under the "Amenities" section under each hotel entry where we have listed **Internet** or **Wi-Fi,** it means you will be charged a fee unless we specify that it comes free with your stay.

Casas Particulares

Aside from official hotels and resorts, the other principal lodging option in Cuba is a ***casa particular,*** or a private apartment or home. An official *casa particular* should display a small plaque or sticker declaring it to be a government-sanctioned *casa.* The symbol is a blue capital "H" set on its side, with slightly bent horizontal lines, and the top horizontal line longer than the bottom one. (It looks like an anchor.) It should also say *Arrendador Divisa,* which means the owner of the house is allowed to rent rooms for *divisa* (hard currency). Houses with red symbols can only rent to Cubans for *moneda nacional.*

Casas charge from CUC$15 to CUC$50 in low season and CUC$20 to CUC$50 in high season. Private apartments cost more. The most expensive rooms are in houses in Havana's Vedado and Miramar neighborhoods. In addition to the season, price variations depend on the number of guests, the length of stay, your status (students often receive discounts), the location of the house in the country (for example, the more remote or less touristy the area, the cheaper it may be), and the amount of tax owners pay on the rooms (dictated by the number of rooms they rent, the square meterage of the house that tourists use, and the location of their house). Those with impressive colonial homes often charge more. ***Note:*** I have not supplied rates for any *casa* in Cuba in the CUC$20–CUC$40 range, mainly because those rates fluctuate quite a bit in low and high season. I only supply fixed-rate prices for high-end *casas* or private apartments.

During low season, do negotiate for a lower nightly rate and always try to negotiate a lower rate for a long stay. Note that it is very difficult to get a discount for single travelers. Pairs/couples and families with children under 18 who share the same room enjoy the most value.

On arrival, *casa* owners must ask for your passport and enter the information into a registration book that must be taken to the immigration office within 24 hours of your arrival. You will be asked to sign next to your information in this book. If you are not asked to sign or are not asked for your passport, your *casa* may not be legal.

Most houses are quite modest—you are basically living with a Cuban family. Rooms for rent mostly have their own private bathroom or a bathroom shared with other tourists, not with the family. Your room will likely have air-conditioning; if not, you should pay less. The minimum facilities you will receive are clean sheets, towels, and toilet paper, probably a bedside lamp, a wardrobe closet, and a sideboard. Some *casas* now have security boxes, TVs, and stocked "minibar" fridges. Most houses provide locked rooms with a key. You may or may not be given the keys to the house depending on the rules of the owners. Some *casas* have independent entrances, which appeal to some travelers. Many of the most attractive colonial *casas* do not have ensuite bathrooms because of the configuration of the houses.

The biggest advantage of staying in a *casa* is that it is a great way to meet and interact with Cubans, something you cannot really do at "official" hotels and resorts. Most owners will also bend over backwards to assist you with your plans—whether that means answering your questions, arranging transport, or making phone calls for you. Most *casas particulares* also serve huge, varied, and tasty meals (breakfasts and dinners) at very reasonable prices.

If you have a reservation for your *casa,* your hosts should honor it. Similarly, if you make a reservation, you must turn up; losing CUC$25 on a no-show is a small fortune to a Cuban. Please respect this system—those who don't are forcing Cubans not to respect reservations. If you just turn up without a reservation and the house is full, the owner will often farm you out to a friend or relative at a nearby house. You are not under any obligation to take these places, but they could save you a lot of hassle—just be prepared to pay a commission that will be added to your nightly room rate. Even with a reservation, it is wise to make a follow-up confirmation by e-mail or phone a day or so before your arrival. *Casa* owners are happy to phone ahead to your next *casa* to tell the future host you are on your way.

Be aware that if you show up at a *casa particular* on the recommendation of a taxi driver or *jinetero,* the driver will expect a commission of between CUC$1 and CUC$5, which invariably is added onto the bill at your *casa particular.*

Warning: Be wary of *jineteros* (hustlers), who may try to dupe you into staying in a *casa* that they recommend so that they can earn a commission. One of the biggest jokes in Cuba among *arrendadores* (*casa particular* landlords) is that since late 2010, the job of *jinetero* has been legalized through the "gestor de viajeros" permitted legal job (travel rep), which means they can show you a license. Sometimes *jineteros* will just tell you that the *casa* you have a reservation in is full; others will take you to the door, put the "key" in, and pretend it's locked, saying that the owner is away; others will tell you the owner of the *casa* you have a reservation in has moved, died, or gone abroad and they can take you to a similar house nearby (from which they'll receive a commission). In this desperate economic climate, *jineteros* will stop at nothing until they collect a commission. Be on guard, and do not be deterred by these scams. If you have a reservation, be confident and insistent that you stay at the *casa particular* where you have a room reserved.

Frommer's has received reports of the occasional theft from *casas particulares.* This is an extremely rare occurrence, since renting rooms to tourists is the main source of hard currency for Cubans. Putting this at risk is, quite frankly, idiotic in Cuba's economic climate. That said, it is always smart not to put temptation in the way of anyone. Lock money and valuables away.

Credit cards cannot be accepted in *casas.* Since spring 2015, U.S. travelers allowed to visit Cuba (see the 12 OFAC categories under "Entry Requirements," p. 264) have been able to book rooms through www.airbnb.com. For other *casa particular* sites, see www.cubacasas.net, www.cuba-junky.com, and www.cubacasa.co.uk.

EATING & DRINKING IN CUBA

Cuba's culinary scene has undergone a sea change since late 2010. You can now eat well in Cuba, especially in the major touristic centers, and exceptionally well in a handful of top *paladares* (private restaurants). The state has conceded that the private sector does better food, and very few state restaurants have opened in recent years. Yes, a handful of good state restaurants do exist, but my advice is to avoid them in the main. In the vast majority of cases, you will eat better food and experience more creativity and better service in the private dining options. Bland food and poor service still exist in vast swaths across the country, however, and there is nothing to do but to grin and bear it.

Paladares are not able to sell lobster, but many of them do; they also cannot accept credit cards for payment. Some restaurants automatically add a 10 percent service charge to bills.

Be warned: Be on the lookout for overcharging (accidental or otherwise), either in the form of phantom charges or inflated prices, and double-check your change. If you show up at a *paladar* on the recommendation of a taxi driver or *jinetero* (hustler), you can expect to pay a commission via the "commission menu" (p. 62).

Given the unique economic and social conditions of Cuba, there is little **street food** to speak of, aside from a few odd pizza, churro, and ice-cream vendors. Cuban street pizza has heavy dough, with a molten mess of sauce and gooey cheese topping, served as small individual disks on wax paper. Peanuts (*maní*) sold in newspaper cones or a peanut-and-toffee bar are also popular.

Local Cuisine

Cuban, or *criolla,* cuisine is a mix of European (predominantly Spanish) and Afro-Caribbean influences. The staples of the cuisine include roasted and fried pork, beef, and chicken, usually accompanied by rice, beans, plantains, and yucca. Oddly, Cubans do not eat large amounts of seafood, although fish and lobster dishes are on the menu at most restaurants. In general, Cubans do not use aggressive amounts of spice or hot peppers, although onions, garlic, and, to a much lesser extent, cumin are used fairly liberally.

With the exception of breakfast, most meals are accompanied by some combination of white rice and beans. *Arroz moro,* or *moros y cristianos* (Moors and Christians), is the common name for black beans mixed with white rice. *Congrí* is a similar dish of red beans and white rice already mixed. Sometimes the rice and beans are served separately.

The national dish, which, unfortunately, you won't often find on restaurant menus (but is worth sampling if you do), is *ajiaco,* a chunky meat and vegetable stew. *Ajiaco* comes from the Taíno word *ají* for chile pepper, although the dish is seldom prepared very spicy. You're much more likely to find *ropa vieja* (literally, "old clothes"), a sauté of shredded beef, onions, and peppers; or *picadillo,* a similar concoction made with ground beef and sometimes featuring olives and raisins in the mix.

La Bomba

If you want to order papaya, remember to call it *fruta bomba.* In Cuba, the word *papaya* is almost always used as pejorative slang referring to a woman's most private part.

In Baracoa, in Cuba's far east, coconut milk infuses much of the cuisine.

If you're looking for a light snack, try a *bocadito,* literally a "little bite," which is what they call a simple sandwich, usually made of ham and/or cheese.

Aside from the Coppelia ice creams, it's generally slim pickings for dessert. Flan is popular, but seldom outstanding. I feel similarly about *natilla,* a simple sweet pudding that usually comes in either chocolate or coconut flavors. Many dessert menus will feature some sort of sweet marmalade, usually *guayaba,* papaya, or coconut, accompanied by cheese. Unfortunately, the cheeses are generally bland and nondescript.

Wetting Your Whistle

Most Cubans simply drink water or any number of popular soft drinks, including Sprite and Coca-Cola, whose locally produced equivalents are called Cachito and Tukola, respectively. While many hotels and restaurants serve freshly squeezed orange juice for breakfast, you'll have a harder time finding other fresh fruit juices than you'd expect in the Caribbean tropics unless you are staying in a *casa particular.* One of the more interesting nonalcoholic drinks is *guarapo,* the sweet juice of freshly pressed sugarcane, and *pru,* a refreshing combination of fermented sugar, spices, pepper leaf, and roots.

Cubans also drink plenty of coffee, and they like to brew it strong. Order *café espresso* for a straight shot, or *café con leche* if you'd like it mixed with warm milk. Ask for *café americano* if you want a milder brew.

Cuba produces a small handful of pretty good lager beers. Cristal, Bucanero, and Mayabe are the most popular. If you want something slightly darker and stronger, try Bucanero. Cuba does produce excellent rums. Most visitors soon have their fill of *mojitos* (light rum with lime juice, fresh mint, sugar, and club soda) and daiquiris. Another popular cocktail is the *cuba libre* ("Free Cuba"), which is simply a rum and Coke with lime.

Wine is imported. Wine parading under the Cuban Soroa label is cheap French table wine bottled in Cuba.

Note: When entering a cafe, roadside cafe, or bar, *always* ask for the drinks' menu; if you don't, I can guarantee you will be overcharged.

Also note: If you are staying at a beach resort, some a la carte restaurants close in the low season.

[FastFACTS] CUBA

Business Hours There are no hard-and-fast rules, but most businesses and banks are open Monday through Friday 9am to 5pm. Some businesses and banks close for an hour for lunch. Shops and department stores, especially those that cater to tourists, tend to have slightly more extended hours and are usually open on Saturday and Sunday mornings.

Customs & Etiquette Cubans are friendly, open, and physically expressive people. They strike up conversations easily and seldom use the formal terms of address in Spanish. Be aware that many Cubans who start a conversation with foreigners in the street are hoping in some way to get some economic gain out of the relationship. *Jineterismo,* or jockeying, is a way of life in Cuba. This may involve anything from offers to take you to a specific restaurant or a *casa particular* (for a commission) to direct appeals for money or goods.

Dress is generally very informal, thanks in large part to the tough economic times faced by the broad population. Suits are sometimes worn in business and governmental meetings, although a simple, light, short-sleeved cotton shirt, or a *guayabera,* is more common. The *guayabera* is a loose-fitting shirt with two or four outer pockets on the front and usually a few vertical bands of pleats or embroidery. The *guayabera* is worn untucked, and is quite acceptable at even the most formal of occasions.

Perhaps the greatest etiquette concern is about what you say. Open criticism of the government or of Fidel or Raúl Castro is a major taboo. Don't do it—especially in open public places. The police, community revolutionary brigades, and reprisals for vocal dissent are an ongoing legacy of Cuba's political reality. One effect of this is that while Cubans you meet will often be very open and expressive with you, they tend to immediately clam up the minute another Cuban unknown to them enters the equation.

Doctors & Hospitals Contact the **International Association for Medical Assistance to Travelers (IAMAT;** www.iamat.org) for tips and for lists of local, English-speaking doctors. The website **www.tripprep.com**, sponsored by a consortium of travel medicine practitioners, also offers helpful advice on traveling abroad. You can find listings of reliable clinics overseas at the International Society of Travel Medicine website (**www.istm.org**).

A full list of international clinics, international drugstores, and opticians is available on the **Servimed** website at www.servimedcuba.com. The **Clínica Central Cira Garcia,** Calle 20 no. 4101 on the corner of Avenida 41, Playa, Havana (www.cirag.cu; ✆ **7204-2811**), is the largest center in the country catering to foreigners. It is also possible to have medical treatments, cosmetic surgery, and undergo drug-addiction programs in Cuba for a fraction of the cost elsewhere. All the details are listed under the Servimed website.

Asistur, Prado 208 between Calles Trocadero and Colón (www.asistur.cu; ✆ **7866-4499**), will help you with medical reports and the management of medical expenses if you end up in the hospital. Its addresses outside Havana are available on www.asistur.cu/mapa.html.

Drinking Laws Cuba has no firm or clear liquor laws. Beer, wine, and liquor are served at most restaurants and are available at most gift shops and hard-currency stores. Drinking and driving is against the law.

Electricity You will find a mix of electrical currents and plug types used in Cuba. Around 90 percent of the hotels and *casas particulares* use a 110-volt current with standard U.S.–style two- or three-prong outlets. However, some outlets are rated 220 volts, particularly in hotels that cater to European clientele and some *casas particulares.* These are usually marked and sometimes accept only two-prong round plugs. For all intents and purposes, you should have personal appliances rated for 110-volt current, with U.S.–style prongs, or the appropriate converters. It is also essential to carry a three-to-two-prong adapter for any appliance you have that has a three-prong plug.

"Cut-outs" are frequent in Cuba, although the black-outs (*apagónes*) of the1990s are gone. My advice is to constantly charge up your appliances rather than wait.

Embassies & Consulates All major consulates and embassies are in Havana. The embassy of **Canada** is at Calle 30 no. 518, at the corner of Avenida 7, Miramar (http://havana.gc.ca; ✆ **7204-2516**). The Consulate of Canada is at Hotel Atlántico, Suite 1, Guardalavaca (✆ **24/430-320;** consulate.gvaca@gmail.com); and at Calle 13, corner of Avenida 1 and Camino del Mar, Varadero (✆ **45/61-2078;** consulate.vdero@gmail.com). The embassy of the **United Kingdom** is at Calle 34 no. 702, between Avenida 7 and 17, Miramar (http://ukincuba.fco.gov.uk; ✆ **7214-2200**). The **United States Embassy,** Calle Calzada between Calles L and M, Vedado (http://havana.usembassy.gov; ✆ **7839-4100**). There is no Australian embassy in Cuba; the Canadian embassy will officially assist.

Emergencies In most cases, you will want to dial ✆ **106** for any emergency. This is the number for the police. Alternately, you can dial ✆ **104** for an ambulance and ✆ **105** for the fire department. At none of these numbers can you assume you will find an English-speaking person. For legal emergencies, contact your diplomatic representation. All U.S. citizens can find assistance at the U.S. Embassy (see above), with no questions asked about licenses.

Family Travel Cuba is an excellent destination for families, particularly if you want an all-inclusive beach vacation with a broad range of tours, activities, and entertainment options. Toward this end, Varadero would probably be your top choice, with a wealth of watersports activities and land-based adventures, including nearby caves to explore. The beach destinations of Cayo Coco, Cayo Guillermo, and Guardalavaca are also worth considering. If you do go the all-inclusive route, be sure the resort you choose has a well-run children's program, with a full plate of activities. If your children are old enough, they should enjoy the colonial wonders of La Habana Vieja (Old Havana), including its forts and castles.

Hotels and attractions throughout Cuba often give discounts for children under 12 years old, as does the tourist bus service, Víazul. However, hotels with regular, dependable babysitting service are few and far between. If you need babysitting service, make sure your hotel provides it before you leave home.

Health Despite ongoing economic troubles and shortages, Cuba's health-care system remains one of the best in Latin America. The country takes extremely proactive steps toward preventive public health. Malaria has been eradicated, but there have been cholera and dengue fever outbreaks in the last few years. You don't need any vaccinations to travel to Cuba, unless you are coming from a region with cholera or yellow fever, in which case the Cuban authorities will require proof of immunization.

Staying healthy on a trip to Cuba is predominantly a matter of common sense: **Know your physical limits** and don't overexert yourself in the ocean, on hikes, or in athletic activities. Cuba is a tropical country, so limit your **exposure to the sun,** especially during the first few days of your trip and, thereafter, from 11am to 3pm. (It is often much hotter in Cuba btw. 2–4pm than at midday.)

Due to the U.S. embargo and other problems, common medicines are restricted or routinely unavailable in Cuba. It is wise to bring a full medical pack containing basic medicines. Travelers may also want to consider carrying ciprofloxacin if they are susceptible to stomach bugs that need treating with an antibiotic. Having said that, Cuba has a well-established network of international health clinics for emergencies, but it's still wise to bring what you need with you, including all prescription medicines.

Tropical Illnesses Cuba does experience dengue outbreaks from time to time, so keep your ear to the ground about this.

Dietary Red Flags

Overall, while **water** is potable throughout most of Cuba, I recommend you stick primarily to bottled water, just to err on the side of safety. Every hotel and restaurant catering to travelers will carry bottled water. Ask for *agua natural* (still) or *agua con gas* (sparkling water).

Bugs, Bites & Other Wildlife Concerns

Cuba has no poisonous snakes. In terms of **biting bugs,** your standard array of bees, wasps, mosquitoes, and sand fleas are present. Sand fleas are a slight nuisance at most beaches if there's no offshore breeze to clear them, particularly around sunrise and sunset. While there are also ticks and chiggers, so far Lyme disease is not considered a problem. Bring repellent and wear light, long-sleeved clothing.

Sun Exposure The tropical sun in Cuba is extremely fierce. The highest sun-protection factor, hats, and protective clothing should be worn. Stay out of the sun between 11am and 3pm and drink plenty of water to avoid dehydration. Use sunscreen, and reapply often. Remember that children need more protection than adults do; look for a sunscreen with zinc oxide or titanium dioxide for full coverage.

Extreme Weather

Hurricanes can occur between June and November in Cuba, but they do not arrive every year. The **National Hurricane Center** (www.nhc.noaa.gov) offers details on any storms in the Caribbean basin. In the event of a hurricane, Cuba has a very well-organized preparedness program. In the event of extreme danger, thousands can be evacuated, minimizing or avoiding deaths completely. Listen to all authorities in the event of an emergency.

During the rainy season, tropical storms with plenty of lightning are common. According to the Cuban Meteorological Institute, around 65 Cubans die each year from lightning strikes. During a storm, stay inside or in your vehicle. Move out of the sea and away from the beach and move away from high ground.

Water It is safer to drink bottled water, sold as *agua mineral sin* or *con gas* and made by Ciego Montero. Foreign sparkling water is now available. If you wish to drink the national water, it is better to ask for "*agua con gas nacional,*" since the default position is to bring out the more expensive foreign import. Ditto Tu Kola (*cola nacional*) versus Coca Cola. Ice is safe to drink in state and private restaurants. There have been a few cholera outbreaks in the last few years, so it is probably smart not to drink the local water (which locals always boil).

If You Get Sick Cuba has a nationwide system of hospitals and clinics, as well as international clinics, and you should have no trouble finding prompt and competent medical care in the case of an emergency. (See the "Orientation" section of the individual destination chapters, or "Fast Facts" for specific recommendations. The system is entirely free for Cubans, but foreigners are charged for services.) This is actually a significant means of income for the country; however, fees for private medical care are relatively inexpensive by most Western standards. If you are hospitalized, you may find that support staff, like nurses, are lacking. You may need to have someone bring your food, clothes, sheets and other necessities, and if you are traveling alone, this could mean informally paying a Cuban—perhaps a *casa particular* owner you've met—to help.

The country has a network of pharmacies, though due

to the U.S. embargo, certain medicines are restricted or often unavailable. That said, it is always a good idea to carry a sufficient supply of any necessary prescription medicines you may need (packed in their original containers in your carry-on luggage), and a small first-aid kit with basic analgesic, antihistamine, and anti-diarrhea medications. You might also bring a copy of your prescriptions, with the generic name of the medication in case the pharmacist doesn't recognize the brand name. Don't forget an extra pair of contact lenses or prescription glasses—although opticians are available if necessary.

If you suffer from a chronic illness, consult your doctor before your departure. For conditions like epilepsy, diabetes, or heart problems, wear a **MedicAlert identification tag** (www.medicalert.org; ✆ **800/432-5378**), which will immediately alert doctors to your condition and give them access to your records through MedicAlert's 24-hour hotline.

Insurance All visitors and non-Cuban residents must hold a medical insurance policy. Failure to carry the correct documents could result in the visitor having to purchase mandatory coverage at the airport through Asistur (see below). Non–U.S. citizens are often only asked to show their insurance documents at the point of extending (*prorrogar*) a tourist visa at an immigration office. If you don't already have insurance and want to extend your stay, you would be wise to purchase through Asistur in Havana before attending immigration. U.S. insurance companies may now sell travel insurance (under a Global policy) to authorized U.S. travelers to Cuba (see OFAC regulations under "Entry Requirements"). That said, visitors are not always asked to present proof-of-insurance documentation on entry but are requested to present it if they extend their visa. To be safe, you should take out an insurance policy before you arrive in Cuba. If you do need to purchase insurance at the airport, contact **Asistur** (www.asistur.cu; ✆ **7866-4499**).

Internet In all cities outside of Havana, head to the main **Etecsa** telephone office, where you will find a small bank of computers on the Nauta system and the main point at which to buy the nationalized (Nauta) Internet cards. A large number of hotels in the provinces and beach resorts also offer Internet access and, increasingly, Wi-Fi on this system. In Havana, outside of the Etecsa offices, nearly all hotels offer Internet access, and some offer Wi-Fi. Some hotels do not operate Wi-Fi on the Nauta system (including the Nacional and the Melia Cohiba, which charge more than the official Nauta rates), and others hotels like to rob tourists by charging them nearly double the official Nauta price (e.g., the Hotel Sevilla, but it is not alone). The **José Martí International Airport** in Havana also has Wi-Fi on the Nauta system.

Internet access on the Nauta system (via a terminal or Wi-Fi) costs CUC$2 per hour. If you buy cards at an Etecsa office or Joven Club, you'll need to show your passport to register and get a card. The credit-card-size card comes with a login number and a scratch-off password, which will allow you to login at any Nauta interface around the country. One card is valid for 30 days. If you do not use the allotted time in the same setting, you must log off with the following: http://1.1.1.1. Then you must disconnect from the system; otherwise you lose your remaining time. The system has much improved in the last 2 years; speeds have gone up, but the system occasionally slows, fails, or is overloaded with overuse.

The Spanish word for @ symbol is *arroba* and is found by pressing Alt 6 + 4.

Language Spanish is the official language of Cuba. English is spoken at most hotels, restaurants, and some attractions. Outside of the tourist orbit, English is not widely spoken, and some rudimentary Spanish will go a long way.

Indigenous and African languages have had a profound and lasting influence, and you will find many words—like *cigar, barbacoa,* and *conga*—tracing their origin to indigenous and African sources used widely across the island. Various African dialects are still widely used in the songs and ceremonies of Santeria and other syncretic religions, although almost no one speaks them conversationally. In a legacy from the Soviet days, some Cubans speak Russian. Also, see "Cuban Spanish Terms & Phrases," p. 300.

LGBT Travelers Homosexuality is not illegal in Cuba, but in general, Cuba has a poor record on gay and lesbian rights, and while the situation has improved somewhat, there are still high levels of homophobia and broad societal rejection of gays and lesbians. For decades following the Revolution, gays and lesbians were closeted and persecuted. (Read Reinaldo Arenas' horrifying account in *Before Night Falls.*) The harsh measures they faced included forced labor and prison. The blockbuster movie *Fresa y Chocolate* (Strawberry and Chocolate) certainly brought the issue to the forefront, yet not much has changed in the prevailing views of this macho society. However, Fidel Castro has now taken responsibility for the way homosexuals were treated in the 1960s and 1970s. Cuba has only a couple of accepted gay and lesbian establishments (see Santa Clara; p. 143), and few of the established gay and lesbian tour operators run trips to the island. However, **Out Adventures** (www.out-adventures.com), based in Canada and working with Intrepid travel, offers a "Comfort Cuba" tour.

Santa Clara (p. 143) is perhaps the most openly gay city in Cuba and hosts an annual gay and transvestite carnival in the middle of May. Raúl Castro's daughter, Mariela Castro, heads the National Center for Sex Education and champions homosexual, bisexual, and transgender rights. In May 2008, the state-television network transmitted *Brokeback Mountain* on TV, the first time a gay film had been broadcast in Cuba. Cuba has also held an anti-homophobia day for the last 9 years, promoted by Mariela Castro. The legalization of same-sex marriage has also been discussed. In addition, sex-change operations were legalized in 2008, and in 2010, Cuba's first transsexual appeared in a documentary publicly detailing her transition for the first time.

While travelers are generally not hassled in Cuba and given some leeway in terms of social mores, same-sex signs of physical affection are rare and frowned upon across the country. Gay and lesbian couples and singles should take the prevailing social climate into account when traveling in Cuba. Gay travelers should also take care. A gay friend of mine was mugged for his camera and left with broken bones on a night out in Vedado. Homosexual love-crime murders have been known.

The documentary film, ***Gay Cuba,*** by Sonja de Vries (Frameline Films; www.frameline.org), is an honest look at the treatment of gays and lesbians in modern Cuba.

The International Gay and Lesbian Travel Association (IGLTA; www.iglta.org; ✆ **954/630-1637**) is the trade association for the gay and lesbian travel industry, with an online directory of gay- and lesbian-friendly travel businesses.

Legal Aid If you get into legal trouble, immediately request to be put in touch with your embassy. All embassies have round-the-clock emergency numbers. **Assitur** (www.asistur.cu) may also be able to help. Its emergency numbers are ✆ **7866-8527,** ✆ **7866-8339,** and ✆ **7866-8920.**

Mail A post office is called a *correo* in Spanish. You can get stamps at post offices, gift shops, and the front desk in most hotels. The Cuban postal system is extremely slow and untrustworthy. You can count on every parcel and piece of mail being opened and inspected. The cost of a postcard or letter to the U.S. or Canada is CUP$.65 to CUP$.85, and it takes about 4 weeks for delivery. A postcard and letter to Europe costs CUP$.85 to CUP$.90. A package of up to 1 kilogram (2.2 lb.) will cost CUC$10 to CUC$20 to ship, depending upon your destination country, but can only be dealt with at principal post offices.

However, it is best to send anything of any value via an established international courier service. **DHL,** Calle 26 and Avenida 1, Miramar, Havana (www.dhl.com; ✆ **7204-1876**), provides broad coverage to most of Cuba. ***Beware:*** Despite what you may be told, packages sent overnight to U.S. addresses tend to take 3 to 4 days to reach their destination.

Maps Most car-rental agencies and many hotels will give you a copy of very basic nationwide and Havana road maps. The Cuban Geographic and Cartographic Institute publishes a couple of much more detailed maps; most tourist gift shops and Infotur kiosks carry these maps. If you're buying a map before your trip, try to get the **International Travel Map: Cuba** (ITMB Publishing; www.itmb.com), the **National Geographic Cuba** map, or the new **VanDam** Cuba and Havana maps (www.vandam.com). Anyone doing any serious driving should purchase the indispensable **Guia de Carreteras,** available irregularly in Havana.

Mobile Phones & Cuban Phones In Cuba, cellular service is controlled by **Cubacel,** Avenida 5 and Calle 76, Edificio Barcelona, Centro de Negocios, Miramar (www.cubacel.cu; ✆ **7266 8364**). Cubacel has offices at the José Martí International Airport (open daily 8:30am–7pm) and in Havana and most major cities and tourist destinations. Cubacel offers two possibilities to foreign travelers: renting SIM cards for CUC$3 per day for a fixed period or the purchase of a permanent SIM for CUC$40 with credit of CUC$10 included. The permanent SIM line will only expire if you fail to recharge within an 11-month period. You are able to top up Cuban phones outside of Cuba through companies like ezetop.com. A couple of times a year Cubacel offers to double the credit if you top up outside of Cuba, so the line can be maintained even if you are not in-country. ***Note:*** Any phone with a SIM from a U.S. provider will not work in Cuba.

Cubacel works with both TDMA phones and GSM systems. Prepaid calling cards are sold in denominations of CUC$5, CUC$10, and CUC$20. Rates inside Cuba run between CUC10¢ and CUC35¢ per minute for outgoing calls, depending on the hour of day. (***Note:*** If a fixed landline calls your cellphone, you pay for the call. If you receive a cellphone call marked with the prefix **99,** the caller is expecting you to pay for the call.). Rates to the rest of the world run between CUC$1.40 and CUC$1.80 per minute. Text (SMS) messages are free to receive, but cost CUC9¢ to send within Cuba and CUC$1 to send abroad. (Remember to dial Cuba's country code of **53** before any area code and the number you wish to dial in the country before using your own phone in Cuba.)

Multicultural Travelers Africans and African-Americans used to be hassled quite regularly by the police, who mistook them for Cuban citizens. Thankfully, with the change in apartheid rules in Cuba in February 2008, this is much less common. The advantage of ethnically blending in also leads to less hassle and scams (see "Race Relations in Cuba," below).

Newspapers & Magazines The nationwide Spanish-language official organ of the Communist Party daily, *Granma,* is a thin paper with sparse coverage of local and international news and a strong party-line editorial bias. The paper is not nearly as widely available as daily papers in most other countries, but some street vendors and many hotels do have copies each morning. English-digest versions of *Granma* come out every few days and are available at many hotels. A handful of other daily and weekly newspapers are published, and are usually even harder to find than *Granma.* These include *Trabajadores, Juventud Rebelede,* and a host of regional rags. No international newspapers or magazines are sold in Cuba.

Pharmacies Called *farmacias* in Spanish, drugstores are relatively common throughout the country, although not necessarily well stocked. Those at hospitals and major clinics are often open 24 hours. Many hotels, particularly larger ones, have either a small pharmacy or a basic medical clinic on-site. A 24-hour pharmacy is at the **international terminal** of Havana's José Martí International Airport (✆ **7266-4105**).

Police Nationwide, you can dial ✆ **106** for police, although you shouldn't expect to find an English-speaking person on the other end of the line. In general, the police are quite helpful and not to be feared. Bribery is not an issue. In the event of robbery, the police are your best bet, but for physical emergencies or other threats of serious danger, you are probably best off contacting your embassy.

Safety Cuba is an extremely safe country. Street crime is relatively rare. With the recent upsurge in tourism, there have been some reports of pickpocketing and muggings in Old Havana and Centro Havana and around the gay hangouts in Vedado, but these are by far the exceptions to the rule. Most popular tourist destinations have a strong security and police presence, and even outside the well-worn tourist routes theft and assaults are quite uncommon. Having said that, news is heavily censored, so real crime statistics are unknown.

That said, you should still use common sense. Given the nature of Cuba's socialist system, a huge disparity in wealth exists between the average Cuban and any foreign visitor, even budget travelers. Don't flash ostentatious signs of wealth, and avoid getting too far off the beaten path, especially at night. Don't leave valuables unattended, and always use the safe in your hotel room or at the front desk.

If you are robbed, you will need a police report for insurance purposes. If you don't speak Spanish, go accompanied by a Spanish speaker; otherwise, you will make little headway.

The U.S. State Department (**http://travel.state.gov**) and the U.K. Foreign and Commonwealth Office (**www.fco.gov.uk**) issue updated advice for travelers.

Meddling in drugs and firearms brings stiff penalties. There are also prohibitions relating to blood products, obscene or pornographic literature, or any anti-state literature. Getting on the wrong side of the law is not advisable in any way.

Solo women travelers can go out at night with no fear for their safety, but it's always best to be careful. Walking home alone in small provincial towns is quite safe. Also see "Women Travelers," below.

Senior Travel Cuba is a comfortable destination for senior travelers. Seniors are treated with deference and respect in Cuba. Moreover, it's a particularly safe country, with low levels of street crime, and the food and water are generally safe as well.

Mention the fact that you're a senior when you make your travel reservations—some hotel chains and package tour operators offer senior discounts. Don't expect to find senior discounts once you arrive in Cuba, however, where you will be lumped into the category of rich foreigner and gouged as much as possible, like all the rest.

ElderTreks (www.eldertreks.com; ✆ **800/741-7956** in North America and 0808-234-1717 in the U.K.) is a Canadian-based company that arranges small-group (up to 16 people) adventure trips for those 50 and older to Cuba. In the U.K., trips to Cuba are offered by **Saga,** The Saga Building, Enbrook Park, Folkestone, Kent, CT20 3SE (www.saga.co.uk; ✆ **0800/096-0078**).

Single Travelers Cuba is generally extremely safe for travelers. Single travelers face no real specific threats or dangers. That said, don't throw common sense out the window. Single travelers—and women in particular—should still be careful when walking alone at night, both in Havana and in other more remote destinations.

I have never felt unsafe traveling on my own, and there are few other countries in the world where I would consider taking an illegal taxi with a strange man for hundreds of kilometers down

Race Relations in Cuba

The Cuban population is—very conservatively—estimated to be about one-third black or mixed-race (in reality, the percentage is probably closer to two-thirds or more). Cuba officially declares itself to be color-blind, and (at least on the surface) the obvious mixed-race heritage and strong presence of Afro-Cuban culture seem to support that notion. Although as a society Cuba is much less racist and male-dominated than it was before the Revolution, racism still exists, even if much of it is under the radar. Economic racism is widespread; relatively few black Cubans occupy positions of authority in the government, state-enterprise, or tourism sector. Racist comments are as regrettably common as they are in other countries. Many Cubans assume blacks to be the majority of *jineteros* (male hustlers) and *jineteras* (female escorts), even though the reality is that hustling in Cuba is universal. Most Cubans also believe that the police harass blacks to a disproportionate degree, and travelers of African and Hispanic descent may experience the same.

—Neil E. Schlecht

back roads (like I did here). Remember also that Cubans face severe repercussions for committing crimes against tourists.

Perhaps the biggest issue facing single travelers is that of ***jineterismo,*** which is a way of life in Cuba. In its most disturbing form, it has become synonymous with prostitution. Sex tourism and prostitution flourish in Cuba, and single travelers of both genders and any sexual persuasion will encounter constant offers for companionship, and usually more. In some cases, the terms are quite clear and a cash value is set. In others, the *jinetera* or *jinetero* is just looking for restaurant meals, drinks, store-bought clothing, food, daily necessities, and sometimes even a good time. Many are looking to cement relationships with foreign tourists that could lead to marriage and a means of improving their standard of living on a long-term basis, either on island or abroad.

Smoking Although Fidel gave up smoking years ago, Cuba remains a major producer of tobacco and tobacco products. Many Cubans smoke. Cuba introduced a nonsmoking ban in enclosed public places in February 2005, but it is not really enforced. Most restaurants have non-smoking areas.

Student Travelers Students with an **International Student Identity Card** (www.isic.org) can pay a reduced fee in some museums. Student discounts on Víazul are not available.

Taxes There are no direct or specific taxes on goods or services in Cuba. Some tourist restaurants and *paladares* add a 10-percent service charge onto their bills.

Telephones Cuba is slowly erasing area codes from national numbers. Havana's former city code (7) is now part of telephone numbers. Meanwhile area codes are one or two digits across the country; individual phone numbers can range from five to seven digits. You do not need to use the area code for local calls, but you must dial **01** followed by the city or area code for any long-distance call within Cuba or to a cellphone, except when calling to or from Havana. Calling from Havana to any other province or from a province to Havana, you would dial only a zero before the area code. Thus, a call from Trinidad to Pinar del Rio would start 01-48. A call from Havana to Pinar del Rio would begin 0-48. The same rules apply for a cellphone call. All Cuba cellphones begin with a 5. To dial a cellphone from a fixed line in Havana, dial 0-5, then the rest of the cellphone number. If you call a cellphone from any other province, dial 01-5, then the rest of the cellphone number. If you dial cellphone to cellphone, just dial 5, then the rest of the cellphone number.

To call Cuba: If you're calling Cuba from the United States:

- First dial 011, the international access code.
- Then dial 53, the country code.
- And last, dial the area code and then the number.

The whole number you'd dial for a number in Havana (area code 7) would be 011-53-7XXX-XXXX.

To make international calls: To make international calls from Cuba, first dial 119 and then the country code (U.S. or Canada 1, U.K. 44, Ireland 353, Australia 61, New Zealand 64). Next dial the area code and number. For example, if you want to call the British Embassy in Washington, D.C., you would dial 119/1-202-588-7800. You can make collect calls to Canada, Spain, the U.S., France, Italy, and the U.K.

For directory and operator assistance: Dial ✆ 113 if you're looking for a number inside Cuba and for domestic help, and dial ✆ 180 for numbers to all other countries and for help with collect calls.

Nearly all hotels and some *casas particulares* have phones in their rooms. Dialing instructions should be available in rooms; if not, contact the reception desk. Cuba has a wide range of **public telephone booths** where Cuban pesos *(moneda nacional)* and a variety of cards can be used. Most older sky-blue phones have been phased out, but the ones remaining—and the newer royal-blue phones with a coin slot—take *moneda nacional*. This is the cheapest option, where you can talk for a very long time for 1 peso. However, most of these phones are now used by callers with prepaid calling cards (*propia*) with set values; with these cards, you can make telephone calls by first dialing an access code (166), then dialing the number on your card, followed by the hash key, and then the phone number you want to dial. These cards are available in CUC and in *moneda nacional* and may be worth purchasing if you plan to make a lot of local calls on your trip. Note that international calls made from these CUC calling cards run between CUC$1 and CUC$1.50 a minute.

To dial an international number from a CUC prepaid calling card, you must dial 166 followed by the card code followed by the hash key, followed by 119 (international code) followed by the international area code, then the number you wish to call, followed by a hash key.

New royal-blue phones can be used for these calling cards expressed in CUC (from CUC$5) and *moneda nacional* (from $10MN).

Note that if you stay in a *casa particular* and wish to confirm your subsequent *casa* in another town, your *casa* owner will make this courtesy call for you. Prepaid calling cards can be used from landlines in *casa* homes too.

Tipping Most Cuban workers earn incredibly low salaries in dollar terms—around CUC$18 to CUC$20 a month—so tips are an extremely important and coveted source of supplemental income. With the rise in tourism, all sorts of workers now expect and work for tips, including porters, waiters, guides, and restaurant musicians. Taxi drivers, especially in Havana, tend to overcharge tourists; taxi drivers do not expect tips. Porters should be tipped CUC$1 per bag. If you stay in a resort, you should tip the maid around CUC$1 a day, and also tip the waiters who serve you every day in the all-inclusive resorts, as they are on miserable salaries.

Toilets Public restrooms are hard to come by. You must count on the generosity of hotels and restaurants or duck into a museum or other attraction. In broad terms, the sanitary condition of public restrooms in Cuba is much higher than those found in the developing world, although at many establishments, toilet seats are often missing, and in cheaper restaurants and bus stations they are pretty filthy. Always bring toilet paper with you wherever you go, and always deposit the paper in the basket and never in the lavatory bowl. It's also wise to bring antibacterial gel to Cuba.

Many restrooms have an attendant, who is sometimes responsible for dispensing toilet paper. Upon exiting, you are expected to either leave a tip or pay a specified fee. If the restrooms are not clean and you do not take the toilet paper, do not feel obliged to tip. Otherwise, the official cost of a bathroom visit is CUP$1 (despite the large silver CUC$1 coins floating in the basket to encourage foreigners to leave more).

Travelers with Disabilities Cuba has been very forward-thinking in the recognition of the rights of people with disabilities. Still, overall, it's not an easy country for the disabled. While some hotels are equipped for travelers with disabilities, these are far from the norm. Moreover, there's no private or public transportation service geared toward such travelers. The streets of Havana are rugged and crowded, and sidewalks in particular are often either totally absent or badly torn up. Provincial towns suffer from the same disrepair. The Cuban people, however, are quite conscientious and embracing in their treatment of people with disabilities.

Asociación Cubana de Limitados Físicos-Motores (The Cuban Disabled Association), Calle 6 no. 106, between Avenidas 1 and 3, Miramar, Havana (www.aclifim.sld.cu; ✆ **7209-3099**), is a Cuban organization charged with ensuring accessibility and lobbying for rights. The association is a member of the Disabled Peoples' International (DPI) and the best contact for travelers with disabilities in Cuba.

The Society for Accessible Travel & Hospitality (www.sath.org; ✆ **212/447-7284**) offers a wealth of travel resources for those with all types of disabilities and informed recommendations on destinations, access guides, travel agents, tour operators, vehicle rentals, and companion services.

Vegetarian Travelers Cuba is not a society geared for vegetarianism. Still, vegetables are more plentiful than they used to be, and fruits and eggs are widely available. Peanuts *(mani)* are sold on the street. Fish can be found in abundance. Travelers should locate the small vegetable markets *(agromercados)* where private trading of products is allowed. Rice and beans *(moros y cristianos)* are plentiful. Dairy products are not always available. Cartons of fruit juices and biscuits and tins of olives are always for sale in town supermarkets. In short, a vegetarian won't starve, but this is no place to come for any innovative vegetarian cuisine.

Visitor Information

Tourism is one of Cuba's main sources of hard currency, and the government is actively involved in promoting tourism internationally. As a result, there's a network of tourism boards and agencies in major cities around the world; some are better than others. Some offices are run by the Ministry of Tourism, others by one of the major state-run agencies like **Cubanacán, Havanatur,** or **Cubatur.** No matter the bureau, the focus is almost entirely on organized tours, but they can give you some basic information. Agencies to contact include the **Cuba Tourist Board Canada,** 1200 Bay St., Suite 305, Toronto M5R 2A5 (www.gocuba.ca; ✆ **416/362-0700**) and the **Cuba Tourist Board Great Britain,** 154 Shaftesbury Ave., 1st Floor, London WC2H 8HL (www.travel2cuba.co.uk; ✆ **0207/240-6655**).

A host of other information is available online. The **Latin America Network Information Center** (http://lanic.utexas.edu/la/cb/cuba) is the best one-stop shop for helpful links to a wide range of travel and general information sites.

The Cuban government sponsors a number of websites, including **Cuba Travel** (www.cubatravel.cu), **CubaSi** (www.cubasi.cu), **Auténtica Cuba** (www.autenticacuba.com), and (the most useful) **Directorio Turístico de Cuba** (www.dtcuba.com). All provide travel-related information and links.

State-run tourism-agency sites, like **Cubanacán** (www.cubanacan.cu) or **Cubatur** (www.cubatur.cu), are also good places to check for hotels, transportation, and packages.

Infotur (www.infotur.cu), based in Cuba, also provides fairly detailed information on the country's provinces. Two interesting and informative sites are **Cuba Absolutely** (www.cubaabsolutely.com) and **Havana Journal** (www.havanajournal.com).

Several blogs offer an interesting perspective on life in Cuba, including **www.desdecuba.com/generationy**, **www.alongthemalecon.blogspot.com**, **www.sinevasionen.wordpress.com**, and www.translatingcuba.com. The newspaper set up by dissident Yoani Sánchez of Generación Y—www.14ymedio.com—is blocked inside Cuba.

Women Travelers

Women should be careful when walking alone at night, both in Havana and in other more remote destinations. However, walking home alone at night in smaller provincial towns should be quite safe. Cuba is a somewhat typical "macho" Latin American nation, with an open and extroverted sense of sexuality. Single women can expect their fair share of catcalls, whistles, and propositions known as *piropo*, especially in Havana and Santiago. The best advice? Ignore the unwanted attention, rather than try to come up with a witty or antagonistic rejoinder. Cuban men are pretty persistent, but if you ignore them they'll get the message. If they don't, say *"Déjeme en paz"* (Leave me in peace). If it gets out of control, a swear word usually works.

Single women of all ages, in particular, should not be naive about declarations of undying love. You could just be the desperately dreamed-about ticket out of the country. Remember that most Cubans do not have the economic means to leave Cuba, and the urge to leave Cuba for greater economic prosperity and freedoms has not diminished despite the late-2010 economic reforms and the recent signs of rapprochement with the U.S. government.

12

CUBAN SPANISH TERMS & PHRASES

Cubans speak fast and furiously. There's a very nasal and almost garbled quality to Cuban Spanish. Cubans tend to drop their final consonants, particularly the *s*, and they don't roll their *rr's* particularly strongly, converting the *rr* into an almost *l* sound in words like *carro* or *perro*. Cubans seldom use the formal *usted* form, instead preferring to address almost everyone (except those much older or of particular social or political stature) as *tú*. Likewise, you'll almost never hear the terms *señor* or *señora* as forms of address—Cubans prefer *compañero/a*, *socio*, or *amigo*. Cubans are also direct. They will almost always answer the phone with a curt "*Diga*," which translates roughly as a mix of "Tell me" and "Speak."

BASIC WORDS & PHRASES

English	Spanish	Pronunciation
Good day	Buenos días	***Bweh*-nohss *dee*-ahss**
How are you?	¿Cómo está?	***Koh*-moh ehss-*tah*?**
Very well	Muy bien	**Mwee byehn**
Thank you	Gracias	***Grah*-syahss**
You're welcome	De nada	**Day *nah*-dah**
Goodbye	Adiós	**Ah-*dyohss***
Please	Por favor	**Pohr fah-*vor***
Yes	Sí	**See**
No	No	**Noh**
Excuse me (to get by someone)	Con permiso	**Con pehr meesoh**
Excuse me (to begin a question)	Disculpe	**Dees-*kool*-peh**
Give me	Déme	***Deh*-meh**

English	Spanish	Pronunciation
Where is . . . ?	¿Dónde está . . . ?	**Dohn-deh ehss-tah?**
the bus station	la estación de guaguas	**lah ehss-tah-seown de gwagwa**
a hotel	un hotel	**oon oh-tel**
a gas station	una gasolinera	**oo-nah gasso-lyn-air-a**
a restaurant	un restaurante	**oon res-toh-rahn-teh**
the toilet	el baño	**el bah-nyoh**
a good doctor	un buen médico	**oon bwehn meh-thee-coh**
the road to . . .	el camino a/hacia . . .	**el cah-mee-noh ah/ah-syah**
To the right	A la derecha	**Ah lah deh-reh-chah**
To the left	A la izquierda	**Ah lah ees-kyehr-dah**
Straight ahead	Derecho	**Deh-reh-choh**
I would like . . .	Quisiera . . .	**Key-syehr-ah**
to eat	comer	**koh-mehr**
a room	una habitación	**oon-nah ah-bee-tah-seown**
Do you have . . . ?	¿Tiene usted . . . ?	**Tyeh-neh oos-ted?**
How much is it?	¿Cuánto cuesta?	**Kwahn-toh kwehss-tah?**
When?	¿Cuándo?	**Kwahn-doh?**
What?	¿Qué?	**Kay?**
There is (Is there . . . ?)	(¿)Hay (. . . ?)	**Eye?**
What is there?	¿Qué hay?	**Keh eye?**
Yesterday	Ayer	**Ah-yer**
Today	Hoy	**Oy**
Tomorrow	Mañana	**Mah-nyah-nah**
Good	Bueno	**Bweh-noh**
Bad	Malo	**Mah-loh**
Better (best)	(Lo) Mejor	**(Loh) Meh-hor**
More	Más	**Mahs**
Less	Menos	**Meh-nohss**

NUMBERS

English	Spanish	Pronunciation
1	uno	**ooh-noh**
2	dos	**dohss**
3	tres	**trehss**
4	cuatro	**kwah-troh**
5	cinco	**seen-koh**
6	seis	**sayss**
7	siete	**syeh-teh**

English	Spanish	Pronunciation
8	ocho	***oh*-choh**
9	nueve	***nweh*-beh**
10	diez	**dyess**
11	once	***ohn*-seh**
12	doce	***doh*-seh**
13	trece	***treh*-seh**
14	catorce	**kah-*tor*-seh**
15	quince	***keen*-seh**
16	dieciseis	**dyess-ee-*sayss***
17	diecisiete	**dyess-ee-*syeh*teh**
18	dieciocho	**dyess-ee-*oh*-choh**
19	diecinueve	**dyess-ee-*nweh*-beh**
20	veinte	***bayn*-teh**
30	treinta	***trayn*-tah**
40	cuarenta	**kwah-*ren*-tah**
50	cincuenta	**seen-*kwen*-tah**
60	sesenta	**seh-*sehn*-tah**
70	setenta	**seh-*ten*-tah**
80	ochenta	**oh-*chen*-tah**
90	noventa	**noh-*behn*-tah**
100	cien	***syehn***
200	doscientos	**doh-*syehn*-tohs**
500	quinientos	**kee-*nyehn*-tohs**
1,000	mil	**meel**

DAYS OF THE WEEK

English	Spanish	Pronunciation
Monday	lunes	***loo*-nehss**
Tuesday	martes	***mahr*-tehss**
Wednesday	miércoles	***myehr*-koh-lehs**
Thursday	jueves	***wheh*-behss**
Friday	viernes	***byehr*-nehss**
Saturday	sábado	***sah*-bah-doh**
Sunday	domingo	**doh-*meen*-goh**

MORE USEFUL PHRASES

English	Spanish	Pronunciation
Do you speak English?	¿Habla usted inglés?	***Ah*-blah oo-*sted* een-*glehss*?**
Is there anyone here who speaks English?	¿Hay alguien aquí que hable inglés?	Eye ***ahl*-gyehn ah-*key* keh *ah*-bleh een-*glehss*?**
I speak a little Spanish.	Hablo un poco de español.	Ah-bloh oon poh-koh deh ehss-pah-***nyol***

English	Spanish	Pronunciation
I don't understand Spanish very well.	No (lo) entiendo muy bien el español.	**Noh (loh) ehn-*tyehn*-do mwee byehn el ehss-pah-*nyol***
The meal is good.	Me gusta la comida.	**Meh *goo*-stah lah koh-*mee*-dah**
What time is it?	¿Qué hora es?	**Keh *oh*-rah ehss?**
May I see your menu?	¿Puedo ver la carta?	***Pweh*-doh vehr lah *car*-tah?**
The check, please.	La cuenta, por favor.	**Lah *kwehn*-tah, pohr fah-*vor***
What do I owe you?	¿Cuánto le debo?	***Kwahn*-toh leh *deh*-boh?**
What did you say?	¿Cómo? (colloquial expression for American "Eh?")	***Koh*-moh?**
I want (to see) . . .	Quiero (ver) . . .	***Kyehr*-oh (vehr)**
a room	un cuarto or una habitación	**oon *kwar*-toh, *oon*-nah ah-bee-tah-*seown***
with (without) bathroom	con (sin) baño	**kohn (seen) *bah*-nyoh**
We are staying here only . . .	Nos quedamos aquí solamente . . .	**Nohs keh-*dahm*-ohss ah-*key* sohl-ah-*mehn*-teh**
one night	una noche	***oon*-ah *noh*-cheh**
one week	una semana	***oon*-ah seh-*mahn*-ah**
We are leaving . . .	Partimos (Salimos) . . .	**Pahr-*tee*-mohss (sah-*lee*-mohss)**
tomorrow	mañana	**mah-*nya*-nah**
Do you accept . . . ?	¿Acepta usted . . . ?	**Ah-*sehp*-tah oo-*sted*?**
traveler's checks?	cheques de viajero?	***cheh*-kehs deh byah-*heh*-ro?**
credit cards?	tarjetas de crédito?	**tar-*hay*-tas de *kray*-dee-toe?**

TYPICAL CUBAN WORDS & PHRASES

Almendrón Collective classic car taxi in Havana
Asere! Que bolá? Hey mate, what's up? (what's the gossip?)
Ay Mi Madre Oh my mother! (exclamation of frustration)
Babalao Afro-Cuban religious priest
Bachata Informal party, hanging out
Bárbaro Great, fabulous
Bicitaxi Bicycle carriage
Bodega Store
Bohío Traditional, palm-thatched rural or indigenous dwelling
Botero Private-car drivers licensed and not licensed to carry passengers
CADECA Acronym for *casa de cambio* (currency exchange office)
Carro particular Privately owned car
Casa de la trova Traditional music club
Casa del campo A simple country house

Casa particular A private home with rooms for rent
Cerveza Beer
Chama Child
Chavito Cuban Convertible Peso
Chévere Cool, excellent
Coche Car
Coche de caballo Horse-drawn carriage
Cola Line or queue
Comida criolla Cuban creole cuisine
Compañero/compañera Literally, "partner," most common form of an address, as opposed to *señor* or *señora,* which are almost never used
Compay Friend
Consumo Price inclusive of food and drinks
Coppelia National ice-cream chain, almost synonymous with ice cream
Cuba libre Cocktail with rum and Coke
Cuentapropista A self-employed person
Diga Literally, "speak"; this is a very common phone greeting
Divisa U.S. dollar/Cuban Convertible Peso
Efectivo Cash
Fanoso Cheapskate
Fruta bomba Papaya
Fula U.S. dollar (slang)
Gallego/a Foreigner
Guagua Bus
Guarachar To hang out or party
Guayabera Loose-fitting, embroidered and pleated men's shirt
Hacer botella To hitchhike
Jinetero/jinetera Literally, "jockey"; used to refer to anyone hustling a foreigner for money
Lucha Daily struggle to find food and goods
Mango Good-looking person
Mangon Exceptionally good-looking person
Máquina Collective classic car taxi
Mata Tree
Mojito A rum cocktail
Muchacho/a Young man/young woman
Orisha Santeria deity
Paladar Private home restaurant
Paradero Transport stop
Por nada You're welcome
Puro Cuban cigar/older respected man
Santero Afro-Cuban Santeria religious priests
Socio/a Literally, "member," used to address close friends
Villas Towns or settlements
Yuma Originally an American; now used as a term for all foreigners

Index

See also Accommodations and Restaurant indexes, below.

General Index

G

H

I

R

S

Accommodations

Restaurants

NOTES